WITHDRAWN
UTSA Libraries

Beyond Bureaucracy: Mary Elizabeth Switzer and Rehabilitation

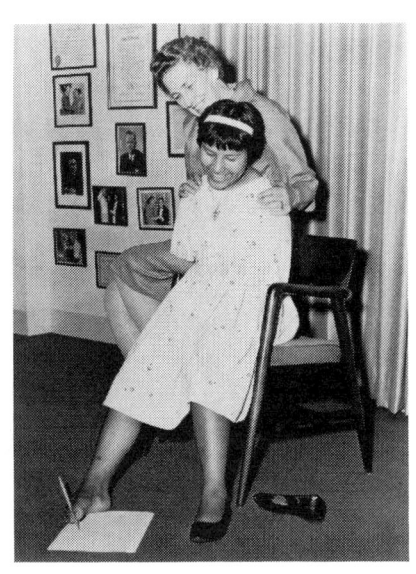

Foreword
by
Elliot Richardson

Martha Lentz Walker

UNIVERSITY
PRESS OF
AMERICA

LANHAM • NEW YORK • LONDON

Copyright © 1985 by

University Press of America,® Inc.

4720 Boston Way
Lanham, MD 20706

3 Henrietta Street
London WC2E 8LU England

All rights reserved
Printed in the United States of America

Library of Congress Cataloging in Publication Data

Walker, Martha Lentz, 1935-
  Beyond bureaucracy.

  Bibliography: p.
  Includes index.
      1. Switzer, Mary Elizabeth, 1900-   . 2. Rehabili-
  tation—United States. 3. United States. Social and
  Rehabilitation Service. Rehabilitation Services
  Administration—Officials and employees—Biography.
  4. Women government executives—United States—Biography.
  I. Title.
  HD7256.U5S938   1985   353.0084 [B]   85-9056
  ISBN 0-8191-4732-X (alk. paper)
  ISBN 0-8191-4733-8 (pbk. : alk. paper)

All University Press of America books are produced on acid-free
paper which exceeds the minimum standards set by the National
Historical Publications and Records Commission.

LIBRARY
The University of Texas
at San Antonio

Beyond Bureaucracy:
Mary Elizabeth Switzer and Rehabilitation

Life is faith and love,
but most of all hope.

The motto of the Department of Health, Education, and Welfare was Spes Anchora Vitae: Hope, the Anchor of Life.

(Courtesy Margaret Washington.)

for Adelle

Table of Contents

	Introduction	xi
I.	That Foreign Element, 1900-1917	1
II.	Across the River to Respectability, 1917-1921	13
III.	One Step at a Time, 1921-1933	23
IV.	A Ship Board Look, 1933-1938	43
V.	The Luckiest Thing That Ever Happened, 1938-1939	67
VI.	The New Reformers, 1939-1942	81
VII.	Bureaucratic Leapfrog, 1942-1949	101
VIII.	Offspring of The Brains Trust, 1946-1950	111
IX.	Taken By The Nape of The Neck, 1950-1952	125
X.	Embattled Advocate, 1953	141
XI.	The Joy of Craftsmanship, 1954-1959	155
XII.	Categorical Jungle, 1960-1965	175
XIII.	There Are Victories, 1960-1967	189
XIV.	Problems of Plenty, 1965-1967	211
XV.	A Rescue Mission, 1967-1970	231
XVI.	The Wind at Her Back, 1970-1971	253

Illustrations

1. Mary Elizabeth Switzer iv
2. Indian child, severely disabled by polio x
3. Swedish Fellows and Switzer, 1957 xvii
4. Margaret Moore Switzer and twins, Anastasia and Arthur, 1904 xviii
5. Michael Jeremiah Moore, ca., 1900 3
6. Mary Elizabeth Switzer, 1904 6
7. Mary Elizabeth Switzer, 1911 12
8. The first national gathering of rehabilitation workers, 1922 42
9. U.S. Public Health Service Survey, 1935 66
10. Mary Elizabeth Switzer and Public Health Service Officialdom, ca., 1939 80
11. Mary Elizabeth Switzer awarded Medal of Merit, 1946 100
12. Mary Elizabeth Switzer on the day she became Director of the Office of Vocational Rehabilitation, 1950 130
13. Switzer, Howard Rusk, and Omar Bradley at Bulova Watch Company, 1951 154
14. Mary Switzer stages Rose Garden Celebration with President Kennedy, 1962 179
15. Switzer "barnstorming" in Barrow Alaska, 1960 203
16. Switzer and "Snowshoes" in her Alexandria home, 1967 208
17. Switzer meets with President Johnson, Secretary Gardner and Undersecretary Cohen, 1967 210
18. Switzer and students at Christian College, 1966 228
19. Switzer becomes Administrator of the Social and Rehabilitation Services, 1967 234
20. Switzer and Wilbur Cohen meet with Hosea Williams and the Southern Christian Leadership Conference, 1968 241
21. Switzer with six Secretaries of the Department of Health, Education, and Welfare, 1970 252
22. Secretary Finch awards Mary Switzer the Flag of the Department of Health, Education, and Welfare, 1970 258
23. Switzer and Teodoria Martinez Silva of Boliva, 1964 *(Courtesy The Schlesinger Library, Radcliffe College)*. 268

Foreword

When Mary Switzer retired in 1970, her host of friends took huge satisfaction in the record-shattering aspects of her career in public service. From the perspective of 1985 her achievements seem even more remarkable. The intervening years, sadly, have seen a demoralizing decline in general esteem for career public servants, and the species is close to being endangered.

Throughout almost half a century in Washington, Mary Switzer prided herself on being a bureaucrat. By precept and example, she taught that to be a good bureaucrat is to make the machinery of government responsive to the needs of people. For me as for the countless others whose careers she influenced, this was an enormously important-- and deeply rewarding--lesson. Her dedication to seeing promises become programs is all too rare today.

A woman who came to Washington when Harding was President and retired during the Nixon administration, Mary Switzer witnessed the acceptance of Federal involvement in the welfare of American citizens, and, later, the denial of its limitations in meeting burgeoning needs.

As this absorbing biography makes clear, there were turning points in the evolution of the Federal role during her tenure in Washington that invite speculation as to what might have happened had she been a little further along in her career, or a little luckier. Mary Switzer was present when the Social Security Act was written in 1935, marking the first extension of Public Assistance to the nation's needy. She frequently reflected upon that time, wishing that the rehabilitation philosophy had been grafted onto welfare programs then, not in 1967.

She was a staff assistant to three Administrators of the Federal Security Agency, precursor of the Department of Health, Education, and Welfare, when agency-wide planning was an actuality. One wonders what might have happened [had she been elevated, when the Department was created in 1953, to sub-Cabinet level] or: [had she in 1946 been made head of one of the Agency's functional bureaus.] Mary Switzer believed in the generalist's approach to agency operation. She saw health, education, and welfare as inextricably related. But she was not promoted, and the pressure to select assistant secretaries who represented interest groups continued to build.

I wonder, too, what might have been the result if Mary Switzer had been made an Assistant Secretary of Health, Education, and Welfare earlier in her career, before the rising costs of public assistance made welfare the target of public outcry. She could drive the categorical nail as relentlessly as anyone, as she had shown in directing rehabilitation programs, but she also valued crosscutting efforts in the Department she cherished.

Mary Switzer's intelligence and strength of character made the switch from staff to line officer an easy one for her. As a witness before Congressional committees she had remarkable range. Her compassion and warmth were linked to toughness and a capacity for indignation, and this combination, laced with humor and charm, made her influence on the Hill almost legendary. As the foremost advocate for rehabilitation, she was a force with whom all Secretaries of Health, Education, and Welfare were forced to reckon.

My own regret is that my term as Secretary of Health, Education, and Welfare began six months too late to work with Mary Switzer as Administrator of the Social and Rehabilitation Services. I came to admire her style and commitment when I served as the Assistant Secretary for Legislation in the latter years of the Eisenhower administration, and I tremendously enjoyed the association. She could be hard to keep in line, though, and I used to tease her about the way she managed the alliance between her office, the National Rehabilitation Association, and the Hill.

It helped our relationship, perhaps, that we both came from Massachusetts. Beyond that, we shared a deep-rooted belief in the significance for each individual of a sense of personal identity and worth. And because work is not only part of who we are but a means both of maintaining independence and of contributing to society, to restore another's ability to work is to restore that person's self-esteem. For Mary Switzer the goals of rehabilitation were centered on these fundamental values.

Mary Switzer affected disability policy in this country as no other person has done before or since. She totally enjoyed the exercise of all the skills that could be brought to bear in achieving a result. She would use every resource: charm, humor, tenacity, orneriness, and sheer savvy to get what she wanted.

Mary Switzer's career was the career of a great bureaucrat. Such careers have seldom been scrutinized. We have many biographies of elected and appointed officials in the Federal government, but too few of great bureaucrats. This book makes an important contribution toward filling that void.

What do I mean by a great bureaucrat? First of all, someone who has demonstrated throughout a lifetime of increasing responsibility in public service the ability to achieve a creative balance between professional accountability and appropriate responsiveness to political leadership. To be counted great, a bureaucrat must be sensitive to the line beyond which legitimate compromise becomes the sacrifice of principle and must be resourceful to avoid capitulating such pressures. And at the heart of the great must lie a self-trancending commitment to the public interest.

To be effective, these indispensable attributes of the great bureaucrat require the backing of an array of highly developed operational skills. She must know exactly where and how her own agency fits into its larger governmental setting. She must be able to deal successfully with the congressional process, with the many satellite institutions and associations that cluster around the agency, and with the means by which its activities are reported to the public. Because the carrots and sticks at her command are limited, she must be prudent in marshalling and deploying her resources lest they be unavailable for the next objective. Among the essentials are balance, flexibility, and footwork. Like a good boxer, a good bureaucrat must know when to back-pedal and when to attack, when to press for victory and when to seek accommodation, when to jab and when to duck.

Mary Switzer had all the moves. The history of her unparalleled service to her country is the history of the development of social programs in the United States.

Elliot L. Richardson

March 14, 1985

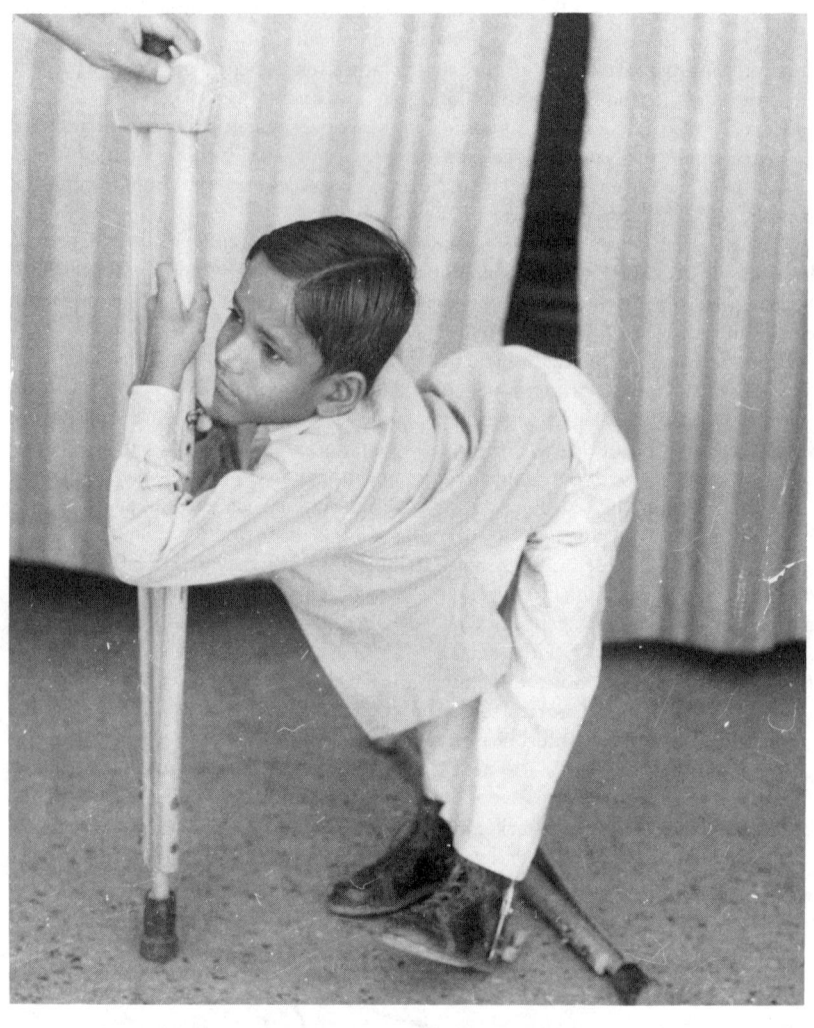

Indian child, severely disabled by polio.
(Courtesy Martin McCavitt, National Institute of Handicapped Research.)

Introduction

The mountains surrounding the Kulu Valley allowed only a narrow road between the Indian villages. On this May morning, children began another journey to school, appearing suddenly along the dirt road.

For one child progress up the road was slow. His friends ran back and forth, seeming to be joined to him by a rubber band that brought them back before the next turn in the road. He came to school each day on all fours, but they arrived together.

The sound of a motor scooter grew louder, and the riders passed, turning to look at the child who crawled to school. The scooter stopped, and the woman rider asked the child if he would like to stand as straight as his classmates. But he had never stood or walked, he explained. He had been very ill, before he could remember, and he was accustomed to dragging himself along the road to school.

The woman gave him a note, with instructions to take it to his father that afternoon. The note said where treatment could be found.

A month later the boy was at Ludhiana, where the Christian Medical College and Hospital carried out the work of rehabilitation. Within three months, the child's contracted knees and hips had been surgically straightened, and physical therapy restored motion. While his legs were being strengthened, the child was also attending school. He found a typewriter a marvelous tool. Other patients seemed as incredulous as he, to be surrounded by doctors, nurses, teachers, and therapists who seemed so full of hope.

When his three months stay was done, the child had another journey to make. Fastening his new braces, he swung his legs over the side of the bed. He stood beside his hospital bed for the last time and quickly walked down the long hallway to say goodbye to the woman he had met that May morning four months ago. He was returning to the Valley and the friends who would no longer have to slow their pace for him.

Thousands of miles away, in an office that looked out on the dome of the United States Capitol, Mary Switzer had begun her day with a ritual she loved. Two graduates of a training program in rehabilitation of the Hard of Hearing and Deafened had finished their work and were returning to Sweden. She awarded the certificates and shook each hand, representing the United

States Government and its program in international rehabilitation.

Several years earlier, Mary Switzer had found a way to help persons all over the world who perhaps needed only the simplest assistance to go back to life and work. She had proposed that funds which had accumulated in other countries through the sale of U.S. surplus commodities be utilized for rehabilitation research and training. Such a law was passed, and it was funds from the International Rehabilitation program that brought doctors, teachers, and therapists to the United States to learn rehabilitation techniques and sent them back to discover persons who could be helped. The woman who rode a motor scooter through the remote valleys of India had received such training and had felt the warmth of Mary Switzer's large hand around hers.

Millions of disabled persons were being helped because this woman, a bureaucrat, influenced public policy. She dared to think of the welfare of the whole human race and had made the Federal government a partner in a quiet revolution, the inclusion of disabled persons in the work and play of a nation. Rehabilitation led the way, through its very practical programs and belief in the individual to make a better life.

Mary Switzer savored the power she wielded. This part of the Department of Health, Education, and Welfare was known as "Switzerland." Her climb to this office with a view of the Capitol dome had taken her more than forty years, but she had made her point. Through government the numbers of people helped to overcome difficulty were greatly multiplied. Through a bureaucrat, worthy programs were promoted and protected so that quiet revolutions occur. Just as the women social reformers made childhood a twentieth century standard, personhood became the standard for the disabled, due to Mary Switzer's statecraft.

The two rehabilitation workers received their certificates, unaware of the micropolitics that created the chance for them to study. The child who now stood upright in the Kulu Valley would never know the woman administrator whose dreams make walking possible for him. Mary Switzer seized every chance to view the direct results of the policies she had shaped, for her influence was hidden by its nature. Rehabilitation was the acid test of the humane functions of government. Bureaucracy existed to serve people.

The story of how Mary Switzer came to Washington, how she coped with transitions of eight Presidents, and how she emerged as one of the most honored women in the United States is the subject of this book.

The change that buffeted Boston and Mary Switzer as a child contributed to the positive expectancies that guided her thinking. Mary Switzer was born in 1900, in an Irish immigrant community. Her father was a laborer for "street car" factories, her mother died of tuberculosis before Mary was eleven years old. Settlement houses, workmen's compensation, child labor laws were being adopted in many states as objections to exploitation of wageworkers. The Irish rebellion was brewing, and Mary Switzer was the favored niece of

Michael Moore, Irish warrior for the better life.

Uncle Mike became the strongest influence on Mary Switzer, exposing her to "revolutionary forces of the time" and his standards of justice. It was Michael Moore who took Mary to meetings of the Gaelic Society and to Ford Hall to see Helen Keller and Anne Sullivan Macy. Mary Switzer left Ford Hall knowing she must make a success of her life. No obstacle could exceed what had faced Helen Keller.

A second standard of beauty and intellectual achievement was established in Mary Switzer when she attended Radcliffe College. As one of her teachers said, she "had a hard row to hoe" to earn money to supplement the scholarship her high school French teacher had helped her capture. Radcliffe accentuated Mary Switzer's dual motives of improving the world and achieving personal security. There she met Harvard students and joined the Liberal Club, which claimed Walter Lippman and Scott Nearing as advisors. At Radcliffe Mary Switzer met men and women accustomed to wealth and privilege. She wanted the cultured life she glimpsed in her classmates, yet her revolutionary spirit also responded to George Grafton Wilson, Professor of International Law.

Elizabeth Brandeis, daughter of the "Peoples' Attorney," was also a Radcliffe student and a friend of Mary Switzer's. Through Elizabeth Mary Switzer found her way to Washington and the reconciliation of her personal and political goals.

During her first years in Washington Mary worked for liberal causes. The District Minimum Wage Board, the Carnegie Endowment for International Peace, and the Women's International League for Peace and Freedom offered temporary employment. The futility of reformers and revolutionaries like her Uncle Mike led Mary to the decision to work for change from within the social structure. Mary took the civil service examination and went on the Treasury Department payroll. The bureaucrat was launched; Mary Switzer's unbroken career as a civil servant began when she was twenty-two years old. She became the ultimate insider.

Single women often lived in womens' clubs, and Mary Switzer lodged at the University Club on H Street. On one of her first evenings in Washington, Mary met Tracy Copp, a new member of the Federal Board of Vocational Education, responsible for Vocational Rehabilitation. Tracy wove Mary into one of the most fascinating women's networks in Washington. The "Trade Union Women" had been central in the progressives' war against poverty. Florence Kelly was the foremost authority on the actual conditions of labor in industry. Rose Schneiderman had helped organize strikes in the New York ladies' tailoring industry. Elisabeth Christman was a leader in Massachusetts of the Consumer's League, an organization that rallied women who shopped in department stores to win better working conditions for salesgirls and children who worked there.

Tracy also infused Mary with interest in rehabilitation. Mary accompanied Tracy on several trips to the mid-West. Tracy wanted rehabilitation to be a "monument of this wonderful civilization of America," and she kept Mary informed about rehabilitation's growth until she retired in 1949.

A second woman entered Mary Switzer's life during those early Washington years. Isabella Diamond, nine years older than Mary, was one of the "Treasury bunch." Here was another network of influence, women who worked with the Treasury Department. There were few of them in those days, and Isabella worked in the Library of the Treasury. Perhaps it was Isabella Diamond who kept Mary Switzer in Washington. The two became housemates in 1928 and remained so for the rest of their lives. Isabella supplied much of the culture Mary needed in her personal life. Their home was comfortable, tasteful, and intellectual. Mary was moving up in the bureaucracy. She described the bulk of her work as "routine," but she was learning how an administrative directive could guide policy as surely as a statute. For fifteen years Mary Switzer accepted the personal obscurity of the classic bureaucrat, in order to learn the craft of humanizing government.

New networks were constructed during the New Deal, with more women appointed or elected to office than at any previous time in history. Mary Switzer had been in Washington long before the "New Deal" women arrived, and she stayed long after they left, for government service for the appointed or elected was usually a temporary stop. Still, this network strengthened Mary Switzer's hand.

One of the appointed officials was Josephine Roche, Assistant to the Secretary of the Treasury for Public Health. Mary pursued the position of the "first woman assistant to the first woman Assistant Secretary." The Public Health Service was as traditional and male as any Federal organization could possibly be. Josephine Roche hoped to use the Public Health Service as a means of controlling medical costs and equalizing medical care in the United States. Although Josephine Roche's fight for a national health plan failed, Mary Switzer began an association with physicians that continued throughout her lifetime. She became the unofficial emissary of the Federal government to medical leaders.

In 1939, when Roosevelt formed the Federal Security Agency, predecessor of the Department of Health, Education, and Welfare, Mary Switzer was named Assistant to the Administrator. Because Mary Switzer understood the process of political compromise bargains were made that advanced government involvement in social welfare. She coordinated the procurement and assignment of health personnel for the Armed Services during the Second World War and became the comrade of the medical and military elite.

When the war came to an end, Mary Switzer was seen by the medical community as the channel to Federal recognition. Mary applied her knowledge and contacts to the cause of national health. Whereas physicians had earlier resisted Federal control, they welcomed Federal dollars. Mary Switzer knew the combination to the Federal treasury. She helped draft the Hospital Survey and Construction Act of 1946 and the National Mental Health Act of 1946. The Federal government had become a principal partner in financing the operation of American medicine. Mary Switzer pointed the way for organized medicine and government to function as partners.

Mary Switzer had served thirty years of apprenticeship. First dedicated, then enterprising, the bureaucrat now wished to be recognized. She wanted a program of her own; she had been assistant to enough administrators.

A small, manageable program needing someone with expertise in the medical area was just what Mary Switzer required in 1950. Mary had followed the fortunes of Vocational Rehabilitation through her friend, Tracy Copp. The program had remained small through its specific goals and selective eligibility criteria, and although its services had been greatly expanded through the Vocational Rehabilitation Amendments of 1943, the current Director was having difficulty understanding medical rehabilitation.

Mary Switzer had a great supporter in Howard Rusk, a physician whom she had met during her days of procuring and assigning medical officers for the Public Health Service during the Second World War. Howard Rusk had great dreams for a public rehabilitation program. Rusk wanted the public program to equal the one he directed for the Air Force, but was meeting resistance from specialists who did not understand the needs of disabled persons as being broader than one function. The idea of having Mary Switzer as Administrator of an agency that could purchase services from fledgling rehabilitation hospitals was most appealing. Howard Rusk went to work on the Administrator of the Federal Security Agency, Oscar Ewing, and Mary Switzer was named Director of the Office of Vocational Rehabilitation on December 1, 1950.

The remaining twenty years of Mary Switzer's career gave her the opportunity to span three stages of public attitudes. When she first met Tracy Copp, the nation's response to disability was compassion without action. For forty years, the nation was willing to act for economic reasons, to make "taxpayers out of taxeaters" through rehabilitation programs. By 1967 the measure of humanity seemed to be the restoration of all disabled people to the fullest extent possible, regardless of economic benefit.

The strategies Mary Switzer employed as leader of the rehabilitation program were learned during her years of ascendency as a bureaucrat. Her last 17 years stretched over the administrations of eight Secretaries of Health, Education and Welfare. The number of persons rehabilitated annually rose from 66,000 in 1951 to 241,000 in 1969. John Gardner asked Mary Switzer to infuse welfare with a rehabilitation philosophy, and overnight she went from administering a budget of 300 million dollars to one of six billion. Dedicated, enterprising, revolutionary were words often used to describe this bureaucrat with "fire in her belly." She seemed to be a combination of Ethel Barrymore and Eleanor Roosevelt.

Mary Switzer saw beyond bureaucracy to the services it could provide those citizens of the world who had lost hope.

In that office in "Switzerland" the evidence of Mary Switzer's success and the clues to her motives awaited the two students from Sweden. On a bookshelf a photograph of Tracy Copp was displayed prominently. On a lower shelf a Shakespearean quote had been carefully lettered: "The first thing we do, let's kill all the lawyers." This was a bureaucrat who cut red tape, and believed that the business of the bureaucrat was to serve people well.

Within two display cases were mementos of her travels to other countries, her 27 awards, including the Baruch Medal, the Albert Lasker Award, Hadassah Myrtle Wreath, and a life membership in the Mended Hearts. The text of the 14 honorary degrees she had been awarded were also displayed. No one could doubt that Mary Switzer had made something of herself, and through the bureaucracy, had improved the world.

Another award was later added to the display, this one perhaps the most valued. From Radcliffe College, where a sculpture of Helen Keller now stood just within the walls of the Yard, Mary Switzer received the Founders Award on June 11, 1969, with this testimonial:

> Firm believer in the potential of all human beings, advocate and encourager of the handicapped, this distinguished public administrator has served the nation for nearly five decades in successively more responsible posts. Radcliffe salutes an alumnae who has directed the forces of government to creative and constructive ends.

Rehabilitation was Mary Switzer's measure of the humanity of government. After her administration, nothing would ever be the same again for disabled citizens.

Swedish Fellows and Switzer, 1957.
(Courtesy Martin McCavitt, National Institute of Handicapped Research.)

Margaret Moore Switzer and twins, Anastasia and Arthur, 1904.
(Courtesy Anastasia Switzer.)

I

That Foreign Element
1900-1917

Everybody works at our house...
Mother takes in washing
Sister works all day
Everybody works at our house
But my old man!

Irish saying

The clapboard house on Elliot Street had only one advantage over the identical dozen crowded there. It was a shorter walk to the tavern where Irish workers gathered each afternoon. Mary Switzer's father was one of these Irishmen who depended upon hourly wages and feared unemployment despite what seemed unbridled growth. The reputation of being hard drinking men followed the Irish, and the child's jingle captured the pathos of many an Irishman in 1900.

Boston was well acquainted with the immigrant problem, and by 1900 was the seat of labor unrest. Irish immigrants who entered the great port of Boston in 1840 through 1850, as respite from the potato famine, had proved a major shock to Boston economic and social structure. The residents with colonial origins who enjoyed inherited wealth based on trade, fishing, finance, and manufacturing combined forces with the skilled artisans, tradesmen, shopkeepers, and civil servants in the resentment of the Irish influx.[1]

The immigrant society within the Boston society initially crowded into ghettos of South Boston. This first wave of displaced persons was too spent to continue further into the promised land, collecting along the harborfront. Irish were followed by Italian and Jewish immigrants. By 1920 Boston was second only to New York City in the number of foreign white stock listed as residents. The Irish dilemma, being neither respected citizen nor immigrant,

1

continued through the 1920s.[2] Emergence from illiteracy and poverty was slow for the Boston Irish, noted most frequently by moves to sections of Boston where skilled tradesmen were needed, and the drab two and three story houses bore a depressing similarity to any New England mill town.

Upper Newton Falls was just such a community in the year of Mary Switzer's birth. Along Elliot street homes were built for families who worked in the Pettee factory. Boston Irish found employment in the 35 industries located in Newton. By 1898 some 2900 Irish had moved to housing similar to that constructed by the Pettee Company. Newton was a great magnet to industry, as there was a convergence of three lines of railway at Nonantum Square. A building boom began in 1890 in Newton, producing boulevards, parks, and street railways operated by electric power.[3]

Among the Irish living on Elliot Street in 1891 was Michael Jeremiah Moore. He had been born in Inskiddy, Cork, Ireland in 1856. The Moore family were survivors, first of the potato famine, then of the slums of Boston. Michael preceded the remaining members of his family to America. Michael Moore boarded on Elliot Street and Chestnut from 1891 until 1897. His friend and co-worker, Julius Switzer, boarded in the same house and worked as a moulder in a machine shop.[4] The need for skilled tradesmen had attracted Michael Moore and Julius Switzer to Newton. By 1900 a close-knit Irish community existed in Upper Newton Falls.

Michael Moore had sent for his mother and sisters in Ireland as soon as he had saved enough for their passage. Margaret Moore was the youngest of his three sisters, a stunning young woman who met and married Julius Switzer. The couple established their own home at 19 Chandler Place, and within the year Margaret gave birth to Mary Elizabeth Switzer. The Switzer home on Chandler Place and the Moore home on Cottage Street were multiple family dwellings, where single men also boarded. John Nolan and Richard Welch shared the Moore home, as many Irish laborers did in 1901.[5]

Newton was not only known for its construction boom, it was also known for its famous residents. Horace Mann, Cardinal Spellman, Ralph Waldo Emerson, and Nathaniel Hawthorne were among its most famous citizens. The Stanley twins were also prominent in Newton and affected the lives of Michael Moore and Julius Switzer directly. The Stanley Steamer and the Stanley Motorcar Company were co-owned by the Stanley brothers,[6] and Julius and Mike worked for the Stanley Motorcar Company as motormen in the early 1900s.

Work was uppermost in the minds of Newton's Irish citizenry, but in their spare time, politics was their passion. The legacy of the Irish in their survival of British dominance was an improvised, intensely personalistic brand of politics. Politics was the only inroad to respectability Boston Irish had discovered, and John F. Fitzgerald's mayoral victory attested to that accomplishment in 1909. Rejection by Brahmins and Yankees only

Michael Jeremiah Moore, ca. 1900.
(Courtesy Anastasia Switzer.)

intensified the Irishman's dedication to politics, and Michael Moore was a prime example of this visionary tradition.

The impression Michael Moore conveyed in his dress and demeanor had much to do with Mary Switzer's conviction that he was the primary influence on her life.[7] Somehow, he managed to dress impeccably for forays into Watertown or Boston. His high, starched collar and six-button vest made him look the substantial citizen. His gold watch chain, arranged symetrically on his vest's second button, made it seem his time was very valuable. Although he was a small man, he stood tall, with his chin jutting. He looked very much the politician.

Testimony to Michael Moore's mettle was his candidacy for Alderman-at-Large from Ward 1 in December 1916.[8] Newton was primarily a bedroom community for the wealthy Bostonian, with the exception of those zones of emergence such as Ward 1. The political sentiment of the majority of Newton was ultra conservative. As late as 1914, prejudice toward the Irish was evident in the Newton newspaper:

> It is evident that the foreign element at Nonantum, Thompsonville, Upper Falls, and West Newton will receive the usual quantity of beer and light wine, which are used as other classes of people use tea and coffee.[9]

This was a community that opposed women's suffrage, saying it postulated a society in which the individual rather than the family is the unit, in other words, socialism.[10] And socialism was just what Michael Moore espoused. Mike Moore would be classified as a feminist, by today's standards, as he encouraged Mary to develop her talents, without regard to any duties to the family.

Although Michael Moore felt alienated from the white collar citizenry of Newton, he found support at the Newton Free Library. It may have taken 30 years, but in 1935 the librarian at the Newton Free Library ordered a book about Russia at Mike's request. He had found the title in *The Daily Worker*, and was anxious to read it.[11] Any book that dealt with social change interested him; he was a student of Marx and Engels.[12] This was hardly the reading taste of most of Newton's populace.

Michael Moore also felt alienated from the only institution in Boston that exerted Irish power: the Roman Catholic Church. Archbishop O'Connell, Boston's influential cleric, set out to make the individual Irish American respectable in the eyes of the Boston Brahmin by building a parochial school system that solidified the Irish community.[13] Mike's mother and sisters were strong Catholics, but Mike had been captured by another view. Socialist leaders of 1900, Martha Moore Avery and David Goldstein, had made a conquest for socialism, and Michael Moore became a great admirer of Eugene Debs, the country's foremost radical.[14] To be a Socialist in 1900 was to be viewed in the Irish Catholic community as "a child of the devil."

Had the church or Newton conservatives understood Mike's fervor for socialism, they might have agreed that there were worse addictions. This warrior for unpopular causes was used by Mary Switzer to illustrate rehabilitation and the importance of outside pressure in the process:

> He was a very heavy drinker in his early years, and around 1900 his drinking became such a problem that his mother--my grandmother--said to him that he would either have to stop it or leave her home. As he tells the story, he stopped immediately, and then went out to seek something to take the place of the frustrations that led him to alcohol.[15]

Mary Switzer did not have a "League of the Cross" to teach her lifelong values, as Mike had. Instead, she had his example to guide her. His strength of character in overcoming alcoholism caused her to call him the "perfect example of rehabilitation." Mary tried to describe his influence:

> He was an extraordinary character, and there were many hundreds like him that made the fiber of American life in the first three or four decades of this century—staunch and strong. His contribution to me was not only the gift of straight thinking, the necessity for continuous education by reading and mastering difficult material, the establishing of standards by which to judge the events of the world as they pass you by, but also the quality of personal character that made him such an outstanding member of the human race.[16]

This outstanding person never married, never owned a house or a car, yet seemed in touch with the most serious issues of his time. Mike's style was to seek out people who would reflect and debate. He always seemed to be stirring something up in the neighborhood, or bringing controversial figures into their home. For that view of the world, Mary Switzer was grateful.

> I find that the exposure I had to revolutionary forces of the time when I was growing up has been of enormous value, because unless a person has really been exposed to this and has listened to the lingo and the kind of arguments, thinking and forces that make for revolutionary ferment, you just do not understand what is going on in the world even today.[17]

As Mary felt her way along the bureaucratic trails of Washington many years later, she realized that her awareness of policy and of the importance of leadership was a bequest from her bachelor uncle. Throughout Mike's life, he and Mary carried on a correspondence laced with discussion of international events, from Manchuria to Ethiopia.[18] They also made recommendations for reading to each other, with Mary often sending along books for "the winter." As Mike aged, he taught Mary new lessons:

> The figure of the fight you have always made is perhaps the most outstanding quality of your whole character, and maybe I will always remember most poignantly the active years when you were out in the front ranks as part of the organized minority fighting for a better life. But in these last years the thing that has impressed me most forcibly is the great ability you have shown to make use of your time, on not only the fight for the ideals you have always cherished, but also to broaden the scope of your own knowledge and to maintain serenity of spirit.[19]

Such a constant and forceful influence as Mike was a great blessing for Mary, for he was the only male figure in her early life. Julius Switzer is, in

Mary Elizabeth Switzer, 1904.
(Courtesy Anastasia Switzer.)

comparison, a shadowy figure. Julius Switzer was a Protestant and frowned upon by his wife's family for not converting to Catholicism and for continuing his drinking. Mary remembered little of her father; no arguments between him and her mother, but also no particular intimacy. She had a vague memory of her father coming home drunk, but not being unpleasantly drunk.[20] Little is known of life in the Switzer household between the years 1900 and 1911, although the birth of twins, Arthur and Anastasia, in 1903, must have taxed the energy and the income of the family. Mary Switzer recalled her mother as being a stunning person, with an alabaster complexion and heavy black hair. Margaret Switzer enjoyed taking Mary and her friends to the Boston Museum on Sunday, or reading to Mary when there was a moment of quiet. In late 1910, Margaret Moore Switzer was diagnosed as having "galloping consumption" and left the house to go to the sanatorium. Mary Switzer remembered the date clearly, Columbus Day, 1910. Margaret Moore Switzer returned to die at home on the 26th of April, 1911.[21]

Michael Moore dominated Mary's memory of her mother's last years and her death. A closeness developed between Mike and Margaret during the last years of her life. Margaret responded to Mike's intensity and loved to listen to him talk about speeches he had heard on the Boston Common. Mary remembered the night Margaret Moore Switzer died:

> My uncle that evening was scheduled to preside at a rally in Boston at which Milwaukee's Mayor, Victor Berger, was to speak. I remember my uncle talking to my mother who urged him to go ahead, to go to the meeting, preside over it, talk about it, and come back and tell her about it. I can remember the eyebrow raising on the part of the other members of the family to think that he would leave under such conditions, but of course this was just what my mother wanted him to do. I remember when he did come back, his face was aglow and the evening had been a great success. He had a red carnation in his button hole, which was given to all those taking a prominent part in the meeting. The memory I have of the evening my mother died is tied up with that episode rather than the usual moanings and groanings that go on in an Irish family waiting for death.[22]

Mary had no memory of her father during this time of her mother's illness, but realized even as a child, that the Moores held Julius Switzer responsible for the tuberculosis that claimed the life of Margaret. Julius had not proved a good provider, had lost a series of jobs, and the Moores felt he had neglected his wife.[23]

For several months following the death of Margaret Moore Switzer, Julius attempted to keep the household intact. A housekeeper came and went, the children helped with daily chores, but finally the Moore aunts moved to gain custody, and were granted guardianship of the three children. Julius Switzer retaliated by taking his son, Arthur, to New York and never returning to see his daughters or the Moore family.[24]

Initially, the upbringing of Mary and Stacia (as Anastasia was called) fell to Mary Moore, the only remaining grandparent. Mary Switzer remembered her grandmother as a typical Irish woman, "matriarchal" in her view. She always had a pocket full of molasses peppermint brown candies. It seemed a magic pocket to Mary. Grandmother Moore had many children, but few had survived. Her daughters, Mary's Aunt Ann and Aunt Bridget, shared the house. In 1913, when Mary Moore died, the aunts took over the rearing of Anastasia and Mary.[25]

Mary remembered her aunts as very frugal persons, never incurring any debts, but always having a good Christmas with "a Christmas tree, dolls, and things."[26] Aunt Ann worked as a housekeeper for a wealthy family, passing on to Stacia the discipline of the housekeeper. Mary was viewed as the scholar of the family, and her sister remembered having to do the ironing and cleaning while Mary studied. Stacia also recalled Mary playing a maternal role with her, wheeling her around and often protecting her from Aunt Ann's discipline.[27]

Meanwhile, "Uncle Mike" had taken on as his student and favorite the young girl who had been named for his beloved mother. The only male remaining in the household recognized the intellect of his niece and committed himself to seeing that she had a good education and was well launched in life.

Mary remembered Mike as being insistent in his argument. The talk was basically about the responsibility of society for people and the neglect of the capitalist system. Mike took young Mary with him to the Socialist headquarters in Park Square in Boston, where she heard the leaders and met Eugene Debs.

> I saw him several times in Boston—mostly when he came to speak to rallies organized by the Socialist Party, but once or twice intimately as he and my uncle, Michael Jeremiah Moore, would be talking over the political situation. My memory of him is warm, and cozy, for a great hero and a man who really was a symbol of the revolutionary ferment in this country during his life. He was a singularly affectionate, easy-to-reach person. At least as far as a little girl was concerned.[28]

Although the youngster Michael Moore was so systematically educating did not remember the topics in detail, Mary Switzer emerged from these experiences with gratitude for having had the chance to "touch the circle of the self-less devotion to causes."

It must have been confusing for Mary, who was being trained by day at a parochial school by Dominican nuns and by night and weekend by this intrepid uncle. While the sisters taught Mary Switzer to speak with her heels together and feet pointed outward,[29] her mind recorded another style—that of Eugene Debs holding an audience in a trance with his tall figure and long arms waving.

Michael Moore instilled in both Mary and Stacia the importance of real work, in support of a worthy cause.[30] Mary remembered the Alderman race well, for she had been up at 4:00 A.M. to stick up flyers on posts, fences, and under precinct doors. Mike's sometimes diabolical humor was remembered by Mary through an incident in the Alderman's race. There was a retired army colonel in the neighborhood who had the reputation of making passes at little girls. Whom should Michael Moore assign to attach Socialist propaganda to the colonel's fence and house but the two young Switzer girls?[31]

Mike's sisters and mother had long been accustomed to the intensity of his enthusiasms, and apparently saw no harm in the Switzer girls being exposed to his thoughts and actions. Perhaps the Moore family had learned from Margaret Moore Switzer, who had cherished Mike's ideas and energy.

The family seemed to recognize the bond between Mike and Mary. The strict aunts allowed Mary to meet Mike after a day's work and carry his lunch pail home.[32] Mary was released from many household duties to read and study and to attend special lectures or cultural events Mike thought important for her education. Even shopping trips made for family purposes were turned into opportunities to listen to revolutionary ideas being discussed. Mike would head for Faneuil Hall with Mary in tow. Once the meat had been chosen and Chase and Sanborn coffee purchased, the duo would end up at the Socialist headquarters to listen to the forensics.[33]

Mary's world was soon to expand greatly, for she entered Newton Classical High School when she reached the age of 14. This was Mary's first exposure to the secular educational institution, and she quickly made a lifelong friend, Miss Gertrude Myles, the French teacher. The High School was classical in the sense of coursework that stressed foreign language, literature and critical thought. Mary found just the niche she wanted in the debating team. Competition between three schools in the Newton area was keen, and Mike gave Mary pointers that honed her speech and delivery. "Know your facts," he warned. [34]

While Mary prospered in intellectual pursuits, Mike sought to enrich her awareness of theatre and aesthetics. Mike had a friend, Eugene Hough, who helped Mike expand Mary's cultural horizons. Hough was also a liberal, having met Mike through their activities with the Fabian society, a socialist group founded in England by George Bernard Shaw and John Stuart Mill. Although Hough shared many of Mike's ideas, he provided a balance for Mary. When Mike became adamant, Hough pointed out the weaknesses in his argument. Often Hough would buy theatre tickets for the Switzer girls. Mary recalled seeing Julius Caesar in the old Boston Opera House and being smitten by the handsome and debonair Antony. Mike wanted Mary to be exposed to the fine things in life, and he depended upon his friend Hough to point out any he missed.[35]

One winter night Mike invited Mary to accompany him to Ford Hall in Boston to see Helen Keller and her teacher, Anne Sullivan Macy. As they made their way to the auditorium, Mike explained that Helen Keller had made a great success of her life, and that Anne Sulivan Macy was the person who had saved her from utter oblivion.[36] Mary could always conjure up the scene of the two women on the stage at Ford Hall, just as the moral of the evening never left her: make something of your life.

Mary was growing older quickly, and Mike wanted her to feel proud of being Irish. Each Sunday for several winters Mary and Mike would go into Boston for meetings of the Gaelic League. Volunteers taught Gaelic on Saturday and Sunday, and Mary found the language quite difficult to master. It was here, however, that Mary heard conspirational talk. Occasionally, Mary attended lectures in the halls of south Boston, halls reverberating with Irish anger.

> I would listen to the talk, the planning and the plotting. Sometimes I would get a little bored, listening to the old socialists trying to get the revolution underway. Often I would go to one of the big lecture halls. I remember one in particular, where the widow of Mayor Skeffington came shrouded in black, after his execution. She had a very pale face and expounded on the sacrifices made to bring freedom to Ireland. Con Lehane, Jim Larkin, Connolly, and Pierce, all of them at one time or another, with the exception of Pierce, had been in Boston, sometimes secretly, often at our house, to plan what could be done to keep the revolution alive.[37]

By 1914 Britain had passed the Home Rule Bill, giving Ireland powers of self-government. World War I and a change in the British cabinet delayed home rule from being implemented. Irish revolutionaries saw the war as an opportunity to cast off British rule forever and began to agitate in Ireland and abroad.[38] The revolutionary point of view was carried to Boston, where the Gaelic Society hosted speakers, such as the ones Mary described. Michael Moore, the Irishman from Cork, attended these sessions regularly. The full weight of Mike's activities on the revolutionary fringe of Boston became known to Mary in 1916. She was at home, studying for a Latin entrance examination to Radcliffe, when two men visited the house on Pearl Street. Mike had just left the house for his customary evening stroll. The agents from the Department of Justice went through Mike's room, explaining that Mike had been dispensing anti-draft literature. Mike was not arrested, but the entire family was shaken by the visit. Mike made his protests a little less obtrusive as a result of the unannounced call.[39]

Even toning down his revolutionary activity was hard for Mike in 1916. Martyrs for Irish self-government were easily found, following the tradition of Sir Roger Casement. This English hero was converted to the Irish cause after uncovering Belgium atrocities in the Congo. He tried to keep Ireland out of World War I by enlisting the help of Germany and Irish volunteers who planned to overthrow the British. In one of the first uses of a submarine, he landed in Ireland to unload arms. He was arrested and hung, which set off the Easter Sunday rebellion. Many of the rebels were shot, including the Mayor of Dublin.[40]

The Irish American, and certainly, Michael Moore, was shocked by the outcome of the Easter Rebellion and subsequent questioning of Irish patriotism by Presidential candidate, Woodrow Wilson. To the Irish American, England was the worst of foes, and a small band refused to accept the English as American allies during World War I. Suspicion of the "foreign-born" was publicly expressed by Wilson and acted out by the barring from the mails of newspapers such as *The Gaelic American*, the *Irish World*, and the *Freeman's Journal*. Secret service men began to attend meetings of Irish organizations. Irish Americans responded at the polls by voting against Wilson in 1920, and *The Gaelic American* claimed full credit for the outcome.[41]

Although subdued, Mike continued his support of the Irish cause. His niece had seen enough and heard enough to identify also with Irish independence. Later, when she went to Radcliffe, Mary registered her protest by not buying Liberty Bonds in her freshman year.[42]

The revolutionary causes of Michael Moore left a deep impression on Mary, as did his style of life. Mike insisted on his own physical fitness and swam from the L Street Beach in South Boston.[43] Mike was a strong swimmer and believed taking care of himself was a moral obligation, for he had to live long enough to see his favorite niece succeed.

Many years later, Mary described the impression Michael Moore left upon her.

> The influence of my growing up was largely on the positive side, and I believe that it left me with two rather conflicting motivations, not always conscious. One was the desire for financial security, the desire not to be in a situation where you would be out of work... And the other motivating force was this consciousness of one's obligation to do something to make the world better. I think this was unconscious for a long time, but I think that it had a great influence on the causes I espoused and the things that I tried to do as I was growing up both in college and in the years that immediately followed.[44]

As well as conflicting motivations, Mary had acquired the excitement and cost of a cause, and the hard work and loneliness required of a leader.

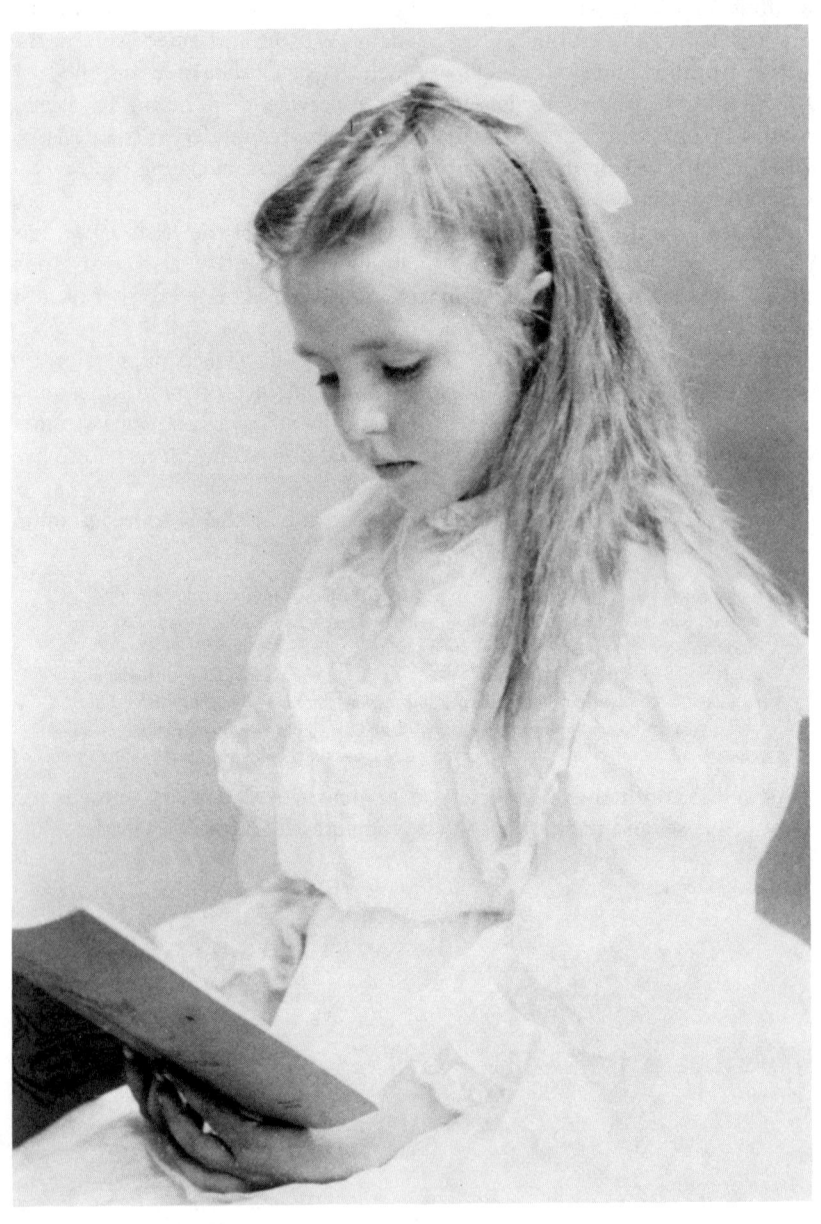

Mary Elizabeth Switzer, 1913.
(Courtesy Anastasia Switzer.)

II

Across the River to Respectability 1917-1921

Mary Switzer is another of those Radicals for which Radcliffe is famed. She's always got the axe out for something in this present social order.

Radcliffe Year Book, 1921

Respectability was for Irish immigrants the elusive prize of social, political and economic equality in America. Mary Switzer was well aware of ethnicity as she grew up in Upper Newton Falls, and the gap between the native Bostonians and immigrant groups was painfully obvious to a young woman seeking higher education. By 1912 segregation was accomplished through the club system of Boston. The upper class of Boston was essentially a business aristocracy, and clubrooms became caucus rooms for Boston's financial leaders.[1] Whereas politics had failed as the lever of inclusion, Mary sensed that education might offset kinship.

Across the Charles River from Upper Newton Falls stood the most respected educational institution in the country, Harvard University. In 1917 women were excluded from study there, but Radcliffe College had been authorized since 1894 to "confer on women all honors and degrees as fully as any university or college in this Commonwealth" with the approval of Harvard. Mary had met other girls at Newton Classical High School who planned to go to Mount Holyoke, but she found two reasons to choose Radcliffe instead. Mary's French teacher, Gertrude Myles, had graduated from Radcliffe in 1906 and assisted Mary in obtaining a $100 scholarship to Radcliffe. And Mary was very conscious of the cost of a boarding school such as Mount Holyoke. If she chose Radcliffe, she could live at home and travel by streetcar to college each day.[2]

Although the trees and shrubs have grown much taller, the Yard at

Radcliffe today is largely unchanged. Most of the Radcliffe Yard had been purchased by 1917, and the Radcliffe Library, Agassiz, Hemenway Gym, Fay House, Vaughan, and Browne and Nichols ringed the spacious lawn.[3] Today each building can be entered from the Yard by stone steps that serve as lunch sites for Radcliffe students on sunny days. High brick walls surround the Yard, and a tourist can easily walk past this haven unaware of the activity within. The contrast between the clamor of Harvard Square, only two blocks away, and Radcliffe's Yard was probably as striking in 1917 as it is today. Women in 1917 typically had little contact with males, except for those in their families. At Radcliffe students had only to step outside the Yard to meet men impressive in their intellect. The excitement of Harvard Square, with its variety and freedom to meet and talk with Harvard men was a great change for freshmen entering Radcliffe.

For four years Mary Switzer crossed the bridge over the Charles River into Watertown, where she could board the streetcar and travel half an hour into the center of Cambridge. Once within the Radcliffe Yard, no one knew whether she boarded or was a day student, and Mary's pedigree was known only to those she wished to tell. The strategy was a good one; Mary "passed" into respectability during the four years of her work at Radcliffe.

In 1917 the women who entered Radcliffe were considered somewhat unusual by most standards of the time. If a woman chose Radcliffe as her college, she was frequently cast as a "Bluestocking." In the 18th century "Bluestocking" was the name of literary clubs, where women could find intellectual stimulation. In 1917, "Bluestocking" was used with a measure of scorn, but this seldom disturbed Radcliffe students. Women who chose Radcliffe realized that Harvard faculty taught most Radcliffe courses, often the same course they taught to much larger groups of Harvard students across the Common. A segregated system suited a Radcliffe "Bluestocking" nicely, since it produced more individual attention for women from prestigious Harvard professors.[4]

World War I began in 1914, and the freshman class in 1917 joined their elders at Radcliffe in support of the war effort. There were not only groups that made and folded bandages, but the majority of Radcliffe women spent the summers between terms at farms reaping harvests now beyond the reach of men. Mary Switzer deviated from this norm, but did so in such a way as to escape attention. Her picture is not to be found in the extracurricular groups at Radcliffe who did their part for "the boys overseas," nor is she remembered for having worked the farms during the summer.[5] The Irish heritage from across river did not allow her to participate in anything connected to World War I, but Mary wisely kept her views to herself during that first year at Radcliffe.

Although guarded in revealing her ethnic identity, Mary did not fit the stereotype of the shy freshman. Classmates remember her fearless approach to professors whose thinking Mary wished to hear after class. That same pluck surprised classmates when Mary established a friendship with Elizabeth Brandeis, youngest daughter of Justice Louis Brandeis and a Senior and President of Student Government at Radcliffe in 1917. It was obvious that Mary was different; she knew she wanted to go places. There was purpose behind her selection of friends and coursework. A classmate said:

> Mary was one of the very highest motivated. She had a vision of what she wanted to do. By the time she came to Radcliffe, there was something about her. . . she was no longer anybody's girl. [6]

Mary had heard of Louis Brandeis and was drawn to his daughter because of the Judge's reputation, and her Uncle Mike's respect for the "Peoples' Attorney." She may also have sensed in Elizabeth the pain of having known ostracism, for the Brandeis family had lived in Dedham, a Boston suburb that tolerated neither his Jewish heritage nor his liberal philosophy. Louis Brandeis had left his practice in St. Louis at the request of a Harvard Law School friend, Samuel Warren, and had come to Boston to form a partnership with this assured member of Boston society. Although Warren sought Brandeis as a professional peer, the sanctions of Boston class structure remained in social situations. The barrier of Brahmin society was made clear to Brandeis when he was not invited to his new partner's wedding.[7]

Louis Brandeis returned the insult to Boston society by taking on a series of cases that sought to rein in the power of the industrial giants. Railroads, public utilities, and insurance companies felt the bite of his intelligence. Although alienated from Boston society, Brandeis earned enough visibility to be appointed to the Supreme Court in 1916. Opposition was instant and chiefly centered in those financial interests which Louis Brandeis had earlier thwarted.[8] The battle for confirmation was hot and long, with Brandeis finally winning and entering the conservative citadel of the law.

Long before Brandeis received national attention, he became one of Michael Moore's heroes. In 1894 Louis Brandeis met John O'Sullivan, a Boston labor leader who became President of the Central Labor Union where the Fabian Society met to talk.[9] Louis Brandeis increasingly identified with the Boston Irish, spending many evenings with the Irish labor leaders and learning about unions. It was not surprising that Brandeis received only one vote from the New England contingent of the Senate when he sought confirmation. Brandeis may have made it onto the Supreme Court, but never into the Boston elite.

Mary Switzer was fascinated by the reformer and by his daughter. Elizabeth Brandeis was the President of the Student Government at Radcliffe and strengthened Mary's interest in government.[10] After struggling through required courses in mathematics and science, Mary met George Grafton Wilson, professor of history. The remaining two years of Mary's study are evidence of her devotion to both Dr. Wilson and the study of government.

Years later Mary wrote:

> When I began to think about what to do after college, I became tremendously interested in international affairs. This was due in large measure to taking courses with a fascinating teacher. This professor of international law was so interesting that he made my desires to be a diplomat very burning. [11]

Dr. Wilson taught Mary the art of scanning and clipping, a skill that brought her to the attention of men in high governmental positions. Dr. Wilson required students to follow discussions printed in newspapers and to draw implications from them for action.[12] The exercise was called a "clipping thesis." Years later Mary taught another woman in the Federal government this same skill, and subsequently the "clipping thesis" became the modus operandi for the Central Intelligence Agency.[13] In addition to learning a new skill in Dr. Wilson's class, Mary also became acquainted with the new ground women were breaking in professions in government. What she heard began to shape her vision of her future. The importance of Dr. Wilson and his interest in International Law was embellished in Mary Switzer's memory as years passed. Although she prided herself on being the first graduate in International Law at Radcliffe, and that major appears under her photograph in the 1921 yearbook. In actuality, there was no such major during 1917-21.[14] Mary had leaped to that distinction from her devotion to the subject and teacher, not the official curriculum of Radcliffe. Records show that Mary majored in Government, History and Economics. She had elected courses in Government that emphasized elements of international law and negotiations, even successfully petitioning Harvard to allow her to take a graduate course from George Wilson.

Mary's interests were more intense than the typical Radcliffe student. Her classmates may not have known Uncle Mike, but they recognized Mary for her powers of argument. "The Why is plain as the way to the parish church" was the quotation *Yearbook* editors chose for Mary. By Mary's Senior year she had assumed a leadership role in the Liberal Club. While classmates struggled with decisions about whether to attend hockey games, song practice, or tea dances, Mary was organizing a conference that would draw students from many colleges on the East coast and attract the attention of Calvin Coolidge. Two of the larger factions of the student body argued between the images of Radcliffe as a "grind college" and of an institution encouraging social and dramatic activities.[15] Mary found such campus isolation from world events intolerable, and during her last two years in college tried to bring herself and others out of the cloister.

Radcliffe had a well-developed club system in which every student who registered was implored to participate. On registration day booths would be set up by students to take new members' dues. One of these clubs was the Civic Club, which included two smaller groups, the Debate Club and the Liberal Club.[16] By 1921 the Debate Club and the Civic Club was all but defunct, but the Liberal Club had never been more vital. Regular meetings were consumed with speeches by members, often focusing on the condition of the downtrodden foreigner. This approach was too sedate for Mary Switzer, and she joined forces with "about half a dozen young radicals in Cambridge from Harvard and Radcliffe and sought the counsel of our idols of the day."[17] To this small group the world seemed materialistic, complacent and boring, and they planned to change the world around them.

On January 21, 1921, a letter from Mary Switzer to Radcliffe College appeared in the *Radcliffe News*. She reported a movement that had been underway since June, 1920 to unite all college Liberal Clubs into an Intercollegiate Organization. Efforts had been made to amalgamate the Intercollegiate Socialist Society and Young Democracy with the student body of the Intercollegiate Conference for Democracy. Mary, and members of the Harvard-Radcliffe contingent, thought this would "avoid duplication of effort and overhead expense." Already Mary was applying bureaucratic principles.

There was a problem, however. Members of the other groups had not seen the need for such an organization, or feared for their "identity," and so a delegation had set out the weekend before to convince the leaders of the two groups being courted. Four Harvard students, two Radcliffe students, and one Wellesley student had traveled to New York, spending "forty-eight hours of incessant discussion" attempting to achieve their goal. The difficulty of getting groups to work together was one of Mary's first lessons in bureaucratic procedure.

The effort failed, but the stalwart group laid plans for a conference of Liberal Clubs to be held in March. A committee was formed to include students from Harvard, Radcliffe, Princeton, Barnard, and N.Y.U. Law. The new organization was announcing its purposes through the upcoming conference and these purposes: to promote the open mind in the college; to fight for academic freedom; and to encourage intelligent ideals of citizenship. The hidden agenda was to develop enough support that a "field secretary" could be hired to open up liberal clubs, like the one at Radcliffe, in other colleges. The Conference was a resounding success, drawing 250 students to the Harvard Union, with 45 colleges represented. Several hundred "older folk" sat on the sidelines of the Conference, noticing the sense of responsibility and unity of purpose in the student delegates. The definition of the Liberal which was accepted by the group was a person who, however conservative or radical his views, keeps his mind resilient, inquiring and tolerant. Speakers at the Conference included Radcliffe's President Briggs, Walter Lippmann, and Walter Fuller, the Editor of the *Freeman Magazine*.[18] Mary Switzer had had her first taste of mobilizing support for a cause, and she found that organizing others was a heady experience.

By April the editorial page of the *Radcliffe News* was full of the aftermath of the Conference. An opposition campaign was launched by a conservative organization, called the National Security League, and the *Radcliffe News* Editor asked a plaintive: "Where shall we stand?" By May the Editor reported that Radcliffe had been indicted with the abuse of Vice-President Coolidge. Quoting from an article in the *Delineator*, the Editor quoted Coolidge as warning that the "reds are stalking," that there was a Liberal Club at Radcliffe, that courses were offered in trade-unionism, and that editorials in the *Radcliffe News* defended Harold Laski for his support of the Boston police strike and criticized the deportation of undesirable aliens. In sum, Coolidge warned citizens that adherence to radical doctrines is destructive of character. Elegantly, the Editor responded to the criticism by writing: "The country needs students who stand and watch, who analyze dispassionately, who are not afraid to turn the search-light of knowledge on the headlong action of the moment."[19] Both Mary Switzer and Michael Moore must have enjoyed the fracas thoroughly.

Mary was grateful for those idols who offered counsel and wondered if they ever realized the influence their encouragement had on this handful of young men and women who wanted to help shape a better world.

> We were trying to come out of the cloister... These were the years when the League of Nations was dying or dead, when the Disarmament Conference was about to be organized, when labor strife was never far below the surface, and when it seemed the major forces around us were materialistic, complacent, very boring, or altogether not of a stripe that we would want to be associated with. [20]

The classic struggle between isolationism and a broad world view was in full tilt, this last year of Mary's college life.

The support of elders was apparent in the spring of 1921, nowhere better illustrated than by the rebuke of an alumna of Radcliffe, who when asked for assistance by the National Security League, self-appointed watchdog of American values, wrote a long reply:

> Why do you consider the Intercollegiate Liberal League a 'grave danger?' The only definite charges you advance seem to be that liberal is the 'latest camoflage' for a variety of socialism. This would seem to require proof.
>
> Have you no more substantial charges to make? . . .
>
> You would prohibit 'the use in all public and private schools of any language other than English as the basic medium of instruction.' 'Every citizen of the United States must think, talk, act American.' Contrast this attitude with that of the Liberal League, the attitude of open-minded consideration and free discussion. Which sounds Prussian? Which American?
>
> Dignified conservatism merits respect and consideration, but illiberalism and hysteria will only render you absurd in the eyes of educated women.[21]

The educated woman who rendered the National Security League absurd with her letter was Eleanor Stabler Brooks, Phi Beta Kappa, summa cum laude in Biology,[22] was representative of the alumnae of Radcliffe who followed college and political events closely and prized intelligent thought.

The support of alumnae and of liberal leaders provided Mary with a devotion to writing her criticism of political or community events, and underscored Uncle Mike's conviction of the power of "straight thinking."

Although Mary Switzer was viewed by her classmates as unusual in becoming uncloistered and described her in the 1921 *Yearbook* as "a radical,"[23] this group of women who graduated in 1921 also valued spirited discussion. More than one man had been "rendered absurd" by their intellect and inquiry. During the Presidential campaign of 1920, the Radcliffe student body had invited candidates to campus for a debate. Democrat and Republican candidates declined to come, thinking the audience of 399, which was the limit of Agassiz Hall, too small to consider. Instead, they sent the typical local politicians, who found to their great dismay that the Farmer's Labor Party was represented by Swinburn Hale. Had Eugene Debs not been in the Federal penitentiary in Atlanta, he might also have appeared. Hale was an accomplished orator, and the contrast between the candidate and the substitutes was painfully clear. A straw vote was taken at the close of the debate, and Radcliffe women overwhelmingly supported Hale.[24] The newspapers once more carried the shocking news of this radical Radcliffe, but the women had conveyed their message to the major parties: no substitutes accepted. Although both Mary and her classmates saw her as being more involved in political and social concerns of the day, she was with a group more like than unlike her. Fifty years later her friend recalled the times and the women:

> When we entered Radcliffe, in 1917, the country was at war and our thinking and goals reflected the serious moods and ideologies of the times. We were dedicated to the idea of 'making the world safe for democracy,' of fashioning it into a better place in which to live. Both the professions and vocations we entered and the avocations we selected were centered around 'good deeds,' 'noble thoughts,' 'service.' [25]

This alumna, chosen to speak at her 50th Reunion, called the Radcliffe influence a "vitalizing" one, which she and others had felt ever since they had "drunk of the College's waters." Mary felt the same loyalty to Radcliffe, keeping in touch throughout her career.

> Every course I had at Radcliffe counts for something and always has. Most have helped quite directly at some points in my career. Many have had a direct bearing on the decisions I have made, and have been responsible for choices among alternative fields of work. A few have opened doors that would otherwise have been closed to me.[26]

The prizing was reciprocated. Mary was made an honorary Phi Beta Kappa by the Radcliffe chapter in 1946. She served on the Board of Trustees for more than ten years, calling that more frustrating than being a member of a "bureaucratic committee."[27] Actually, she enjoyed that honor greatly, and was complimented by Helen Gilbert, another Trustee, for having "brought wisdom from her position in Washington to give decisive thinking to some major and vital decisions before the Board."[28] Helen Gilbert was Acting

President of Radcliffe, when President Bunting was called to serve on the Atomic Energy Commission.[29]

Mary's memories of Radcliffe were not entirely serious. The love of theatre begun by Michael Moore's rather crude promptings was fed by Mary's experiences at Radcliffe. While powerful world and national affairs shadowed the class of '21, this period was also one of excitement in a developing national theatre. At Harvard and Radcliffe, some of the people who would become fine playwrights were getting started. Eugene O'Neil was one example.[30]

Yearbooks from 1917-21 contain pictures of Mary, taking part in college plays. "The Adventure of Lady Ursula" may not have brought down the house, but Mary found the acting much to her liking. Forty years later, Mary wrote:

> When I was in school, most of this (joy and appreciation of the arts) could be had only through the personal effort of the individual. There was the feeling that the process of creation was closely tied to the enjoyment itself. In Cambridge, because we had the great teacher of the drama, George Pierce Baker, who did his teaching through a drama workshop--in writing, producing, seeing, we were perhaps more conscious of the theatre than in other college communities. We had the chance to work in all phases of theatrical production. This gave us a never-to-be-forgotten insight into what it takes to make a good play.[31]

Play-making became important to Mary Switzer in her personal life and influenced many of her professional decisions. Dramatic entries became her hallmark when she delivered testimony before Congress many years later; films and plays about disability were well-funded in the days of her administration. Radcliffe, in this less serious opportunity, had molded Mary for the future.[32]

College staff, in particular, Eva Mooar, the Director of the Appointments Bureau, made concerted efforts to keep Mary Switzer at Radcliffe. Mary was constantly in need of financial help while there, and Miss Mooar saw to it that notices of employment for students were routed to Mary. When summer approached, Miss Mooar stretched her ties to find something that would help Mary. Mary invariably received inquiries during the spring, by dint of Miss Mooar's efforts. It was a privileged clientele that wanted summer help, as one letter addressed to Mary reveals:

> Miss Moore thinks you may be willing to assist me for two to three months with four children, the eldest 9 years, in Chilmark, Martha's Vineyard--old farmhouse, lovely sea beach, fresh water bathing, rowing, swimming, picturesque hills, not a summer resort. Family is myself, mother, children, cook, and second girl. We wish to go on Friday next. Terms to be agreed upon, mutually satisfactory. Telegraph reply.[33]

Mary accepted such offers at least twice during her college years, once going to a resort on McMann Island in Maine, and once to the Breakers in Spring Lake, New Jersey.[34] Although the families and the environment may have been pleasant, Mary learned something important about herself: she did not feel comfortable with young children. Teaching was a usual occupation for women at that time, and this insight was unsettling. She reported:

> I did not really have what I would consider now a good feel for children, although, you know, I managed. But I did not have much imagination about how you could play with them, dreaming up games, and that sort of thing. That was something that was left out of my own make-up, I guess. Some people have a natural aptitude for children and dealing with children and organizing play for them, even though they have had no training for it. I just do not happen to have it, but it filled a gap and I was able to get the money I needed.[35]

Although Mary was one of a handful of women at Radcliffe in need of such employment, her need did not embarrass her. It might have been easy to feel intimidated by the wealth of most of the students surrounding her, but Mary thought she had been prepared for the disparity.

> Our family gave us the sense of our own human dignity. I think my sister and I have done whatever we had to do and never felt one way or the other that it made any difference.[36]

Mary's one regret in her years at Radcliffe was that she often had to choose between the practicality of earning needed money and broadening her experiences. As with the decision to attend Radcliffe and not Mount Holyoke, Mary felt a bit cheated of wider social experiences. She seldom had time for social encounters with males, and she thought a boarding school might have been different.[37] The summer jobs Miss Mooar helped Mary land did not add to Mary's social sophistication, but they certainly firmed up her ideas about a career.

One such idea was of continued study as a Carnegie fellow. The competition was fierce for that goal, and Mary called upon faculty members to write recommendations to the Carnegie Endowment Committee. President Briggs wrote as strong a letter as he could, calling attention to her special circumstances.

> Miss Switzer's record here is distinctly good, though her marks are not so high as they would have been if she had not been obliged to work hard in order to support herself in college. Wherever she worked people wanted her again. She is excellent material, and I feel sure that she will make good use of the scholarship, if she is fortunate enough to get one.[38]

Miss Mooar filed away the letters of recommendation in hopes that Mary would be chosen. Most of the faculty remarks had less to do with Mary's scholarship than with her personality and involvement in extracurricular activities that required "common sense, initiative, and reliability."[39] Perhaps these virtues were not in high demand by the Carnegie Endowment Committee, or perhaps they wanted a combination of high grades and good character. The Fellowship went to another candidate, and Mary began to look elsewhere for a place to begin. Her friend, Elizabeth Brandeis, proved the link she needed to make the first step out of college. Elizabeth had been in Washington since her graduation from Radcliffe, and now she was in charge of the District of Columbia's Minimum Wage Commission. It seemed a perfect beginning for a woman who knew she did not want to teach, but was fascinated with government and international law. Elizabeth promised her a job for the summer, and with that frail a future, Mary decided to head for the seat of government in the United States.[40] In 1921 it was no small thing for a woman to travel from Boston to Washington. The best transportation was the Federal Express, which left South Station at 7:30 every evening. Members of the family or a special male friend customarily accompanied a young female graduate as far as Back Bay. For this traditional leave-taking, the companion paid 24 cents to travel for 12 or 15 minutes before saying goodbye to his friend. Mary Switzer chose a Harvard friend, Hallowell Davis, to accompany her on that prelude to departure. Hal was in medical school, a son of a Quaker mother, and brother of a survivor of the Intercollegiate Liberal League wars. Horace Davis had been an even closer associate of Mary Switzer's, but Hallowell was her choice. He continued to be a friend throughout Mary's life.[41] As the train pulled away from Mary's last tie to home, she realized how dependent she was on Elizabeth Brandeis, but how excited she was about starting in work that befit a liberal.

Radcliffe had been the way out of Upper Newton Falls for Mary Switzer. Her life was greatly changed from her experiences there. Seven years later, when asked by the Alumnae Office if she would chose Radcliffe again, she answered affirmatively, and for several reasons. Its standards of scholarship were the most stimulating of the women's colleges; it had less of the "so-called college spirit than in most places," thus prompting individuality in students; and it was close to a city, which added variety to the student body and decreased insularity. Aside from the academic reasons, Mary mentioned "contact making" as an important contribution Radcliffe had made to her. It had opened up "broader avenues of social intercourse."[42]

Gratitude for the education that promised equality for Mary was expressed through unbroken contact with Radcliffe for 50 years. The daily crossing of the Charles, from Upper Newton Falls to Cambridge, was rewarded. Nativism could be bested by education, and the significance of that victory never slipped from Mary Switzer's memory.

III
One Step at a Time
1921 - 1933

A good memory and a good set of files will serve you well.

Michael Jeremiah Moore

Among Mary Switzer's possessions as she rode the Federal Express, bound for Washington, was a note from Scott Nearing. Nearing was one of the well-known radicals Mary had met at Radcliffe, when he had been one of the Liberal League's advisors. Mary had heard Nearing debate and thought him a man of Uncle Mike's ilk. Nearing's criticism of the leaders of the country gave her destination special meaning.

> The American Way was not based on life, liberty and the pursuit of happiness, but upon the determination of business men to hold down wages and push up profits. The American Way was designed to make the rich richer while it kept the poor in their places. Who was responsible for this policy? The very best people: those who owned the show and ran it, in their interest and for their own profit. In the capitalistic United States, the 'best people' were bankers, manufacturers, merchants, and their military retainers.[1]

Such candor had gotten Nearing fired from the Wharton School of the University of Pennsylvania, and only his popularity as a speaker and policies of free discussion at such institutions as Chautauqua, in New York, had kept him afloat financially.[2] For his protégée, Nearing offered debarkation advice wrenched from his own tumultuous career. His note steadied Mary in her adjustment to the "best people" in the nation's capitol.

> Go easy.
>
> Even the swiftest take only one step at a time, and remember that the mere expenditure of energy, the mere physical motion is not progress.
>
> We must make people happier and better or more correctly, we must do the things that give people a chance to be happier and better. All cults, creeds, and theories are subject to that basic proposition.

So be sure each time you turn your hand or lend your strength that it counts.[3]

The work Elizabeth Brandeis was doing with the Mimimum Wage Board seemed to meet Nearing's criterion; it was designed to give people a chance to be happier. Mary Switzer was depending on Elizabeth Brandeis for her chance to lend her hand to liberal causes. In 1921 this was a great vote of confidence in her friend, for the country was in a state of flux. Many liberals would have been discouraged by the atmosphere in Washington.

The Republicans had won an overwhelming victory in the Presidential campaign of 1920, with promises of lower taxes, less government interference, and more frugal administration. Wilson's hopes for a better nation and a better world were deemed futile by the majority of voters, and Democratic candidates Cox and Roosevelt were badly defeated.[4] For liberals and progressives, 1921 was a time of despair, and Mary Switzer was joining the liberal flotsam created by the new administration.

Progressives in Washington maintained their commitment to a better social structure through the leadership of men like Louis Brandeis. The liberal Justice of the Supreme Court lived with his wife in an apartment on Connecticut Avenue, and his home became an important oasis for liberals in the twenties. Young disciples and old friends gathered in the Brandeis home regularly to hear the Justice discuss his favorite themes: the importance of the individual to create change in any large community or organization and the excitement of having an intelligent plan for human institutions. Mrs. Brandeis presided at afternoon teas, the "at home day" expected of wives of important members of Washington officialdom.[5] As Elizabeth's friend, Mary Switzer was invited to the afternoon teas and occasional dinners at the Brandeis' apartment. Mary had found lodging at the Women's University Club on H Street and had begun her work with the Minimum Wage Board, and the Brandeis' home was a mooring during her adjustment to a city also in transition.

> *During that summer, as I went around inspecting the various restaurants, laundries and other shops in the city for compliance with the Minimum Wage Law, I saw a side of life in the Capitol that was quite a contrast to the atmosphere that I enjoyed as a junior member of the Brandeis family. Tea in the afternoon was a heady thing in those days, with the Justice probing the minds of those who came to call, and the young ones like me listening wide-eyed on the fringes.*[6]

Brandeis related politics to morality and interpreted the rise of Harding and Coolidge as evidence of America's moral decline; but in drawing around him young persons with ideals similar to Mary Switzer's, he fought the despair of Liberals of the 1920s, encouraging them to continue the struggle.[7] In 1921 liberal goals were very simple: they wanted to use the powers of the state to curb the dominance of the strong, to protect weaker groups.[8] A great barrier to government regulation, the control of state legislatures by powerful interest groups, had been overcome in 1913, when United States Senators were required by the Seventeenth Amendment to be elected by direct vote of the people, not the legislatures of states. In 1920 women became entitled to vote, largely due to the efforts of liberals and national gratitude for the efforts of women during World War I. Perhaps due to her involvement in the Radcliffe Liberal League, Mary found her beliefs quite compatible with those of the Brandeis coterie.

One of the "liberal" causes had gotten its start about the time Mary was finding the Liberal League so interesting. Rehabilitation of disabled citizens had only been deemed a national responsibility in 1920. In 1921 it was considered a liberal cause because it seemed altruistic. Conservatives viewed altruism as an individual virtue but a dangerous practice for government. For a country in a depression, having expended dollars and men in a World War, enough had been done to "save" other people or countries. Out of gratitude to the doughboys, the Soldier's Rehabilitation Act had been passed unanimously by both House and Senate in June of 1918. A civilian agency, the Federal Board for Vocational Education, was authorized to serve disabled men who were in hospitals and encampments. The demilitarization of rehabilitation proved quite controversial. The Surgeon General of the Army would not allow the civilian agency to contact any hospitalized servicemen, for he thought disabled soldiers should be physically restored to noncombat duty in the army. The civilian agency took a more generous stance, saying there could be other vocational objectives for the injured serviceman; he did not have to return to the military. Delays in service resulted from thousands of men being discharged from Army hospitals to civilian status without knowing of the services available through the Federal Board.

Making a "liberal" idea operational continued to be difficult. Protests from veterans groups resulted in the formation of a Veterans Bureau in 1921, an independent agency whose director was responsible to the President. This solution was also fraught with problems, as Republicans were charged with bad management, neglect, and favoritism within the Veterans Bureau. As the presidential election of 1924 approached, the Veterans Bureau became a campaign issue. Republicans found their reputation of a businesslike administration to be sullied by this result of Congressional philanthropy.[9]

It was fortunate for the civilian disabled that the problems of administering a veterans' rehabilitation program were part of the country's future in 1918. As it was, the legislation to provide rehabilitation services to disabled veterans prompted the introduction of bills to provide vocational rehabilitation programs for civilians "disabled in industry or otherwise." This was considered "bolshevist" by opponents, since it did not limit services to persons disabled in industry or some "legitimate" occupation. Since a precedent had been established with the legislation for veterans, the civilian bill passed, despite additional arguments of states' rights and charges of impracticability.

On June 2, 1920, President Wilson, himself disabled by a stroke in September 1919, signed the first Federal act to provide vocational rehabilitation services for disabled civilians.[10] From that moment on there was no question about the propriety of Federal involvement in humanitarian and welfare problems of the states.

Mary Switzer was soon to be educated about this unknown liberal cause, rehabilitation. Her choice of a local residence was a building owned by an association that later became the American Association of University Women. Meals were served guests in a central dining room, and permanent guests like Mary Switzer met many women of the day who were traveling and stopping briefly at the H Street club. It was pure chance that Mary met Tracy Copp and learned of the cause that would one day be hers.

> No place could have been more conducive to setting a high standard of living for me and opening the doors to the friendship of fine women, many of whom lived or passed through that club in those days. It was presided over by a darling little person we called Miss Piper, a wee dresden china type with white hair and bright blue eyes. It was in that club, almost the first night of my arrival, that I met Tracy Copp, who had herself just come to Washington to be part of the new program for the Vocational Rehabilitation of the civilians injured in industry that had just come into the then revolutionary program of vocational education, enacted as a result of the dramatic needs for this training turned up in the First World War.
>
> I can see Tracy now, and from that day until the day she died she never changed much in appearance as far as my eyes could see. She was always the handsome, serene, composed, delightful person that was my ideal all of my life. Perhaps because we were both alone, although I did not think of this at the time I was so flattered by her attention, we were drawn together in a close friendship that grew with the years. I used to think that at her age if I could be like her my life would be complete and I would have reached the zenith of accomplishment. That ideal remained with me always.
>
> Of all my Washington friends in the orbit that is now important, Tracy Copp had a more profound influence than any, because had it not been for my acquaintance with her, I would never have known anything about the program of vocational rehabilitation, I would not have grown up in the knowledge of it through many years, on the periphery to be sure, but nevertheless close to it.[11]

Rehabilitation and Mary Switzer were maturing at the same time, with the help of the same woman, Tracy Copp. Had she not been one of Mary's chance encounters within days of arriving in Washington, rehabilitation might have been unknown to Mary for at least two more decades. As it was, Tracy confirmed Mary's hopes that a woman could lend strength where it counted. During those early, vulnerable days in Washington, hope was essential for Mary's survival in Washington. Mary's belief in social progress was challenged by her own faltering career. The summer job with the Minimum Wage Board lasted from July until September, with Mary earning $133.33 a month. Mary wrote her supporter, Miss Mooar at the Appointments Office at Radcliffe, about her work:

> Every inexperienced woman and all minors in the printing and mercantile and hotel trades have to be registered at our office and receive a certificate (issued in triplicate) stating what salary he must get and for how long, according to experience.
>
> ... So there is enough interviewing to break any monotony. An adding machine is nothing in my life at all, and a typewriter—why I might have been professional for years.[12]

The summer of investigating and recording was exciting for Mary. Mastering a typewriter and an adding machine made her feel competent. The National Clubhouse of the American Association of University Women was always interesting, and her friendship with Tracy Copp was thriving. Unfortunately, this foothold proved temporary. Mary wrote Miss Moore on August 26, 1921:

> This is just to tell you that I am finishing my work with the Board about the fifteenth of September. I am looking here for something else, but I may have difficulty in getting just the right thing. If you should hear of anything in the line of industrial research or teaching south of New York I should be grateful to hear of it. If it became necessary to take a position before the fifteenth, I think I could arrange to leave here sooner.
>
> I can now type quite proficiently. I have a great hankering to teach, somehow, you have not the University of Texas on your list--or some place similar?[13]

Impending unemployment certainly broadened Mary's career objectives. Although she knew she did not want to teach children, perhaps there were college teaching jobs available. On September 13, 1921, an even more urgent letter arrived in Miss Mooar's office:

> When this reaches you I shall be among the "unemployed" as I expect to finish my work here by Thursday. Just now everything looks very black! The government is not taking on any more people, except in one or two cases where a civil service examination is essential. I shall take the one for 'Special Field Agent' for the Womens' Bureau sometime this month. Even if I should be successful in that, the appointment would not go through until January.[14]

None of Mary's inquiries proved fruitful, and in September she returned to Newton. During the fall and winter her family worried about her future while Mary struggled along with any work she could acquire in Newton. In April Mary made one more attempt to get her footing in Washington. She returned to work with Elizabeth Brandeis at the Minimum Wage Board. Although she knew what a precarious position the agency was in, it seemed worth a try.

A battle had persisted for twenty years over the constitutionality of minimim wage laws. Louis Brandeis had served as unpaid counsel to the Consumer's League in their fight to have minimum wage laws accepted.[15] When he was appointed to the Supreme Court in 1916, the fight continued. Justice Brandeis felt he could not vote in 1917 or in 1922, when the issue was brought before the Supreme Court, because of his earlier involvement. His abstention was critical in 1917, for without Brandeis the vote was a tie. When the issue was reintroduced in 1922, the vote was five to three that the minimum wage law was unconstitutional.[16] Elizabeth and Mary thought it a great irony, and it was not long before Elizabeth left Washington to study Economics at the University of Wisconsin. Her young friend was once more out of work.

When her Radcliffe friend decamped, another took up Mary's case. Professor Wilson was successful in persuading the Carnegie Endowment for International Peace to hire Mary temporarily. Although the purpose of the work Mary was asked to do was disarmament, a subject dear to the young liberal's heart, the long afternoons at Jackson Place, pouring over documents, was not what she had imagined she would be doing. The work was tedious, but the editing of the monograph concerned with decommissioning of Japanese ships was finally completed.[17] At least the job had given her an opportunity to make some additional contacts, and these led to another brief job with the Women's International League for Peace and Freedom.

As Executive Secretary to the Board of the Women's International League Mary met Jane Addams, Florence Kelly, and Mary Church Terrell. Jane Addams had been a delegate to the International Congress of Women which was held at The Hague in 1915, a meeting that produced a proposal for a negotiated peace settlement of the First World War. The fifteen hundred women who attended the Congress asserted that internationalism does not conflict with patriotism and urged the governments of the world to bring an end to bloodshed. The Women's International League for Peace and Freedom was founded at the Hague in 1915, and in 1922, when Mary Switzer went to work for them, the League continued the pressure for international responsibility.[18] Although she was strictly a secretary, at least Mary could watch other women apply some of the concepts she had heard discussed in Professor Wilson's class.

The Board of Directors of the Women's International League in 1922 was composed of women leaders of social reform in the early 1920s. Florence Kelly met Jane Addams when she travelled to Chicago in 1891 to Hull House. Both Jane and Florence were daughters of abolitionist families who later supported equal suffrage for women. These strands of social justice were integral parts of their concern for the weak against the strong. Florence Kelly made her contribution at Hull House, where she canvassed a square mile area around the settlement house and found tenement work the rule. As a result of her research, the first factory law was passed in Illinois. An eight hour day was prescribed and the employment of children under 14 was prohibited. In 1899 Florence Kelly was asked to head a new organization known as the Consumer's League. For the remainder of her life, Florence Kelly marshalled consumer power to improve working conditions.[19]

Supporters of liberal causes seemed to gravitate to this organization of internationalists. Mary Church Terrell was the wife of one of the first black District judges, and was herself the first black woman to graduate from

Oberlin College. The founder of the National Association for the Advancement of Colored People, along with Florence Kelly, Mrs. Terrell was active in Washington supporting education and political action among black women.[20]

The Board was alive with liberal thought of the day, and Mary Switzer felt awed by the presence of these determined women. One of Mary's responsibilities as the young secretary was to organize an annual meeting of the League. Innocent of some Washington traditions, Mary made her preparations:

> One of the events planned for in this meeting was a luncheon at the Dodge Hotel, which had been opened that year under the auspices of the YWCA. It was a beautiful hotel, with a dining room that opened onto the lobby. I was taking reservations for the luncheon, and naturally, tickets were sold to all those who attended the meeting. I remember vividly being accosted by the manager, Miss Lindsay, when I arrived just before the luncheon. 'How long have you been in Washington?' she asked. I had to admit, for a very short time. She said: 'Don't you know that we do not have mixed eating in this city? I hope we will have no untoward events as a result of your selling tickets to the negro members of WIL.'

> I was shocked and horrified since the thought had never occurred to me and I was not conscious of the color line in Massachusetts. We had negro girls in our class at Radcliffe, and thought nothing of it. Mrs. Terrell was a Board member, she naturally had a table. She had organized her table and sat right in front of the door leading into the lobby of the hotel. I've always carried in my memory the picture of Mrs. Terrell's table of six perfectly beautiful young negro women, dressed far more stylishly and colorfully than any other group in the dining room. They were carrying on their business and their conversation quite unconcernedly, it seemed to me. But I imagine deep down inside they must have had a real chuckle, and then grateful for a young novice who had not learned to be wary and not to follow the instincts on which she was reared.[21]

Mary Switzer remembered the job with the Women's International League for Peace and Freedom as one she did not do well. The luncheon was a painful memory of her brief period as Executive Secretary. Often Mary felt diminished by the power of the women of the League. The way of the liberal was not exactly as Professor Wilson had painted it.

By August 1922 Mary was seriously looking for another job, this time a more secure one. Radcliffe's course structure was difficult to explain; employers took a dim view of Mary's year in economics having been directed by a tutor. Still, Mary stressed her background in money and banking, trade unionism and labor organizations, political and economic theory and international law.[22] The problem was that there did not seem to be much demand for urbane fare, at least not for a 22 year old woman with no family connections.

The Brandeis family continued to be a comfort to Mary. As unsettled as her career seemed destined to be, her first two years in Washington were memorable for the exposure she had in afternoons at the Brandeis home to men with like interests, but of higher position. She admired Dean Acheson, the handsome young law clerk for Justice Brandeis. Mary described Acheson as "one of the glamour boys of the capitol" and enjoyed watching him from the periphery of Justice Brandeis' drawing room.[23]

Except for these weekly interludes, life in Washington was rather lonely and tenuous for Mary, until her loneliness was relieved by meeting Wright McCormick. Although not as glamourous as Dean Acheson, Wright McCormick had his share of allure, particularly for an Irish woman. Son of an old Washingtonian, McCormick had fought in World War I and returned to become a newspaperman. When Mary met McCormick he was working for the Friends of Irish Freedom, an organization garnering support for the Irish Revolution. Years later Mary analyzed her attraction for McCormick:

> It was real fun to come on someone who knew the language of the Irish rebellions, for I was brought up in that atmosphere. I often think that part of the attractiveness of Wright McCormack was the fact that he and I could identify so quickly this background that we had in common.[24]

Although the feelings of kinship were strong, they were overruled by Mary's determination to get a job in Washington and Wright's need to find work as a newspaperman. The Friends of the Irish was not a stable organization and had little to offer a man who wanted to marry and support a family. Wright left Washington in search of steady work; Mary stayed in Washington in search of the same. Both hoped the separation was only temporary.

Mary's first courtship ended abruptly. Word reached her that Wright had been killed in a mountain climbing accident in Mexico. There was no tolerance in Mary Switzer for the "moaning and groaning" she had seen at Irish wakes. Instead, she grieved quietly, explaining to friends who knew how deeply she felt about Wright, that "he had fallen off a mountain," and she must rebuild her dreams.

Another dream came to an end at almost the same time. Mary had hoped to step directly into the battle for peace and equality, but she did not like the work open to a rank beginner. The road to becoming a diplomat was difficult; it was time to be practical, to look for work in more established places. Although she might have to begin with boring job duties, at least there would be security in a government job. After eighteen months of uncertainty, Mary was hired as Research Assistant in the Treasury Department. The research bureau of the Treasury had just begun and Mary was in the Statistics Section. Once more Mary felt unsuited for a job. She was no more a research worker than she had been an Executive Secretary, but she worked at learning. One of her liberal friends in Cambridge wrote his condolences: "Oh dear, what a terrible thing, you are going into the Treasury, the very heart of the present system."[25] For the Radcliffe senior who had had an axe out for the social order, this was quite a change.

The Junior Economist, as Mary was officially titled, struggled along for six months, but on the day the Graf Zeppelin flew over Washington, she was fired.[26] Someone recognized her general ability, however, and took her back as a mimeograph operator. Mary always thought the Treasury was "paternalistic" in that moment, and was grateful for the largess.

The Treasury was both "the heart of the present system" and paternalistic in 1923. For the privilege of signing all the paper money the government printed, the Secretary of the Treasury was charged with the management of national finances. A more complete job description showed that the Secretary was responsible for the collection of revenue, keeping public accounts, reporting to the Congress on the condition of public finances, controlling the building and maintenance of public buildings, the coinage and printing of money, and the administration of the Coast Guard, and the Public Health, Prohibition, and Secret Services. For this job, President Harding had appointed Andrew Mellon, a Pittsburgh banker known to be the third richest man in the United States.[27]

Although the Treasury and Andrew Mellon were aversive to Mary's liberal friends, the new job promised Mary a stability she had not known since coming to Washington. President Harding was having his problems with the national finances. In June of 1921 a Budget and Accounting Act had been passed that created a Budget Bureau in the Treasury Department. All requests for appropriations went to the Bureau before going to Congress. The Treasury was the heart of the Harding administration, and Mary was now a civil servant, safe at last from termination of her job. Mary's description of the Treasury reflects her relief and pride to be on the Treasury payroll.

> The Treasury was the apex of the Washington scene. The building symbolized the strength of our government and seemed very protective. The beauty of the views across the back lawn of the White House from the rooms on the south and west of the old building were breath-taking when enjoyed on that first day, and continuously satisfying as the years went on. You did not know until much later that the excitement of your own first Treasury day was matched in personnel history by one of the great moments in the struggle for good government. You were not completely aware either that you entered on your government service in a period of change and reconversion.
>
> The Treasury Department was established on that day as one of the bulwarks against the scandals that swept other departments during the Harding administration. The political Assistant Secretary, Elmer Dover, resigned by request after a very short term. He wanted a 'clean sweep' of all possible Treasury jobs that had been filled under the Democratic administration in the years before. Many hundreds of Collectors and Deputy Collectors of Internal Revenue and Customs which traditionally had turned over with a change of administration--these and many other jobs Mr. Dover felt he needed to pay 'party debts' and gather the friends of the party about. Mr. Andrew Mellon had been in his office in the Treasury Building long enough to catch its atmosphere. He had met his staff and found them competent and willing. He had glimpsed the problem of converting the department from war to peace. The Bureau of Internal Revenue was hardly established. Some of the older bureaucrats suggested the difficulties that would confront his office if Treasury staffs were depleted wholesale. The Secretary probably turned in his chair and looked out of his southwest windows at a glowing sunset across the White House lawn. He thought, 'The Treasury is a far-flung department with a great tradition. I cannot run it alone or with strangers.' He went instantly to the President and told him Mr. Dover would have to go or he would resign.[28]

Secretary Mellon won Mary Switzer's loyalty with his devotion to competence and continuity. At last she felt safe. Less than a year after the Junior Economist began work at the Treasury, President Harding succumbed to a stroke. The news of the President's death had minimal personal impact on Mary, as did the efforts of Calvin Coolidge to continue Harding's initiatives. From Mary's position, far down in the Treasury, there was little evidence of Coolidge's influence as a leader. Mary was much more interested in Mrs. Coolidge, due to the Secret Service man assigned to protect her. Mary would follow Mrs. Coolidge's activities just to watch what this "movie actor type" did.[29] Grateful to have a secure job at last, Mary's interests in government were tempered by her interest in the opposite sex.

The Treasury was small in 1923, and those who worked there came to know one another well and later to call themselves "the Treasury bunch." Mary's loneliness was lessened by one of the Treasury bunch, Isabella Diamond. Isabella was nine years Mary's senior, a Bryn Mawr College graduate who had found her way to Washington and work in the Treasury some years before Mary arrived. Correspondence between Bryn Mawr and the War Trade Board suggests that Isabella may have begun her career in New York as an Assistant to the War Trade Board,[30] an agency charged with the administration of the Espionage Act of 1917. It is not clear what brought Isabella to Washington, but she was an old hand at the Treasury when Mary began. There were many similarities between Mary Switzer and Isabella Diamond. Both had been the favorites of maternal uncles, as John Stevenson of Fulton, New York, was Isabella's guardian. Neither had fond memories of their fathers, and did not know their mothers beyond early childhood. Both had attended prestigious women's colleges and had been exposed to wealth and culture during their college years. Although the Dean of Bryn Mawr took a reserved position in recommending Isabella, the reference had satisfied employers:

> Miss Diamond has not done brilliant work but has been a faithful student and ought to succeed. Her major subjects have been English and Latin. She has also had work in Biology, Philosophy, Psychology, Economics, and Politics, a year of Spanish, and other elective courses. She is well-liked by her instructors and classmates and is undoubtedly the sort of person who would be pleasant to work with.
>
> I shall quote statements from two of her professors. Professor Wheeler of the Latin Department says: Miss Diamond's scholarship is not above average. Her personality is pleasant and cheerful. She would be a faithful, conscientious worker, I believe. She is not at all brilliant, but she is not slow, and after she has had a little experience, I believe that she will do her work well. She is good tempered and is not likely to be ruffled by vexatious occurences. Professor Chew of the English Department says: Miss Diamond's scholarship is fair. I should think she would have a good deal of energy and enthusiasm in business.[31]

Perhaps it was the energy and enthusiasm that appealed to Mary, or perhaps there was enough in the backgrounds of Mary and Isabella to cause them to become fast friends and to eventually enter into a "Boston marriage," a respectable life-style for upper middle class and professional women of the time. The practicality of two single women combining households outweighed the possibility of more intimate reasons, making this an acceptable alternative for Mary and Isabella. Chance meetings had profound effects on Mary Switzer's life. Like Isabella Diamond, Tracy Copp just happened to be in Washington when Mary arrived, and her dedication to rehabilitation was transmitted to Mary.

Life had not been easy for Tracy Copp in the nurturance of an infant and "liberal" program. She had begun work in rehabilitation as a factory inspector for the Wisconsin Industrial Commission, under Governor Robert LaFollette. She had come to Washington when the Federal Board of Vocational Education was charged with administering Public Law 236, a new grant-in-aid program for disabled citizens.[32] Tracy was one of six staff members in the Washington office of the Federal Board of Education, and her greatest responsibility was to encourage states to accept the assistance of the Federal government. She traveled regularly to thirteen states.

It must have been a hard program to sell, for by 1924 twelve states had still not availed themselves of the cooperative program, largely due to the indifference of State departments of education where vocational rehabilitation programs would be administered. Determined travel and attention to details in making the new program operational taxed the stamina of the small Washington staff. Policies, programs, staffing, management of Federal funds and a reporting system had to be developed within each cooperating state, most frequently with an undercurrent of mistrust of Federal aid to education.[33]

The vision was clear in the minds of the Federal staff. They saw rehabilitation as a highly individualized service that might not result in returning all clients to work, but would help them achieve some self-care goals. Federal law was much more restrictive, but this handful of leaders pressed ahead, urging state agents to expand their services. The fact that Federal funds could only be used for training, not medical intervention, required agents to call upon private sources for aid in meeting client needs. Physicians were asked to perform surgery without pay; clubs were implored to donate funds for client room and board.[34] One had to be flexible and persuasive to work for the state board of vocational education in 1924.

Tracy shared her experiences and a few of her travels with Mary Switzer. Some of the leaders in older state programs had been successful because those particular states had distinguished liberals in elected offices. William Faulkes of Wisconsin had begun operating a rehabilitation program for individuals injured in industry in 1918.[35] The senator from Wisconsin at that time was Robert M. LaFollette. LaFollette had been a progressive reformer since the turn of the century, first serving as governor of Wisconsin for six years, then as United States Senator for twenty years. Married to Belle Case, the first woman to graduate from the University of Wisconsin Law School, Bob

LaFollette and his family championed a series of social causes. The intensity and zeal of the LaFollette family carried the Senator into the Presidential election on the Progressive ticket, although Bob LaFollette would live only one more year. The Brandeis and LaFollette families were close, with Justice Brandeis being called "Uncle Louis" by young Bob LaFollette.[36] Wisconsin supported the progressive thought and actions of the LaFollettes for many years; it was not surprising that the combination of William Faulkes' determination and the progressive spirit of the LaFollettes made Wisconsin a model of what could be accomplished in rehabilitation.

Tracy Copp introduced Mary Switzer to some of the "key characters in the rehabilitation drama," among them, William Faulkes. She also exposed Mary to state officials of a different stripe--the mercenaries of state government.

> And then there were the other characters who were colorful but not what might be called leaders in rehabilitation. I remember one named Herb Battle in the Chicago office of the Illinois agency. In those days the government of the State of Illinois and the City of Chicago was considered a caricature in the political world of the time. Mayor Thompson and all sorts of weird people were in positions of authority. Public jobs were on the auction block for the highest patronage bidder and no one had a job in Illinois unless they were very much involved in the political activities of their party. And usually they dressed and comported themselves as the cartoons of the day depicted them--shiny brown shoes, checked coats, a cane with a gold handle, poor grammar even if college graduates, and all the rest of the show that is put on often by very intelligent people. [37]

It seemed to Mary that there were contradictions here, just as she had noticed in the Women's International League for Peace and Freedom. She watched Tracy deal with limited persons in order to reach a large goal. Liberal philosophy seemed so simple; how did it become so distorted in application? Despite the heroic efforts of state and Federal workers like Bill Faulkes and Tracy Copp, rehabilitation was still viewed as a trial program in 1924. Public Law 236 was scheduled to expire in June 1924, and the Chief of Vocational Rehabilitation, John Kratz, had a near single-handed battle to convince both the Federal Board of Vocational Education and Congress that the Act should be extended. The Act was extended for six years, but Congress adjourned before appropriating money for the vocational rehabilitation program. Salvaging the work of three years and the six idealists in the Federal office became Kratz' urgent task. Kratz asked the help of state agency directors, who agreed to continue state operations as best they could without Federal funds until December, when Congress would reconvene. President Coolidge was petitioned by the Board for permission to deficit spend the administrative funds necessary to maintain the Federal staff until December.[38] The demise of the Federal vocational rehabilitation program and Tracy Copp's job was narrowly averted, but the near miss served an interesting purpose.

All 39 states cooperating in the state-Federal rehabilitation program kept their programs alive until December, except Missouri. The sudden loss of Federal funds caused many states to reexamine their dependence on Federal support and to organize the first national conference on vocational rehabilitation. From this conference the National Rehabilitation Association evolved in 1927, an organization of early rehabilitationists who believed Vocational Education had not and would not grant the status and priority needed for a program for the rehabilitation of disabled people. After all, John Kratz had been forced to wrest an appeal for the program from the Federal Board of Vocational Education. The National Rehabilitation Association intended to remove reliance on an indifferent agency and establish vocational rehabilitation as far more than an extension of vocational education.[39]

Those early rehabilitation leaders, and certainly Tracy Copp, developed an allegiance to a program that was so personal in its approach that the statistics of cases rehabilitated never obscured the persons who had been helped. The Wisconsin "agent" could not forget the client who lost his left hand in a fodder shredder at the age of 57, yet returned to work as a one-armed blacksmith. The Florida "agent" recalled the lineman whose foot was crushed, gangrene developed, and his leg was amputated. With vocational rehabilitation aid, the lineman received an artifical leg, and climbed utility poles for 35 years longer, wearing out 14 artificial legs in the process. The Tennessee "agent" treasured the record of a typist who was blind, yet produced 300 letters without error in her job at a hotel in Chattanooga.[40] For these rehabilitation pioneers, services were a right, not a privilege or gratuity. By 1925, the United States Secretary of Labor was echoing this belief:

> *Vocational rehabilitation is making it possible for each member of society to pay his own way. This is a moral obligation of organized Government and should be developed on that basis, rather than on the basis of impulsive charity or misdirected sentiment.*[41]

These were survival years for rehabilitation, and the threat of extinction hung over the collective heads of state agents and Federal staff alike. Despite the dramatic results in individual cases, Congress was still concerned with the economic results of the program. It fell to Tracy Copp to answer these persistent questions, and in 1928, the product of a year's work collecting information on persons rehabilitated between 1921 and 1924 was published by the Federal Board. Among the facts noted in the study was that it cost $300 to $500 a year to maintain a person in a poorhouse or custodial institution; vocational rehabilitation of a disabled individual cost an average of $250 per person.[42] Years later, Mary Switzer would follow Tracy Copp's lead in collecting information to spur the growth of a program.

Tracy was a model for Mary in many ways. Early photographs of rehabilitation workers reveal how outnumbered Tracy was by men. Tracy had begun her career as a teacher of "tuberculous children," but she soon was attracted to the employment problems of persons with disabilities and moved to the Wisconsin Industrial Commission, and was responsible for women's activities. At the state level she became accustomed to being a solitary woman, and thought little about the disparate sex ratio. As vocational rehabilitation was starting in Wisconsin, Tracy joined the Department of Vocational Education as an "agent." Like Mary Switzer, Tracy was influenced by her friend, Mary Anderson, to come to Washington when the staff of the Vocational Rehabilitation Division of the Federal Board of Vocational Education was being formed.[43] Mary Anderson, known as Chief of the Women's Bureau in the U.S. Department of Labor, had known Tracy Copp since Wisconsin days. Tracy was the sole woman in the Federal staff for many years. Mary Switzer took note of Tracy's work in a man's world:

> There was never any question about her wholehearted loyalty to the program, but she did not influence it at all, really. She did not influence it in any way because it was a man's program... She had friends among the men and they were always very loyal to her and so on, but they did not look up to her as . . . a leader. . . As far as the development of the program, the changes that took place in it when she was associated with it--she was really not in that inner circle—she was a woman in a man's world and the men were not her kind of people anyway. And she did not socialize with them very much, except when it was necessary. They were not companionable in the sense that people go together and work together.[44]

Although Mary worried that Tracy was not viewed as a leader by the men with whom she worked, she also understood that Tracy had indirectly affected the course of rehabilitation with her field investigation. One of the stated purposes of the study, in addition to influencing Congress, was to reassure rehabilitation workers that their own accomplishments were worthwhile. Tracy's study was the first evidence that the rehabilitation process could be a "monument of this wonderful civilization of America."[45] And, as Mary Switzer's "first friend in Washington," Tracy also convinced Mary that rehabilitation was "the most romantic work in government."[46]

Mary's earlier love for the theatre was reinforced through her friendship with Tracy. Although Tracy was thoroughly dedicated to her work, she arranged a balance in her life that impressed Mary Switzer:

> I also remember during one of the trips we made to Chicago going to the first of the Wagner operas that I had wanted to see—Lohengrin, put on by the Chicago Opera Company. I was always conscious with Tracy of the way in which she organized her life and resources to enjoy everything. She saw all the best plays, went to all the concerts in the cities where she traveled, she went to opera, she went to Europe and encouraged me to go on my first trip in the late 20's. She had beautiful clothes and beautiful appointments in her apartment. She entertained with grace and style, everything she did was tinged with beauty and with an unflagging sense of excellence. In this she was outstanding among our many friends.[47]

This first friend introduced Mary to other women in Washington, including Mary Anderson, who in turn introduced Tracy and Mary to "Trade Union women" from New York, like Elisabeth Christman and Rose Schneiderman. Although it had been hard initially for Mary to enter a society in Washington that provided stimulation and enjoyment, while she worked in a routine job, the circle widened through Tracy Copp.

Mary's jobs became less routine as she worked her way up the bureaucracy. Her point of entry to the Treasury on September 16, 1922, was the lowest possible civil service rating, as well as being an inappropriate slot. Being a research assistant, or "Junior Economist," as she was titled, tried Mary's ability to adapt. She was so unsuited to the job that she was fired,[48] but was so well liked that a position was found for her as a clerk in the Office of the Secretary of the Treasury.[49] On July 1, 1924 Mary was moved to the Office of the Chief Clerk and there began to make herself noticeable and indispensable. Professor Wilson's clipping thesis had taught Mary a most useful skill for a woman in a routine job. Mary was assigned the task of sorting and classifying the clippings that had accumulated in the Secretary's office since Andrew Mellon's appointment by President Harding in 1921. In six months, working half days, Mary had constructed a permanent file. Then, she began a current file. Apparently, she put the press clipping service out of business, although she had been asked by a superior to justify the amount of time she was spending in this service:

> After I had achieved a current file, it developed that the press clipping service was not satisfactory, so I undertook to keep the file going by my own efforts. I began scanning magazines and papers regularly for material of interest to the Secretary... I have been reading eight or ten of the larger papers daily, clipping all the news of interest to the Secretary and sending it to him as soon as possible in the day.
>
> Were it not for the fact that I am a prolific reader interested in this field, and have developed a certain technique in the work, and in addition have access to specialized libraries, I should not be able to accomplish it. It may interest you to know, in this connection, that during the three weeks I was on annual leave last summer, a period during which the Secretary was in Europe, I spent 37 hours by actual count, gathering material for the file.
>
> It is clear, therefore, from the fact that I spend only the hour or so every morning, the occasional hour or two I go out for intensive browsing at Bretano's and the few minutes I occasionally take at luncheon to purchase a particular periodical, that most of the work is done outside of the seven hours I am at the office.[50]

One almost pities the Mr. Birgfeld who had asked for an accounting of the unusual activities of the clerk in the Chief Clerk's office. Mary had seized an opportunity, provided a valuable service for the Secretary, thus enlarging a clerk's job to one of a special assistant. Nevermind if the supervisor in the Chief Clerk's office resented the arrangement! Mary was moving up in the Treasury; within three years she became a Principal Clerk. Four years, and two promotions later, the young woman who had come to Washington so fascinated with International Law was handling most of the correspondence that came to the Secretary of the Treasury.[51] Mary was part of a women's support group that helped her up each step. Although Mary was a fast reader, she could never have continued her clipping responsibilities without the help of Isabella Diamond. One of those specialized libraries to which Mary had access was run by Isabella Diamond. Knowledge of what was happening in government traveled fast along the channels of the Chief of the Women's Bureau and the League of Women Voters. Still, Mary must have wondered: "Must it be this slow?"

It helped to have the balance of a personal life that was increasingly interesting. Mary was an excellent tender of friendships and corresponded consistently with Radcliffe and Harvard friends. She was also a loyal family member, and she traveled frequently from Washington to Boston to visit with Uncle Mike, her aunts, and her sister, Anastasia. Prosperity was part of Mary Switzer's life between 1922 and 1927:

> As I went back and forth between Washington and my home in Boston, I made New York a regular stopping place. There, through friends I had met in college, I had a very rich friendship with people in the theatre, or close to it, and in the publishing field. Those were the years when Horace Liverwright was one of the shining lights in the publishing world and even today my library shows the results of my deep friendship with him. All I had to do was mark up a catalogue and the books would come from Liverwright. And Alfred Wallerstein, who introduced me to the Theatre Guild, and his daughter Bertha, who was my dear friend. [52]

The entrepreneur in the clerk's job was equally enterprising in her social and personal activities by 1927. As 1928 and another Presidential election approached, Mary could look back on the last seven years and claim having made her effort count, even in seemingly insignificant or disliked tasks. The brief job with the Women's International League for Peace and Freedom brought Mary into contact with leaders of the Quakers, who had organized the National Council for the Prevention of War. Among the persons Mary came to know was Clarence Pickett, who later became Executive Secretary of the American Friends Service Committee. Jane Addams, Grace Abbott, chief of the Children's Bureau, and Clarence Pickett were social reformers whose pacifist views and pleas for social reform later influenced Eleanor Roosevelt. And Mary Switzer knew them all, at least from afar. Although her association with social reformers was tangential, Mary thought it purposeful:

> As you look back over your life and the threads that come together in one period, if you really stop to think about it and face the facts, you can see that one thing leads to another in fairly logical sequence. [53]

The threads of international concern, government service, women's leadership, pacifism, and rehabilitation were all being woven into the fabric of Mary Switzer's life by 1927. These same causes were unpopular with the American public as 1928 began. Citizens still believed that there was work for all who wanted to work, because farmable land had always been available in the United States for anyone willing to work. The national government was largely undeveloped due to the frontier psychology of the early twentieth century. Federal domestic legislation was sparse indeed. Poverty was considered the result of imprudence; private charity the means of dealing with the poor.[54]

The nominees for President of the United States in 1928, Herbert Hoover and Alfred Smith, epitomized the poles of political belief. Hoover represented all the conservative virtues: an engineer, thrifty, self-made. The prosperity of 1927-28 provided Hoover with justification for refusing to debate Smith. Hoover fostered the image of being above politics, standing for "tranquility, prosperity, and purity." Alfred Smith had established a reputation in New York as a knowledgeable and progressive legislator. Son of an Irish immigrant, Smith was Catholic and gained strength through the political machinery of New York City. All these qualities made Smith suspect to the majority of Americans.[55] Mary Switzer was keenly aware of the polarities of background and persuasion of the two candidates for President. At the Brandeis home, on the occasion of a family dinner enlarged for political discussion, Mary recalled:

> I remember one night before the 1928 campaign when six of us were there, including Senator Walsh of Massachusetts, and it was a great shock to the conservative, aristocratic Democrats to have to support Al Smith, particularly because he was a "wet." I used to caution my friends in those days, not to think he was too great a liberal, although he had been a fine liberal Governor in New York State largely because of the people he associated with him and because of his belief in being able to make a good government. Dealing with national matters of great theoretical concern he might not have been as great a President as his strong admirers and promoters, of whom I was one, believed at that time.[56]

Mary's reaction to Smith, that he was not the pure liberal to whom she was accustomed, was prophecy of the election results. Although Hoover won by a margin of 6 million votes, Smith won the votes of citizens who had voted to stay with a "sure thing"; 15 million voters, primarily in mining and industrial counties, supported Smith. The voice of new immigrants was surprisingly loud in the election of 1928.[57]

The irony of the Republican slogan, "Hoover and Happiness or Smith and Soup Houses," shaped the years that followed the stock market crash in 1929. Hundreds of thousands of jobs were eliminated when companies failed. Disabled persons who must now compete with hundreds of able-bodied applicants might have been sacrificed in the struggle to survive the Great Depression. Somehow the small, insecure public program survived. In 1930 Hoover signed the renewal Act for Public Law 236, providing for a three year extension of the program. Renewed again in 1932, the program received no changes in support levels until 1937.[58] The fiscal restraint of the times is reflected in this long growth hiatus, but the program survived a national calamity of dimensions that shook the social and economic structure of the United States.

The budget of the United States in 1930 was prepared and passed before the stock market crash. Within that budget there was a requirement for the promotion of public health, with an allocation of 19 million dollars. Combined expenditures for health and education, with nothing for welfare or social security was 31 million, less than one percent of the Federal budget.[59] Within that context the scope of the vocational rehabilitation program in 1930 seems much less modest. In 1930 forty-four states were participating in the state-Federal program. There was a total of 143 rehabilitation workers in those 44 states. Between 1921 and 1930 only 45,000 persons had been rehabilitated and 12 million dollars had been expended in ten years.[60] Although the workers in rehabilitation were zealous and had sworn independence from the Federal Board of Vocational Education, the threat to survival was so real in 1930 they were forced to retrench and wait.

The young Administrative Assistant in the Office of the Chief Clerk of the Treasury was called upon to act as a "rehabilitation agent" in an unofficial capacity. The Depression rocked the Treasury, and Andrew Mellon would sometimes become aware of a family that needed assistance but would not turn to charity. David Finley, Mellon's Special Assistant, contacted Mary Switzer in October of 1930, asking her to visit a family and report the circumstances to Mellon, so that he might make a personal contribution to the family's welfare. Having been approached because of her "excellent judgment," Mary wrote to Mr. Finley in December:

> The case is not one for charity as the family is not in dire need, but rather in one of those very low periods of discouragement that any family would find themselves in after a long period of sickness and heavy doctor's bills... My personal impression about this case is that the family is the victim of poor management and weak wills. I should not advise any large monetary contribution. On the other hand, this being the Christmas season, it might not be detrimental to send, for instance, a suit of clothes for the men... I got the impression that the neighbors felt she was in no distress. It would be my judgment that this was not a case for charity, and I should not recommend that the secretary make any contribution.[61]

Apparently the Secretary and his close staff knew and trusted Mary Switzer. Tracy Copp may have advised her on this rehabilitation problem, or she may have been influenced by her own family's reaction to hard times, but Mary had little sympathy for someone unwilling to be active in their own rehabilitation. In addition to investigating requests for help, Mary was practicing a craft she would continue to perfect during her career. Although a devoted liberal, given to those dynamic teas and dinners at the Brandeis' home, and girded by friends of consonant thought, she adopted the "long view." She would work with whomever was in office, for she intended to be there long after the elected or appointed left. Having established herself as a clipping expert, she soon endeared herself to President Hoover:

> Mr. Hoover had a passion for the printed word and for broad-scale look-see at the press of the country and he organized a press clipping service, which was financed in large part by his Cabinet by personal assessment and by the Republican National Committee. And the only contributed government funds were staff--and I was a member of the staff. For four years, I was one of the group who helped to analyze the editorial comment and other things that came into this little office that we had. It was an annex to the White House and every afternoon at 4 P.M. these results of the day's culling were taken over to Mr. Hoover--cartoons and circulation of papers that said these things, and so on.[62]

It must have been painful reading for President Hoover, but perhaps the comments contributed by his clipping staff diluted the public sentiment. At least something led Herbert Hoover to run again for the Presidency in 1932.

Republicans had approached their convention with something akin to dread, while the Democrats were jubilantly anticipating their first opportunity since Wilson to regain the leadership of the country. Hoover had no real opposition to nomination and continued to stand by his belief that the Federal government should only provide encouragement to business, which would eventually restore American abundance. Roosevelt had a more difficult time winning the nomination, but accepted with the speech in which the words "New Deal" occurred for the first time. It was a speech with the old phraseology of progressives. Later in the campaign Roosevelt spoke more pointedly: government should act as a guarantor of the common good within the existing economic system.[63]

The man with the fly-paper mind, as Roosevelt's "Brains Trust" advisor Rex Tugwell described him, was elected by a wide margin.[64] Change was once more at hand for Washington bureaucrats. Onto this stage walked a President who had experienced rehabilitation, who had learned from progressives, and who knew the public was waiting for the "New Deal".

The first national gathering of rehabilitation workers, May 1922. John Kratz (11), William Faulkes (44), and Tracy Copp (45), are present. *The Rehabilitation Record*, 1970.

IV
A Ship Board Look
1933 - 1938

Perhaps because I am Irish and incurably romantic, all my life I have had idols--teachers, friends, characters in novels and history, who somehow in their person and the way they performed in the world, seem to be worth striving to be like.

Mary Elizabeth Switzer, 1959

With the New Deal, many women came to Washington to function in elected or appointed offices. Among these women, Mary found mentors. It may have been Irish luck that she continued to find wise counsel and companionship, but her first secretary, Josephine Coe, thought it was her "Irish outlook," her inclination to view everyone as nice.[1] Mary felt she differed in her positive outlook from her Uncle Mike and her sister, Anastasia. They seemed to be more the "Black Irish" strain in the Moore family, stirring up conflict without even trying hard. Mary described herself as pleasure-loving, happy-go-lucky, and "easy," a trait that made her transition into the New Deal administration much easier.

Mary made allowances for the ousted Republicans. Even Andrew Mellon, who had depended on Mary as "clipping specialist" and personal emissary to needy families, was excused by Mary for income tax evasion. She found it unbelievable that he had solicited direction from the Bureau of Internal Revenue for ways to avoid paying tax, and had then used five of the 10 devices they suggested in his own tax returns.[2] When Mellon was convicted in 1934, Mary's new boss used the incident to castigate the Republican rich and to close tax loopholes. Meanwhile, Mary felt as if a tornado had hit Washington.

And, of course, it had. The Treasury was the eye of the storm, from the night before Roosevelt's Inauguration until 1937. Roosevelt had dissociated himself from Hoover's economic policies and allowed the banking crisis to develop. On the eve of Inauguration, Treasury officials were pleading with governors of New York and Illinois to close the banks to prevent expected runs the next morning. The new Secretary of the Treasury called for swift action, and Roosevelt answered by signing an emergency banking act that granted him new powers over banking and currency that kept the banks closed. A display of action followed, so swift that it became known as "the hundred days." Bills were drawn by Presidential advisors working in hotel rooms and were passed into law within two months.[3] The transition from the legislative to the executive branch of government as the center of reform was accomplished in this whirlwind of activity.

Although the philosophy of the New Deal was similar to the ideals of earlier progressives, the magnitude of the crisis and the pressure for centralization of government took Mary by surprise. The New Deal had three objectives: relief, recovery, and reform, and the Treasury stood at the center of each objective.

A port in the storm for Mary was the new Secretary of the Treasury, William Woodin of Pennsylvania. Roosevelt's second choice, Woodin was neither a radical nor intimidated by the prospect of Roosevelt's unorthodox fiscal policies. Mary found Woodin "a sweet man,"[4] although in 1933 he questioned the necessity for the clipping service she had so lovingly built. Woodin's Undersecretary was none other than Dean Acheson, Mary's acquaintance from the Brandeis home, who came to her defense with Secretary Woodin, and the service continued.

Any shelter from the storm of executive power was razed with the controversy over the gold standard as a base for currency. Some of Roosevelt's advisors saw the reduction of the gold value of the dollar as the surest way to restore prices to a pre-depression level. Roosevelt took several actions: he stopped the outflow of gold to Europe, forbade the hoarding of gold and required the delivery of all gold held domestically to the Federal Reserve Banks, and advocated the elimination of the required payment of Government debts in gold. Finally, Roosevelt announced he would buy newly mined gold in the United States for prices he and his advisors set. In the midst of this revolutionary change in monetary policy, a dying Secretary Woodin had left an inexperienced Dean Acheson to manage as best he could. Acheson was opposed to manipulating the currency and stood his ground, irritating Roosevelt increasingly. Feeling that he was being asked to do something contrary to law, Acheson resigned and was quickly replaced with Henry Morgenthau. Secretary Woodin felt badly about Acheson being pressed to resign, and resigned himself in January 1935 to make way for Morgenthau.[5]

Old loyalties to Mellon, Acheson, and Woodin gave way to new opportunities for Mary Switzer. Henry and Elinor Morgenthau were the

Roosevelt's closest friends among the Cabinet.[6] A New York appointee of Governor Roosevelt, Morgenthau had come to Washington as head of the Farm Credit Bureau, but both before and after his appointment as Secretary of the Treasury, Morgenthau involved himself in other Cabinet members' assignments. Although Morgenthau's willingness to do Roosevelt's bidding, regardless of territorial domain, endeared him to Roosevelt, it maddened other Cabinet members. Harold Ickes, Secretary of the Interior, often ran afoul of Morgenthau, thinking him a Roosevelt toady.[7] But for Mary Switzer, Morgenthau's bond to Roosevelt accelerated her climb up bureaucratic steps, and she had kind words for him:

> Mr. Morgenthau had been a farmer in upstate New York, a gentleman farmer, but most of all he was Mr. Roosevelt's mouthpiece and 'Man Friday.' Everything Mr. Roosevelt wanted done, he was prepared to do. He was also a person who knew how to gather around him men of ideas. One of the most significant things he did was to build himself a good staff in the Treasury which had been a very, very light staff up to that time. There had only been one or two lawyers to advise previous Secretaries--now there was a large General Counsel's office established--people in charge of public relations. Herbert Gaston, one of the editors of the old New York World, who had come to Washington with Mr. Morgenthau from Albany, was one of his most delightful appointees.
>
> When he came to the Treasury, he had little understanding of the Treasury mechanics and the outstanding atmosphere appeared to be one of the recalcitrance of bureaucrats. The Treasury represented to Mr. Roosevelt, I am quite sure, a rather monolithic pillar which just was immovable. No one knew exactly what was going on or what made the Treasury tick and Mr. Morgenthau came in determined to find out. And one humorous thing happened. Naturally, what he thought he would like to do would be to find out what was being sent out--press releases and reports of all kinds. So he issued an order to have all reports centralized and cleared with his office before they were issued. Well, he forgot that the Coast Guard was part of the Treasury Department and had important weather reports that were issued periodically; and then there were the Public Health Service's vital statistics reports that were routine and he had never thought of that, of course. So he got a very bad press in the early days and he used to be very troubled about it. I can remember one day when he came back from the White House and told his staff: 'Well,' the President said, 'Ole Hanky boy, you've got to go up, you can't go down.'[8]

Determined to go up, Morgenthau asked Gabrielle Forbush, a friend of his wife, for help. Gabrielle, a Vassar classmate of Elinor Morgenthau, had come to Washington in 1933 to assist Morgenthau in the Farm Credit Administration. When Morgenthau moved to the Treasury, Gabrielle went along.[9] Mary was in the business of "building her fences" those days, for she had had no particular assignment since the dismantling of the Press Bureau under Woodin. "Just fiddling around and trying to land on my feet" was how Mary described her work in the Treasury between 1933 and 1935.

Thinking Gabrielle an excellent possibility as a connection to the New Deal leaders, Mary invited her to lunch on the roof of the Washington hotel. An innocuous exchange ended with Gabrielle's saying, "We must get together," but Mary did not hear from her again. Some time later a desperate Morgenthau, unwelcome in the Treasury and unable to locate even a pencil, asked Gabrielle if she knew anyone who could help him. Gabrielle recalled her lunch with Mary and suggested Mary to Morgenthau. Asked if she could be loyal to him, Mary's reply was: "Of course, I can be loyal to you, I am a civil servant."[10]

Tired of the cold shoulder within the Treasury, Morgenthau not only wanted to learn his way around internally, he wanted to know what people were thinking and writing him. Gabrielle was told to organize a Correspondence Section to deal with the voluminous correspondence that came to the Treasury. Questions about taxes, foreclosures, home loans, and requests for help poured into the Correspondence Section. Mary composed form letters for some of the concerns, used her knowledge of government to get help for everyone possible, and frequently visited people in need.[11] Morgenthau soon found himself with a splendid public relations instrument. And Mary found herself part of the inner circle of the New Deal.

Garden parties at the White House were open to intimates at the Treasury, due to Mrs. Morgenthau's friendship with Eleanor Roosevelt. Mary frequented such occasions, firming her relationship with Gabrielle and the Morgenthaus. Morgenthau had brought his private secretary, Henrietta Klotz, to Washington with him.[12] No one reached Morgenthau except through Henrietta Klotz, and she was greatly feared and generally disliked because of her power. Present at every meeting, privy to Morgenthau's thoughts, Miss Klotz spoke for the Secretary at the Treasury and attended all social events. Mary's estimate of Henrietta Klotz was "that she was not an interesting or widely informed person, but so thoroughly sincere that it was apparent she was invaluable to the Secretary."[13] Mary won Henrietta Klotz through social contacts, including dinners with the Forbushes and cocktail parties with "newspaper pals." Now she was one step closer to the Secretary.

One afternoon in the summer of 1935, the "fence building" paid dividends. Gabrielle Forbush had informed Mary months earlier that a Vassar friend of Mrs. Morgenthau's, Josephine Roche, was about to be made Assistant Secretary of the Public Health Service. Mary had told Henrietta Klotz about her early desire to be a doctor and conveyed her hopes of being able to work with Miss Roche. Again, there was no immediate response, and Mary was kept in suspense. A Morgenthau tea for Department executives was held at the Morgenthau home. Mary proceeded through the receiving line, where Morgenthau was flanked by Gabrielle, Henrietta Klotz, and Elinor Morgenthau. As approached, Mrs. Morgenthau reminded the Secretary that he had something to tell Mary. Without any amenities, Morgenthau said, "I'm making you Josephine Roche's assistant." Mary broke into tears and Mr. Morgenthau hugged her, saying, "I gather the answer is 'yes.' "[14]

Why would Morgenthau release an assistant who had become valuable to him? Morgenthau had a suspicious nature and had acquired the habit of assigning a staff person whom he knew would represent his point of view to any new appointee whom he did not know personally. Although Josephine Roche had been a college friend of his wife, he did not yet trust her, so he placed Mary in a position to be his "eyes and ears." Josephine Roche had an equal amount of mistrust in Henry Morgenthau, and this posed a problem for Mary. Miss Roche did not like her private comings and goings known, and Morgenthau was so possessive of employees' time that he insisted on knowing Miss Roche's whereabouts.[15] After a period of mutual testing, Mary proved worthy of Miss Roche's confidence by protecting her from Morgenthau's inquiries.

Unwittingly, Morgenthau had connected threads in Mary Switzer's life that stretched to the past and into the future. Josephine Roche had been president of a coal company in Colorado that had early been unionized. Josephine Roche was well-acquainted with the United Mine Workers, John L. Lewis, and the progressive values of the labor movement. Josephine Roche had also run for Governor of Colorado in 1934, daring to be one of the first women to seek public office in that state. Mary's liberal beliefs, acquired through Mike Moore and her Radcliffe days, were compatible with Miss Roche's history. The thread of the future lay in the nature of Josephine Roche's new post. Hers was the task of supervision of the health of the nation, and through the Public Health Service Mary Switzer began to make contacts that would become her most powerful constituency.

Josephine Roche was a tough-minded woman, and she had much to teach Mary Switzer about negotiation. In 1927 Josephine Roche had inherited large holdings in the Rocky Mountain Fuel Company, the second largest coal producer in Colorado. Mary loved the story about the way Josephine Roche handled the violent strikes in the company she had inherited. "Her truly phenomenal Joan of Arc performance, as the champion of the forces of labor," Mary called Miss Roche's "iron-hand-in-the velvet-glove" tactics with Colorado coal barons.[16] In November of 1927, when guards for the Rocky Mountain Fuel Company killed seven striking miners, Josephine Roche went to the mine, forced the guards to throw their machine guns down an abandoned shaft; and then stood on a woodpile, telling the angry miners that such violence was over for good at the Rocky Mountain Fuel Company. She signed the first agreement with the United Mine Workers. She had done this, she said, to "substitute reason for violence, confidence for misunderstanding, integrity and good faith for dishonesty."[17] Quite a heroine for Mary Switzer!

Frances Perkins, Secretary of Labor, had called on Miss Roche for help in 1933 when President Roosevelt invited individual coal operators to the White House to agree on a code to protect them against unfair competition of the large coal operators. Miss Roche was included in those invited to the White House, primarily because Secretary Perkins thought she would vote "yes." Miss Roche not only voted "yes," she gathered a group around her to do the same, proving her usefulness to the Roosevelt administration.

At the age of 48, Josephine Roche announced her candidacy for governor of Colorado, running on the platform of "Roosevelt + Roche = Recovery." When the votes were counted, Josephine Roche had lost by a margin of 10,000 votes. Although she had been defeated, she had waged a tough and close battle, and Roosevelt beckoned her to Washington as Assistant Secretary of the Treasury. Newspapers called Miss Roche the "baby member of the Brains Trust." She became part of the President's entourage and confused the press.

> Miss Roche does not fit the ordinary conception of the dominant, efficient female. Extremely feminine in dress, manner and appearance, she is one of the most popular and attractive women in Washington... Her face is entirely her own unretouched by powder, rouge or lipstick... her fingernails, while carefully filed, have not been shaped into menacing points.[18]

As Josephine Roche's assistant, Mary studied her effect on the press and members of Roosevelt's administration. She called it a "thrilling assignment" that made her "long, more or less bureaucratic career thoroughly justified." She was the first woman assistant to the first woman Assistant Secretary in any department,[19] and she was an avid understudy.

Mary was now a thirty-six year old woman, with a "den mother personality."[20] What rewards did this assistant-to-the-Assistant job bestow to balance the years spent arriving?

Mary gravitated to power and drama. With Josephine Roche there were seemingly unlimited opportunities to witness history happening. Developments in the labor movement were swift in 1935 and 1936, and Josephine Roche was privy to them all. The United Mine Workers were thoroughly disenchanted with the American Federation of Labor. The National Recovery Administration, the agency created by Roosevelt to resuscitate industry, had been disappointing to the smaller producers in industry. Organized labor, represented by the American Federation of Labor, had been ineffectual in recruiting unskilled and semi-skilled workers to the union, and had become known as "the aristocracy of labor." In turn, the National Recovery Administration had difficulty enforcing codes enacted for minimum pay and better working conditions for other than the craft unions. The struggle to organize the unorganized developed into a clash of personalities: President of the American Federation of Labor, William Green, and the United Mine Workers' John L. Lewis. As Josephine Roche's assistant, Mary had a front seat for one of the most theatrical moments in the conflict, and she described it in detail.

> The day the UMW walked out of the AFL over in Constitution Hall, Miss Roche was on the platform and I was in one of the boxes and saw the whole dramatic episode unfold... In the first place, knowing the background of controversy between Lewis' group and the old Federation, I could appreciate how strong the feeling is between them and the actual

> speaking that was done was merely the last play and just an outward expression of what had already taken place. Green, of course, did not have a chance with that group who are dominated by Lewis' magnetic leadership and by their firm conviction that craft unionism is out of date and there is strength in the industrial set up. Green was fighting, grasping at a straw. His speech was too long, he degenerated to personalities, instead of sticking to the one issue that had any validity, namely, solidarity. He also did the unforgiveable thing of throwing up to the miners the contributions that had been made to them by other unions when the miners were down and out. He neglected to say also that no group is more generous than the miners when they have it. Their own record for helping down and out organizations, whether union or not, is one of the really exciting things about them. They have been particularly helpful in the unorganized women's strikes in the South. Well, the crowd was wooden. Green talked for an hour and ¾ and didn't really make the slightest impression on them. He was desperate, excited, and nerve wracked. It was a difficult position for him to be in for he is not a strong character and merely carrying out the mandate of the Executive Council. That was the psychological part of it.
>
> The dramatic move that Lewis made when he called for a show-down right after Green's speech was, of course, very effective, but the thing that ran through my mind was the clash between the old craft unionism and the new industrial unionism. Lewis on the one hand being smart enough to see today the need for a change in emphasis but not sufficiently wise to see the foundations of the present industrial set-up. However, the union that he heads and the plans of industrial organization that he believes in now are much more logical and much more impressive from the point of view of future planning than the old craft lines. Furthermore, he does provide a certain amount of dynamic leadership and has gathered to him such left wing elements as there are in the old Federation. I think this will give an opportunity for some new leadership to develop in the younger unions; that is all to the good.[21]

Mary's perspicacious analysis of this dramatic event was delivered to please Uncle Mike, the man who insisted Mary have her facts, but the emotional undertone of the letter reveals her pleasure in observing that colorful episode. At last Mary was in a position to meet the major players and see them in action, and that had been worth the long wait.

As Josephine Roche's understudy, Mary made immediate use of her new knowledge of labor relations. Mary's exposition at the Brandeis home was now fertile and welcomed by the Justice. Brandeis was considered the "dark angel of the Wilson administration" by influential Presidential advisors, and he had very tenuous ties with the Roosevelt Cabinet. Brandeis and his former student, Felix Frankfurter, found Morgenthau a disgrace as a Secretary of the Treasury.[22] Although Dean Acheson's forced resignation affirmed Brandeis' view of Morgenthau, the resignation made Brandeis' influence on fiscal policy even more difficult.

The Treasury Department was important to Brandeis and Frankfurter because they viewed taxation as the key to recovery. Brandeis deplored the creation of the National Recovery Administration as a recovery measure because the concept of government-business planning "partnership" rang warning bells of bigness--the curse he had long decried. In May of l935, the Justice had his revenge. A unanimous Supreme Court decision declared the

National Recovery Administration unconstitutional, asserting that Congress could not delegate legislative power to the President to exercise discretion in the making of codes. The opinion of John L. Lewis and Josephine Roche that business had had a greater voice and more control of the situation under NRA rules was passed to Brandeis through Switzer channels. Mike Moore was following the struggle between labor and management and wrote his view of the Supreme Court decision in June 1935:

> Some changes have taken place since I last wrote you about the Supreme Court on the NRA. I can see how that is going to hurt Roosevelt, for instance, the NRA was conceived by the dominant sections of the Capitalist Class. It was designed to increase the power of the monopolies, legalize company unions, freeze wages at the low levels of the minimum allowed by the codes, and increase the profits of the capitalists at the expense of the living standards of the workers. In these objectives of the capitalist class the NRA succeeded well. The small business man was driven to the wall, some three to four million workers were herded into company unions and real wages of the workers fell six percent.[23]

Mary's knowledge of the labor movement from her new perspective was of use to Justice Brandeis and of great interest to Michael Moore. Proximity to a pioneer in labor-management relations increased Mary's value to both of the men she had long respected.

The development of the New Deal philosophy dominated much of Mary Switzer's correspondence and discussion during 1935-36. Judge Brandeis was specific in his criticism of programs and attempted to influence Secretary of Agriculture Wallace in his crop-retailment program, known as the Agricultural Adjustment Administration. Although Brandeis supported this Federal agency, he was concerned about the Southern tenant farmer or share cropper forced to move from his pitifully small farm due to a reduction of cotton acreage. The "nine old men" of the Supreme Court had split in close votes on decisions regarding vital parts of the New Deal. On January 3, 1936, Justice Roberts read the Court's opinion on the constitutionality of the Agricultural Adjustment Act. By a vote of six to three, the judges held that Congress had invaded the reserved rights of the states to regulate and control agricultural production. Brandeis was one of the dissenting votes, holding that the power to tax and to spend includes the power to relieve a nationwide economic maladjustment by conditional gifts of money.[24] Mary tried to assess the results of the decision, quoting to Uncle Mike a letter from "the West" that she had received:

> Had quite a chat with our County Farm Adviser yesterday and he tells me that most of the Stephenson County farmers were strong for the AAA and felt and appreciated that it had done the very much needed things that had gotten them a very much improved price from farm products.
>
> He feels that the farmers are terribly disappointed over the decision and that if there was a radical leader in the Country now there might be trouble as many of them are in a much disturbed frame of mind. The farm Bureau are all rather conservative and in this County will probably control the sentiment and keep it from radical dominance. . . One of the

farmers arguments that influences them greatly is that industry had had a protective tariff for years and the farmers have also backed it up while the farmer never had any protection until the AAA gave it to him and that industrial protection is legal, why shouldn't agricultural protection also be legal. One of the fallacies of the decision is that the Federal Government went beyond its powers in regulating agriculture in the States and thus took a power that belongs to a State. Agriculture can not be regulated by independent States as it is a national affair. The price of farm products is not governed by State markets but by large central markets of both this country and Europe. We out here are very fearful that this decision is going to lower the farm income and in this agricultural section that means a lowered income for all concerned in this agricultural section. We are all hoping that some method will be found to continue the work of the AAA that will not conflict with the Constitution. For one I am quite confident that such a method will be found. [25]

While Mary Switzer pondered the implications of the Supreme Court's decision, Roosevelt smouldered. His plans for relief, recovery, and reform were being thwarted by the Federal judiciary. Challenged by conservative entrenchment, Roosevelt announced to his Cabinet a bill to appoint a new justice for every justice who failed to retire six months after reaching seventy. But Roosevelt had miscalculated the support he would have in the Senate and House, and the bill was defeated.[26] Reform was taking time; redistribution of power among the branches of government was temporary.

Social reform was a world issue in the early 1930s. Mary Switzer's connection to Josephine Roche brought her into the broader theatre of change. The United States had withheld moral approval of the Bolshevik government since 1920. When the United States recognized the Soviet Union in 1933 after labored efforts to resolve financial obligations and trade negotiations, a concert was held in Constitution Hall. Josephine Roche and Mary Switzer attended, fascinated by the scene of the Russian Ambassador Litvinov and his wife seated in one box, with Eleanor Roosevelt and her party seated in a box across the hall. The national anthems of both countries never evoked such warmth as on that evening. Josephine Roche also took Mary to the reception at the Russian Embassy for Ambassador Troyenevsky, whom she had known previously. Mary was enthralled by the pageantry of the Ambassador and his wife at the head of the wide Embassy stair, and by the presence of Prokofiev, who played that evening.[27] Although Mary was new to such grandeur, she was well-acquainted with Russian affairs--Uncle Mike had kept her informed. In 1934 he wrote of attending the May Day celebration in Boston, a pilgrimage he made each year.

All fases (sic) of the political and econmic (sic) and industrial were described from the angle of the working class against the capitalist class. My old friend Bieden done one fine job. You remember him long ago when you went to here (sic) him at the Dudley Opra (sic) House about 1920 or 21. He remembered me all right. All the speakers were good. . . there was about 25 or 30,000 and banners of all descriptions including the Russian flag. A large force of police were on the Common where they were practicing with blank boms (sic). The people as a hole (sic) did not take much notice of them and I think they looked disappointed. [28]

Mike's spelling and grammar did not dull his message, and Mary kept up a running exchange of political opinion with her uncle. Their correspondence ranges from the Spanish Civil War to the sugar beet industry in England. Mike craved reports from Mary on what she had seen, heard, and thought. At 80, Mike was still inviting dialogue; six months before his death Mary wrote a typical treatise:

> Of course I have been quite interested in the new Soviet Constitution. Everyone has naturally been tremendously interested in following the kind of political change which would take place as the Russian dictatorship merged into some of the more democratic forms of government. The impression one gains from studying the draft of the Constitution and the articles concerning the remarks made by its authors convinces an objective reader that the seriousness of purpose behind the establishment of the U.S.S.R. in the first place is also motivating this particular change.
>
> I have also found it illuminating this year to note the amount of space which the New York Times has given to the proceedings of the Communist Convention in New York. Much of the change in attitude in newspaper publicity has been due, I think, to Browder's ability to capture the attention of the people in the American way. He is a very unusual character and his talks during the convention and his method of publicizing the principles of communism as applied to American life will have wide influence. He is what has been needed ever since Debs left the scene in the left wing of American labor movement. He has such a realistic sense of what is needed practically to bring about a real workers' party. He appreciates the necessity for control of small office holders and does not mistake the noise and large arena of a national campaign for the achievement that must be had through office holding if any permanent gain is to be effected. I am very much impressed with the manner in which he has lead the Communist Convention. I presume he has been the influence behind the publicity which has gone out in regard to the Farm-Labor fight and the place of Lewis' industrial union. I think it is most hopeful for the building of a real left wing party that he has such a practical grasp of political principles. There is no question in my mind as I have often said that he has the capacity to translate Marx's theories into the American necessities.[29]

Mary's forecast was inaccurate, for Browder had a short tenure as Secretary General of the Communist Party of the United States, and American labor never accepted Russian dogma of the worker as peasant or slave.[30] American relations with the Soviet Union occupied newspaper editorials in the early part of the Roosevelt administration, just as discussion of Soviet ideology laced Mike and Mary's correspondence.

While Mike Moore and his revolutionary ideas represented Mary's past, Josephine Roche served to sheath Mary's axe for the social order. By example, Josephine Roche revealed to Mary her consummate skill at quiet reorganization. Her confrontation with organized medicine was to be her second "Joan of Arc performance."

As Assistant Secretary of the Treasury, in charge of supervising the Public Health Service, Josephine Roche plunged into a strong current of history. The United States Public Health Service began with the signature of John Adams on the Act for The Relief of Sick and Disabled Seamen on July 16, 1798.

Beginning with the care of sick seamen, developing through a system of military hospitals, toughening with the crusade against contagious disease, the Public Health Service was a major battleground for social reform in 1934, when Josephine Roche arrived.[31] Dr. Hugh Cumming, Surgeon General of the Public Health Service, had announced his opposition to the report of the Committee on the Costs of Medical Care. The Committee had been established by the American Medical Association in 1928 and had toiled to produce a monograph representing the five year effort. The majority report considered medicine a municipal service supported by public funds; the minority report insisted that medical programs and policy be determined by county medical societies, essentially the American Medical Association. The monograph, "Medical Care for the American People," polarized the medical community, and the majority report was discounted by conservatives as the creation of "Medical Soviets."[32] Josephine Roche was Roosevelt's hope of salvaging a Federal health program from the fiery wake of the Committee's report.

Miss Roche's debut was less than desirable. Dr. Cumming was in Buenos Aires attending the Pan American Sanitary Conference when President Roosevelt announced his appointment of Josephine Roche as Assistant Secretary of the Treasury on October 31, 1934. Rumors flew among the delegates to the Conference that Dr. Cumming would soon be replaced because his views differed so from those of Miss Roche. It took a public denial from Treasury Secretary Woodin to staunch the gossip that Dr. Cumming would be supplanted.[33] Despite this unfortunate prelude, Miss Roche's adroitness caused Dr. Cumming to remember their association as cordial, and Mary Switzer remembered Dr. Cumming as a "real, old Virginia gentleman."[34]

Josephine Roche had a near-impossible assignment. Tension had built as a committee composed of both liberals and conservatives attempted to solve the problems of the high cost of medical care and the absence of modern medical facilities in many sections of America. Preliminary reports of the Committee were denounced as propaganda for socialized medicine. The final recommendations of the majority brought the controversy to a crescendo.

Under the majority report plan, voluntary health insurance would be made available to every member of the community; public appropriations would care for charity patients, and each community of 15,000 would have a nonprofit municipal health center using contractual medical services. Many members of the medical profession were adamantly opposed to health insurance proposals that would lead to salaried arrangements, group practice, or collective, prepaid service. An outstanding theoretician of social insurance, Isaac Rubinow, suggested that the psychology of the physician was based on the speculative hope of exceptional success, and that this individualistic orientation made him hostile to any suggestion of cooperative medicine. The medical community divided into those physicians identified with entrepreneurial practice and salaried physicians, medical administrators, and health officials. Within the medical world, solo practitioners held higher status than those concerned with public health. Seventeen physicians had signed the majority report, predictably members of teaching forces of hospitals and pioneers in public health. The eight dissenters were led by officers of the American Medical Association.[35]

These opposing forces were awesome enough, but the issue went beyond health to social welfare. Roosevelt's Cabinet members were themselves divided on the best approach to meet the nation's most basic needs. Between 1933 and 1935 the response had been Federal intervention through relief funds administered by Harry Hopkins' Federal Emergency Relief Fund. The question of control of social welfare programs was intimately related to the fight for control going on in medicine. Hopkins had lost faith in the states' ability to efficiently and equitably administer public welfare early in his career. Frances Perkins, on the other hand, was a strong supporter of the states' ability to manage social welfare programs. The experience of two states, Ohio and Wisconsin, was used as models of each position. Wisconsin had passed a law that created incentives for employers to reduce unemployment. Employers who laid off fewer workers paid less into the employment fund than less "safe" employers. Elizabeth Brandeis' husband, Paul Raushenbush, a professor of economics and consultant to the Wisconsin Industrial Commissioner, was Frances Perkins' chief supporter. Hopkins had Isaac Rubinow on his side, stressing that the Wisconsin approach was irrelevant in an age of mass unemployment.[36] Instead, money must be channeled quickly into workers' hands. In Ohio, contributions were collected from workers and employers and placed in a state fund, and benefits lasted only so long as the state fund was intact. For both social welfare and health, the issue was self-help and prevention versus other goals of social insurance. Local administration was viewed as the key to self-help.[37]

Roosevelt refused to decide between the two opposing approaches to a national social welfare plan. Despite the urging of Louis Brandeis and the Wisconsin group, Roosevelt remained aloof. He sent a message to Congress on June 3, 1934, appointing the Committee on Economic Security to formulate a program and to write a comprehensive economic security bill. The cast of characters grew instantly, and the activity of the Committee between June 1934 and August 1935 when Roosevelt signed the Social Security Act was bracing.[38]

At Frances Perkins' suggestion, Roosevelt required that Committee members also be Cabinet members, knowing it would then be under his control. Frances Perkins was appointed Chair of the Committee, and Harry Hopkins was the only non-Cabinet member. Secretary of Agriculture Henry Wallace, Secretary of the Treasury Morgenthau, and Attorney General

Cummings were the remaining Cabinet Members. Perkins then organized two subordinate agencies: a Technical Board and an Advisory Committee. Wisconsin was well represented in the Technical Board's staff. Arthur Altmeyer, former chairman of the Wisconsin Industrial Commission, chaired this group of government experts.[39] Edwin Witte, labor law specialist from Wisconsin, arrrived on Altmeyer's heels accompanied by his twenty-one year old assistant, Wilbur Cohen.[40]

Roosevelt chose Perkins as chair because he knew she believed in social insurance. Secretary Perkins was one of Florence Kelley's converts to social welfare. While at Mount Holyoke, Perkins had heard Kelley describe the sweatshops of the clothing industry and had taken up work with the Consumer's League. While working in New York City, Perkins had witnessed the Triangle Fire in which 146 shirtwaist workers died. Perkins had never forgotten the horror of the fire or Rose Schneiderman of the Shirtwaist Makers Union, speaking to a group which later forced the creation of the New York Factory Investigating Commission. Through the years that passed, Perkins had excelled in organizing labor and management for minimum wage laws and industrial disease and accident. Roosevelt had appointed Perkins his Industrial Commissioner in New York when he was Governor, and she had won the appointment to the President's Cabinet by popular demand from women's groups around the country.[41]

It had not been easy to be the first woman member of the Cabinet. No one in the Labor Department greeted her when she arrived in Washington for the Inauguration, and she had had to fend for herself to reach the platform outside the Capitol. Aside from such snubs, Perkins had begun with disdain for her predecessor, William Doak, whose policy of deporting aliens was legally questionable. Perkins had personally evicted Doak's investigative group, when she found them late one night rifling the files. Other Cabinet members found Perkins to be equally tough. Secretary Garner had accepted her on the grounds that she did not interrupt at Cabinet meetings, but when the President asked her opinion, she gave it loudly, distinctly, and succinctly.[42]

Perkins' reputation for strength would be tested as chair of the Committee on Economic Security. Support came through the substitution of Josephine Roche for Secretary Morgenthau on frequent occasions. Henry Morgenthau often deferred to his assistant, as he was otherwise occupied in the closing of tax loopholes. And it was Josephine Roche's assistant, Mary Switzer, who prepared Miss Roche's notes for the Committee meetings.[43] Meetings of the Committee were held in Perkins' office, usually at the lunch hour. Roosevelt's wisdom in appointing a few Cabinet members was evidenced by the speed and unanimity with which the Committee functioned.

The formation of the Advisory Committee was much more worrisome and finally caused Perkins to adopt a principle of administration that limited a committee to specific questions submitted to a responsible official. In that way she hoped to avoid public advice on subjects she could not afford to air. Twenty-three persons represented labor, industry, social work, and the public on the Advisory Committee. The outrage from the medical community had been so strong at the announcement of the purpose of the Committee that the AMA formed their own Medical Advisory Committee and presented a report to Secretary Perkins.[44]

At the request of Morris Fishbein, Editor of the AMA *Journal*, neurosurgeon Harvey Cushing and AMA President Walter Bierring agreed to serve on the Medical Advisory Committee. Cushing's brilliance as a surgeon, celebrity as the biographer of Sir William Osler, and his broad range of medical activities made him an impeccable and powerful influence. The Committee presented a unanimous report to Frances Perkins, stating that preventive, not curative medicine should be emphasized, advocating the construction of hospitals, and requesting more time to reach a decision about health insurance. Privately, Cushing advised President Roosevelt to combine all programs dealing with health into a department whose chief would have Cabinet rank. President Roosevelt thought that a poor political move, and the idea was dropped. The AMA's confidence in Cushing quelled their strident criticism of social security. The committee's reluctance to recommend changes in the financing and organization of health services as the Chairman, Edgar Sydenstricker wished, caused health and disability insurance to be left out of the Social Security Bill.

On a December night, Hopkins, Wallace, Witte, Altmeyer, and Josephine Roche entered Perkins' home, had the door locked behind them, and a whiskey bottle set on the table. For six hours they poured over the draft of the bill. On August 14, 1935, the Social Security Act was signed by President Roosevelt. It represented the first use of Federal funds for permanent assistance programs. Aid to dependent children, elderly adults and blind individuals, unemployment and old age insurance were included. Nothing in the act addressed health insurance or permanent disability.[45]

The medical profession had delayed and obstructed any action on health insurance. The island of individuality remained inviolate. A new awareness of the political power of the medical profession sank into all the reformers' consciousness, including Mary Switzer.

One member of the Committee on Economic Security Technical Board, I.S. Falk, who had been assigned to study health and disability problems, did not give up easily. Although he argued for a separation of health insurance from disability insurance and developed far-reaching plans for the administration of such programs, he had no data to prepare a permanent disability proposal. Falk contacted Josephine Roche and Harry Hopkins, asking that the government undertake a national health survey that would collect such data.[46]

Josephine Roche agreed and assigned Mary Switzer to assemble canvassers in cities across the country to conduct a door-to-door health survey.[47] The first such attempt to measure health conditions employed Hopkins' WPA workers as the surveyors. The effort yielded rich results. There was a significant number of Americans who suffered from illness and long-term disability. The numbers were large enough to suggest government intervention, just as Falk had hoped.

Although the data collected changed little immediate social policy, Mary's travels across the country to direct the health survey changed her sphere of influence. Public Health officials and medical school faculty members were impressed with the efficient bureaucrat. During the summer of 1936 Mary was a candidate for Dean of Women at the University of Georgia and corresponded with a professor there regarding national health issues.

> *Personally, I cannot look at the figures for Federal aid for services for the last ten years and feel that we can ever again leave this load to the localities. This in spite of all the psychological advantages of having localities keep this side of their life for themselves. I remember a year and a half ago, when the Social Security Act was being discussed and I was talking with Judge Brandeis about the Public Health end of it, that he said even $8,000,000 was too much for the Federal Government to put into localities for health work. His point was that if you could not get localities to support such appealing things as health and social services, what could you get money for? My answer was: that you don't get it for anything. His rebuttal was: Look what the State of Tennessee put into roads and things connected with automobile transportation. Given a limited amount of money, choice does have to be exercised in the disposition of this money.*
>
> *. . .If we are one country, and one region benefits by exportation of population from another region, we must admit that the region benefiting should bear its share of the overhead. This presumes a very much more centralized form of control than we have been willing to admit we wanted. I do not see how we can continue to put Federal money into health work and similar services without exercising very much more direct control than we have in the past. The balance to be struck between local responsibility for Federal funds and local responsibility for providing as much local funds as possible is a very meager one and it is very easy to sit here in Washington and legislate or administer in such a manner that local initiative and responsibility becomes less keen and as a result you have the scandalous and loose administration that accompanied so much of the far flung distribution of Federal money under WPA.*
>
> *I personally don't think you can enforce anything on a Federal scale. I think you have to devise some mechanism whereby local machinery can be utilized to maintain standards, set by Federal influence if you will. In the exercise of police power the Federal government cannot be any more successful in the field of social service than it was in prohibition.*[48]

A growing dichotomy in Mary's thinking became clear as her correspondence with the Georgian professor continued. She saw the need for centralization, but she was quite conservative on issues of control.

If I do not go as far as you in the feeling of Federal spending, it is perhaps due to two things. First, conditioned thinking and reaction as a result of twelve years in the Treasury bureaucracy, and the instinctive feeling as the result of that, that things can't be quite as bad as they are painted. Second, the very definite belief, and this is probably due to my New England background, that the more you can stimulate locally, the more effective the job can be. But apart from those two considerations, I see no way to avoid spending as much Federal money as can be appropriated in the places that can absorb it most effectively.

. . . It is very clear as the problem of medical care and more complicated work in communicable disease control progresses, as for instance, in the field of venereal disease treatment, unless the State Health Departments are prepared to take hold and go ahead, other agencies will step in and these departments will become purely sanitary inspection plants. The latter, I would not like to see develop, since I think there is a great tradition behind the development for public health in the United States and a fairly effective machinery exists for absorbing some of this new material. The old boys are very conservative, however, and the program may pass them by.[49]

Mary was well aware and troubled by the opposing views on social welfare problems. She saw the businessman's approach with government as financier, but she feared for the quality of service provided without control over how the money was spent. While Mary was concerned about the preservation of the local health departments and their preventive programs, her survey results were being compiled to dramatize the need for a national health program.

Roosevelt's next move in justifying Federal intervention was to create another committee, chaired by Josephine Roche, to bring about coordination of the government's activity in the health field. The Committee was to publicize the need for a national health and disability program. [50] Mary Switzer's friend, Tracy Copp, and Bill Faulkes had convinced Edwin Witte in 1935 that the rehabilitation program should be included in the Social Security bill. John Kratz had testified before Congress of the necessity to save this worthwhile program from being destroyed by the depression. The "piggyback" action made Vocational Rehabilitation a permanent program and through the subsequent increase of grants from the state government, Federal planners became more aware of vocational rehabilitation.[51] As the Interdepartmental Committee to Coordinate Health and Welfare assembled, Tracy counted on Mary's influence to preserve the rehabilitation program as a model of effective Federal intervention in disability problems.

While Mary studied her mentors from labor relations, Josephine Roche, and Frances Perkins, and their adaptation to an all male world, two women physicians were fighting concurrent battles for health reform in America. Although she was not placed for daily observation, Mary watched the women battle for health issues.

Martha Eliot, an outstanding pediatrician who had become Assistant Chief of the Children's Bureau in 1934, had researched the impact of social factors on maternal and infant mortality after the Great Depression. Believing that the minimum living standard should be maternal and child health, Eliot prepared recommendations for Josephine Roche's committee that outlined a National Health Program to acquire a uniform standard of medical care for all citizens throughout the nation. Alice Hamilton, Perkins' advisor on industrial medicine described working conditions and occupational hazards that could lead to serious disabilities. Hamilton advocated labor legislative reform as the road to improvement of industrial health. The two physicians publicized the nation's needs and provided backing for a National Health Conference to meet in July of 1938.[52] The stage was set for yet another confrontation of organized medicine and social reform, and Mary Switzer was to be the stage manager.

Roosevelt wrote Josephine Roche on July 15, 1938 with his regrets for not being able to speak at the National Health Conference, and congratulated her on the acceptance of invitations from medical and public representatives. While sailing away on his cruise, he embellished the importance of the Conference:

> Nothing is more important to a nation than the health of its people. Medical science has made remarkable strides, and in cooperation with government and voluntary agencies it has made substantial progress in the control of various diseases.
>
> But when we see what we know how to do yet have not done, it is clear that there is need for a coordinated national program of action. Such a program necessarily must take account of the fact that millions of citizens lack the individual means to pay for adequate medical care. The economic loss due to sickness is a very serious matter not only for many families with and without incomes, but for the nation as a whole.
>
> We cannot do all at once everything that we should do. But we can advance more surely if we have before us a comprehensive, long-range program... I hope that at the National Health Conference a chart for continuing concerted action will begin to take form.[53]

Roosevelt hoped he had played his cards correctly, bringing in Committees and advisors to divide the responsibility for whatever national health policy was adopted. His command, mixed with his blessing, heightened the pressure on Josephine Roche and Mary Switzer.

The Conference convened on July 18, 1938 at the Mayflower Hotel in Washington. As Josephine Roche's assistant, Mary was largely responsible for decisions about invitations and program. This was her first experience in mixing volatile constituencies. Mary's view of the Conference was that it had been successful, primarily due to participant composition. Representatives from professional and lay groups had been invited, and all had been seated alphabetically in semicircles. From organized medicine came both conservatives and liberals; lay groups included labor and women's groups representatives. For Morris Fishbein, Executive Director of the American Medical Association, Mary felt some compassion. After all, his position was paid. She dismissed his influence as superficial, saying he was a skillful debater, prancing like a featherweight. Mary thought Fishbein would change his mind; "inherent tories" were a different matter. The long prepared papers, read by the Technical Committee were a mistake, Mary thought. Much more important was the exchange between lay and professional participants. Mary's prediction was that the desperate need for medical benefits, voiced by lay members, would have a profound effect on the medical profession, if not on the official policy of the American Medical Association. Antagonism between Hugh Cabot and Olin West, the liberal and conservative leaders of organized medicine, dominated part of the conference, but leadership emerged from surprising sources during the closing hours of the Conference. C.E.A. Winslow, an old public health warrior "galvanized" the audience by describing the Conference as the culmination of a dream public health workers had had for half a century. By the time Josephine Roche stepped to the platform, a near-religious spell had been cast over the audience. Mary had helped prepare the summary Miss Roche delivered, and she listened anxiously. Even Mary, the behind-the-scenes technician for the Conference, felt uplifted. Everyone was deeply moved. In a letter written a month after the seeming triumph, Mary was less sure of Roosevelt's commitment to the health and education field than she was of the Conference was the end of an era in health. Specific proposals had been advanced; now they rested with the medical professionals.[54]

All the high hopes of Mary Switzer and Josephine Roche vanished when the trustees of the AMA met prior to the House of Delegates Assembly on September 16th. Those who had attended the National Health Conference were referred to as an "infinitestimal portion of the 110,000 physicians who constitute the membership of the AMA."[55] The concept of a national health plan was cast as theoretical and impractical. The AMA's counterproposal, drawn by the House of Delegates during the two-day session, opposed any type of national health insurance or any plan to establish government treatment centers.[56] The proposal was delivered to Josephine Roche, who immediately requested a conference with AMA delegates. Their October meeting ended in a deadlock. Even the cunning developed in the Colorado coal mines could not penetrate the intransigence of the AMA.

By November, Mary knew that the exhilaration of the conference had been false. She was bitterly disappointed about the reversal of the Conference plan by the American Medical Association's House of Delegates. She agreed with

Elizabeth Brandeis that this had indeed been a "revolt," and there was no doubt what Mary Switzer thought of the physicians who had ignored the work of the Conference:

> I love your comment about the AMA revolt. It is a healthy thing to have the battle lines drawn, but I agree entirely with your reaction to the statement of principles. The problem of providing medical services for any segment of the general population is so expensive and difficult to administer on a national scale that it staggers you even to think of it. There is a subcommittee of the Interdepartmental Committee considering what should be the next steps in the problem. My own feeling is that while we do have to provide a certain amount of medical care and hospital treatment for the actually indigent and medically indigent groups, the most important thing is to make the general public aware of the death grip organized medicine has on the service that it as a trade gives them and to loosen up the tight professional grip. This point, I think, The Citadel brought out very effectively. I thought it was a very interesting novel and perhaps its great lesson was that doctors are just a cross section of the human race, motivated by the same economic urges that drive the rest of us; those with integrity and standards go one way, the racketeers go the other way. They have a well-knit trade union, much more unscrupulously run than the worst of the building trade organizations, and the public is its victim as are a large percentage of its members.[57]

The defeat of the concept of a national health plan was particularly hard for Public Health Service officers. Along with physicians in academic medicine, they were considered avant garde by the majority of the American Medical Association membership. Many of these career officers in the Public Health Service had served on the Technical Committee on Medical Care that outlined a program for the Interdepartmental Committee. They had gone so far as to recommend the financing of health programs through general taxation or specific insurance contributions from potential beneficiaries.[58] From their perspective, they knew a national health plan would work. Dr. Alice Hamilton was one of the physicians associated with maternal and child welfare who joined Public Health Service officers in depicting the Federal government, not as a hostile power, but as "ourselves organized."[59]

The President of the American Medical Association and Morris Fishbein scoffed at the concept of a national health plan. These were theories that "no practical health administrator could possibly approve."[60] Thomas Parran, the man who had succeeded the conservative Dr. Cumming as Surgeon General of the Public Health Service, had already established himself as a man of courage.[61] He had found the Public Health Service dominated by conservatives like Warren Draper, who believed firmly in the military personnel system and its accompanying esprit de corps. After all, awarding commissions to physicians had resulted in a mobile corps, subject to assignment anywhere, anytime.[62] Parran often ran afoul of Draper and other conservatives as he attempted to expand the numbers of commissioned public health officers.

Parran had made his reputation by persuading doctors that it was their responsibility to remove the secrecy that surrounded the transmission of syphilis. He had been successful in challenging this social taboo. Parran's fame as a public benefactor was strengthened by his leadership in the improvement of living conditions in the United States.

> During the early days, before the passage of the Social Security Act, funds out of the Emergency Relief appropriation and out of the WPA were channeled into the Public Health Service for the development of . . . well, there was a Privy Building Campaign and all kinds of fundamental public health facilities were built, and I can remember the shock that I had when I first learned of the extensive existence of outside toilets in this country. It was a great eye-opener. [63]

Posters distributed by the Public Health Service in the early 1930s show lanes lined with privies, and warnings that "Sanitary Privies are Cheaper than Coffins," or "The Flies that You See in the Privy will soon be in the Dining Room."[64]

Despite what seemed such obvious need to Mary Switzer, Josephine Roche and Thomas Parran, Parran would need all the courage and commitment he could muster to extend a national health plan. Parran prevailed upon the developers of the Social Security Act to provide for the build-up of state and local health departments, and met with some success. Through Title VI of the Act, the Public Health Service could make general support grants to states to upgrade weak public health organizations; through Title V the Children's Bureau made grants to state and local health departments for maternal and child health services.[65] While money began to flow into states for public health, Parran also had his eye upon an experimental program being operated in the dust bowl.

Destitute farm families in the Dakotas and Oklahoma were struggling to pay their doctor's bills. The Farm Security Administration, a rural relief project of the New Deal, provided loans and technical aid to farmers in need. Dr. Ralph Williams of the Public Health Service set up a corporation in each of the Dakotas to which the Farm Security Administration paid funds for the medical care of FSA clients. Medical directors were appointed in each state, bills from local physicians were sent to the medical director and were paid according to an amount allocated by the two medical corporations. Dr. Parran was convinced from this project that Federal medical care was feasible, and he had wholeheartedly supported the recommendations of the Technical Committee on Medical Care. Unfortunately, Dr. Williams' proof that the medical cooperatives were handled locally with the cooperation of county medical societies and the State Medical Association carried no weight with the American Medical Association House of Delegates. The grand experiment continued for some years in the Dust Bowl, proving Parran and Williams quite practical as health administrators, but the opposition of the American Medical Association removed the Public Health Service as a means of controlling medical costs and equalizing medical care in the United States.[66]

Roosevelt's rather passive response to the defeat of the concept of a national health plan surprised Parran and Roche. Apprehension about upcoming elections had softened his stance.[67] Although he was concerned about education and health, his primary goal was economic security for the nation. In 1936 Republicans had used the Social Security tax to arouse worker's ire. Factory placards, concealing the fact that employers were also contributing to a pension fund, announced that workers had been "sentenced" to pay a weekly tax deduction for the rest of their working lives. The tactic had been unsuccessful, particularly with ethnic groups, and Roosevelt's reelection was viewed by many analysts as the victory of his ideas. By 1938, however, the businessmen's opposition and the liberals' disenchantment worried Roosevelt.[68] The son of Robert La Follette, grand old liberal of Wisconsin, was organizing a new progressive party. They had had enough of relief; they wanted jobs and security. Health was relegated to a low priority. At least the court challenge of the Social Security Act had been defeated. The majority opinion supported Congress in spending to promote the general welfare. Roosevelt would wait until America strengthened its belief in government power and until the Chamber of Commerce and the American Medical Association mellowed in their opposition.[69]

Mary Switzer, minor character in this beginning of the social welfare era, had begun 1935 with apprehension, confiding in a friend, "I do not feel that any of the seemingly important legislation is going to pull us out of the doldrums."[70] By 1938 Mary had seen her mentor foiled and the raw power of organized medicine frustrate the sanguine Parran. Josephine Roche resigned, ostensibly to return to Colorado and the care of Senator Costigan. Parran worked on in the Public Health Service, hampered now by a more militant American Medical Association and the declining fortunes of the New Deal.[71]

Mary Switzer's loyalty to the Public Health Service survived the shock to her idealized version of leadership. She was grateful for having been in a place where the "New Deal was at its best."[72] The Public Health Service had been free of "very extreme people."[73] She had gained intimate knowledge of the Public Health Service, had served on a committee of the Treasury traditionally composed of men, and she considered working for Josephine Roche as a major landmark in her career.

> *Miss Roche was always, it seemed to me, on the right side. She was very liberal but very tough. She was impatient with fuzzy-mindedness and with people who were not sure of their facts or not willing to sit down and think things out in a logical manner. She brought the skill of the negotiator in labor relations, and salary and wage efforts... her influence and the fact that she was an educated, disciplined person made quite a different person out of me.*[74]

By 1938 Mary had endeared herself to many of the officers in the Public Health Service. Chief among her admirers was Warren Draper, Assistant Surgeon General. Draper, like Parran, had joined the Public Health Service immediately upon his graduation from medical school. Draper had also had experience as Commissioner of Virginia's State Health Department and in rural sanitation through the "Hygienic Laboratory" of the Public Health Service. A Harvard graduate and a member of the American Medical Association's House of Delegates for twenty-one years, Draper epitomized those physicians who viewed collective programs and contract practice as a solution to the nation's health needs.[75] The coincidence of Mary Switzer and Warren Draper having been born in Newton, Massachusetts and having been educated at Radcliffe and Harvard gave them mutual interests, as well as a common philosophy. Mary described Warren Draper as:

> . . . one of the most delightful members of the Surgeon General's staff. He missed being Surgeon General himself just by the chance that Dr. Parran happened to have known the President in Albany, and had that slight personal edge over him. Which of the two men would be better is a toss up. No others were even considered, which is also a tribute both to the President and to the Service. He has been a wonderful help to me in my present job--patient, and understanding of my sky rockets which shoot high and come back to rest, perhaps not below the ground, but almost to the ground, as sky rockets have a way of doing.[76]

The sky rocket was resting almost below the ground when Josephine Roche left the Treasury. Although Mary had many friends in the Public Health Service, she did not know how to build upon what she had learned. Elizabeth Brandeis Rauschenbush was also concerned. "What kind of opportunity will you now have in the Treasury?" she wrote.[77]

"The Treasury without Miss Roche and my job without her is even more different than I had imagined, and I thought I had forecast in my mind most of the low places," Mary confessed.[78] Mary was loathe to desert the program Miss Roche had planned, and described herself as "completely absorbed in the public health program and its alliances in and out of government."[79] "I couldn't conceive of going back to a purely routine Treasury job. . . my best interests are served by sitting tight."[80]

Victor Weybright, editor of the *Survey Graphic* and friend of Mary and Isabella, gave Mary an opportunity to gain perspective on her changed position by interviewing her regarding civil service. She was a career civil servant, surrounded by almost 100,000 persons who had been appointed between 1935 and 1937 without regard for civil service rules. Emergency activities of the New Deal had been converted into permanent government agencies.[81] Neither vacillating standards nor the loss of Josephine Roche dimmed Mary Switzer's romance with civil service. "My guess would be that you will find the administrative people much better off and realizing it, than if they had been in a private industry," she told Weybright.[82]

Weybright used suggestions Mary gave him for interviews with members of the Civil Service Commission to write an article about the growth of government service during the New Deal.

> Because of the state apportionment system for civil servants not in the field service, Washington is actually a cross section of every cross roads in the U.S. The flocks of minor bureaucrats who scurry across the streets in front of your taxicab resemble folks in a county seat town rather than city crowds such as you see in Chicago's Loop or New York's downtown streets, or even in informal Los Angeles.
>
> The administrative civil servants have a different air. Even those who have come up from the ranks have a sort of shipboard look, a quizzical atmosphere of being engaged with important and slightly mysterious affairs. They assist in drafting bills, prepare profound reports, hire, fire, audit, investigate, administer, summarize, research, teach . . . If they are dulled by routine or dunned by creditors they do not admit it; neither do they admit that they are probably doing as well as they would have done in business.
>
> . . . Paradoxically, a career can be started in the government much more readily than it can be moved along. The pay to clerical and manipulative workers is a little better than paid by business; but in the higher grades the government has never competed with business. Prestige is one compensation; and a fair, if not magnificent, retirement annuity system is still another. Most administrative salaries run around $5000 and seldom reach more than $7500, and in the long years before that the salary may hover well below $5000.
>
> Politics and luck still play a considerable part in promotion. Death and transfers, quite unforeseeable, create vacancies. Politics in the civil service is not partisan, but personal. Internal shake-ups are just as drastic and alarming when a cabinet member is replaced within as when election changes party lineup. Often such intra-department politics are motivated by lofty intentions--but they are seldom fair to loyal, capable civil servants who just by chance failed to come to the attention of a Cabinet member's personnel advisor.[83]

The year Weybright wrote his article, Mary Switzer earned $4600. She had played the personal politics of the Federal civil servant, and had edged upward to meet influential persons who would remain life-long friends. She had also lost some of her liberal idealism, having witnessed the might of organized medicine. She deserved her "shipboard look," Weybright's sure clue to the civil servant.

U.S. Public Health Service Survey, Detroit, Michigan, 1935. Clark Tibbits, George Parrott, Mary E. Switzer, Charles Duffield, and Stuart Walker gather data for framing health proposals. (*Courtesy the Schlesinger Library, Radcliffe College.*)

V

The Luckiest Thing That Ever Happened 1938 - 1939

Of all the satisfactions there are in a lifetime of devotion to a cause, the one that is greatest is related to the conviction that you chose the right road and were able to keep it clear and move it to the end.

Mary Elizabeth Switzer, 1967

Mary knew she could not go back to a less exciting position than she had held as Assistant to Josephine Roche, but she did not know just where she could go. The Treasury still represented security; she was just as proud of being one of "the Treasury bunch" in 1937 as she had been in 1923. Her loyalty to the Public Health Service and its tradition of working with state and local health officials was deeply ingrained. Elizabeth Rauschenbush wrote "the Social Security Board would be very lucky if they could get you to act as a liaison with the Treasury and other government departments. . . I'll tell Arthur Altmeyer what an opportunity he has!"[1] Mary thanked Elizabeth for her suggestion, but was not overly enthusiastic.[2] The Social Security Board was already viewed as a cohesive organization, with a pride that equalled that of the Treasury.[3] Building allegiances with the Social Security Board would mean starting over for Mary. She preferred looking within the Treasury for advancement.

Letters and telegrams continued to flow from Mary to Josephine Roche, now home in Colorado. Throughout 1938 Mary kept Josephine Roche abreast of Treasury happenings. Mary's secretary, Josephine Coe, searched for missing correspondence; Mary conveyed her worry about the "haphazard manner in which the Chief's papers are being handled. . . if we can get them all away from the present holder, we will guard them with our life."[4]

Mary held tightly to the past, conjecturing about the rumors of reorganization that seemed most interesting of all possibilities. The reorganization Mary mentioned had been discussed within the bureaucracy for some time. Rather than leaving health, education, and welfare concerns in Departments that had been organized occupationally, Roosevelt was considering grouping agencies according to function. Older departments such as the Treasury and Interior did not convey the Administration's interest in social welfare.

But the reorganization seemed very slow in coming, and Mary thought she saw a more expedient solution for a career move. Throughout her career with the Treasury she had been appointed to the Budget and Improvement Committee. Bureaus within the Treasury submitted budgets to this Committee before going to the Secretary for approval. Mary had inspected budgets from the Bureau of the Mint, the Bureau of Narcotics, and the Coast Guard. This rather tangential responsibility gave Mary some understanding of the Bureau of the Mint, and made an opening as Assistant Director of the Mint quite appealing. In late 1938, while reorganization was still only a subject of discussion, the Assistant Director "Miss O'Reilly who was a very dignified Dresden-china like person who knew the Mint from top to bottom" retired.[5] Miss O'Reilly's position happened to be the top Civil Service job held by a woman, a fact that made the job even more appealing to Mary Switzer.

The Director of the Mint was Nellie Tayloe Ross, "someone who had been Governor of Wyoming and had to be taken care of when the New Deal came." Mrs. Ross had not been well received because the staff felt she was upstaging Miss O'Reilly. Mary had already demonstrated her ability as an Assistant Director, and this would keep her in the most stable part of the Treasury. Despite her love for the Public Health Service, Mary set her cap for the job.

> I felt that it was very much my right to be considered for it because I was one of the older and more experienced civil servants, and I was a woman, and I had given a good deal of time and thought to it, and I wanted it. So, Mr. Morgenthau said 'no,' he was not going to give it to me for one very simple reason—Mrs. Ross didn't want me, and Mr. Morgenthau was not about to listen to all her gripings and her dissatisfactions. Everything that went wrong would be blamed on me and on the Secretary for appointing me, so he just didn't give it to me. But I felt abused and very much let down, I felt that I had been unfairly treated and I guess all of this was probably true, but of course, it was the luckiest thing that ever happened, because had I taken that job I'd still be stuck there... So these things we have little control over and sometimes things that appear to be the greatest disappointment one can have turn out to be blessings in disguise.[6]

Not getting what she had wanted turned out to be the luckiest thing that ever happened, for it kept Mary in a holding pattern until the long awaited reorganization became a reality.

Mary was assigned to the Bureau of the Budget in the Treasury, in anticipation of the reorganization that had been proposed by Roosevelt's Committee on Administrative Management in 1937. Three able men, Louis

Brownlow, Luther Gulick, and Charles Merriam, had studied the outmoded structure of the government and suggested changes that would lessen the fragmentation of functions within old departments. The report had also suggested that the President be permitted to submit reorganization plans to Congress that would be approved within sixty days, if Congress did not reject the plan. On April 3, 1939, Congress passed such a law, giving the President greater control over the executive branch of government than had ever been the case.[7]

Within three months the Committee presented Roosevelt with a specific plan for reorganization that included three major changes: a new Executive Office of the President was created, into which the Bureau of the Budget would be moved from the Treasury; a Federal Security Agency was constructed which would encompass the Social Security Board, the National Youth Administration, and the Civilian Conservation Corps, as well as the Public Health Service, the Office of Education, and the United States Employment Service; and a Federal Works Agency was established to consolidate public works programs.[8]

Working alongside Mary in the Bureau of the Budget, which was soon to be moved from the Treasury, was Wayne Coy. Coy was working on an organization that would be appropriate when the Committee on Administrative Management's plan became effective.[9] It happened that Coy was also a supporter of Paul McNutt of Indiana, who had been encouraged by Roosevelt to run for President in 1940. Governor McNutt had no idea that Roosevelt, as part of his strategy for re-election, was also prompting Harry Hopkins, Alben Barkley, Cordell Hull, Henry Wallace, and Harold Ickes to enter the race. Sheer clutter would make his renomination a certainty, Roosevelt rightly reckoned.[10] As evidence of his support, Roosevelt appointed McNutt Administrator of the newly created Federal Security Agency.[11]

Mary Switzer had hoped Roosevelt would appoint Josephine Roche, and had bet Wayne Coy that she would be the choice. When Paul McNutt was chosen, Wayne Coy hurried to tell Mary that they wanted her to join them.[12] Both Mary and Wayne Coy were appointed Assistants to the Administrator. Wayne Coy's health declined, and Mary Switzer became second-in-command for the new agency of Departmental status, that now supervised the activities of both the Public Health Service and the Social Security Board. Mary Switzer's disappointment in being passed over for the position of Assistant Director of the Mint lasted less than a year. Her new position elevated her above all her former associates.

The *Radcliffe Quarterly* carried the "great news," quoted from the August *Survey Mid-monthly*:

> The most significant acts of the new Federal Security Administrator, Paul V. McNutt, have been his appointments. All of them are technically well qualified and of undoubted competence. For example, Mary Switzer, assistant to Mr. McNutt, was right-hand lady to

> Josephine Roche in the Treasury Department and was assistant to the chairman of the Inter-departmental Committee.[13]

Mary had been cited as one of the outstanding career women in government service. Her pride in her new position was obvious when she wrote the *Radcliffe Quarterly*.

> After seventeen years of ingrown devotion to the Treasury Department, I left it last July to move over to the newly created Federal Security Agency as assistant to the Administrator, Governor Paul V. McNutt. In a way this position followed logically out of the one I had been holding in the Treasury Department for the last three of four years, namely, that of Assistant to the Assistant Secretary in charge of Public Health, Josephine Roche. My duties in the new position are a little broader than in the old and I have considerably more independent responsibilities. Needless to say, I am very much excited at the opportunities in the new position and although I thought I should always want to remain in the fiscal branch of the Treasury, I find that my fiscal background, with its administrative experience, was one of the things in my favor for consideration in the new agency. My experience in the Treasury has given me an opportunity to combine with what I like to think is a social point of view, some of the realistic and more hardheaded considerations of a strictly fiscal organization like the Treasury.[14]

Mary Switzer, Wayne Coy, Paul McNutt and Michael Collins, from the Bureau of Accounts and Deposits in the Treasury, on July 1, 1939, unlocked the door of a small marble building on the Naval Hospital grounds, where the Federal Security Agency was housed temporarily.[15]

Having a boss who hoped to be the next President of the United States was exciting for Mary Switzer. She joined McNutt Clubs, and tried to persuade her friends that he was the prime candidate for the 1940 election. Some of Mary's more sophisticated friends could not go along with her suggestion.

> Frankly, the more I see of the white-haired boy from Indiana, the more I realize that he is an outstanding administrator and has a fine mind, but that he simply has not got the touch that this country hungers for, without which we cannot carry on with any national unity. Frank, for all his faults, has had that magic touch and will go down in history as the man that kept our souls alive when everything else went to hell on a tobaggan.[16]

Mary's ambitions were probably never higher than when she thought she might be advisor to the next President of the United States. It became clear rather early in the campaign that "the white-haired boy" was a pawn in the election, however, and Mary Switzer scaled down her aspirations accordingly. What she discovered confirmed what Roosevelt said privately about McNutt: "He is good only if he has a definite assignment."[17] Mary Switzer became indispensable to McNutt, preventing him from making embarrassing mistakes as Administrator. "Governor McNutt felt comfortable with me," she said,[18] finding his dependence flattering and somewhat familiar. Morgenthau had also relied upon Mary for good judgment and fierce loyalty.

Mary Switzer had reached a new degree of political maturity in 1939. For the next six years she served Paul McNutt ably, transferring her devotion to his two successors, Watson Miller and Oscar Ewing.

She had to keep her road clear without the aid of her closest advisors. While these years were ones of career consolidation and advancement for Mary, they were also made significant by the loss of persons who had guided her throughout her earlier years in Washington. Death, retirement, and her own personal advancement dominated Mary Switzer's life in the late 1930s.

Michael Moore had relished Mary's involvement in political affairs and kept up a lively correspondence with his niece until his death in 1936. Mary missed his philosophical letters and wrote a friend of Mike's:

> He was 80, as you know, on his last birthday and very proud of his fine health and spirits almost until the end. He was really ill only about six weeks and suffered very little pain. Most of his discomfiture was from his difficulty in breathing on account of the strain on the heart. He died as he had lived, full of optimism and a realistic belief in the future of mankind. He was cremated at Mount Auburn, simply and without any services, as he wished.
>
> His sister, Mrs. McLaughlin, who was left alone in the home after his death died last March after an illness of only a few days. And so the family of that generation is gone now.
>
> You might be interested to know that Mike's library, my sister and I presented to the Newton library where it will be made a part of the general collection. Mike had gotten very friendly with the librarian during the last few years when he used to spend his winters at home in Newton and a great part of the day in and about the library. We like to think that the books that meant so much to him and to so many of us will be read and studied by interested neighbors and friends.[19]

No records have been kept at the Newton Free Library of the donated volumes from the Moore collection,[20] but the correspondence between Mike and Mary conjures images of the most liberal writers of the time. The librarian, after all, had subscribed to the *Daily Worker* at Mike's request. Although his reading tastes were known to the librarian and his friends and family, Mike Moore's books have probably not enjoyed too wide a distribution in the Newton community. Mike's obituary was as brief as his cremation:

> Michael J. Moore of 30 Capitol Street Newton died on Oct. 20. He was born in Inskiddy, Cork, Ireland 80 years ago and had resided in this city for about 50 years. He formerly resided in Newton Upper Falls and was employed at the Pettee Machine Shop. In later years he resided at Newton and for 22 years was employed by the Stanley Motor Car Company.[21]

Uncle Mike would have been pleased to know that the liberal legacy he imparted to Mary continued to be her philosophy. Although more realistic after being educated by the American Medical Association, Mary's insistence on liberal beliefs remained. She sounded like Eleanor Stabler Brooks when she defended the Civil Liberties Union.

> I think that the most important contribution that such an organization as the Civil Liberties Union can make is not in the field of philosophical abstraction, but rather on the front of activity and by the nature of things their chief concern should be with freedom of

speech for the groups to the extreme left or for such submerged minorities as cannot lift their head without help. The fascists, and the manufacturers associations, and Henry Ford do not have any difficulty at all in getting their views before the public. Neither do any of the organized religious groups. At the present time the Catholic point of view is amply represented and so is the Jewish.

I think we are more aware than ever in this country of the need and desires for religious freedom. I think, on the other hand, that those of us who are less religious but more humane than strong religionists might wish to have a little less noisy presentation of the extreme religious view and a little more of the relaxed tolerance of a real liberal. The ease with which it is possible to take a person as being a communist is apparent; for instance, when a nominating committee of the Washington Lawyers Guild presented Fowler Harper's name for office in the Guild, there was considerable controversy over it because it was alleged he was a communist which shows how easy it is to fall into the trap which is being set all around us.[22]

The uncle who had offended his Catholic sisters by insisting on being cremated, who had made yearly trips to celebrate May Day with the Communist Party on the Boston Green, was represented in Mary's plea for freedom of speech and the relaxed tolerance of a real liberal.

The other important influence in Mary's moral development lived only a few years longer than Mike Moore. Louis Brandeis resigned from the Supreme Court in January 1939, at the age of 83. During his twenty-three years on the Supreme Court he had rendered 528 opinions. The range of issues was wide: federalism, administrative law, patents and copyrights, bankruptcy, monopoly and the restriction of trade, labor relations, and civil rights.[23] After his retirement, Brandeis continued to advise Roosevelt, his chief concern being fascism.[24] Mary Switzer, like many other men and women who visited the Brandeis home, depended upon Judge Brandeis for guidance and inspiration. Mary and Josephine Roche visited Judge and Mrs. Brandeis during the two years between his retirement and his death on October 5, 1941. Mary wrote Elizabeth Brandeis Rauschenbush that her father and mother seemed "in good spirits" and that Judge Brandeis had discussed "how things are now" at length with Miss Roche.[25]

Mary listened intently to the eulogy Dean Acheson delivered at Justice Brandeis' funeral.

> ... Our relationship was far more than that between young men and one of the greatest and most revered figures of our time. What gave it life, what gave it endurance was the depth of affection which the warmth of his interest and solicitude for us inspired. Throughout these years we have brought him all our problems and all our troubles. A question, a comment, and the difficulties began to disappear; the dross and shoddy began to appear for what it was, and we wondered why the matter had ever seemed difficult.
> ... But to him truth was less than truth unless it were expounded so that people could understand and believe. During these years of retreat from reason, his faith in the human mind and in the will and capacity of people to understand and grasp the truth never wavered or tired. In a time of moral and intellectual anarchy and frustration he handed on the great tradition of faith in the mind and spirit of man which is the faith of the prophets and poets, of Socrates, of Lincoln.[26]

Mary had been one of those who brought her troubles to Justice and Mrs. Brandeis. Although Elizabeth had long since moved to Wisconsin, the bond between the Brandeis' family and Mary held. As Mary moved up in Federal responsibility, she disagreed with Louis Brandeis and his daughter. Neither trusted Federal jurisdiction. Still, all three, and certainly Elizabeth's husband, whom she met at the University of Wisconsin, Paul Rauschenbush, believed unstintingly in the individual. Brandeis had been both mainstay and gadfly in the development of Mary's beliefs; she missed his counsel sorely.

During this period of change, Mary also observed the retirement of some of the women who led social reform efforts at the time Mary came to Washington. In May of 1935 Mary attended an anniversary party for Jane Addams. The intensity of Hull House had reached into every corner of the country during the 1920s and 1930s, drafting women for the cause of minimum wages, child and maternal health, better working conditions. Florence Kelley, Alice Hamilton, Frances Perkins, Grace Abbott had directly or indirectly come under the spell of that original "settlement worker." Settlement living, as a means of communication between favored members of society and their destitute fellowmen, had been easily transplanted from London to Chicago.[27] The crusader was honored 46 years after the opening of Hull House, and Mary Switzer attended the event, wondering at change.

> All the old war horses were out. The virtues of the pioneer of Hull House were extolled, her character, and her courage and her gracious fellowship, until after the speeches by Secretary Ickes, Gerard Swope, Oswald Villard, Mrs. Roosevelt, Dr. Hamilton, etc., etc. one felt the rarified atmosphere of a very shadowy figure. Through it all Miss Addams sat until it was time for her to reply. When it was she did so with a chuckle bringing everyone down to earth by the solid homey metaphor she uses so effectively. I was thinking, as it went on, of my own brief tenure as Secretary of the W.I.L. and how we all started out as propagandists and reformers, and how much that is good in our approach to life is due to the influences we ran up against while we were having that experience. But I was struck also, very forcibly, by the extent to which the instruments of radical reform and education change. As we were all gathered around to do homage to Jane Addams, and the associates that made her and Hull House and the movements that emanated from there so very much the vanguard of social reform, I was struck with the inadequacy of the instruments that these pioneers had created. How the W.I.L.--useful though it is--could no longer be the thing that ignites the imagination of the people today who are really left-wingers. I suppose it is a truism to say that when an organization in our country becomes so popular that the wife of the President and the associates of the administration grace its meetings its lowest common denominator is too flat.[28]

The occasion had been tinged with regret for Mary, and her shrewdness in perceiving the shelf-life of a social movement depicts her as an observer constantly abstracting principles for her own use. The irony of the anniversary dinner preoccupied her, for she added a postscript to her letter describing the event, saying the afternoon papers reported that Mrs. Roosevelt received the members of the W.I.L., then went on to a reception of the Army-Navy League. This, she thought, proved her thesis regarding the lowest common denominator.

Mary was surrounded by change, the deaths of her heroes, the distortion of a social movement, and increasing inter-departmental conflict. In her new position within the Federal Security Agency there was never any question about Mary's loyalty to Public Health Service friends, however. It was a difficult time for public health. Its bureaucratic competitor, the Social Security Board, viewed the Public Health Service as captive of the medical establishment. Even the Surgeon General saw his organization as a "gentleman's club," and chafed under the regulations that slowed the process of approving officers for the Public Health Service. The dreams of the Public Health Service for health legislation had been successfully sabotaged by the American Medical Association. The compromise that emerged was based on the Public Health Service's tradition of working with local authorities. Had the Social Security Board not been demoted in the reorganization to form the Federal Security Agency, health care might have been more federalized, as was Social Security. Arthur Altmeyer, leader of the Social Security Board, wanted to unite Federal money with Federal administration, but he no longer reported directly to the President. Instead, he reported to Paul McNutt and his assistant, Mary Switzer.

The policy battle was waged within the Federal Security Administration, between the Social Security Board and the smaller Public Health Service. The Public Health Service was walking a tightrope of preventive medicine, so as not to invade private practice and stir up the American Medical Association once more. By trying to avoid conflict, the Public Health Service was increasingly cast as conservative.[29] Warren Draper, although a conservative in hiring protocol, was a believer in social medicine. Draper was as skilled a tightrope walker as the Public Health Service had to offer. As delegate to the American Medical Association from Public Health, Draper consistently attempted to interpret the Public Health Service's position to both camps of disdainful critics: the Social Security Board and distrustful members of local medical societies.

> ... it seems to me quite futile to discuss 'socialized medicine' unless the particular persons taking part in the discussion are in in agreement as to exactly what is meant when they use the term. 'Socialized medicine' may mean one thing to one person or group and an entirely different thing to others. It is my experience that when the term 'socialized medicine' is used in a medical gathering, a sort of aura is created and everyone wants to fight with only a hazy conception of what it is he wants to fight.
>
> ... The Public Health Service has neither proposed nor endorsed any plan for the practice of medicine in the future ... What we in the Public Health Service are earnestly hoping is that the medical profession will attend to the formulation of a plan which will insure that the health-preserving, life-saving functions of modern medicine are made available to all who need them without in any way tending to weaken or destroy the principles that have enabled this country to attain the highest standards of medical service that exist anywhere in the world.[30]

It was heartening for Warren Draper when Mary Switzer moved up to be Assistant to Paul McNutt. They had forged a permanent connection, and

Draper knew the Public Health Service was understood and respected by the new Assistant. When Draper wrote Mary Switzer his congratulations on her new position, he acknowledged the bittersweet nature of the change.

> While I cannot for a moment believe that you will not occupy a position in the Federal Security Agency of equal or greater importance in its relationship to us than the one you have held in the Treasury, the fact remains that with our transfer today the old association ends.
>
> I wish that we could express to you adequately the gratitude and appreciation which we in the Service feel for your devotion to the work and the invaluable cooperation and assistance you have given. We have marvelled at your ability to understand and to aid in the solution of our administrative problems, to gain the confidence and friendship of our personnel, and to add to our effectiveness by the wisdom of your counsel and advice.
>
> We shall need you more than ever in the time that is to come and I hope that you may find it to your liking and advantage to join us speedily in the new department.[31]

The old association had ended, but Mary's confederacy with Warren Draper continued. In the uneasy aftermath of reorganization, Mary was the Public Health Service's advocate with the Administrator.

The influence Mary applied varied with issues and personalities, however. She admired Thomas Parran and his crusading spirit, but she was closest to Warren Draper, and sometimes the two men took opposite positions.

Careful screening of physicians before commissioning them as officers in the Public Health Service was a tradition Warren Draper protected. For Surgeon General Parran, the process was often too slow to meet the demands made by the war for medical personnel. Parran was undaunted by protocol and, on several occasions, wrote orders to commission physicians without observance of the stringent routine. As Warren Draper's ally, Mary Switzer was in a position to countermand Parran's orders, which is just what she did. Skillfully, with logic and a dash of threat, she bracketed Parran between herself and Draper.

> Certainly the Agency has only one objective in scrutinizing closely the appointments in the Reserve, namely, that of safeguarding the integrity of the Corps as a whole and protecting you and the Administrator from any possibility of criticism in connection with its use.
>
> It is the general policy of the Administrator's office to limit the commissions in the Reserve to the classes of scientific and professional personnel covered in the regular Corps. . . In view of this settled policy, it is necessary to examine exceptions closely.
>
> The question of whether it is more or less desirable to have civilian educational programs conducted by a commissioned officer in uniform is one which we have never explored. My own feeling on this point is that it is far better for the present and future of the Public Health Service to build up the standing of its scientific and professional personnel in a non-commissioned status rather than to give temporary recognition by transfer to the Reserve, thereby psychologically increasing the gap between the two groups. Any other policy tends to depreciate those who do not get commissions. We cannot afford to depart from the conviction that it is not necessary to be a commissioned officer to do a first class job in the Public Health Service even in wartime. I know you agree with me. It would be unfortunate if we felt differently on this very fundamental issue.[32]

Mary strengthened her position as buffer between McNutt and the Public

Health Service, and Parran soon gave up any hope of going directly to Paul McNutt. Instead, he began to rely more heavily on Mary Switzer for advice regarding speeches, the text of annual reports, and proposed policy changes.[33] By 1940, Mary reported to other Federal Security Agency staff that she had "no difficulties whatever" in contacts with the Public Health Service. The only problem was "situations sometimes created by other branches of the Administrator's office going to the Public Health Service directly." "Multiple contacts at the staff level" were disliked by the Public Health Service, she said.[34] This was her domain, and Mary Switzer enjoyed using her status with Paul McNutt to advance the Public Health Service.

Mary maintained the networks she had previously constructed, in formal and informal contacts. Her move to "senior faculty" of the administration did not change earlier allegiances, it increased her use of those resources. In addition to the Public Health Service, there was a sisterhood of women in government service that transcended agencies and reorganizations. This network of women, located in a wide variety of government departments, passed information to one another that might aid their friends in other departments.

The communication channels are evident in correspondence between Mary Switzer and other women in government positions. Two distinct groups of women existed, one associated with health, the Children's Bureau, and public assistance, the other was composed of women involved in the labor movement. Mary Switzer straddled both groups, due to her work in the Public Health Service, but she felt closer to the labor contingent.

The schism between the two groups of women became evident during the New Deal, when Frances Perkins had attempted to combine the Children's Bureau with the Women's Bureau. Both Grace Abbott, head of the Children's Bureau, and Mary Anderson, head of the Women's Bureau, had welcomed Perkins to Washington, but both were horrified at the suggestion of combining bureaus. Mary Anderson was so shocked that a serious lack of communication resulted, and observers attributed the distance between Perkins and Anderson to differing educational backgrounds.[35] Mary Anderson's hurt was fully understood by Mary Switzer, however, who had also experienced the distinction between social workers and all others. The shadow of Hull House fell between those women whose background was social work and those who had entered government from the working class and labor concerns.

In 1939 through 1940, Mary Switzer demonstrated the strategies used by women in high-level positions to assist other women in the network. She had been lucky, now she intended to pass some of that luck along. Her purpose was to capture an honorary degree for Mary Anderson, who had directed the Women's Bureau since 1920, but had never received such recognition.

The composition of the 1939 "Mary Anderson Degree Committee" reveals the membership of the network of women in government service, less known than the health-social work group. The Chair of the Committee was Louise Griffith, who along with Edith Rockwood and Gladys Harrison, worked in the Labor Department and were leaders in the League of Women Voters. Mary La Dame was also a Labor Department member. Tracy Copp, from the Office of Vocational Rehabilitation in the Department of Education, Jo Coffin, an Assistant to the Public Printer, Jewell Swofford of the Employee's Compensation Committee, and Isabella Diamond of the Treasury comprised the membership. Elisabeth Christman, one of the top labor leaders in the garment industry and Executive Secretary of the Women's Trade Union League, functioned as Secretary of the group.[36]

It was Mary Switzer who provided the strategy for the Committee. Since neither Radcliffe nor Bryn Mawr awarded honorary degrees, she wrote President Comstock of Radcliffe to ask her advice in the project. President Comstock replied with specific suggestions, and Mary Switzer then enlisted the help of President Park of Bryn Mawr. The correspondence to President Comstock reveals Mary Switzer's diplomacy and admiration for Miss Anderson:

> Friends and associates of Miss Mary Anderson, Chief of the Women's Bureau, Department of Labor, would like to have an honorary degree bestowed upon her, if possible, within the next year. We would like to have that mark of recognition given her for a number of reasons, and at this time, because while she is still active in her work, she is approaching the age when her retirement is inevitable. I do not know whether you are acquainted with her or not but I know that you will appreciate what her career has been from the point of view of a woman and from the point of view of an American woman.
>
> Miss Anderson came over from Sweden as a little girl and settled in Chicago. She became a boot and shoe worker and early in her career joined her trade union and became one of its active workers. As she grew up in Chicago she came into contact with Mrs. Raymond Robbins, Miss Jane Addams and other Chicago women who were interested in helping women workers to organize and in generally improving working conditions. Sometime before the last war, the Women's Trade Union League was organized through the efforts of Mrs. Robbins who conceived the idea that an organization like the League had a definite place in American life for the purpose of combining organized women workers with interested sympathizers who were not actually in the factories but who could influence the public and legislatures to improve working conditions. With some of the work of the National Women's Trade Union League I know you are familiar.
>
> In working in this League and organizing it, Miss Anderson achieved quite a reputation and did many courageous things in promoting better conditions for women-- state minimum wage laws, hour laws, and so on. During the war she worked for the War Labor Policies Board along with many others. When the Women's Bureau was created Mary Van Kleeck, you may remember, became its director. When she left she recommended Mary Anderson to succeed her. This was back in 1920. She has been the director of this Bureau ever since and has had a unique place now in the minds of many of us Government women.
>
> A good many things about her make her an extraordinary person. First of all she occupies, as head of a technical research and investigation bureau, a place without the usual professional qualifications, and does this job in a manner which would bring distinction to anyone. She has demonstrated the ability of non-professional personnel to hold this kind of a public job and has combined the best of her labor experience with a

broad human experience to promote innumerable programs for the common good. Much honor has come to her, for while there are now many women in Washington with positions of equal importance to that of Miss Anderson's, when I first came almost twenty years ago and for ten or twelve years after that, she was one of the very few women occupying positions of prominence. During these ten years she made friends with many youngsters like myself, stimulated them, was kind to them, and in every way used her position and her home and her generosity to expand the horizons of those with whom she came in contact.

We feel now that it would be a fine thing to have some recognition given to her in the form of an honorary degree because we naturally think of that as carrying the kind of dignified distinction we would like to bestow.

You have had degrees yourself and you have undoubtedly been called upon to suggest people for degrees and perhaps to advise someone, like myself, who is interested in helping secure one. I should like to have your advice, first on the feasibility of the idea and its appropriateness, second, on the kind of institution that would seem to you to be most plausible, and third, on the mechanics of getting a candidate for an honorary degree before those who should consider it. Is it necessary to organize a campaign of interested people who have influence with the institution? In short, if you have the time, it would be a great favor to me and to many of us here if you could give us the benefit of your advice.[37]

Within the week President Comstock answered Mary Switzer's letter, indicating her surprise that Mary Anderson had not yet received an honorary degree and identifying Smith and Mount Holyoke as the women's colleges most likely to recognize Miss Anderson's services. Offering to suggest Miss Anderson to Smith, and instructing Mary to "assemble a few letters from authoritative people," President Comstock ended her reply by saying: "Your letter to me is exactly the kind of letter which should be presented to a committee on honorary degrees."[38]

The network broadened when letters of support were needed. Marie Obenauer, a well-known economist, Estella Ford Warner, the first woman physician to be commissioned in the Public Health Service, Caroline O'Day, Congresswoman from New York, all forwarded letters to President Comstock. Josephine Roche, retired, but active as National President of the Consumer's League, also wrote in support of Mary Anderson. Finally, Mary Switzer asked Frances Perkins and Alice Hamilton, Special Advisor to the Labor Department on Industrial Medicine, to recommend Mary Anderson for the honorary degree.[39]

Ada Comstock telegrammed Mary Switzer nine months later, saying: "The deed is done, but of course it's a secret."[40] And Mary Anderson received her honorary degree from Smith College in 1941, three years before her retirement.

This same strategy was used within the women's network to advance each other. Several years later, it was used to nominate Mary Switzer as a delegate for the International Health Conference.[41] In addition to furthering individual causes, this less visible network continued to promote the Women's Trade Union League, bringing Mary Switzer into contact with benefactors and prominent national leaders.

When requesting money for the education committee of the National Women's Trade Union League, Mary discovered the Albert and Mary Lasker Foundation in the year it was founded.[42] No one could foretell the role Mary Lasker would have in the development of health research during the late 1940s, but Mary recognized Mrs. Lasker as more than just the wife of a wealthy advertising executive, who had coined the terms "Kotex" and "Kleenex." The women's network provided access for Mary Switzer to Mary Lasker. Mary was also asked to help keep the national office of the Women's Trade Union League intact, and once more happened upon an individual who became her friend. While giving Elisabeth Christman aid, Mary contacted Clarence Pickett, a man who continued as Mary's advisor for many years.[43] Helping a woman or a woman's cause in the network seemed to have a boomerang effect; Mary Switzer's career was advanced by the contacts she made in promotional efforts.

As she bridged the change of decades, Mary Switzer relished her new role. She was in a position to help her friends and to cultivate influential persons who would help her "keep the road clear" in her escalating career. She could congratulate herself on her timing and her choices. The new Federal agency seemed to offer her broader exposure. She took with her the philosophy of her uncle and Justice Brandeis, the history and allegiance to the Public Health Service and a special women's network. Roosevelt's re-election and the threat of war dominated the start of the 1940s, but Mary Switzer believed she had taken the "right road."

Mary Elizabeth Switzer and Public Health Service Officialdom, ca. 1939. (Courtesy The Schlesinger Library, Radcliffe College.)

VI
The New Reformers
1939-1942

That you care enough to come, that you remember what you see, that you keep your promises--this is important.

Mary Elizabeth Switzer, 1964

Mary Switzer's new job as Assistant to the Administrator of the Federal Security Agency kept her close to old friends in the Public Health Service, for the Service had also moved from the Treasury. The new grouping introduced Mary to the National Youth Administration.[1] Roosevelt had chosen Harry Hopkins to establish a public works program, and the National Youth Administration was one of Hopkins' newest and most successful attempts to put people back to work. It provided funds for part-time employment of students and encouraged the development of worthwhile leisure-time activities.[2] Mary learned quickly about vocational guidance and apprenticeships, depending upon Margaret Weisman of the Consumer's League of Massachusetts for information on the workings of the National Youth Administration in Boston.[3] The women's network functioned once again as a pipeline of information, helping the new Assistant to the Administrator keep close watch on local program difficulties. Weisman's intelligence reports were direct and colorful, advising Mary "not to show her hand," and dismissing a candidate for an administrative job there as having a "loose-looking countenance and his eye still wanders."[4] Paul McNutt could depend upon Mary Switzer to identify problems with the program.

Although it was a different program with very different personalities, Mary identified with the philosophy underlying the National Youth Administration. Harry Hopkins engraved those beliefs on the cornerstone of the Works Projects Administration at the 1939 New York World's Fair:

> *The foundation upon which this nation stands is the dignity of man as an individual. . . his right to free expression in politics and religion, and in the labor by which he builds his way of life. Work is America's answer to the need of idle millions. . . Work, not charity . . . peaceful work, not regimentation to build machines of war . . . useful public work, to benefit us all.*[5]

The reformers Mary Switzer met when she first came to Washington had been just as certain of the health, safety, and educational needs of the American people. The note of peace was also familiar; Jane Addams could have spoken in very similar terms. As the person who was to be the "eyes, ears, and voice of the Administrator,"[6] Mary had to get the facts and advise the Administrator. Responsibility for the NYA brought a man into Mary Switzer's path who would remain her confidante for 28 years.[7] McCloskey and Mary Switzer were kindred in spirit and history, for Mark McCloskey was the son of Irish immigrants, born in New York's tough West Side. Mark's father had been a truck driver whose treasured volumes of Shakespeare, Burns' poems, and the Bible (although Mark insisted that the Bible was used for its literary value only) accompanied him on his routes. Determined to be free of the succession of flats his family of nine inhabited, Mark worked his way through Princeton and eventually earned a master's degree in sociology at Columbia. In 1935 McCloskey was appointed NYA Administrator for New York, where he placed thousands of girls as assistants in settlement houses and kindergartens and convinced the public schools to remain open at night for adult recreation. In 1941 McCloskey arrived in Washington to organize off-post recreation for servicemen, later shifting to create planned communities in warboom towns. Finally, McCloskey succeeded Charles P. Taft as Director of the Office of Community War Services, one of the Federal Security Agency programs,[8] and he and Mary Switzer became fast friends.

Mark believed in recreation as a right in the pursuit of happiness, as neither a means of culture nor a cure for delinquency, but as plain fun. And although he was a staunch believer in home products and local development of recreation, he also believed no child in America should be afforded an opportunity to play by dint of someone's philanthropy. Recreation was a common need of America; it should come from the common purse of America.[9]

Mark McCloskey was successful in planning recreational facilities for Oak Ridge, a city built for the Atomic Energy Commission during the Second World War.[10] He believed fervently that the Federal government should similarly organize when peace came. Mark McCloskey and Mary Switzer had similar dreams, as a result of their successful wartime ventures. Mark McCloskey combined swift technical assistance and the financing of the Federal government as an investment in a community. He was in pursuit of the happiness of the nation; Mary Switzer still yearned for a national health plan.

The two administrators were so like-minded that they complained at times of "working with pygmies."[11] Mark called Mary Switzer a good administrator, one with "fire in her belly," who mastered material and then "gave it a drive and a warmth."[12] Mary Switzer counted Mark McCloskey as one of the new reformers and promoted him in 1946 as a candidate for the Medal of Merit for his services to the United States.[13] With her responsibilities, Mary Switzer was privy to many opportunities.

A second reformer, one the "incurably romantic" Mary Switzer had longed to meet, was soon encountered. On March 25, l940, the FSA Administrator received a letter from Eleanor Roosevelt asking if he would allow a representative of Social Security to serve on the Arthurdale Committee.[14] Although Mary was not responsible for the Social Security Board, she was appointed rather than Jane Hoey, a note had been handwritten on the White House invitation, addressed to Paul McNutt: "Governor, Mary would like to do it."[15] As a member of the Advisory Committee, Mary rejoined an old friend, Mrs. Morgenthau, and began her association with Jennings Randolph, Eleanor Roosevelt, and Clarence Pickett.[16]

Mary had again relied on personal politics to intercept the request for representation and insure her chance to work with Eleanor Roosevelt and her "pet project." Mrs. Roosevelt's enthusiam was not shared by everyone, for Senator Byrd called Arthurdale a "Tugwellian experiment, the most costly ever conducted in this country, based on a Russian form of communism."[17] But in 1940, Arthurdale seemed to many to be the sort of useful public work that was America's answer to human dignity.

Unemployed miners were being relocated on subsistence homesteads, and Arthurdale was an example of the grand experiment. Located in Logan County, West Virginia, families occupied prefabricated cottages that circled a village complete with a general store, barber shop, post office, meeting hall, handicraft workshop and a "filling station." The homesteaders had been selected on the basis of their need, ability to work, and health status. The average annual income was $467 per family.[18]

By June Mary was taking an active role in this "rural renewal" project. She had visited Arthurdale and was finding work for an assortment of carpenters, painters, stone cutters, blacksmiths, tractor operators, and plumbers. Working with the Employment Service, Mary attempted to find jobs for adults in expanding defense industries, and vocational training for young people through NYA resident projects.[19] Eleanor Roosevelt's column "My Day" in the *Washington News* began to carry news of trips to Elkins, West Virginia, and Mary Switzer's name appeared alongside Mrs. Morgenthau's and Clarence Pickett's.[20]

Mary Switzer considered her association with Eleanor Roosevelt one of the most important forks in her route to the top of the bureaucracy. She was "growing up in public service," and she watched Eleanor Roosevelt's way with "peoples' problems."[21]

Eleanor Roosevelt found the subsistence homestead idea appealing because it was "simple, sensible, and practical."[22] Mrs. Roosevelt believed people could be moved away from unfavorable locations and overcome insurmountable obstacles. A sometimes tongue-tied Mary Switzer traveled on the overnight train from Washington to Arthurdale, alongside Mrs. Roosevelt and Mrs. Morgenthau, listening to the wives "chat about their husbands."[23] When they arrived in the early morning at Arthurdale, a ritual visitation began.

The head of the Homestead Bureau met the three women and accompanied them around the projects where crafts were being sold and trades were being started.[24] Mary Switzer watched Eleanor Roosevelt work her magic, talking to young people,

> finding out about their families, their dreams, what they had done since her last visit, taking in at a glance what was going on--some of the obvious things that needed improvement and repair, and some of the lackadaisical ways the public agencies did not follow through on what they promised to do.[25]

Mary Switzer learned at Arthurdale what a simple visit could do: "that you care enough to come, that you remember what you see, that you keep your promises"[26] was the first lesson from Eleanor Roosevelt.

The second insight that remained with Mary Switzer, long past the demise of the Arthurdale Subsistence Homestead, became fundamental in her philosophy of administration.

> To win a battle of thousands, the battle of the individual must be won first. The person who can keep contact with the individual is the one who in turn gives confidence to the individual. No amount of paper pushing across the desk is much use unless it results in getting service to someone.[27]

Mary Switzer was never closer to the Presidency than in her association with Eleanor Roosevelt. Each tidbit of conversation, each insight was shared with Isabella Diamond when she returned from her journeys to West Virginia. Clippings from the West Virginia newspapers were proudly filed. Mary and Isabella cited Mrs. Roosevelt as their standard whenever they took on the problems of people in their neighborhood. Mary had seen Eleanor Roosevelt treat persons as special cases, if they came to her attention, and she thought the special treatment that resulted was an indication of Mrs. Roosevelt's compassion.[28] When associates told Mary that she reminded them of Eleanor Roosevelt, she responded that the only similarity she could dare claim was an honest caring.[29]

Mary Switzer was a beneficiary of Eleanor Roosevelt's style and interest, and the involvement with the Arthurdale project produced another association that kept Mary in step with reform. Clarence Pickett, head of the American Friends Service Committee, became involved with miners. The Quaker's dream was that people could improve their own lives, and the Quakers taught native crafts, supplied mattresses for families who slept on the floor, and tried to give these victims of poverty a vision that life could be improved.[30] Clarence Pickett had interested Eleanor Roosevelt in Arthurdale, and he was chairman of the Advisory Committee. When the Arthurdale Advisory Committee was dissolved in 1942,[31] the friendships of the group of advisors continued. On the night President Roosevelt died, Eleanor Roosevelt was to have attended a dinner hosted for her by several of the Advisory Committee.[32]

The work of the American Friends Service Committee continued along other peaceful lines, with Clarence Pickett and Mary Switzer often corresponding on subjects of mutual concern. The war years brought problems for pacifists who were assigned to Civilian Public Service Camps because of their objection to the war. Clarence Pickett took on the responsibility for managing the placement of conscientious objectors as they began work "of national importance." Although some of the conscientious objectors worked in forestry programs, others wanted to share the danger with combatant brethren.[33] The problems of getting passports through the War Department for seventy men who wanted to join the Friends Ambulance Service in China became insurmountable.[34] Clarence Pickett called upon his friend, Mary Switzer, for help. Mary knew how to get the job done, convincing Surgeon General Parran that the Public Health Service could be the conduit for the Friends Ambulance Unit in China.[35]

The work of Clarence Pickett and the American Friends Service Committee won the Nobel Peace Prize in 1946.[36] No note was made of the role a bureaucrat played in furthering the cause of peace, but the correspondence of Pickett and Switzer reveals that she had helped with "making way for individual conscience."[37] Pickett asked Mary to help him with other social planning efforts, realizing she knew how to get things done.

A committee was formed to review the reports of researchers who collected data in "derelict areas" of the country, cutover land in Northern Michigan or the lead and zinc mines of Missouri. Many of the problems of relief were unfinished, interrupted by the war. The displacement of workers to war boom towns created a new problem. One of the researchers, a public health nurse, presented an unconventional report of conditions in a West Virginia county.

> Had som lan, lan didn't grow much--
> Had a mule, mule wouldn't plow.
> Loved a gal, sweet and handsome--
> Didn't want to leave no how.
> Charlstons a lonesome place fur a poor man
> Wish I didn't come. Wish I wouldn't stay.
> Dey comes and dey goes but deys all a walkin'
> Walkin' in de night, Walkin' in the day.
> Jobs is easy come by, I got me one.
> Got money in my pocket and I earn it hard

> But I'm still a poor man sleepin in de station.
> Got nuffin but my job in de Navy Yard.
> Effen she'd come--still I couldn't bring her
> Dis ain' no place for my sweet chile.
> She come sick and what we do den?
> Not know a frien' for a thousand mile.
> A man on a corner fin's it easy picking
> White girl, black girl, der dey stan.
> Dey'll go if a man's got a bed to give dem
> An ebbry man's got money en his han.
> De streets is hard but ders nuffin on 'em
> Nuffin I want, cept when I eat.
> I got a puzzlement an my haid hurts me.
> I got a misery in my feet.
> Dey say, "Leave your lan, and come yere."
> Dey say, "Dis yere's a job for you."
> I look at de bus and de trains a comin',
> And I think, "What these people agoin to do?"
> What's dis war and what it doin?
> Dats what I'm thinkin night to noon.
> Somebody got a make a plannin--
> Somebody got a tell me soon."[38]

The report described a new kind of starvation in the United States. Clarence Pickett's concern for derelict areas now had to be spread to cities where the natural resources of the soul had been stripped.

Mary Switzer added information to the Committee. Through her contacts with the National Women's Trade Union League, she became aware of problems of women workers and produced the evidence for the committee. She argued for equal pay for equal work, saying many of the women workers were "practically illiterate as far as a knowledge of the importance of collective bargaining and decent working conditions."[39] The trade union people seemed to consider women as poor substitutes for the men now at war. Because of low pay, women who came from rural communities were easily prostituted. "It is my belief that much of the free and easy attitude on the sex side can be traced to a desire for a little extra cash for small consideration, coupled with a desire for romance and adventure," Switzer wrote.[40]

The problems shifted in peace and war, the programs came and went, but the Assistant to the Administrator of the Federal Security Agency became even more convinced that lasting reform occurred within government. Domestic concerns gave Mary Switzer an opportunity to know three new reformers and to study their beliefs and approach to planning for healthier communities. Through Mark McCloskey, Eleanor Roosevelt, and Clarence Pickett, Mary Switzer was exposed to the needs of the poor and the displaced and to the strategies of new reformers.

These great leaders gave her a personal sytle well-suited to the tier of influence she now entered through the demands of the Second World War. War produced a demand for the commodity Mary Switzer had accumulated-- the knowledge of administration and administrators in the Government and in medicine.

Mary embellished the role she had seen Henrietta Klotz play with Henry Morgenthau when the New Dealers arrived in Washington. Paul McNutt might not have known what an opportunity he had as Administrator of the Federal Security Agency, but Mary Switzer knew precisely what the consolidation of agencies concerned with the nation's welfare could mean. Although she had never had primary responsibility, Mary had seen the force of a Bureau chief, and believed in Federal authority.

The path Mary had taken, leading further into the bureaucracy, was opposite that of her friend, Elizabeth Brandeis Rauschenbush. Elizabeth had opted much earlier for the investment of her energies on the state and local level, not in the Washington limelight. In 1942 Elizabeth Brandeis was writing about the war's effect on the thinking of the nation. Centralization of government had been accepted by the populace as a necessary accomodation to external threat, but Elizabeth Brandeis warned of accepting the proliferation of administrative agencies in Washington as a long-range solution to government.[41] It was better, Elizabeth argued, to retain administration on a state basis, where private citizens could function effectively in the government process. Concerned about the effect of her beliefs on their friendship, Elizabeth penned a nervous note on a copy of an article for the *Survey Graphic* sent to Mary: "Hoping you will agree."[42]

Although Mary respected Elizabeth Brandeis greatly, and corresponded in an appeasing tone throughout the 1940s, she certainly did not agree. She was a declared bureaucrat who spread the gospel of Federal leadership and partnership with local communities at every opportunity.[43] A list of Mary's "Speaking Engagements" from 1936 to 1941 attests to her missionary zeal.[44] Speeches on national health programs, national defense, technical and interdepartmental committees, functions of Federal agencies were regularly delivered to audiences of teachers, students, officials and voluntary organizations. Perhaps it was the peaceful use of Federal power that captured her loyalty, or perhaps it was being an eye-witness to the growth of the Federal bureaucracy that convinced Mary of the inevitability and necessity of bureaucracies in modern political structure. Mary Switzer believed the Federal government was a prime instrument of reform, despite her friend Elizabeth's persuasion.

Washington had been tranformed in the years since Mary Switzer and Elizabeth Brandeis arrived. The New Deal not only produced a plethora of agencies, it brought newcomers who changed the intellectual and gender balance of the Federal government. A peak of appointments for women occurred with the inauguration of the New Deal.[45] By 1939 turnover in government positions had lessened and the growth of Federal agencies had stabilized; few jobs were available for women. By 1940 many of the less prominent women in the New Deal inherited leadership positions. Grace Abbott and other social reformers retired and replacements were not forthcoming. Women seemed less interested in careers in public service, instead they moved to occupations newly open as a result of the war effort.

Mary Switzer was a survivor of the many changes that had come to Washington. She described herself as an "old bureaucrat" who had been able to take on the "protective coloration" of the locales in which she worked.[46] Being Assistant to the Administrator required surface conformity to the code of the bureaucrat: to be a person and no person; to be all things to all men at all times. Mary did not perform as the textbook bureaucrat, as the traffic light that functions without regard to personalities or influence. Although she publicly cast herself as the "eyes, ears, and voice" of the Administrator, she was far more than the "amplification and synthesis" of his personality.[47] In actuality, Mary was the Administrator's trouble shooter and ambassador.

The flavor of the bureaucratic locale of the 1940s prompts respect for the seasoned bureaucrat who shepherded the Administrator of the Federal Security Agency through the war years. Within three months of the bombing of Pearl Harbor a dinner for government agency representatives was held at the Cosmos Club by the Common Council for American Unity. Among the guests were J. Edgar Hoover, Alan Cranston, and Mary Switzer, Mary representing the Federal Security Agency. The mistrust of the public in November 1941 is represented by the Council's objectives:

> Detecting active disloyalty, espionage, sabotage and subversive activity and protecting the country therefrom;
> Eliminating discrimination on account of national origin, race, creed, and, so far as possible, alienage.
> Encouraging an attitude of acceptance and friendly understanding on the part of Americans in general, toward the newer elements in our population.[48]

Friendly understanding was in short supply, and its furtherance depended in part upon the skill with which the Federal Security Agency could meet military needs for health and medical personnel without sacrificing civilian safety. One of the Public Health Service physicians who knew Mary Switzer in her role as Assistant to the Administrator, described her as having a "den mother personality."[49] Mary Switzer furthered friendly understanding wherever she represented the Administrator. She also enjoyed being called "Miss Mary," a title that had patrician associations for her.[50] Some of the problems Mary had to solve were quite a contrast to the Boy Scout or aristocratic aura she promoted. The provision of health and sanitary facilities for communities with increased populations resulting from proximity to military camps came under Mary's authority. "Miss Mary" had to deal with "social protection" services, to control the spread of venereal disease.

The scope of the problem and the attitude of the public in the early 1940s is evident in the fate of a film produced by Universal Studios in cooperation with the Venereal Control Division of the Public Health Service. Venereal disease was considered a national menace to public health, and actors, including Jean Hersholt, donated their services to complete a film that could be released through commercial theatres. The National League of Decency previewed the film and protested to the Surgeon General on the grounds that "sex hygiene and venereal disease were not subjects for motion pictures."[51] The embattled Surgeon General asked his Advisory Committee for an opinion, and fear of Legion of Decency influence prevailed: the film was never distributed to commercial theatres.[52] Although venereal disease was a public health emergency, the public was not to be educated through film.

The Mexican border was a particularly troublesome area, but the sanitary requirements of each city were stringent. In towns where Mexicans outnumbered Americans, prostitutes were examined once a week for disease. City officials required each "inmate" to provide a pitcher full of water, a basin, a slop bucket, a bottle of liquid soap, a quart bottle of potassium permanganate, a jar of calomel ointment (30% strength), and absorbent cotton. In the room of each known public woman a conspicuous placard was posted saying: "Visitors are requested to use the means of cleanliness by order of the City Health Officer." When necessary, Mary Switzer could become a technical expert on any subject, as the specificity in her office correspondence suggests.[53] Her tenacity is also evident in memos supporting the decision of the Civil Service Commission refusing to employ persons with venereal disease, and advocating the criminal prosecution of persons involved in interstate travel having venereal disease.[54]

Mary Switzer's personal reputation for being tough was furthered by her imperturbability and her ability to anticipate problems. Within the Federal Security Agency, the range of problems that might have developed was enormous. Where there were legal implications, Mary sought legal advice and formulated a statement before bringing a problem to McNutt's attention. Adroitly, she sorted and defused possible crises.

The Federal Security Agency was responsible for delivering civilian war assistance to those left without resources as a result of enemy action. Emergency assistance was provided on the East and West coasts to thousands of repatriates. Local facilities were expanded to provide as one service whatever was needed to help war victims re-establish themselves in normal lives. A scrap of accounting from July 1942 illustrates the need for emergency services for civilians. Medical services, amounting to $221.25, were provided 25 passenger survivors of the steamship "Robert E. Lee" which was sunk by enemy action off the Louisiana coast. The cost of fourteen burials of unidentified bodies recovered from ships sunk by enemy action was borne by the FSA.[55]

Another population for which the FSA had medical and health care responsibility was aliens interned in the United States. Value judgments required of the Surgeon General and the Administrator were difficult, and Mary Switzer buffered both with legal and folk wisdom. In 1943 the "War Relocation Centers" were experiencing a continued drain on the medical personnel available to internees. Originally, the 10 centers had 86 Japanese physicians to care for 150,000 internees. By 1943, 40 Japanese physicians "had been permitted to relocate." Surgeon General Parran expressed the need to either recruit American physicians and nurses to care for internees, or to retain Japanese doctors in the Centers. With American communities experiencing dire shortages of medical personnel, the issue was heated. Mary Switzer came forward with a recruitment and relocation plan that resolved the dilemma and prevented embarrassment for the Administrator.[56]

Mary Switzer thrived in this role that called for merciless completion of dirty jobs and eloquent descriptions of what had been accomplished. The details Mary attended to during the war years rivaled the mounds of uncooked garbage whose dispatch was just one detail she engineered. Whether the problem was the interstate shipment of garbage for feeding hogs and the resulting danger of trichinosis or the destination of psychopathic enemy aliens, Mary Switzer finished the job.[57] And, after finishing the job, she would describe the process in such terms of glorification that the stench of the task never reached the Administrator.

Mary thoroughly enjoyed one of the responsibilities of being the Assistant to the Administrator. This was her relationship with Surgeon General Parran. She had worked under his direction before she and the Public Health Service became part of the Federal Security Agency. Once Parran had asked Mary to "work up material" for Josephine Roche on very short notice. Parran had established a pattern of asking Mary to write letters for his signature, edit the annual report that bore his name, and to drop everything when he needed her consultation. Like a good civil servant, Mary met Parran's demands, although she seized any opportunity to lecture Parran and reveal his lack of knowledge. One of her prissy replies to Parran was occasioned when Parran asked for a list of drugs derived from opium and cocoa leaves. Mary responded: "A categorical reply to this question is fraught with difficulty and possible misinterpretation" and went on to supply two pages of detail on the subject.[58] Parran's obedient servant could expose his ignorance when she chose, which was just often enough to remind him of her worth. Now everything that went up and out of the Public Health Service to the FSA Administrator had to go through Mary Switzer. Parran found his correspondence scrutinized, his speeches edited, and his travels approved by the woman he once supervised. It was sweet revenge for Mary to telegram Parran in 1944: "Please do not release any copies of your speech until we have had an opportunity to discuss."[59]

Mary enjoyed her authority over Parran for private reasons also. Parran had gotten the job Mary hoped her friend Warren Draper would be granted in 1936, and this increased her resentment toward Parran. Having the authority to officially correct Parran was a plum for Mary Switzer.

Mary became known as a responsive listener to complaints about the Public Health Service, and as Surgeon General Parran was often overseas or was occupied with larger problems, Mary became adept at settling sticky situations. Freedman's Hospital was just such a concern. An inheritance of the Civil War, the hospital provided medical service to black citizens of the District of Columbia and served as the teaching hospital for Howard University. The Public Health Service was responsible for its operation, and complaints were usually directed to Mary. As the hospital was in critical need of staff, space, and equipment, the complaints were frequent. Mary continued her efforts for several years, approaching the Kellogg Foundation for money a Senate Committee refused to appropriate for a study of the Hospital.[60] Medical education for blacks was important to Mary Switzer, and she worked diligently to improve the resources at Freedman's Hospital.

A similar sort of clean-up operation became Mary Switzer's introduction to another institution that had been moved from the Department of the Interior to the Federal Security Agency, Saint Elizabeth's Hospital. Since 1855 Saint Elizabeth's had been charged with the responsibility of the treatment of the insane "of the Army and Navy of the United States and of the District of Columbia."[61] In 1939, Saint Elizabeth's had 6500 patients and 2000 employees. The Superintendent of the Hospital was Winfred Overholser, who managed a Federal budget appropriation of about one million dollars in caring for the patients. In 1943 there was some talk of the Hospital being administered by the Public Health Service. In a politically astute move, Dr. Overholser welcomed Mary Switzer to the Board of Visitors, the supervisory body appointed by the President which was composed of nine citizens of the District of Columbia.[62] Hoping that the Administrator's Assistant would be a supporter of the independent status of the Hospital, Overholser brought the subject to the Board for discussion.[63] The Board, with Mary Switzer in the lead, gave tentative support to independence, but asked for a "further definition of the functions of the Hospital."

A study of the Hospital was not what Dr. Overholser had in mind, but it was standard operating procedure for Mary Switzer. Her principle was: when change seems imminent, gather the facts. The Board of Visitors and a small committee of psychiatrists and physicians began separate studies of Saint Elizabeth's. What they found was not consistent with Dr. Overholser's appraisal.[64] The questions used by the committee capture the state of psychiatric care in the mid-forties.[65] The range of treatments explored included electro-shock, prolonged sleep, artificial fever, lobotomy, and hypnosis. Two psychiatrists submitted reports, listing the most urgent problems as "woefully inadequate physical facilities" and the lack of "extra-psychiatric" medical staff. One of the psychiatrists recommended the demolition of all buildings, after seeing the battle between attendants and roaches in the basement of one building.[66] The same psychiatrist noted that in some instances, the Hospital served primarily as a prison, not as a hospital.

A week after the Administrator received reports from the psychiatrists, Mary Switzer sent a brief memo to the Assistant Administrator, Watson Miller. She made it very clear that the problem with Saint Elizabeth's was Dr. Overholser, who had resisted change. She directed the Administrator, saying: "I believe you and I can help the Superintendent look objectively at some of the problems that need immediate attention."[67] The problem had the potential of becoming much worse, as Mary feared the Navy might make other arrangements for their patients if conditions were not corrected.

Mary's prediction came true. Dr. Overholser wrote a rather pathetic letter to McNutt, on stationery titled "United States Department of the Interior" which had been struck through and amended with "Federal Security Agency." The outmoded tone set by the letterhead was echoed by the long letter that recited the history of Saint Elizabeth's and struggled to supply reasons for its continued service to Navy patients. Dr. Overholser had received copies of letters addressed by the President to McNutt and the Secretary of the Navy, instructing them to "see what can be done as soon as possible about discontinuing the use of Saint Elizabeth's Hospital by the Navy." Blaming crowding on wartime conditions and inadequate buildings on the budget, Overholser claimed there was room at Saint Elizabeth's for the care of veterans, and hinted at the lack of gratitude for the service rendered since World War I. Realizing what the departure of the Navy would mean to the Hospital, the Superintendent asked McNutt to bring the facts he presented to the President's attention.[68] The crisis produced a record of bureaucratic efforts to keep the public peace.

One of Mary Switzer's administrative tactics was to record telephone conversations that dealt with important matters. Her secretary would then transcribe the conversations for the record. On July 23, 1945 Mary called Dr. Overholser following the appearance of articles regarding Saint Elizabeth's in the Sunday *Star* and Monday *Post*. The conversation reveals Mary as crisp and subtly accusatory.[69] Two patients had died under mysterious circumstances, and reporters had visited the Hospital and Dr. Overholser to fill in details. In his effort to downplay the deaths, Overholser had supplied information to the reporters regarding the Presidential directive to discontinue the use of Saint Elizabeth's by the Navy. Everyone involved in prior discussions was furious that the Executive Order had been made public, and Mary Switzer was determined to find out how much Overholser had revealed and to insure his future silence.

Beginning with a direct question, Mary asked if the Superintendent had had any discussions about Saint Elizabeth's with the newspapers. Overholser replied carefully: "In a general way. Told them they should check with Budget." Mary followed with another direct question: "Do you think what you said might be considered the basis for the article?" Again, Overholser replied in an offhand manner: "Might be."[70] Overholser was quite sure that Mary Switzer had been the link that precipitated the President's directive. It was she who visited Fort Worth, where the Public Health Service and the Navy operated a hospital jointly. It was she who reported to Watson Miller that such an arrangement might be a way to satisfy the Navy's desire to abandon Saint Elizabeth's, using the Public Health Service network instead. The hostility communicated over those telephone lines was distilled in Mary's last remark to Overholser, a remark that informed him of her knowledge of his activities, and demanded full disclosure.[71] All in a day's work for a woman who was accustomed to seeing that the leading actors of the day remained unencumbered by necessary, but "dirty" work. When Paul McNutt described Mary's "outstanding performance" he labeled such work as "the many ramifications of the operation of a group of units of which the FSA is composed."[72]

One of those units for which Mary functioned as go-between for the Administrator was the Food and Drug Administration, and it too had its trouble spots. During the war it fell this agency's duty to maintain the nation's food and drug supplies in the face of "strong incentives to relax sanitary controls and resort to substitutes."[73] Mary Switzer loved the challenge of technicalities, and the scope of the statutes affecting the Food and Drug Administration proved a worthy challenge. She also enjoyed the role of the investigator, and the trials and tribulations of the FDA during the war years afforded her fertile ground for ferreting instincts. Standards were being set for ice cream, canned products, waxed paper, fluorine, pasteurizing, and the labeling of products like Lysol and Hadacol. Mary had voluminous sources with whom she could check before issuing a statement or advising the Administrator. She could change her tone from officious to solicitous, depending upon the situation. In one skirmish with pear growers who had sprayed with lead arsenate twice the usual tolerance, Mary put off the FDA official wanting clearance on a statement saying the pears would not be seized until she could consult a technical advisor.[74] Impatient with lukewarm advice, Mary called on outside scientists to study the problem. Before noon Mary contacted the nervous FDA representative, delivering her firm message in a solicitous manner:

> Well, now, I have been thinking about this little memo. I honestly don't see how any of us could go along with you and give you any assurance in saying there would be no seizures made. I spent quite a while talking with the PHS. We are going to try to fix it up as quickly as we can and to get an announcement out, but I don't see how we could even informally take responsibility for that statement.[75]

Despite a plea for the growers, whom the FDA representative said were fast losing their ranches in the West, Mary stuck to her guns and vetoed the statement that would have reassured growers of being able to sell their produce.[76]

During the years of observation and adulation, Mary had acquired strategies from the best of players. Her position now allowed her to dampen or magnify information before it reached the Administrator. The accumulated wisdom of Tracy Copp, Henrietta Klotz, Josephine Roche, and Eleanor Roosevelt heightened her confidence. Mary's greatest weapon was her repertoire of responses; she could change instantly from the gracious diplomat to the penetrating inquisitor.

Paul McNutt not only had an able Assistant in the maintenance of health and medical care of civilians during the war years, he also depended upon Mary Switzer as Executive Officer in his dual role as head of the War Manpower Commission. Prior to Pearl Harbor an Executive Order created the Commission to insure the orderly procurement of health personnel for the Armed Services. A Board of prominent doctors and other professional personnel developed policies by which every state and county in the United States approved induction of health personnel into the Armed Forces.[77]

As Chairman Frank Lahey explained the function of the Central Board, it was to provide a safe supply of physicians, dentists, and veterinarians for the armed forces, and also enough physicians for the civilian population. The plan was to review the status of every physician in the United States at the county level, for "essentiality." That decision was then reported to state chairmen, and finally, to the Central Board in Washington. Men under 45 who were scrutinized as nonessential were requested to seek commissions in the armed forces.

By the close of the war, the Procurement and Assignment Service had classified every physician within the United States, surveyed the needs of all hospitals, medical schools, clinics, industries and communities, and had rearranged and readjusted assignments until they seemed fair to both the armed services and civilians. Drawing evenly from all parts of the country was difficult in itself; requisitions for physicians during the war years complicated the distribution problem greatly. In July of 1942 the Air Force had requested 6,100 physicians. Two months later it asked for 2,400 more.[78] Dr. Lahey attributed much of the success of the Procurement and Assignment Board to the help it received from Paul McNutt and "his department."

Photographs of the Board make obvious the showcase this responsibility became for Mary Switzer. Surrounded by men in uniform, she is the only woman present in formal portraits. It was a contrast that suited her plan well. Now that it was impossible for her to be overlooked, Mary described herself as responsible for negotiations resulting in the cooperation between organized medicine and government interests.[79] Doctors, nurses, dentists, and veterinarians were secured and allocated during the war years without a filed complaint. Of course, the same strategies that were working well for Mary in her civilian efforts enabled her to declaw attackers before a formal complaint could develop.

Mary Switzer was now the comrade of the medical and military elite. Dr. Frank Lahey, was the former President of the American Medical Association, adding credence to the group. In a rather folksy fashion, the Board met every Saturday to direct national policy and to listen to reports about the mobilization effort.[80] Mary was trusted by the physicians and the military and used her position to extend her influence. Rear Admirals wrote underlings to announce her forthcoming visits to military hospitals and to urge a royal welcome. Mary became a familiar face in an all-male world, and she prided herself on being part of the "healing profession" when working as part of the "war machine."[81]

Dr. Lahey found Switzer's bureaucratic abilities invaluable, although he was not as theatric as she about the task. Her capacity to deal with the technical and technicians amazed him. Mary could prepare, with seeming aplomb, extensive memos delineating a problem, describing alternative solutions, and influencing decision through the logic of her rationale. When a critical shortage of nurses faced the Board, it was Mary who laid out the legislative picture and calculated the costs and benefits of drafting women for military service.[82] When the public criticized doctors and medical educators for continuing their civilian duties, rather then going off to war, it was Mary who suggested a button to be worn in the lapel attesting to the essential nature of their assignment.[83] Dr. Lahey knew his task would have been impossible without Mary's guidance through the maze of official procedures and personalities in Washington.

Having seen the effectiveness of Federal control of health planning in her work on the Procurement and Assignment Board, Mary became increasingly frustrated with the lack of cooperation between government and organized medicine for peacetime purposes. The cold war between the medical establishment and government had been overshadowed by the war in Europe and the Pacific, but it continued with little improvement. A determined Senator Wagner of New York had proposed a national health act in 1939 which was defeated, and had combined forces with Senator Murray of Montana and Representative Dingell of Michigan to propose social legislation calling for compulsory health insurance in 1943. It never emerged from committee debate.[84] Morris Fishbein sent Mary Switzer a galley copy of his article accusing the measure of developing a government controlled medical service by making the Surgeon General of the Public Health Service a "gauleiter" of American medicine.[85]

Asked what the Public Health Service's stance was, Warren Draper said the PHS had taken no stance, but his opinion was that legislation should be formulated that would insure health-preserving, life-saving functions of modern medicine being available to all.⁸⁶ Mary was reminded of the stalemate of 1938. Would the forced cooperation of the war make a difference?

Mary's rhetoric in the closing years of the war emphasized the need to make medical care available regardless of accidents of wealth or geography. In letters to her medical friends, she continually emphasized the success of the Procurement and Assignment Service and suggested it as a model for distributing medical personnel throughout the country once the war ended. "The close camaraderie working together of medicine in and out of government" would be a requirement of such an operation.⁸⁷ Organization and a common purpose had been the key to wartime success; organizational genius and trust could work the miracle of assuring medical care for post-war America.

Mary's persuasion was accompanied by two other strategies. With Morris Fishbein, who was the most outspoken opponent of any sort of "socialized medicine," she practiced her old "clipping thesis" act. Mary would send Fishbein articles or information about the PHS and Warren Draper's accomplishments in Europe, encouraging Fishbein to send her working drafts of his articles. She would react to the articles, gently diluting the vitriolic content.⁸⁸ Through flattery, Mary maintained a personal relationship in order to manipulate the mouthpiece for organized medicine.

Regular requests for autographed copies of Fishbein's books came from Mary, as well as suggestions of interesting books she had recently read. Through such wiles, Mary succeeded in muting Fishbein's criticism of a cooperative relationship between government and organized medicine. The second strategy Mary employed was also typical of her style. By the mid 1940s Mary had quite a distinguished following, and she deployed them to further her hopes. Alan Gregg was a physician employed by the Rockefeller Foundation. Mary had cast her spell upon Dr. Gregg. Just as she had organized the campaign for Mary Anderson's honorary degree several years earlier, Mary contacted Gregg, asking him to use his influence in gaining the cooperation of the medical profession. Gregg wrote to influential friends recasting the issue in terms they could not dismiss:

> The real question is whether doctors will as a profession collaborate with laymen or not. If they will, then the situation is one of collaboration and not a struggle for domination. If doctors are unwilling or reluctant to collaborate, then, it is true, the situation invites a fight and organized medicine will probably repeat the policies and the experience of the utilities companies during the past thirty years. The utilities companies assumed they could disregard such things.⁸⁹

Mary hoped to organize support among her physician friends, pattern the organization of medical care after the Public Health Service and the Procurement and Assignment Service, and finally achieve the partnership for common good that had eluded Josephine Roche years earlier. The fact that a succession of men and women had failed continuously during the last decade to pass legislation providing for a national standard of medical care did not discourage Mary. Her experience on the Procurement and Assignment Board had been so successful that she was confident she could organize a similar program for peacetime health care. By 1945 Mary Switzer had every right to be confident; she had excelled in every task undertaken. She had even been a successful "secret agent."[90]

Although years later Mary recoiled at her own part in contracting for research in biological warfare, during the war years the substance of the job bothered her much less than the secrecy with which contracts had to be handled. She reasoned:

> I had to do it because, strangely enough in today's light, the Army and Navy couldn't do it. They thought it was contrary to the Geneva Convention. I've often thought how terrible it was, that I did that, although I don't know. I don't see much difference between one weapon and another, though on the scale they're doing it today, it's unnecessary and unreal. Anyway, we developed some good medical information valuable to researchers later on, so I suppose some good came out of it.[91]

Switzer's appearance and routine made her an unlikely carrier of secret information, and she was called upon to meet various scientists, secure information, and deliver it to Surgeon General Parran. Mary's rather ample bosom proved an adequate safety deposit box. When transfers had to be made, she looked the very proper, kindly customer at the Mayflower Hotel dining room. The diners appeared innocent, and important papers went first into Mary's "reticule," then next to her body for the trip home.[92] This most dangerous part of Mary's work during the war only confirmed her belief that she could accomplish anything with planning.

And what she wanted most to accomplish in 1945 was a national health program.[93] Josephine Roche's dream seemed within reach now. Mary did not consider leaving Washington for the Presidency of Connecticut College, instead, she remained in her role as a bureaucrat, feeling that her experience in government should be used to promote the cause of a national health program. Viewing public health as a tool for "keeping the world together," Mary was certain what had been learned and accomplished during the war would be transferable to post-war problems. In part, she was absolutely correct.

The research that had gone on during the war was used in civilian practice. Interest in chronic disease, such as cancer or heart problems, supplanted earlier research thrusts in tropical disease. Having found the research approach productive in war, Congress committed large sums of money in the late 1940s toward the pursuit of answers to illness.

Mary was also correct in predicting dissatisfaction among young physicians who had practiced with modern equipment and techniques during the war when they returned to small towns across the United States. The building of modern hospitals and clinics would be an aftermath of the war, and Mary predicted both the Great Health Crusades and the era of hospital construction as early as 1943.[94]

The war years bound Mary Switzer to health and medicine, tested the capacity of the Federal Security Agency as an instrument of relief for communities changed by military bases and war industry, and readied the government for reorganization. Mary was anxious to apply the strategies she had perfected during the war to peacetime needs for medical care and community revitalization. She had earned a splendid reputation during national emergency; now she set new goals. In 1946 she said with satisfaction that the "government work" she had done for the past 25 years had been the right spot for her.

Few knew what responsibility Mary Switzer had carried during the last five years of her "government work." She had "assisted" in organizing the policies for the withdrawal of health personnel at the conclusion of the war; she had arranged for the disbursement of over one million dollars in research grants to universities and medical schools; she had the full power to exercise the Federal Security Administrator's veto in any of the committees on which she sat.[95]

Frank Lahey knew her value and wrote Paul McNutt his recommendation for Mary's receiving the Medal of Merit.

> To have undertaken a work which was so interrelated with many other departments and agencies in Washington as is the Procurement and Assignment Service would have been almost impossible, without the benefit and guidance and advice of one who is as familiar with channels of procedure and with individuals in high places as is Miss Switzer.
>
> She is not only thoroughly familiar with procedures and personalities but has, in addition, the extraordinary virtue of being completely trusted by them all.[96]

Paul McNutt attached Lahey's letter to his own estimate of Mary Switzer's value during his administration, and a Medal of Merit came from the President. McNutt had nominated Mary with highest praise.

> In all of these activities which were vital to the successful prosecution of the war, and some of which were of the highest secrecy (War Research Service), the knowledge, ability, and initiative of Mary E. Switzer were outstanding. Her intimate familiarity with Government administration, resulting from more than twenty-five years of continuous service, her wide knowledge of important Government officials and of leaders in the fields of science and medicine, combined with the high esteem and confidence which these officials and leaders reposed in her, her indefatigable zeal and energy in responding to the calls of the Director of War Research Service and the Chairman of the Procurement and Assignment Service... were responsible in considerable measure for the high degree of success of both... In my own estimation, Mary E. Switzer is one of the most outstanding women in the service of the Government and without the wise and able representation she afforded me in connection with the above activities, I should have found it practically impossible to comply with the demands for time and profound consideration which they made upon me in my dual capacity of Chairman, War Manpower Commission, and Federal Security Administrator.[97]

On October 15, 1946, a crowd gathered in the Administrator's office. Paul McNutt had resigned, and Watson Miller was the present occupant. But this was the day Mary was to be awarded the Medal of Merit at the direction of the President of the United States. Paul McNutt had asked that he be allowed to present the President's Medal of Merit, and everyone was waiting in the Administrator's office for him to appear. Perhaps Watson Miller would have to make the presentation; the time dragged. Suddenly, applause was heard outside, and the door flew open. Paul McNutt appeared in a white linen suit, handsome as always.[98] Isabella Diamond and Warren Draper were both relieved, for they knew the ceremony would mean much more to Mary, with McNutt officiating.

Mary had been a supporting character in many such awards, but this was her first award after 25 years of government service. These moments with friends, family, and dignitaries saluting her made her want to weep. She accepted the Medal, smiling broadly up at "Governor McNutt." This was another turning point for Mary. She thought of herself as an "old bureaucrat" with the heritage of "uncertain scores," stepping into the Atomic Age.[99]

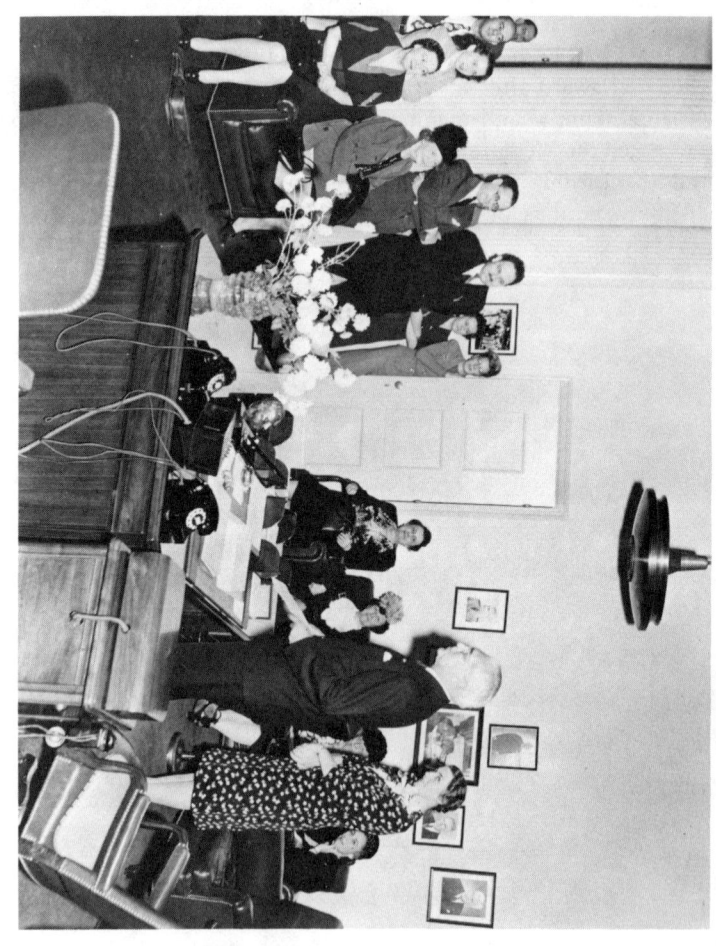

Mary E. Switzer awarded Medal of Merit.
Paul McNutt speaks, Isabella Diamond and Anastasia Switzer watch, 1946.
Diamond to left of McNutt; A. Switzer to right of Mary Switzer.
(Courtesy The Schlesinger Library, Radcliffe College.)

VII
Bureaucratic Leapfrog 1942-1949

The duty of the seasoned bureaucrat in the throes of profound changes is to be a steady anchor, to preserve the equilibrium, to 'stop the rush to the boats' by the way he walks, to be a little paternal and protective of those new services developed in the last decade so as to insure that what is essential will survive this curious phenomenon of democracy.

Mary Elizabeth Switzer, 1946

It had been a long wait for Mary Switzer to have her day in the sun, with Paul McNutt delivering the Medal of Merit. In 1946 her path to future distinction was obscured by a host of factors. Although she had earned a reputation for wise counsel and persistence within the Federal Security Agency, its creator, Franklin Roosevelt, was dead, and Harry Truman was beset with a Republican Senate and House of Representatives. The future of the Federal Security Agency was uncertain. And her closest supporters, physicians with whom she had worked during the war, were not so taken with her ideas about parity for the nation's medical care.

Although Mary was no amateur bureaucrat, profound changes rocked her in the late forties. Mobilization for war had forced the Federal Security Agency as well as the federal watchdog, the Bureau of the Budget, to direct attention overseas. Like the FSA, the Bureau of the Budget had been moved from the Treasury Department during the reorganization of 1939. Unlike the FSA, the Bureau of the Budget had been moved up to the Executive Office of the President, an intimacy that increased its influence markedly. In the aftermath of war, the Bureau of the Budget could now turn its almost undivided attention to increasing the "economy and efficiency" of government, fortified by statutory responsibility for government reorganization.[1]

Reorganization always produced casualties and beneficiaries; Mary Switzer could not predict the outcome of reweaving holes in the governmental fabric. Would her career be furthered by remaining Assistant to the Administrator? If Truman's intent to elevate the FSA to Cabinet level was realized, perhaps remaining in her position would be advantageous. But would the Public Health Service be charged with responsibility for the nation's medical and health care? If so, Mary should angle for reentry to the Public Health Service and realize her dream of employing the tactics of the Procurement and Assignment Service. It was difficult to plot a course for further recognition when reorganization made bureau status uncertain.

Adjustment problems were sure to result from the upcoming changes. Although the Federal Security Agency had been charged with the responsibility for the health, education, and security of the nation at its inception, its structure deviated from logic at many points. The autonomy and organizational integrity of such going concerns as Vocational Rehabilitation were deeply threatened by the possibility of reorganization. The Bureau of the Budget valued functional and effective alignment; a program whose history gave it vigor and identity, yet violated coordination and integration principles of management, was a target for change.

Vocational rehabilitation was a pioneer agency that defied the administrator's logic. A categorical program that offered health, education, and welfare services, such as Vocational Rehabilitation, did not fit neatly under any functional category. Vocational Rehabilitation insisted that in order to serve the "whole person," a variety of needs must be addressed: physical restoration, training, psychological and social adjustment to disability, employment, and financial assistance.[2] The diversity of functions inherent in the process of rehabilitation had made it vulnerable to rearrangers of organizational charts. Vocational Rehabilitation was all too familiar with bureaucratic leap frog.

In 1920, when President Wilson signed the first civilian rehabilitation act into law, Vocational Rehabilitation was assigned to the Federal Board of Vocational Education as a new unit. The Federal Board was composed of the Secretaries of Commerce, Agriculture, Labor and Education as ex officio members and was operated by three salaried members. In 1932 President Roosevelt transferred Vocational Rehabilitation to the Department of the Interior, under the Office of Education.[3] This had not been a setting where Vocational Rehabilitation prospered, instead, rehabilitation leaders found themselves defending the program to educators. Tracy Copp and other Vocational Rehabilitation leaders had hoped to be free of the Office of Education in 1939, when Roosevelt created the Federal Security Agency. Instead, the Office of Education was transferred intact to the Federal Security

Agency, with Vocational Rehabilitation in tow.[4]

Mary Switzer had done her best to see that Vocational Rehabilitation gained visibility in the reorganization of 1939. She had spoken informally with staff members of the Advisory Committee on Education who would advise the President regarding the administration of rehabilitation. And she had enlisted the support of Josephine Roche and Arthur Altmeyer, head of the Social Security Board, in the emancipation of rehabilitation from the Office of Education.[5] The report of the Advisory Committee on Education "indicated cleverly the need for the complete autonomy of the rehabilitation work."

The dream of independence was delayed once more in 1939; reorganization did not lessen Vocational Rehabilitation's hierarchial status, and business was to continue as usual. Knowing bureaucracy, Mary Switzer understood that there would be another day, new reorganizations, and she and Tracy Copp planned steadily to improve Vocational Rehabilitation's position in the administration.

Tracy Copp continued to work on a Coordinating Committee, diligently trying to communicate the needs of the state-Federal program to singularly unimpressed Office of Education administrators, Outhwaite and Reeves.[6] Mary worked at higher levels through an old friend and Budget Officer, Leo Miller, to frame legislation that would accomplish several objectives—including the separation of Vocational Rehabilitation from the Office of Education.[7] Referring to Tracy and herself as "the gold dust twins," Mary produced a bill which she described as their "brain child." She emphasized the importance of the administrative authority as she thought over the final product: "I think we have planned out methods of action which will safeguard the independence of the rehabilitation program itself. The regulations require a full-time director and independence of operation."[8]

The gold dust twins did their work well, for Public Law 113 was adopted by both Houses and signed into law in July, 1943.[9] The law called for a rehabilitation service under the management of a director of rehabilitation appointed by the Federal Security Administrator. No more Office of Education; a direct route to the Administrator had been forged. For the bureaucrat, this accomplishment was equal to the advance of broadening rehabilitation to include physical restoration and the mentally ill as clients, changes also instituted by the passage of Public Law 113.

The gold dust twins knew what slow strangulation by "administrative channels" was. Tracy Copp had labored under the indifference of the Office of Education for years. Thanks to her pipeline to Mary, the frustration of continuing as an agency that merely offered vocational training could be communicated unofficially and with gusto. Mary, in her position as intermediary for the Administrator, was weary of the "orations" of Office of Education administrators who offered little intelligent direction.[10] Liberty in

1943 was a great gain for Vocational Rehabilitation.

In bureaucracies, program visibility gains are temporary, and President Truman seemed quite determined to reorganize the Federal Security Agency so that it could be made a Department and its Administrator a member of the Cabinet. A very thorough study was launched in 1945, with key Federal Security Agency staff submitting suggestions for reorganization. Mary Switzer was one of the eight persons who met daily over a two week period and singled out agencies' programs that should be included in the new department.[11] In the reorganization that resulted, Vocational Rehabilitation escaped resubordination to the Office of Education. Instead, it was placed in the Office of Special Services and no longer enjoyed a direct link to the FSA Administrator.

Losing direct access, Mary Switzer had been a loser in the reorganization also. Her recommendations that functions such as program and policy planning, coordination of Federal-state relations, field operations, research, administrative services be centralized were not followed. More important, Mary had cast her lot with the Public Health faction of the Federal Security Agency, opposing any furtherance of the "Social Security Board group."[12] Mary Switzer properly viewed the leaders of the Social Security Board as a closed group, for the Social Security Board had been transferred intact to the Federal Security Agency. The cohesiveness of Board personnel was deepened by intense rivalry with the Public Health Service, whose philosophy favored local control, while the Social Security Board thought decentralization invited gaps and discrepancies in services.[13] Mary Switzer closed ranks with her friends in the Public Health Service, a program that was already in decline.

When Watson Miller made a statement on July 16, 1946, detailing his plan of organization, it was clear that Mary had been overlooked as an administrator, and that her ideas, except for the disposition of Vocational Rehabilitation, had also been discounted. Rather than centralize, Miller decentralized activities into homogeneous groupings. There would be four branches: Social Security Administration, Office of Educational Affairs, Office of Public Health, and Office of Special Services. Altmeyer would be Commissioner for Social Security, Jewell Swofford Commissioner for Special Services, and Parran and Studebaker would continue in Public Health and Education. Miller created two new staff offices, appointing a director for Federal-state relations and for interagency and international affairs.[14] Although Mary had just returned from an international conference, she was not named for that post, nor had what she coveted come to pass: the combination of the Public Health Service, Food and Drug Administration, Saint Elizabeth's Hospital, and the Children's Bureau under her direction as assistant administrator.

Mary was disappointed in the results of reorganization, but she maintained her equilibrium. Writing to Consumer's League friends, Mary explained the reorganization and its effects upon the Children's Bureau and the Department of Labor. Her words of reassurance were addressed to women of the labor reform movement, but they were also self-reminders: "The first pangs of readjustment are always difficult. But the history of the Federal Security Agency is one of making such adjustments and in so doing benefiting all concerned."[15]

The adjustment period continued for years; Harry Truman was determined to transform the Federal Security Agency into a Department. The Reorganization Act of 1945, which authorized the improvement of the Executive Branch, was to expire in April of 1948.[16] Within two weeks of the announced reorganization of 1946, Truman urged heads of executive departments and agencies to improve their internal organization. Watson Miller hoped his staff had enough energy for yet another study.

With customary resilience, Mary offered her help in the new administrative studies.[17] There were many loose ends about the new organizational structure, and Mary was chiefly concerned about her own role and function. She was no longer at the controls of information sent to and from the Administrator in matters of health. Watson Miller would not use her as liaison in the new system, for fear of creating "conflicts of authority." Mary hoped to be involved in program planning and operations of the activities of the four commissioners. She predicted opportunities for conflict and competition between the units and wanted to facilitate teamwork. The Administrator adopted Mary's suggested job description, saying "the need for coordination has increased as points of inter-dependency have multiplied." In an informal memo attached to his official designation of Mary's responsibilities, Miller said that these more difficult fields of administration will be more important and more comprehensive than her prior work.[18] Some saving and salving was going on during the "readjustment period."

In order for the Federal Security Agency to become a Department, external support was needed as well as the agency remodeling Truman and Watson Miller began. A Committee on a Federal Department of Health, Education, and Security was formed in order to involve the public in the creation of a Department. Twenty-seven members were chosen to represent health, education, social security, and the general public.[19] The Committee requested a listing of advantages of grouping the three fields in one agency,[20] for there was considerable doubt among Committee members that such "bedfellows" should continue to cohabit.

Watson Miller responded with the wartime record of the Federal Security Agency, and with the argument that complex problems are of mutual concern to health, education, and security. By assembling an agency with the capacity of pooling disciplines to meet human need, the specialization produced through new knowledge and the synthesis required by the holistic nature of man could be achieved. Mary Switzer prepared a draft for Miller, stressing the interdependence of the professions and reporting the confidence of Agency staff that "we are on the right track."[21]

As a secondary argument, Miller wrote of the success of Vocational Rehabilitation, a "combined operation." Citing rehabilitation as an exceedingly complex problem, Miller emphasized the relation of rehabilitation to health, education, and economic security. During the past four years varied resources had been mustered for an overall attack. Federal-state partnership had been demonstrated through Vocational Rehabilitation, and the Administrator hoped other programs might follow such an exemplary course of Federal participation in overcoming inequities of birth or geography.[22]

With Mary Switzer's prompting, Watson Miller was heralding the acceptance of the public for government to respond to demands of general welfare. The demand for state and local services was about to burst upon all levels of government in early 1947. Vocational Rehabilitation was used to convince the Joint Committee that a diverse but complementary Department was beneficial, and that complex problems could be addressed through Federal-state cooperation. Mary's familiarity with Vocational Rehabilitation was timely for Watson Miller; she provided him with a program so little known and so heroically depicted that it was just the substantiation needed. Rehabilitation also was one of Miller's interests. From 1923 until 1941 he had served as the Chairman of the American Legion's Committee on Rehabilitation of Veterans. When Miller became Assistant to Paul McNutt, he had brought James Drain, a one-armed veteran, with him to Washington. Miller's knowledge of rehabilitation, particularly the medical problems of disabled veterans, had influenced him earlier in dispatching Vocational Rehabilitation to the Office of Special Services;[23] now Vocational Rehabilitation served as his pièce de résistance while trading up to the Department level.

Perhaps Watson Miller was too occupied with other tasks in 1943 to be aware of how Mary Switzer had changed her view about Federal-state cooperation. The original bill, formulated by the gold dust twins, called for the federalizing of the Vocational Rehabilitation program. Apparently, Mary had as much distrust of the capacities of state and local governments as did staff of the Social Security Board in the early forties. Mary had written Tracy that "it would be better to federalize the existing state program than to delimit it to a small segment of the vocational racket in the states."[24] The bill Senator LaFollette introduced called for much increased power for the Director of Rehabilitation; the Director could cut off funds if a state failed to comply with Federal guidelines.

The bill that became law was substantially changed. States would submit a plan for Federal approval, but state officials would control medical services. This was the first Federal subsidy for medical care. The means by which it was achieved through Public Law 113 was the relinquishing of Federal control. This far-reaching change in social policy occurred without the controversy one would have expected from Josephine Roche's experience of the late thirties. Official testimony hinted at how significant the change was.[25] Compromises had also been struck on other issues that obscured the fact that Senator LaFollette's bill had originally combined veteran and civilian rehabilitation in order to provide a less expensive program. The combined forces of the American Legion, the Veterans of Foreign Wars, and the Veterans Administration soon stripped the bill of its comprehensiveness.[26] LaFollette had done the bidding of the gold dust twins and had called for the certification of training by the Director of Rehabilitation. Superintendents of Public Instruction across the nation had protested this federalization, and the bill was amended to appease the educators.[27] What remained in the Barden-LaFollette bill was a capitulation to special interests as well as a landmark of Federal participation.

Although Mary Switzer's rhetoric carried the day with the Joint Committee and the interested public, there was a contradiction in philosophy and practice that remains. The concept of teamwork and pooling of specialties was sensible and persuasive, but when the score was totaled of winners and losers at the game of bureaucratic leapfrog, those programs that dealt with only one facet of human need fared much better than more inclusive programs.

In the aftermath of the July 1946 Reorganization, Watson Miller had little time to align rhetoric and practice or to reconcile staff hostilities resulting from the changes. By August of 1947 he had resigned and Oscar Ewing became the third Administrator of the Federal Security Agency. A lawyer who had previously been a special assistant to the Attorney General during the sedition trials of 1944, Ewing was also from Indiana. Bureaucrats privately referred to McNutt, Miller, and Ewing as the "Indiana boys." Ewing revived the struggle to make the Federal Security Agency a Department, and asked for background information to explain its exclusion from the President's Cabinet.[28]

The proponents of a comprehensive Department had suffered recent setbacks. A strong medical lobby preferred an independent National Health Agency to the combined model of health, education, and welfare. Once autonomous programs, such as the Children's Bureau and Vocational Rehabilitation, were less than enthusiastic about another reorganization. Everyone was dissatisfied with delegated authority and were fearful of the powers granted the Administrator in reorganizing the Agency and the proposed Department.[29] Katherine Lenroot of the Children's Bureau was apprehensive about the possible division of the Bureau between health and public welfare and approached a senator for support. Senators Taft, Aiken, and Fulbright were promoting the creation of a separate Bureau of Vocational Rehabilitation.[30] Inter-dependency sounded much better than it worked; another reorganization would mean different winners and losers in the game, in the battle for power. Oscar Ewing learned quickly that he did not have the whole-hearted support of his own program chiefs, if he chose to work for the creation of a new Department.

An even older and more dangerous battle soon captured most of Ewing's energies. President Truman had been engaged in a running controversy with Congress over health insurance ever since he took office. The time seemed right for a new approach to the provision of health service, and Oscar Ewing became a spokesman for the Wagner-Murray-Dingell Bill, which would enact the President's program.[31] Mary Switzer was Ewing's advisor in the health field, and he depended upon her to maintain "productive relationships" with voluntary and professional groups in the health field.

When Truman sent Ewing a memo asking that he undertake a comprehensive study of the possibilities of "increasing health levels," Ewing adopted a strategy Mary Switzer had used almost ten years earlier--a National Health Assembly.[32] During the three day conference, 800 professional and lay persons advised Oscar Ewing, and the outcome was the endorsement of the principle of contributory insurance as the basic method of financing medical care. Congress still did not act, and opponents of national health insurance prevented the upgrading of the Federal Security Agency into a Department. They knew precisely where Oscar Ewing stood, and they did not intend to improve his chances of creating a national health program.

Truman's upset victory in the fall of 1948 may have been partially due to his blaming the Republican Congress for reducing social insurance coverage, while delaying a national health insurance system. After all, the Republicans had ignored the advice of the National Health Assembly and the Federal Security Administrator. Mary Switzer, at the elbow of Oscar Ewing, had misgivings about Truman's proposals.[33] Without personnel, facilities, or physicians' cooperation, she felt a national program would fail. This was certainly not the orderly program she had envisioned at the end of the war. Despite her connections with voluntary and professional groups in the health field, she was critical of the American Medical Association for their fierce opposition to national health insurance. Although a decade had passed since Josephine Roche had attempted to negotiate with organized medicine, little had changed. The Truman-Ewing group seemed fated to fail, for in 1949 industry-financed health insurance was allowed as an appropriate subject for collective bargaining.[34] Voluntary health insurance boomed; governmental intervention was shelved.

Mary Switzer may have been relieved that the push for national health insurance terminated so abruptly, but she was apprehensive about Oscar Ewing's devotion to centralization. The drawn-out discussions within the Federal Security Agency concerning the organization of the hoped-for Department were dominated by the Administrator's view that statutory bureaus within the agency were deleterious and that the generalist administrator was preferable to a professional in health, education, or welfare doubling as administrator. Loyalty to a program or to a profession was viewed as destructive in the common direction of professional points of view. The old rationale was trotted out:

> The reasons for creating one Department instead of three rest largely in the fact that we are concerned with the health and the education and the security of the same men and women, and that the needs of these people do not always divide themselves neatly among the professions.[35]

Since the Administrator (and hopefully, future Secretary) would be a lay supervisor and coordinator, appointed by the President, Under Secretaries should also be well-qualified administrators, unencumbered by professional identities.

Detachment from the function of the proposed Department by the key administrators was tied to the equalization of power between the operating agencies and the proposed Office of the Secretary. Administrators wanted advice, not empire-building. As the influence and control of the operating agencies grew, the power of the Secretary was diminished. Oscar Ewing wanted loyalty to the Agency and to him, rather than loyalty to a profession or a program. One way to insure such allegiance was to create a layer of managers. One proposal went even further, allowing the Administrator to abolish units of the Department and to transfer their statutory authority to himself.

Mary Switzer was herself an administrator, not a professional. Still, she reacted strongly to the centralization proposed in planning for Departmental structure and status.

> I think it is dangerous for an agency like ours which has such a vast array of service programs that touch almost every person in the country to take such a strong centralized position. There is much justification for a statutory bureau that can remain stable through unfavorable, changing times. In our complex governmental set up, with an ever-widening range of function, it does no harm to have variety of organization or even competitiveness. As long as the head of the agency has the responsibility for policy formation and the means with which to get joint policy planning and administrative planning, he ought to be able to assert the leadership necessary to carry on.[36]

The existing situation must have been bad indeed, for Oscar Ewing was learning that fidelity could not be forced. Had he been able to look ahead, he would have seen how immutable professional and program allegiance was. The competitors, Social Security and Public Health, would continue their animosity born in the late thirties. As the game of bureaucratic leapfrog would have it, Wilbur Cohen, as Secretary of Health, Education, and Welfare in 1968, relieved the Surgeon General of administrative and policy leadership functions,[37] squaring the score for "drastic reductions" of functions of the Social Security Agency in 1948,[38] while appropriations increased 33% for the Public Health Service. History and emotion proved the most important organization within the Federal Security Agency and the Department of Health, Education, and Welfare.

It was the observation of natural allegiances that caused Mary Switzer to note that the more things change, the more they remain the same. The Federal Security Agency was much larger than when she first knew it, but the personalities transcended all organization charts. Reorganization had been the albatross of the post-war years. Mary's hopes for celebrity had not been realized within the bureaucracy.

VIII
Offspring of The Brains Trust
1946 - 1950

It was as if the 'Brains Trust' that had advised President Roosevelt was now diffused and institutionalized in administrative agencies . . . they were problem solvers and innovators, somewhat detached from bureaucratic routines and rivalries, interested in what might get through the legislature and how it might work . . ."

James Leiby in A History of Social Welfare and Social Work in the United States, 1978, p. 300

During the post-war years, Mary Switzer's attention was divided between internal bids for power and the opportunity to experiment in developing social policy. Internal disappointments were a stark contrast to the success she experienced weaving Federal influence into the developing fabric of social programs. No one realized how symbolic Mary Switzer's accustomed pose in committee meetings was. She always brought her knitting, a metaphor for her function in those years of adjustment to peace. Top priority for the Federal Security Agency in post World War II days was reconstruction of civilian welfare. The woman who had been apprenticed to the "baby member of the Brains Trust" relished the charge. Twice Mary had seen her ideal thwarted. Although the idea of a federalized Vocational Rehabilitation system made perfect sense to her, it had been amputated from the legislation passed in 1943. Passionate as the pleas for a national health program grew, President Truman seemed to be making no more headway than had Roosevelt. Congress and the American people were simply not going to accept Federal control in any recognizable shape. Both the fate of a federalized Vocational

Rehabilitation program and the rejection of a national plan for medical care were lessons in a nation's temperament.

Twenty-five years of training in the bureaucracy had toughened Mary as a technician of policy and innovation. She could see the way out of the stalemate and began to refashion her career goals from that of the generalist administrator to program advocate. As part of the transition, Mary Switzer used her title and role as the Administration's representative to widen her constituency. Voluntary and professional groups were delighted to have "Miss Switzer" at their meetings; she could see possibilities others had scarcely dared imagine.

Since the direct approach to Federal involvement in health care had not worked, Mary aligned herself with members of the medical establishment, choosing practicality over principle. Josephine Roche had spoken of "practical idealism." This seemed a choice time to compromise, using less obvious routes and testing her supports and technique along the way.[1] Mary Switzer became health care's guide to Federal dollars. She trusted that Federal control would follow.

The prominent physicians Mary knew from the Procurement and Assignment Service provided excellent leverage in the indirect approach to the Federal budget. These contacts constituted a "Who's Who" in American medicine: Frank Lahey, Harold Diehl, Mayo Clinic leader who later became Vice President of the American Cancer Society, Max Lapham, later Dean of the Tulane College of Medicine, James Paullin, University of Georgia Medical School Dean, Allen Gregg of the Rockefeller Foundation, Theodore Klumpp and George Merck of the pharmaceutical industry. Mary's wartime assignment resulted in a procurement project of her own, yielding supporters among the most respected men in medicine.

The story of the National Mental Health Act, first postwar piece of medical legislation, is a study of Mary Switzer as trailblazer to Federal expenditures for health. It began with one of Mary's old worries, Dr. Winfred Overholser. As Superintendent of St. Elizabeth's Hospital, that vast creation of Dorothea Dix and only Federal hospital for the mentally ill, Overholser was too conservative for Mary's liking. Still, he was concerned that psychiatry would be overlooked by the Procurement and Assignment Service and asked Mary to arrange a meeting with Paul McNutt and Karl Menninger.[2]

Mary sat in on the meeting of the great evangelist for psychiatry and the Federal Security Agency Administrator. The explanation of the nervous and mental disorders that would result from war was eloquent and simple. Mary left with instructions from McNutt to inform the Board of Procurement and Assignment of this clear need. And Mary also left with a profound impression of Karl Menninger. "His personality made me feel that anything he asked for I would try to get for him with all my might and main."[3] The respect was returned, for Karl Menninger was shrewd enough to see that Mary Switzer could help him. She possessed considerable "might and main."

Percy Priest certainly recognized Mary Switzer's expertise, when she presented him with draft legislation for a national mental health program.[4] The Tennessee Congressman had approached the Public Health Service for information on the problem, and was presented with a near-finished product. David Rapaport of the Menninger Clinic was one of Mary's technical resources in assembling the components of the bill.[5] Once the technical aspects were resolved, Federal Security Agency administrators had to be tutored. Dr. Felix, Chief of the Mental Hygiene Division of Federal Security Agency, had to be briefed, as well as Surgeon General Parran. Confidentially, Mary told Karl Menninger that both Dr. Felix and the Surgeon General "needed a great deal of guidance" before the bill was ready for Percy Priest to introduce.[6]

Through Mary Switzer, Karl Menninger's thinking became the philosophical base for the National Mental Health Act. Lamenting the influence of the "custodial aspects of psychiatry," Menninger saw training as the key to incorporating psychiatric thinking into the repertoire of all medical men.[7] The proposed law was drafted to offer grants for research and training and to provide states with grants-in-aid to develop community mental health services, an emphasis Dr. Menninger felt was critically important.[8]

The next step in ushering through the bill was Congressional hearings. Once more, Mary's medical coterie came in handy. Witnesses included Capt. Frank Braceland, Chief of the Neuropsychiatry Division of the United States Navy, Edward Strecker, Vice President of the American Psychiatric Society, William Menninger, Chief of Neuropsychiatric Division of the United States Army, and Daniel Blain, Neuropsychiatric Division of the Veterans Administration.[9] Not only had the selection of witnesses been guided by Mary, but she had also briefed them on the finer points of the bill.

A figure from the past assisted Mary in the rougher moments of the hearings. The Surgeon General, Thomas Parran, had been Mary's boss before she moved up to Administrative Assistant in 1939. Since the Public Health Service was to administer the grant program, Dr. Parran was also one of the witnesses and came to the rescue of Dr. Felix. During the hearing, questioning by Congressmen became embarrassingly specific. Mary watched apprehensively as Dr. Parran put his hand on Dr. Felix's arm and took over the testimony.[10] Although he had no more detailed knowledge than Dr. Felix, Parran's deft redirection of the discussion to theory and long-range implications reassured the committee.

Everyone was surprised at how quickly the bill was enacted, with very few revisions from the draft. No one who knew how the draft was prepared was surprised that private, nonprofit institutions such as the Menninger Clinic later received funds to perform mental health research and train professional personnel. The practical idealist had found a way to gain the medical profession's support of Federal involvement in the health care of the nation. Within the stipulations of the Act was the appointment of a National Advisory Mental Health Council composed of private authorities from the field. Expenditure of funds was controlled by this body, a group to be appointed by the Federal Security Agency Administrator whose representative with full responsibility and authority was Mary Switzer.[11] And medicine trusted Mary Switzer.

It worked very well for all involved. The Public Health Service acquired a new agency, the National Institute of Mental Health, which by 1950 was receiving 9 million dollars of Federal funds and by 1970 more than 400 million.[12] Karl Menninger saw the number of boarded psychiatrists increase six times in twenty years, and Mary Switzer had blazed a trail for other interest groups to follow.

Another Mary was in the wings, watching the passage of the bill with great interest. Mary Lasker had her own crusade and was depending on Mary Switzer to help find a way to fund research efforts to end disease. Since 1942 Mary and Albert Lasker had promoted a variety of medical research projects through their private foundation, but the desired type of long-term research required a much broader financial base than two wealthy people could provide.[13]

Mary Switzer kept Mary Lasker abreast of legislative developments and Mary Lasker introduced Mary Switzer to Senator Lister Hill and Congressman John Fogarty, the key legislative pins in Lasker's scheme to conquer disease.[14] Senator Hill and Congressman Fogarty were most willing to enhance their political reputations by championing medical research, and as heads of appropriations committees could open the Federal treasury to any medical specialty designated. The rather somnolent National Institute of Health had been in existence since 1939 with several small research laboratories. Mary Lasker, Lister Hill, and John Fogarty changed that with what was derisively called the "disease of the month club," beginning in 1948. The National Heart Institute, the National Institute of Dental Research, the National Microbiological Institute, the National Institute of Neurological Diseases and Blindness, the National Institute of Arthritis and Metabolic Diseases all came into being in rapid succession. NIH appropriations rose from 2.8 million in 1945 to 52.1 million in 1950.[15] The iron triangle of a Federal agency, Congressional support, and an outside pressure group was never more effective. The Public Health Service maintained bureaucratic control, while advisory groups made decisions on how and to whom grants were awarded.

While Mary Lasker was busy with health research, Mary Switzer turned her attention to another battle: the preservation of social science as a legitimate recipient of Federal research support. Pressure for a National Science Foundation had been building for years, and Mary Switzer was familiar with two of the major issues, as she had acted for the FSA Administrator on the President's Scientific Research Board.[16] Summoning up the support of Dr. Felix and Dr. Scheele (Parran's successor as Surgeon General) and the name of Eleanor Roosevelt, Mary insisted that there was "a practical body of knowledge that can be brought to bear on almost every phase of human relations."[17] Mary was only partly successful; social sciences are not included as a basic area of research in the National Science Foundation Act of 1950, but "other sciences" was added to fields of mathematics, physics, biological and medical, environmental, and engineering.

The degree of Mary Switzer's influence in establishing the National Science Foundation is clear in the fight over a second issue: constitution and authority of the Board. Truman had vetoed a bill in 1947, one which used the same strategy devised by Mary Switzer for the National Mental Health Act and for extending the National Institute of Health. The Board would have been composed of private citizens who would determine policy and expend public funds. The third time around Truman apparently saw a potential violation of his authority.

With the additional time the veto allowed, Mary argued for members with "broad vision and wide experience in public affairs," not specialized scientists.[18] Two of her six suggestions for the Board were forwarded to the President, persons she felt could be relied upon to "give penetrating, considered, realistic judgement on the basic issues that are raised by the major role of science in our society." George Merck and Mary Lasker made it; Theodore Klumpp, Hans Clark, Franklin McLean, David Rapaport failed to clear the Administrator's hurdle.[19]

Although not all Mary Switzer's suggestions were accepted by Oscar Ewing, her comments reflect the breadth of her contacts and her conviction about the nature of a government research program. Hans Clarke was Professor of Biological Chemistry at Columbia University. Both Professor Clarke and Mary served on the Medical Advisory Committee of the Polio Foundation. Mary thought him an excellent member of a committee, as well as a wise scientific philosopher. Theodore Klumpp was President of Winthrop-Stearns and a former head of the Drug Division of the Food and Drug Administration. Franklin McLean was Professor of Physiology at the University of Chicago, and Mary described him as a fine liberal and a first-class scientist, who had worked for years to provide graduate training for Negro physicians and graduate students. David Rapaport, a clinical psychologist who had been in charge of research at the Menninger Foundation, was Mary's choice for representation of the social sciences on the Board of the National Science Foundation.[20]

Mary Switzer's hope that the National Science Foundation would not become a technical forum was sustained in the words of the Act. The 25 members of the Board were to be "eminent in the fields of the basic sciences, medical science, engineering, agriculture, education, or public affairs."[21] The bill Truman signed into law made the Foundation director a presidential appointee, as well as the Board members, whose nominations were submitted by scientific and educational institutions. Nowhere is the public distrust of Federal control so clear as in the administration of such a Foundation.[22] Science was clearly to be governed by scientists and paid for by the public.

Mary Switzer wasted little time worrying about compromises that would have bothered her earlier. The consequences of idealism were all-too-evident. President Truman was perennially attempting to institute national health care; Oscar Ewing was exhausting himself and others in the FSA trying to work out a palatable arrangement with organized medicine.[23] Meanwhile, Mary was pointing out the advantages of partnerships between the government and voluntary efforts. Using the Hospital Survey and Construction Act as an example, Mary publicized the benefits of financial aid for the construction of hospitals and amplified the success of intermingling voluntary and public effort.[24] The compromises were working; direct means of improving medical care for Americans were consistently rejected.

One of the hallmarks of compromise during the late forties was the use of advisory bodies to preserve the autonomy of professionals, whether they were scientists or physicians. Mary Switzer and Tracy Copp had tested the sensitivity of local medical communities to government health care programs in the amendments to the Vocational Rehabilitation Act of 1943. That legislation allowed medical treatment to be purchased with Federal dollars. Few people realized that the Federal government was already in the health care business because there had been no opposition from organized medicine to the authorization of funds for physical restoration. What made the change palatable for the medical profession was the provision of a local medical consultant who approved plans for physical restoration, without setting fees. The public was paying for medical care on a small scale, and like scientific research, the endeavor was being governed by the professionals.

Grants-in-aid were a second hallmark of compromise in the increasing amount of government involvement in the field of health.[25] This ploy was obvious in the Hospital Survey and Construction Act, the principal stimulus for the construction of new hospitals for the next twenty-five years. Resistance to direct Federal aid was lessened through the grants-in-aid maneuver, because the state governments were responsible for planning and provision of services. Senator Lister Hill introduced the bill and rode the tide of demand for health facilities to an absolute victory for those desiring construction of health facilities through Federal dollars, but with local control.[26] Watson Miller called attention to the "serious implications" of allowing a Federal hospital council to overrule the Surgeon General on administration of the program.[27] Harry Truman took heed of the Federal Security Administrator's warning and asked that this concession to professional control be removed. The timing was not right to apply brakes, and the Hospital Survey and Construction Act became law in 1946.

By the end of 1946 a patchwork beginning had been made in the Federal provision of health care. Through the "laundering" of Federal influence with advisory committees and/or Federal grants-in-aid, health facilities were built, research and training were supported, and medical service to disabled citizens was delivered. Scattered as they were, the pieces were there. The Federal government took the initiative and the medical establishment took the control. Mary Switzer had helped to assemble the pieces.

With Mary's need to get something done, she did not calculate the possible damage of indirect methods. Achieving national responsibility for the health of all America's citizens was uppermost in her mind. Although organized medicine was being tamed through provision of bricks and mortar for hospitals and training and research for medical specialties, the cost was a shift of medical practice to hospitals, with no change in free enterprise medicine. And while Vocational Rehabilitation got its subsidized medical treatment and labor and management increased fringe benefit programs, the fundamental problem of Federal administration of medical care programs was side-stepped.

Perhaps nothing would have happened if indirect methods had not been employed and private health security had not grown, but the lack of support for Truman's health insurance bill seemed to be directly related to the drain-off of energy and frustration gained by compromisers of Mary Switzer's ilk.

While the public as a whole made little progress toward the desired amount and quality of health care,[28] some sectors of rehabilitation and labor were setting the pace and showing what could be done through comprehensive service patterns. It happened that Mary Switzer had a large part to play in two related "demonstration projects."

Dr. Warren Draper had been a friend of Mary Switzer's for more than a decade. He, too, was disappointed in the response of organized medicine to the needs of the country. A long-standing member of the House of Delegates of the American Medical Association and a medical officer of the Public Health Service since 1910, he prodded colleagues to produce effective legislation to insure availability to all American citizens of modern medicine's "health preserving, life-saving functions."[29]

A Harvard Medical School graduate and much decorated officer of the Public Health Service, Warren Draper had served his last years as Deputy Surgeon General and at age 64 had been deployed to Eisenhower's headquarters in Europe to oversee the health needs of troops and demolished nations.[30] Retirement in 1947 and a brief association with the American National Red Cross left him with a lifetime of experience about to be summoned by Mary Switzer.

Mary had kept in close touch with Josephine Roche, the former Assistant to the Secretary of the Treasury, who had left Washington in 1937 to attend to personal and business matters in Colorado. In 1944 the Rocky Mountain Fuel Company, the business Josephine Roche had inherited from her father in 1925, went bankrupt. At sixty-five, Josephine Roche was named a trustee of the United Mine Workers' Welfare and Retirement Fund. She had been a great supporter of the UMW since the 1920s, and John L. Lewis was an old and loyal friend.[31]

Striking coal miners had insisted on the creation of a welfare and retirement fund, and John L. Lewis drove a bargain with the Department of the Interior that created two separate systems: one that paid miners' sickness, disability, death, and retirement benefits, and one that paid health benefits. This miniature health insurance system was governed by a board of three members, one union, one management, and one neutral representative.[32] A five cent royalty on each ton of coal financed the entire plan. Josephine Roche was to remain a trustee until 1969; John L. Lewis until 1968.

Soon after arriving in her new job, Josephine Roche went in search of a medical officer who could step up the program. Mary Switzer suggested Warren Draper for the post, and he began building a system that would reduce the physical cost of "this brutal industry."[33] Union officials had made the statistics of disabling accidents public: a miner ran a greater risk of being killed or maimed than workers in any other industry. Falling rock, gas and dust explosions, blasting, electrocution, asphyxiation were daily hazards to the miners.[34]

Warren Draper took the job and started learning what problems a disabled miner faced. He found that many miners had received only immediate care following accidents that caused permanent injury. Workmen's Compensation benefits were small and often contested. Some disabled miners had been without medical care for as long as 20 years, living in isolated shacks, fed and cared for by neighbors.[35]

Draper began to build a system that eventually became "a hospital chain 250 miles long,"[36] to reach into the mountains and restore injured miners to useful lives. Union members served as guides for Fund doctors who journeyed into the hills, up creek beds, locating cases and determining the kind of services needed.

What these men found was pain and despair, paralyzed men who had not been out of bed in years, fed and cared for by family and neighbors. What these same agents carried was hope. The Fund would send them to medical centers for relief of suffering and training. Warren Draper set up ten Area Medical Offices throughout the soft coal mining regions of the country to carry out a general medical care program.[37]

These long-neglected workers needed facilities and specialists prepared to deal with the complications of traumatic injury. Warren Draper knew that such specialists existed, and Mary Switzer knew that those specialists needed a battlefield on which to prove themselves.

Howard Rusk was the leading spokesman for the specialty of rehabilitation medicine, and Mary Switzer saw an opportunity to help miners and a struggling new medical specialty. Mary Switzer had met Howard Rusk on a rainy Saturday afternoon when he had appeared before the Procurement and Assignment Board to describe what he was doing in the Air Force with wounded men.[38] "Out of bed and into action" was his maxim, and his attempts to normalize the hospital environment for injured men had caught Mary Switzer's attention and held it. But Howard Rusk had had great difficulty since the close of the war selling his medical colleagues on the "rehabilitation concept." Orthopedists were suspicious of Rusk, thinking him party to a "social service boondoggle" whenever he stressed the point that the whole person needed rehabilitation, not just the damaged part.[39]

Rusk had devoted himself to the promotion of this newest specialty in medicine, physical and rehabilitation medicine. Determined to establish a civilian rehabilitation center, Rusk wrested space from Bellevue Hospital in New York City and began to recruit staff. With space and staff in hand, Rusk was as badly in need of patients as Warren Draper was in need of facilities and trained personnel. Mary Switzer had a match, and she set about furthering the development of both "demonstration projects."[40]

Photographs in the Welfare and Retirement Fund publications make those experimental days of rehabilitation service delivery unforgettable.[41] The legless man sitting on his doorstep with his disconsolate family was shown on the opposite page as "dignified and erect," emerging from an airplane with a properly fitting pair of limbs, walking again for the first time in ten years. A sequence of photographs showed the miner squatting in the mine, vulnerable to slate falls, when he was "jackknifed" and his spine snapped. Paraplegic miners, lined up in a stretcher row at a railway station were loaded onto Pullman cars, where physicians and nurses accompanied them to specialized rehabilitation facilities.

This first step in the rehabilitation of miners never ceased to be dramatic. Some of the injured miners lived a hundred miles away from the nearest train station or airport. Union officials hired ambulances to follow roads to their end, where the driver and an assistant would carry a stretcher to the miner's shack. Ten or twelve miners, summoned for this purpose, would lift the miner from bed to stretcher and then take turns as stretcher bearers through hollows and down ridges until they reached the ambulance.

Occasionally a patient would be so exhausted when reaching the train that a local hospital would give preliminary treatment. One physician described the condition of an arriving miner:

> On admission he was a horrible sight. His legs were useless appendages, horribly deformed and gangrenous. He had a tube in his bladder, and he was saturated with offensive urine. He had lost about everything mortal man ought to possess except the

dignity of his soul. He made a delightful patient. In spite of all his acute suffering, he was always cheerful. His behavior was invariably that of an aristocrat.[42]

Howard Rusk remembered the work of the team and spirit of the injured miners:

> Johnson had broken his back in the middle 30's. He'd even forgotten the exact date. He spent a few weeks in a county hospital and nothing was done and he asked to go back to his cabin in the hills 'to die quiet at home.'
>
> Somebody in the little settlement at the foot of the mountains remembered that he had gone up with his family a good number of years ago, that nobody had seen him for three or four years, at least. Nobody knew whether he was alive or dead. But the team went up. There wasn't any road. You couldn't go up with a jeep. You couldn't go up with a wagon. Mule-back or "shanks-mare" was the only way, but the team went up.
>
> They got to a clearing late in the afternoon, to a slab-sided, two-room cabin high in the pines. Joe had been there four years and he was a terrible sight to see, all but his face. He still had fire in his eyes and hope in his heart, but they counted 19 bed sores that his wife bandaged up with old torn-up sheets she had saved from better days that had been washed again and again and hung in the cool pine-scented air to dry. There wasn't any medicine, just warm water and homemade lye salt and clean cloth for bandages. And as he lay in bed, day after day, his knees seemed to grow up. They were almost to his chin. And they hurt because he couldn't get them down. The team told him about this 'rehabilitation business', that there was hope for him because he had hope and he said he would like to take a try.
>
> The big problem was how to get him down the mountain. That was finally solved by taking two poles and putting blankets between them to make a sling, a kind of hammock. Two of the neighbors became the bearers and they went down the mountain. A wagon met them at the foot of the path and later on a car and then the train, and he came to the Institute.
>
> It was a strange new life for a twisted, sick man covered with sores. And as the examination went on the story was even worse for we found he had stones in each kidney and in the bladder. One kidney was operated on, then the other, then the bladder, then 26 plastic skin grafts were done on the bedsores and four operations on his legs to straighten them out. Eleven months and more than 30 operations later, after the day he arrived, he was ready to start his training, and he trained well. He worked hard but we had to change the diet for him and for the other miners that followed because as he said, 'I ain't used to city vittles.' He just didn't do well on lots of orange juice, spinach, and green salad. He had to have fried meat, turnip greens and corn bread, although he said the corn bread wasn't very good.
>
> He stood on his feet the first time two months later. He had wonderful shoulders and arms that he'd built into pillars of strength working hour after hour each day. . . Just a hundred days after his training, he was ready to go home. Home to a job and the job was the most interesting part of all the story.
>
> Nobody cared much about being sheriff down in this part of Kentucky. The four previous ones in his county had all died of 'lead poisoning.' But he had lots of friends, and he thought he'd like to take a try at 'sheriffing.' So while he was training at the hospital he ran for sheriff on both the Democratic and Republican tickets. And he went home and took office and he's been there ever since. They say there was never a sheriff who had the respect of everybody like him. I guess regardless of how bad and mean you are that you would respect a man with a courage to win the fight like he had won.[43]

Rusk's beloved "Institute" was what awaited the miner at the end of his exodus from the coal country. There were too few and too far such centers, operated by men like Rusk and Henry Kessler, another friend of Mary Switzer's from Procurement and Assignment Board days. The former Navy orthopedic surgeon opened his civilian institute in Newark and practiced the rehabilitation medicine he had begun in military hospitals during the war. Although hampered by the lack of similar, more proximate rehabilitation centers, by 1951, 659 "hopeless" cases had been admitted to rehabilitation centers and had been returned to usefulness.[44]

Warren Draper went on to establish area medical offices in 10 major coal mining communities, demonstrating the potency and practicality of the rehabilitation movement and the possibilities of cooperation between medicine and labor. Howard Rusk and Henry Kessler had a steady supply of patients for their centers and demonstrated what could be done physically and vocationally for injured workers through this new concept of a rehabilitation center. Mary Switzer's connecting the needs of the Fund and of rehabilitation medicine paid great dividends. Both Mary's "demonstration projects" pointed out deficiencies in the delivery of medical care and rehabilitation services, and they provided a platform for her launch into program advocacy.

By employing a member of the American Medical Association's House of Delegates as Chief Medical Director of the Welfare and Retirement Fund, Josephine Roche hoped to allay the fears of organized medicine. Warren Draper found the aim of the fund so admirable he could scarcely imagine disagreement. To "improve wretched health conditions and to make good medical care available to a million miners and their families" was a laudable purpose. Warren Draper expected support and assistance from the AMA, after all, he was one of their own and had been as incensed as other physicians by editorials appearing in the United Mine Workers Journal regarding the medical profession.

Warren Draper began work to provide medical care to miners in 1946; his confidence in the medical profession was shaken during the 24 years he directed the Medical Program of the United Mine Workers Welfare and Retirement Fund. Within three years Warren Draper had been presented with such overwhelming evidence of exploitation and maltreatment of miners by the medical profession that he invited experts from the AMA to visit the mine fields and see for themselves. Listing the charges for the AMA Council on Industrial Health, Draper targeted inferior quality of medical care delivered by Workmen's Compensation, the company doctor, low grade hospitals (known as "butcher shops"), low grade professional work done by unqualified doctors, and abuses of the Fund through overcharges, incompetent treatment, and overtreatment.[45]

Teams of observers were deployed by the AMA and found the abuses Draper had detailed. Still no action was taken against offending physicians, and Warren Draper took matters into his own hands. The Fund arranged for appropriate specialists to see patients before the decision for hospitalization was made. The reduction in rate of surgical operations and hospital readmissions ranged from 30-50%.[46]

Despite the evidence of exploitation, in 1957 the House of Delegates of the American Medical Association adopted a disapproving resolution regarding the new requirement for specialist consultation. Although the procedure had been in effect in Vocational Rehabilitation agencies for several years, the same action on the part of the Fund increased the tension. As a result, local medical societies threatened to "discipline" any members who did not break off association with the Fund.[47]

Warren Draper withdrew to higher ground, choosing a different means of insuring high quality of medical care. Surgeons who were Fellows of the American College of Surgeons would be utilized. The Illinois State Medical Society called this discriminatory. This time Warren Draper did not rescind the rule. The Illinois Society sent patients notice to go to the doctor of their choice and bill the Fund later.[48]

Calling upon the AMA House of Delegates to resolve the controversy, Draper found himself excluded from committee discussions which produced a guide for relationships between the Fund and state and county medical societies. Dr. Draper found unacceptable the stipulation that every physician licensed by the state to practice medicine and surgery be assumed competent in any field he claimed. Writing an old friend, Draper reminded him that he had begun the program with the mistaken assumption that every duly licensed physician was competent, with disastrous consequences.

> While the majority of physicians rendered conscientious, high grade service, there were those who did not, so that it was absolutely impossible to continue upon such a basis without becoming bankrupt or incurring the liability of being declared wasteful and inefficient. . . . Our files contain abundant evidence, both photographic and written, of the grotesque, incompetent and ignorant treatment that many of our beneficiaries have received. . . Much of the surgical treatment was performed in a manner that would make it impossible to convict the physician on charges of corrupt and incompetent practice.[49]

Warren Draper did not intend to go back to a naive assumption of competence, instead, he discarded the guide and continued to operate on the principle that an agency has the right to choose the physician, if it is the agency that pays the bill. The AMA fought back, charging that Dr. Draper had installed a controlled and paternalistic medical care program that competed with community hospitals and the private practice of medicine. Several state medical societies denied membership to physicians working with the Fund, and the AMA Convention was presented a resolution making physician participation in "systems of medical care a violation of medical ethics."[50] After twenty-five supporters of the resolution spoke, a solitary Warren

Draper rose to read a short statement, ending with the warning that "petty persecutions will be settled by legal means."[51] AMA lawyers knew what this meant. They would be meeting John L. Lewis in court. The resolution was withdrawn the next day. Warren Draper was now known as the "Devil's Disciple."

The fact that the medical care program and Miners Memorial Hospitals system developed, despite the opposition of the AMA, is testimony to Warren Draper's stature and John L. Lewis' strength. It was a demonstration of medical and rehabilitation teamwork, of the value of group practice, of the practicality of regional hospital systems. And it was a fine trial balloon for Mary Switzer's emerging plan.

What worked for the injured miner should certainly work for the general populace. Mary knew that there were isolated beginnings of rehabilitation centers, and that a plan had been constructed in 1946 for community rehabilitation service centers. Nevertheless, the plan was gathering dust, despite its auspicious start.

Bernard Baruch, financier, had a physician for a father who was the first teacher of physical medicine in the United States.[52] In 1943 Mr. Baruch created the Baruch Committee on Physical Medicine, to honor his father. The Committee's purpose was the promotion of wartime and postwar physical rehabilitation, and their blueprint for a community rehabilitation and service center was a cartooned diagram showing the sequence of activities necessary for taking "the man from the bed to the job."[53]

The timelessness of the report was a measure of the men who constructed it, all physicians with experience in rehabilitation programs of the armed services and the vanguard of a specialty approved in 1947, the American Board of Physical Medicine and Rehabilitation.

Although the concept was clear, and the members of the committee thought communities would gladly receive their ideas and act on them, only a few localities did so. And those who did were influenced by individuals who were not easily discouraged.

Pioneers in making rehabilitation a community resource added something of their own to the Baruch Committee plan. Each rehabilitation center struggling along during the late forties and early fifties seemed the shadow of an individual's thought, translated by a unique community.

The state of Virginia had as its director of Vocational Rehabilitation a man named Richard Anderson, who believed the prophecy that there would soon be a great expansion of rehabilitation centers for the disabled. Anderson also had a way of recruiting talented staff from the ranks of educators.[54] Frank Birdsall, tall and droll, from Tidewater Virginia, and Corbett Reedy, a counselor who always thought he would return someday to teaching, were two of Anderson's most valuable recruits. Both Birdsall and Reedy stayed in rehabilitation for thirty years, shaping the rehabilitation center concept for Virginia.

Anderson had had his eye on the Army General Hospital at Fishersville, Virginia, which had been declared surplus in the demobilization following the end of World War II. The hospital stood amongst the mountains of western Virginia, and soldiers had been flown from Richmond to Afton, a sequestered spot, for rest and recuperation. After negotiation with the Army, the state rehabilitation agency had the vacant hospital transferred to its possession, and the Woodrow Wilson Rehabilitation Center opened in July of 1947.[55]

It differed from the institutes of Howard Rusk and Henry Kessler in its rural location and its emphasis on education. Corbett Reedy and Richard Anderson were educators, not physicians, and the Woodrow Wilson Center bore their mark. In 1947 there were 17 "students" at the Center, and the vocational training they received paralleled their medical care and physical rehabilitation regimen.

The Center grew rapidly to a capacity of 400. The miners came from West Virginia and Virginia. Tuberculous patients were sent from New York. Frank Birdsall came to direct the Center in 1948 and hosted visitors from all over the country, and later the world. Airlines gradually changed to accomodate wheelchairs, for somehow disabled persons had to reach the rehabilitation centers.[56]

The Woodrow Wilson Center was a demonstration project that dramatically illustrated Mary Switzer's dream. Medical care and vocational training were being delivered to civilians who had never been viewed as reclaimable. The union was embarrassing both the medical profession and legislators. If miners received such specialized care, should not all citizens?

Mary Switzer had prepared the way for great changes in social policy. By the close of the forties, she could qualify as one of the most accomplished of the members of the new, institutionalized, "Brains Trust."

A path to Federal resources had been blazed. Mary Switzer had suggested the use of advisory groups and grant-in-aid formulas to dilute Federal control. Established medicine now welcomed Federal money, which poured into new efforts in research and training. Along with Mary Lasker, Mary Switzer had harnessed the power of voluntary groups for lobbying purposes. The partnership between the community and government would result in expanded health care, of that Mary Switzer was sure.[57]

Interminable luncheons and committee meetings had built Mary's knowledge of and influence with voluntary groups. During this same period, Mary had also strengthened a new medical specialty, physical medicine and rehabilitation, by seeing to it that patients were referred to specialized centers. By suggesting the rehabilitation center as the answer to the rehabilitation needs of injured miners, Mary had established a goal for communities throughout the nation.

Mary Switzer now knew how to get things through the legislature, and she also knew now what she wanted to create. In order to make it work she would have to shed her role as the generalist administrator, and become the program advocate.

IX
Taken By The Nape of The Neck
1950-1952

Mary acted on cynicism as penicillin does on bacilli.

Warren Bledsoe, 1972

Eleven years of giving advice to an administrator were enough. Enough to learn where a start could be made and how the campaign to provide health and dignity for needy Americans could be won. Mary was fifty years old, and she wanted to establish a beachhead of her own.

She had been infinitely patient and watchful. Her range of interests was from patents to the New York Yankees. She knew her job thoroughly, yet she also kept abreast of what was happening in other agencies and within other nations. She had participated in many changes as the faithful civil servant. It seemed the time to cross the line from "impartial" administrator to program advocate.

Her friend, Tracy Copp, urged her to pursue her chance at solving administrative problems independently. Tracy wanted her to take on the Office of Vocational Rehabilitation, where she had worked for 38 years. "The program needs you and will give you the opportunity to take it by the nape of the neck!"[1]

One version of how Mary came to be Director of the Office of Vocational Rehabilitation on December 1, 1950 was that Oscar Ewing looked around in an elevator one day and said: "Why don't you do it, Mary?" Mary was reported to have modestly replied, "But, I've always been a second string person--I'm not sure I can do this."[2]

Another account, as told by Mary at the end of her career, was a bit different. Again, Mary stated that she had not sought the job, but had been looking for a better deal in the Federal Security Agency. As Assistant to the Administrator, she had been involved in the discussions of finding a new Director for the Office of Vocational Rehabilitation. None of the possible candidates seemed to have the right combination of qualifications:

> I can remember the evening so well. We were having dinner at the Army-Navy Club with two or three of the top people in the Federal Security Agency, and Dr. Howard Rusk. We had gone over these people being considered for the position and ruled them out for one reason or another. Coming down in the elevator, almost in a joking spirit, I said: 'Well, it looks as if I ought to take it.' That's how it happened. Dr. Rusk said: 'I think that's a good idea,' and we joked back and forth for a time. The next day they supported the idea, asked if I would really be interested, and it became my assignment.[3]

One of the Administrator's right hand men, John Thurston, did not think the appointment had been accidental at all. He remembered Mary Switzer actively pursuing the job, and Howard Rusk being her strongest supporter.[4]

Mary was very familiar with the VR program and with the 1943 legislation that authorized Federal payment for medical care and physical restoration. She recognized the potential of the program. It had carefully prescribed and measurable outcomes, a budding structure for comprehensive delivery of services, and a philosophy that could be sold to conservatives and liberals.

Mary had made the most of OVR's slow pace, calling it to the attention of Oscar Ewing through her collaborator, Howard Rusk.[5] And Howard Rusk had good reason to want Mary appointed Director. Although the cadre of physicians devoted to rehabilitation medicine had taken the Baruch plan and established a number of physical medicine centers, by the fall of 1948 it was clear that OVR was not utilizing the centers.

Rusk was exasperated with the Federal office for not pushing referrals to rehabilitation centers and sustaining the relationship with local physicians who referred patients to hospitals, not rehabilitation centers. After all, the United Mine Workers Welfare and Retirement Fund Medical Program was showing what could be done for miners. It was the responsibility of the Federal office to take on the more difficult cases who could be helped by a rehabilitation "team" at one of the centers. Although private sources had helped the rehabilitation centers start, only the state of Virginia had put public support behind the concept. The "disease of the month club" approach was gobbling up Federal dollars, while the newer idea and promise for improving community health through regional centers was not even being fed by the agency authorized to do so.

Rehabilitation medicine needed the constant support of the Federal agency; Mary Switzer needed a respected advocate in order to take over the leadership of OVR. Howard Rusk was the right man. Mary Switzer was the solution for Howard Rusk's problem, for she understood the "back-scratch" theory: if you want someone to help you in your area, you must help them in theirs.[6]

The incumbent Director, Mike Shortley, had been brought in as Director in 1943, when OVR was moved from the Department of the Interior to the Federal Security Agency.[7] Mike Shortley's work had been with the Social Security Board, and "old-timers" in the Federal and regional offices of Vocational Rehabilitation had resented Shortley's appointment. John Kratz had been the Director of the agency before Shortley, during the long years of administration in the Office of Education. Kratz was a hero to the administrators who had battled against the misunderstanding of Vocational Rehabilitation as little more than a training program.[8] To have him set aside as assistant to an import like Mike Shortley offended Kratz' comrades in VR's struggle for independence.

Shortley was accustomed to the authority and administrative style of the Social Security Board and compounded the resentment caused by his appointment by infringing on the authority of the state directors. What had once been a free and easy state-Federal relationship became much more formal, with more rigorous financial auditing. Within a few years Shortley yielded to the power of the regional and state directors, leaving them to their own devices.[9] As Tracy Copp put it, "Poor Mike never trusted the old timers, so he let them alone, which gave them a rather placid existence."[10] Shortley's retreat made him vulnerable to the criticism Howard Rusk placed in appropriate ears.

Mike Shortley was relegated to the position of Regional Director of FSA and continued to do a respectable job.[11] Circumstances had brought about his displacement, with a little help from Mary and her friends. For almost thirty years Mary had heard of the Vocational Rehabilitation program from Tracy Copp. The program had existed only one year longer than Mary's tenure in Washington. Tracy Copp had educated Mary Switzer to the concerns and constituencies of the Vocational Rehabilitation program, and Mary considered both carefully.

She knew the leaders in Vocational Rehabilitation, including the old guard who had defied Mike Shortley. W. F. Faulkes, Wisconsin VR Director, was the oldest rehabilitation worker in the country and a prototype of rehabilitation leadership. He had begun as an instructor in vocational education, when physically disabled people were barred from attendance at public educational institutions. Bill Faulkes started the first vocational school in Wisconsin, performing so admirably that he was asked to head the VR program in 1921. The years that followed in rehabilitation made him critical of state vocational education attempts to subsume rehabilitation service. His testimony in 1943 was in part responsible for VR's emancipation from vocational education. At 73, Faulkes was acknowledged as the grand old man of state agency administrators and of the National Rehabilitation Association, a voluntary organization that had also been instrumental in the passage of the 1943 legislation.[12]

Faulkes was representative of a very important constituency for Mary Switzer. The state directors of VR had scored a major victory in the 1943 legislation. Not only had the Federal administration of the program been made distinct from education, a narrow range of services was expanded to a spectrum of needs for the mentally and physically handicapped.

Although the state programs had benefited from the 1943 legislation, the state directors had been under attack since 1944, from Paul Strachan, President of the American Federation of the Handicapped. Strachan had created the National Employ the Handicapped Week in 1945, and had lobbied for the creation of a Federal Commission for the Physically Handicapped to be located in the Department of Labor. Paul Strachan had little regard for the VR program or its administrators, whom he called "Brahmins," more concerned with preserving their caste system than in rendering actual service to the handicapped. Strachan not only lambasted state directors, he dismissed the Federal Security Agency (a "do-gooder" agency), the National Rehabilitation Association ("the state directors' organization which has never had any ideas for national programs") and rehabilitation counselors ("meaningless term, a toga of professionalism not fooling anyone") as self-serving and ineffectual.[13]

Strachan's criticism was voiced at Congressional hearings and at meetings of the American Federation of the Physically Handicapped. Viewing himself as the voice of disabled persons, Strachan believed all that was needed was jobs, and that the Department of Labor could improve services to disabled persons. Strachan was particularly incensed in 1950, when he accused NRA, OVR, and FSA of "gagging" his witnesses before hearings on legislative changes. Charging that "opulent directors" functioned as unregistered lobbyists at taxpayers' expense, Strachan called for a checkrein on the "rehab boys."[14]

Despite Strachan's vehemence, Vocational Rehabilitation continued as usual. The program was not transferred to the Department of Labor, nor was the activity or influence of state agency directors curtailed. The feud was an airing of linen Mike Shortley regretted, but it solidified the FSA, NRA, and OVR alliance. The charge that the Federal-state rehabilitation program was wholly inadequate was backdrop for Mary Switzer's debut as Director.

Two veterans of Strachan's attacks remained in the Office of Vocational Rehabilitation. Shortley's closest associates were Joseph Hunt and Donald Dabelstein. Hunt was the originator of the cost benefit ratio, showing what a disabled person earned after services were rendered. Dabelstein was the "program thinker" who balanced humanity against the accounting system with which VR was both blessed and blighted. Both men had been at Mike Shortley's elbow during his last appearance at appropriations hearings.[16] Both had helped prepare the rather dull, abbreviated testimony that reported a total of 87 state agencies with 2200 employees yielding 59,000 "rehabs" for the previous year.[17] Their request had been for 23 million dollars, yet Strachan called this agency lacking "in capacity, experience, or trained personnel to administer an overall program for the handicapped."[18] Although Strachan's criticism was often as exaggerated as his claim to possessing thirteen disabilities, there was enough truth to his charges to sting.

Vocational Rehabilitation was fraught with contradictions. While the virtues and importance of the VR counselor had been extolled for years, the counselor resembled a purchasing agent more than a case service worker. Other social service agencies provided "soft services" designed to change behavior and proving difficult to measure. The VR counselor was able to purchase "hard" services from providers in the community, building a network of organizational allies and supplying measurable outcomes for state agency directors. The purchase of services had enabled VR agencies to increase their flexibility, control staff size, and create dependent allies.[19] Although the complexity and importance of the continuous service of "counsel and advisement" had been stressed throughout the history of VR, the rehabilitation counselor was still expected to acquire these skills with no special professional training.[20] This contradiction gave too much credence to Strachan's criticism for Mary's liking.

Mary's concept of rehabilitation had been learned from Tracy Copp, who was a past master in getting people to work together so that real help was received by disabled persons.[21] Mary was also aware of the possibility of administrators' preoccupation with production, and the negative effects of a system of measuring program success by the number of clients exiting the system with jobs. As the end of the fiscal year approached, the quality of rehabilitation work sometimes suffered, so that each state would show a substantial number of successful closures. The pressure of year-end statistics sometimes caused the philosophy of rehabilitation, as Tracy Copp had taught it, to be violated. And hurried or superficial casework gave Paul Strachan the evidence he craved. If she got the job, Mary knew she would have to reconcile the contradictions Strachan had so determinedly revealed.

The quality and substance of services would have to be improved. At the same time she would have to win the support of the state agency directors, for they were a formidable lobby. The state agency directors were informed of the change in the Federal leadership by Michael Shortley. His brief message assured the "rehab boys" that Miss Switzer was familiar with the work of the states and of Vocational Rehabilitation.[22] He left his successor his desk and his wish for continued cooperation between the Federal and state programs.

A newspaper release was attached and circulated to all regional and local VR offices citing the cause for Switzer's appointment as "her wide experience and background, as well as her familiarity with Government Administration."[23] From the photograph taken on December 1, 1950, seven pleased persons look out from a stark setting, complete with Venetian blinds and a

Mary Elizabeth Switzer on the day she became Director of the Office of Vocational Rehabilitation, December 1950. *from left:* Margaret Weisman, Father McGowan, Mrs. Krueger, Isabella Diamond, David Pritchard, Josephine Coe, and Warren Draper. *(Courtesy The Schlesinger Library, Radcliffe College.)*

standing waste receptacle. Seated, smiling, and bedecked with a corsage and flowery hat is the new Director. In an equally showy hat, with her arm on the back of Mary Switzer's chair, is Isabella Diamond. Her expression approaches a smirk. Trusted friends, including Jo Coe and Warren Draper, are among the coterie. It is a triumphant occasion; no one seems concerned about Mary Switzer's future as Director.

Only one of Mary's friends fully understood what was ahead. After 26 years in the central office of Vocational Rehabilitation, Tracy Copp had retired in 1947 at the age of 70, returning to her home in Green Bay, Wisconsin. Tracy's "gold dust twin" wrote frequently, sending along office correspondence and asking for counsel. The problem was to build on what was present, and that posed some problems. Mary encountered staff who made condescending comments, telling her it would take some time before she could understand the problems of the office. Tracy resented such pedantry and wrote a sarcastic retort: "You can be forgiven since a galaxy of experts seem to have been in considerable fog."[24] Tracy continued to attend rehabilitation meetings in Chicago and Milwaukee and functioned as Mary's detective. She was also a trusted analyst, outlining the strengths and weaknesses of regional and state staff with no holds barred. "He is stingy in every aspect of his life, his dough, his judgments. He is a really gossipy old man. I do not trust him. He does not have any use for women, or negroes-- classes them together I guess."[25] Tracy provided Mary with on-the-job training for the Directorship, and her wisdom of years of watching regional and state directors at work was enormously valuable to Mary. The role of unofficial advisor was greatly enjoyed by Tracy.[26]

When asked, Tracy could deliver incisive instruction, comparing the behaviors of central office, regional, or state agency staff to their response to John Kratz or Mike Shortley. Management of personnel was delicate, as Mary knew some of the staff was expecting business to go on as usual, and she relied upon Tracy's judgment. "There are some fine individuals connected with OVR, and they should welcome the new attack," Tracy wrote encouragingly.[27] And of Mike Shortley, Tracy said, "I think Mike will be a good sport about it, and perhaps a return to the old group will be a relief. He functions best with a formula."[28]

Mary did not need or seek formulas, but she did need Tracy's judgment. Mary would ask Tracy's opinion of a meeting they both attended, being cautious about the "rave reviews" she heard. Or she would request help in dealing with regional representatives whose careers had overlapped those of John Kratz and Mike Shortley and who took a passive stance with the new Director.

Mary met the "boys" head on, in Executive Committee sessions with state agency directors, where each described their most pressing problems, and by visiting them on their home turf.[29] Corbett Reedy, the State Director of Virginia, invited Mary to address a group of state directors from Region III, and the occasion was her first speech to "rehab people." None of the men knew this "lady" with the public health and Treasury background; all were in suspense about this unknown replacement for Mike Shortley. Mary's speech allayed all fears. Recalling the history of the public program and the importance of the task, she made the tough old-timers sense her determination to lead to a better future for rehabilitation.[30]

To rally the regional representatives, ten men who directed the Federal program in specific geographic regions of the country, Mary instituted a weekly report called "Headquarters News Notes." The first edition emphasized her need for closer rapport with the regional representatives, and the chatty nature of these bulletins seem to bear out her intent.[31]

Those "News Notes" were a Switzer blend indeed. Always written in the first person, and inevitably containing an endearing reference, such as "I was on television, my debut, in New York City"[32] or an account of a luncheon for John Kratz,[33] they also contained information on common concerns and an occasional reprimand. When news of variation in hospital costs between private and rehabilitation patients was reported, Mary labeled it "the Washington situation" and asked regional representatives to send in relevant data.[34] The mixture of the personal touch with administrative control was Mary Switzer's strategy.

Mary was selling herself to each of her internal constituencies: the regional representatives, the state directors, and the central office staff. With 87 state agencies, Mary mixed visits to states or regional meetings with inviting the state directors to Washington. Tracy Copp advised her not to be "too tied down to the Washington office, as it will be so stimulating to the State workers as well as the Regional for you to be in the field."[35] She was concerned with the emphasis the state directors gave placement and used every opportunity to talk about widening the group served and extending the services provided in the states. Mary was well aware of the reluctance of state agency staff to accept difficult cases, as her experience with the UMW Welfare and Retirement Fund had been her teacher. And, of course, Howard Rusk had chafed under the state agencies' tendency to take on easier cases, so that the end of the year showed successful closures. In l950 the states could claim 60,000 successful closures; Mary thought they could be pulled along with additional funds.[36] The 20 million appropriated in l950 would have to be increased if more severely disabled persons received services.

Mary's journeys into various states were carefully planned. An itinerary was prepared on letter-size bond which had been divided into three segments. Her agenda was placed on the left, telephone numbers and names of persons she knew or hoped to contact on the right, and brief facts about the state she was visiting in the center.[37] During the years of solidifying her state and regional constituency, Mary never left the office without her "Fact Sheet" to prepare her to broaden her network of influence.

Money was the predominant issue in the central office. The 25 staff members there remembered the summer of 1951 as "budgets-formula-financing: ceaseless, thankless tasks."[38] Reading the proposals for regional projects, central office staff saw a disquieting contrast. From some regions there were no new ideas, others proposed new programs with qualified personnel. Don Dabelstein labored over the goals of equality and uniformity and prepared for budget hearings in October.

Mary trusted her central office staff to attend to the endless detail of grant administration and concentrated her efforts on "telling the rehabilitation story" to public and private groups working in associated areas. She wrote more articles in 1951 than in any year of her career, publishing in journals of hospital associations, industrial health, religious groups, and physical medicine.[39] She also spoke to as many groups as she could reach, stating simply and emphatically the role of rehabilitation.

> In the past, the physician has thought too much about the physiologic and clinical aspects of the patient's disability. The vocational counselor too frequently has thought only in terms of physical skills which could be utilized vocationally. Between the two there is a wide area through which most physically handicapped persons must go when their medical care is completed but before they are ready to undergo vocational training or retraining.[40]

Having established the gap, Mary would go on to describe the rehabilitation center as the focal point of rehabilitation. Holding up the Woodrow Wilson Center at Fishersville, Virginia as the prototype, Mary would encourage listeners to develop a cooperative plan that would identify the number and kind of rehabilitation centers needed nationally.[41] There was no question about it now, rehabilitation medicine and rehabilitation centers had the support of the Federal office.

Internal loyalty was important in Mary's plan to make this new shop her own. The lure of international travel was too strong to keep her in Washington, but she faithfully dictated records that were mailed to the central office staff when she was away.[42] She wanted her staff to function as a family, and her long discourses on her travels seemed much more personal than professional.

The central office staff seemed to enjoy their new boss; she was colorful and drew favorable attention from legislators and administrators. In April, when she had appeared for the first time before the Senate Appropriations Committee, a liveliness was apparent that neither Joe Hunt nor Dabelstein had seen in her predecessors. Demurely, Mary had begun saying "she would like to try to justify their request for 23 million dollars." Cautioned to "try hard" by Senator Chavez, she said she understood how hard the Committee's job was, since she was an "old bureaucrat."[43] Touching on discrimination against hiring the handicapped in government positions, Mary pressed her advantage.

> The more you serve the severely disabled group, the more expensive it becomes... we are the only agency that can do it--it takes more skill and time... We should serve the people no other agency is set up to do anything about... we should not shy away from things because they are hard.[44]

As if predicting the future, Mary went on to say: "I believe in concentrating at certain periods on certain things, because I think you can make progress faster that way."[45] By the time she had finished her testimony, the modesty had been replaced by near self-righteousness. As she rose to leave, she admonished the senators to think about what she had told them. She had made her points and also her reputation. She was known already as a potent witness in Congressional hearings.

Mary had a great advantage in her friendship with Oscar Ewing, the Federal Security Administrator. Four days before she offered her testimony, Ewing had presented the overall budget of the FSA to the Senate Appropriations Committee. He had many agencies within the FSA which he could highlight, and he used the opportunity to refer to the Office of Vocational Rehabilitation as a place where a small Federal investment was being made to remove people from relief rolls; the restored taxpayers returned $10 for every $1 expended, Ewing stated.[46]

This sort of attention gave Mary credence not only "on the Hill" but among her central office staff. When Prince Feisal of Saudi Arabia visited Washington, Ewing invited Mary to join him and top staff from the State Department at lunch.[47] That sort of company was a real status boost to the small agency, accustomed to being on the periphery of Washington activity.

Mary could turn a friend's favor into a full-scale demonstration of the "rehabilitation story." Following the lunch with the Arabian prince, she escorted the entire group to a public hospital in Washington, where a physical medicine department was working with 700 indigent patients. Mary reported that they "made a great hit" in the Galligher wards; "everyone got quite a thrill out of the spectacle, including your Director."[48]

Her friends in high places bolstered Mary in her new position. Oscar Ewing from above, Howard Rusk from without, and a growing group of admirers from key legislative committees kept her in command. She had been warned that some of her staff in the central office were "waiting eagerly for the effects of your charm as a woman to disappear" and that "'little men' do not like to be supervised by a woman, resenting a woman finding the answers and achieving results when they have proven their inability to do so."[49] Choosing to defend her staff, Mary defused her informant, saying his irritation grew from others not meeting his extraordinary standards and asking him to not think poorly of "our family."[50]

Increasingly, inside the "family," Mary showed herself to be as free with criticism as she was with praise. Memos to staff had a stern note, punctuated with moralisms: "Only by attention to small matters can we expect work to flow smoothly. Therefore, telephones should be covered, communications should not be held, previous correspondence should be consulted, and outgoing communications must be cleared."[51] When problems persisted, a threat resulted: "Unless there is a marked improvement in the spirit of cooperation evidenced by all, serious consideration will have to be given to establishing a central pool for typing services."[52] Mary Switzer expected an efficient family.

By July of 1952, Mary summarized her gains as Administrator of OVR. The recruitment of several well qualified, interested, aggressive staff members and the reorganization of top staff of her office was paramount. Mary was not so pleased with the function of the regional representatives or Federal-state relations.[53] She had spoken to every regional National Rehabilitation Association meeting in the past 18 months, leaving her with the hope that she would not have to make another speech for at least a year, but also with the conviction that the state directors must come to Washington on a regular basis.[54] Mary's most pressing problem was state support, more state money in order to capture increased Federal funds.

Mary knew the ladder of competition she would have to climb in order to enlarge Federal appropriations for Vocational Rehabilitation. The public arena was more competitive than private business. Competition began within her own office, and Mary Switzer backed the staff proposals she deemed of most worth. The next level of competition was with other agencies within the Federal Security Administration; there she must persuade the Administrator that her proposals were more worthy than those of other agencies. Then the Bureau of the Budget must be satisfied, when all departments of the executive branch demanded their share of available funds.[55] It was only with those three battles bested that the program advocate could appeal to particular Congressional committees, hoping to push the budget proposal toward her goal--appropriation of Federal funds.

Only a novice entered that competition without the support of voluntary organizations and state and local backers. Mary Switzer could count on the National Rehabilitation Association as her nongovernmental ace-in-the-hole.

Since 1925 the NRA had rallied diverse groups interested in services to disabled persons. In most recent years, it had been a staunch supporter of the Federal Security Agency and the state-Federal program.[56] The Executive Director, E. B. Whitten, was known to Congressional committees as a sensitive consultant, skilled in preparing legislation.[57] Whitten and three state directors had even met with President Truman to discuss financing, the first time anyone from the NRA or the state-Federal program had met with a president since Hoover.

The motivation of NRA members and leaders may have been mixed, some with firm moral commitment to the rehabilitation movement and some with financial involvement, but the organization had the capacity to mobilize state and local support for rehabilitation appropriations. Mr. Whitten called the NRA "the Poor Man's Lobby," saying it bore little resemblance to liberally financed political organizations.[58] Working quietly and inconspicuously, NRA distributed fact sheets to explain the needs of the program clearly and emphatically.

The virtues of such a nongovernmental group were recognized by sponsors of rehabilitation legislation. In a case study of the appropriations process, one researcher wrote:

> The tools a leader for NRA would have are impressive: A good cause; a good national lobby; very good local organization, which could be coordinated by the congressman and NRA; and, most important, goals that can be met--they don't want the world.[59]

NRA was just what the program advocate needed to boost rehabilitation past the competing program heads and secure a larger share of the Federal dollar.

The regional NRA conferences offered Switzer a forum for rallying support; it also gave her the opportunity to shake up regional or state administrators who had failed to pick up the pace. Reminding listeners that the state-Federal program had had the authority since 1943 to provide needed services, "we impose restrictions on the length and type of training, on maintenance, or of providing comprehensive physical medicine and rehabilitation services to disabled individuals." Challenging NRA members to think beyond the present law, to remove themselves from "silent isolationism" and "don the cloak of dynamic leadership," Mary repeated her message: this group must pledge allegiance to the handicapped, using a multi-disciplinary approach to correctly analyze individual limitations and potentialities and develop the maximum of services authorized under the VR Act.[60]

Mary knew how to bait her audience. Throughout her speeches there were references to the need to enact new legislation that would broaden the content of the present program. Having whetted her audience's appetite for more money and power, she reminded them that such action only resulted when the state leadership demonstrated the urgency of the need.

The newcomer was also adept at increasing her credibility with the grass roots. During her speeches she referred to her experience during the Second World War, when the team approach worked so well in the rehabilitation of men in the Armed Forces or in the UMW Welfare and Retirement Fund rehabilitation program. Mary mentioned her international exposure to rehabilitation, which had convinced her that rehabilitation was the best demonstration of democratic forces at work. Her expertness was most obvious when she scolded. "Recently, in preparing for hearings before the Bureau of the Budget,"[61] she would say, and attention was riveted just in time to hear her report how few severely disabled persons were receiving physical medicine services.

The "poor man's lobby" was being readied for its most important role. Mary Switzer knew she could rely on the NRA for instant and steady pressure on legislators. Her barnstorming paved the way for legislative change; it also gave Mary a good look at each of the states and their programs. For the woman who wrote the National Mental Health Act in 1946 and who was devoted to psychiatry as Karl Menninger described it, it was embarrassing to review the description of cases in 1950 and see that only 6.5% were categorized as mentally ill. And, as a friend of Howard Rusk's, the underutilization of rehabilitation medicine and rehabilitation facilities for the treatment of mobility impairments caused by spinal cord injury, arthritis, cerebral palsy, and stroke, was disturbing. Despite the 1943 Act, things had gone on pretty much as usual, with amputee and orthopedic cases making up almost half of the states' caseload.[62] Mary's determined treks to each of the states, billed as largely ceremonial, gave her first-hand knowledge of the people and programs for which she was responsible. When the barn-storming was over, she knew what must be done.

Each state director kept a weather eye peeled on what benefits neighbor states were receiving from the Office of Vocational Rehabilitation. Each regional director analyzed the budget of the other nine regions to be sure of equitable portions. Now Mary threw in a new bone. Applications would be taken from each state for special projects. States that created projects that involving severely disabled or nontraditional populations were rewarded with Federal funding for the program.[63] Within a short period of time, rehabilitation centers were featured in numerous states, centers that served patients with severe and chronic disabilities, such as multiple sclerosis. Not surprisingly, projects serving mentally ill clients also flourished. Newsletters to the regional directors described the outcome of the competition for funds, reserving one line for the laggards: "None of the State rehabilitation agencies in Region I and VII presented an application for a special project."[64]

This was a swift pace Mary Switzer was setting. Not only was she beating the bushes in the states to understand the problem, build support, and spur action, she was attacking inertia from the top as well.

Howard Rusk had carried on as Chair of the Health Resources Advisory Committee after the end of the Second World War, reporting to the President on the "doctor draft" law and other health concerns. One month after Mary Switzer's appointment as Director of the Office of Vocational Rehabilitation, he wrote Senator Symington, Chair of the National Security Resources Board, reporting a critical need for incorporating disabled persons into the work force, which was rapidly being depleted by defense mobilization. Rusk asked Symington to call this to the attention of the Director of Defense Mobilization, Arthur Flemming.[65]

By April Fleming had responded to Rusk's further suggestion of the creation of a task force to explore the matter.⁶⁶ Rusk had even supplied names of possible members, including the nomination of Theodore Klumpp for Chairman. Dr. Klumpp was President of Winthrop-Stearns Chemical Company and an old friend of Mary's and Howard Rusk's.⁶⁵

Mary Switzer's strategy of focusing attention of an influential Senator and a key executive department representative, while guiding appointments to the Task Force, was never more productive than in this instance. One of Mary's most trusted staff members, Russell Dean, was assigned as special assistant to the Task Force. By May, 1951, ten members had been appointed, including physicians, businessmen, directors of voluntary agencies, and officers of professional groups. The Task Force also had two other components, consultants and a secretariat of experts from several government agencies. Mary Switzer, of course, was a consultant.⁶⁸

The time was ripe; South Korea had been invaded in June of 1950. By September 1951 the Task Force could report that 621,000 young Americans of working age had been inducted into the Armed Forces. A necessary loss to the work force, they said, but also temporary. During the same year, 250,000 workers were lost to the work force, unnecessarily and permanently, through disablement as the result of disease and injury. In their report submitted six months later, the Task Force pointed to the handicapped workers as a tremendous pool of local labor, and suggested an attack on the shortage of manpower.⁶⁹

The Task Force and its report were Mary Switzer's and Howard Rusk's means of getting things going from the top down. There was even proof in the report that the principles outlined were already working, way down in Knoxville, Tennessee. The city had organized for action to combat disability, setting up a permanent community organization that placed more than 100 disabled persons on a job within a year's operation. A community had found a way to use human resources in this time viewed as a "critical international situation."⁷⁰

Hank Smith, Tennessee's Director of Vocational Rehabilitation, had taken advantage of Mary's enticement through "special projects." Identifying a potential labor shortage in a community adjacent to the Atomic Energy Commission plants in Oak Ridge, Smith brought members of the community together to study the facts. How many unemployed handicapped persons lived in the community? What facilities for medical service, job training, and other services existed? What was the employment outlook in the community? "Operation Knoxville" was just the example of teamwork and local involvement that Mary Switzer wanted the Task Force to advertise. Within six months over 1500 disabled persons who had been receiving public assistance had been screened by a team for possible rehabilitation services.⁷¹

"Operation Knoxville" was used as a demonstration of the rehabilitation process and the answer to labor problems produced in communities affected by defense mobilization. While disabled individuals were being interviewed and evaluated for vocational potential, community leaders were organized to identify jobs within local business and industry that would develop with the opening of defense plants and military installations. Training for jobs that would be vacated in the event of a national emergency was offered to disabled workers, many of whom had previously been receiving public assistance.

The rehabilitation counselors in Knoxville used familiar skills to locate disabled citizens. Appalachian men and women were typically close-mouthed, and infrequently visited physicians. It took sleuthing, using Public Health nurses, teachers, and welfare workers to locate families who were in distress because the wage earner was disabled and out of work. Rehabilitation counselors reached into hundreds of neighborhoods, searching for persons who might be eligible for rehabilitation services. Corner groceries, fire halls, and service stations became part of the rehabilitation counselors' route in publicizing what "Operation Knoxville" could do for disabled persons.

Nearly 500 families were found whose income had been adversely affected by disability. Rehabilitation counselors began the interview process, exploring the individual's perception of the disability, as well as the cause and course of the problem. The disabilities were varied: amputations, paraplegia, deafness, respiratory ailments. As the counselors listened, they began to plan medical interventions or assistive devices that could return these persons to the work force. For each person the rehabilitation plan differed. Some required medical treatment for conditions long ignored due to inability to pay, or ignorance and fear. Others required only special equipment, such as an artificial limb or a hearing aid, to be able to meet the requirements of the job. Retraining for a job within clients' physical and intellectual capacities was often the service needed.

As the rehabilitation counselors talked with clients and began to plan for the removal of physical or educational barriers, they were also communicating hope to the clients. For some, long out of work, the idea of learning a new trade and leaving home each day for the workplace was inconceivable. Only when real help was provided, purchased through rehabilitation funds, did clients begin to believe they could return to the working world.

While rehabilitation counselors spent much of their day talking with clients or organizing physical restoration or training programs, they spent an even share with community leaders. All efforts to get clients ready to work would be in vain if jobs did not materialize. Key community leaders were told the problems; newspaper publicity challenged Knoxville to deal with the potential manpower problem by accepting responsibility for its disabled citizens. Employers were encouraged to give disabled applicants "Just One Break," the chance to try a new job.

The results of "Operation Knoxville" were so impressive that it became the model program for rehabilitation as a community affair. Special job applications were developed, and disabled applicants were given top priority. The changes in the lives of Knoxville citizens were dramatic: a paraplegic worked successfully as a glass blower, earning a wage he could never have commanded without the training he received through rehabilitation. The report of the Task Force was distributed and described as a national policy statement. The Task Force had prepared such a forceful document that it was printed by several national organizations and was the topic of the meeting with the state directors. Russell Dean was deployed to frame a companion national manpower statement on the handicapped to be made part of the nation's defense plans. This skillfully designed effort to give Mary Switzer the top level interest she would require had been an unqualified success. The document was a model of needs assessment and rehabilitation philosophy.

The Task Force had indeed been a highlight of Mary's first full year as head of the Office of Vocational Rehabilitation. In her annual report to the Assistant Administrator of the Federal Security Agency, Mary described the report as "one of the most significant contributions to the cause of rehabilitation in more than a decade."[72] But it was by now the end of July. Dwight Eisenhower was home from Europe and his first ballot nomination at the Republican convention in Chicago forecast change. Everything had been timed to build momentum for the rehabilitation program. November arrived, Eisenhower won resoundingly, and for the first time in 30 years, all program chiefs would have to sell their programs to a Republican administration.

Down from Washington to the regional representatives, came this message from Mary Switzer:

> Many of you may be wondering what we in Washington are thinking and feeling in this period of flux. As an old bureaucrat who has seen many changes and lived through many revolutionary organizational shifts, my philosophy is now as it has always been: to keep one's eye on the main objective of one's job and be ready to move the program ahead as one man. Rumors are rife--there is very little authoritative even in the rumor field. It is well to remember that rehabilitation has always had bipartisan support in the legislatures--both national and State--and that there is increasing community understanding all over the country of the possibilities of our program.[73]

Two years had been short indeed to establish herself as the leader of this "program with possibilities." She had worked 18 hour days and traveled to every state to carry the rehabilitation story. It seemed she was just getting her house in order; now the question was whether she could keep it.

X
Embattled Advocate
1953

When I was first Director of our Program of Vocational Rehabilitation, it was during a rather stormy period of our history. . . there was this substitute for activity, which can be an occupational disease of bureaucracy. So, instead of doing anything, all the energies were spent in calling each other names or pointing out what was not being done.

Mary Elizabeth Switzer, 1963

The transition from a Democratic to a Republican administration began on a hopeful note for Mary Switzer. She and Howard Rusk had known Oveta Culp Hobby, the former Commander of the Women's Army Corps who had served with Eisenhower in Europe and now had been appointed to succeed Oscar Ewing. Privately, Mrs. Hobby had told Howard Rusk that she "loved Mary" and would depend upon her.[1] The next seven months, however, were difficult ones for Mary, and her position was clearly precarious.

How ironic it seemed. President Truman had included rehabilitation in a major address in September of 1952, saying that only a fraction of the people in the United States who needed rehabilitation services were receiving them. Two million disabled was the estimate.[2] The Task Force on the Handicapped had done their job well in establishing the need for VR program expansion.

The new President had boldly recommended that the Federal Security Agency be elevated to Department status.[3] Mary remembered the succession of "reorganization plans" that had been prepared for Democratic administrations in the late 1940s. Finally, a popular, newly elected President seemed to have the support to transform the old FSA into a real Department and its Administrator into a Secretary for his Cabinet. Mary had helped with the plans for a Department and with the development of the VR program.

Surely she would be allowed to continue.

While Mrs. Hobby struggled with the name of the proposed department, Senator Robert Taft juggled pressure groups and Presidential advisers in a debate on the role of the assistant secretaries. Neither was an easy task, with the "Department of Welfare," "Department of Human Resources," and the "Department of Health, Education, and Social Security" being discarded in favor of the "Department of Health, Education, and Welfare." Senator Taft was almost successful in providing Mrs. Hobby with a staff free of parochial concerns. Only the health sector managed to have an assistant secretary named for health and medical affairs. The other assistant secretaries were for Legislation and Federal-State Relations, representing the wishes of the Bureau of the Budget, Mrs. Hobby, and Senator Taft.[4]

The compromises in name and organization proved productive, and on April 11, 1953, Reorganization Plan #1 of 1953 became effective.[5] The new Department was the first created since the Department of Labor in 1913, and Oveta Culp Hobby was sworn in as HEW's first Secretary. The creation of a new department was a historic occasion, not to be repeated for more than a decade. Upgrading of the Federal Security Agency into a Department brought new interest from media and the public. Although nothing but the name had changed, the improved status made each of the program chiefs more visible and their jobs more attractive.[6]

President Eisenhower's strength was obvious with the reorganization, and Mary Switzer's friends grew more apprehensive with this show of power. The Republicans were stressing fiscal conservatism, and they knew that administrators inherited from a Democratic administration were vulnerable. Mary wrote friends her thanks for their concern for her welfare. Denying any feelings of insecurity on her own part amidst the activity in Washington, Mary quieted their doubts.

> This program of help to the handicapped is so worthwhile that everyone is for it . . . perhaps I am living in a fool's paradise, but I am keeping a serene spirit and believing that doing a good job honestly does pay off in the end.[7]

The serene spirit did not dispel her supporters' fears, and they wanted Mary to find out what Mrs. Hobby's intent was.

Mary asked Mrs. Hobby if she would be retained, and the answer she received shattered her confidence. "Take as much time as you like, but find something else," said Secretary Hobby.[8] The pressure to convert civil service jobs to appointed positions was great, and the directorship of one of the six agencies comprising Health, Education, and Welfare was a plum.

Mary knew she was in serious trouble, for Mrs. Hobby had already proved herself "an effective operator" by converting FSA into an executive department. The fact that Mrs. Hobby was the lone woman Cabinet member also drew press coverage and rising interest in her decisions.[9] The irony of the situation was that had Mary not decided to become a program advocate, she might have retained her position as assistant to the Administrator for Health and Medical Affairs and remained safe in the bosom of the new Secretary's staff as the only assistant secretary with line functions. But she had chosen to direct Vocational Rehabilitation, and now she would have to defend herself.

Mary was vulnerable in the spring of 1953. She was held responsible for every criticism of the VR program, whether it came from Maine's State Medical Association who saw the medical services provided through Vocational Rehabilitation funds as "evils of socialized medicine,"[10] or from Congressman Busbey from Illinois, who challenged Federal expenditures for laggard states during the appropriations hearings in March of 1953. Mary had her hands full keeping Mrs. Hobby informed about the nature of complaints, and the purpose of various committees or policies, while responding directly to external criticisms. When Mary heard the verdict from Mrs. Hobby, she called in reinforcements.

Howard Rusk responded by flying to Washington from New York City and confronting Mrs. Hobby with the "rumor" he had heard, that Mary would not be appointed as Director of OVR. Clearly distressed, Rusk declared that anyone having the responsibility of being Secretary of Health, Education, and Welfare should have the right to staff of her choosing. "Do you want Mary?" questioned Rusk. With tears in her eyes, Mrs. Hobby said she did, but she had been told she "couldn't have her." Apparently, there was a woman from California who had been active in Nixon's campaign who was slated for Mary's job.[11]

From Mrs. Hobby's office Rusk went to see Sherman Adams, Eisenhower's "Chief of Staff." "If this happens to Mary there will be a groundswell!"[12] Rusk predicted. The 27 million disabled people and their families who respected and trusted Mary would not stand for it. Adams declared that Mary would stay. Rusk was not convinced. His next stop was General Snyder, Eisenhower's physician. Once more he made plain the consequences of dumping Mary, and the good General assured Rusk he would brief the President the next morning;[13] he wouldn't let it happen.

The day was not ended until Rusk called his and Mary's friend, George Merck, to tell him of the threat to the alliance built over the past decade. It was already nine in the evening, but Merck began calling legislators immediately. By seven the next morning Merck called Rusk back to say he had been on the telephone all night.[14] Now her allies waited to see if their counterattack had been effective.

Mary survived, thanks to Howard Rusk's persistence, and distanced herself from the indignity of the threat itself. Several months later, writing George Merck, she sounded coy. "The flurry about me seems to have been very great. Howard told me some of it and I had copies of your letters and telegrams and one or two from Ted Klumpp."[15] Some of the sting was still with Mary, for she noted that they all agreed that "someone of my record should not be thrown out just to make room for someone else."[16]

Although hurt, Mary spoke philosophically of the jeopardy she survived, mentioning to Radcliffe friends that OVR had been retained as one of the five major program constituents of the new Department, and that she had "remained" as Director. "I have always said that no bureaucrat really comes of age until he or she has found the answer to accomodating to successive changes in administration. . . if I am not a 'grown-up' bureaucrat now I will never be."[17]

Mary had her stiffest test of maturity to face within a few days of learning she would not be replaced. Economical government was the new Administration's principle, and a Republican controlled Congress was holding the purse strings. The hearings of the House Sub-Committee on Appropriations were no place for a novice in March of 1953.

The landslide Republican victory in November of 1952 resulted in Republican chairmen for all congressional committees and subcommittees. John Taber of New York chaired the House Appropriations Committee, and Fred Busbey was named chair of the Labor-FSA subcommittee that heard discussion on rehabilitation appropriations. Both men wanted to reduce appropriations, and the House Appropriations Committee appointed a staff of 75 to identify waste in federally supported programs. One such "investigator" had spent three weeks in Mary Switzer's office, just before the hearings began.[18]

On March 11, 1953, Mary Switzer seated herself opposite Fred Busbey in the House Building. Behind her, to act as witnesses, when needed, were four of her staff members: Joe Hunt, Donald Dabelstein, Emily Lamborn, and Russell Dean. M.A. Stephens, Budget Officer for the Federal Security Agency, which within a month would officially become the Department of Health, Education, and Welfare, was also present. Mrs. Hobby's opening remarks to the Appropriations Committee stuck in his mind: "I will cut away every cent that is not producing the results which FSA should be achieving."[19] Although she had been on the job less than five weeks, he believed she meant it.

Chairman Busbey was armed with the report of his "investigator;" Mary Switzer was similarly equipped with her own figures and explanations. The duel began with forced pleasantries. "Miss Switzer, we welcome you back, we always listen with interest to anything you have to say to help us in consideration of this appropriation request."[20]

Thanking the Chairman, Mary introduced herself as one of the "bureaucrats who like to come before the Appropriations Committee." With that Mary submitted her written statement and summarized the progress made during the last year. With a display of tables and amplification by Joe Hunt, Mary made the point that states were beginning to assume more of the cost of rehabilitation. The transcript of this hearing, which might well be called a grilling, due to its length and substance, reveals all of Mary Switzer's "tricks" of persuasion.

Here was the program advocate, embarrassed by her own charts which revealed a rise in federal expenditures since 1943, when the VR Act was changed to allow 100% reimbursement of states for administrative costs and 50% reimbursement for case services. As a program advocate, Mary defended the state directors, saying state laws and state budget officers were the problem.

Mustering her most passionate arguments, Mary attributed the states' dependence on the Federal dollar to community ignorance of the benefits of rehabilitation. Predicting that attitudes would change when states saw the reduction of relief costs as a result of rehabilitation programs, Mary tried to divert attention from the most damaging facts of all.

Chairman Busbey would not be deterred. Requesting a table showing the past five years of financing VR, with state and Federal contributions compared, Busbey pressed his point. Although the Federal share of funding had decreased slightly over five years, the decrease had only been from 73.5% in 1947 to 66.8% in 1952. Mary countered with the point that some states did much better in this regard than others, and she would like to move them all along as quickly as possible.

She had two recommendations to make when Busbey asked what would help. Rather than reimbursing the states for their expenditures, she wanted financing to be on a current basis. For two years she had seen current appropriations eaten away by payments to states for the prior year. She also wanted the authority to allocate money at the beginning of the year. These were not casual suggestions; Mary had been asked by Mrs. Hobby for an analysis of OVR's financing problems and she had requested clearance to present legislation that would improve the situation.[21] Clearance had not come, but the question had, and Mary was prepared.

Busbey was up against a long history of Federal-state partnership, and although Federal agencies might have their differences with state and local agencies, when a threat to their fiefdom occurred, the ranks closed. The relationship was one of mutual dependence, and VR was one of the oldest grant-in-aid programs in the country. Responsibility was hard to fix, even for a Fred Busbey, when the Federal administrator blamed state controls. Governors and state fiscal authorities found it equally hard to win when state administrators pointed to Federal regulations and single state agency requirements. These were really corporations, with charters provided through Federal law. Challenging the state agencies' power and legitimacy in 1953 was as naive as it was ardent.[22]

Busbey, however, had a number of factors in his favor. The political climate favored scrutiny of all budgets, and he was unlike most of his successor legislators. There were few grant-in-aid programs in 1953, and Busbey had made himself something of an authority on VR financing. He had more than a part-time interest in this battle.

Mary Switzer reminded Busbey that the last Congress had considered changes in the financing of VR, but that recommendations similar to the ones she had made did not pass the House. And, again, she said she thought slow progress was being made with "increases in the States."

At this point in the proceedings, the silent Mr. Stephens decided to contradict Mary Switzer. From his vantage point of the last ten years, he thought the Federal administrators had done a good job of selling to Congress and the Bureau of the Budget. From 1943 to 1951, he said, "the Federal Government paid it all." It was only when this Sub-Committee and the Bureau of the Budget started "shoving them around" that the states put in any funds.[23]

Mary could only offer a meek "I know State support is increasing" before Busbey built upon his advantage by saying what his goal was. The office in Washington should be an advisory service only, and the states should take over all responsibility for staffing and case services. Quoting from Mary's prepared statement, Busbey mocked Mary's reference to "the splendid initiative displayed by the States during recent years."[24]

Ignoring the sarcasm, Mary pointed out the need for changing the law, and until it could be changed, recognizing that state agencies expected the federal support to staff their agencies.

The line by line dissection of her written statement continued. Whenever possible, Mary inserted personal accounts of the accomplishments of the program, how a paraplegic veteran had learned watchmaking at the Bulova Company and returned to California to support his wife and child. "When you get low in your mind pushing papers, you look at that and you get new courage."[25] She was in the midst of inviting the sub-committee to Fishersville when Busbey interrupted to continue his examination of the witness.

Busbey accused the states of considering vocational education more important than vocational rehabilitation and challenging Mary Switzer's statement that the Federal-state ratio of support was improving. The dissection culminated in Busbey's charge that money had been spent fraudulently, citing three cases from three different states. Mary Switzer defended each point, claiming that each case left room for a difference of opinion. Busbey finally deferred to other Committee members, saying the hour was getting late. The remainder of the hearing was anti-climatic, with Congressmen Jensen of Iowa and Fernandez of New Mexico asking benign questions and nearly apologizing for the "good going over" the Chairman had administered. Ceremonial hypocrisy was practiced by the opponents as the meeting ended. Mary Switzer said she appreciated the interrogation, that it helped in the development of the program. Fernandez said he thought the Chairman was well-pleased, Busbey said: "We like to have everyone feel happy before the committee." Mary replied, "I'm sure you do."[26]

While Busbey might have wanted Mary to "feel happy" during the Hearings, the Sub-Committee Report was dedicated to a different purpose. In the report, Busbey accused Mary Switzer of maladministration and cited three examples of ineligible persons being served. The "investigator" was a staff member of the Metropolitan Life Insurance Company appointed by Congressman Taber to spend three weeks in OVR offices asking questions.[27] He compiled a list of 25 cases as evidence. Busbey criticized Mary Switzer for inaction on cases that had been identified as audit exceptions.[28]

This was the first time such criticism had been leveled at the program, and Mary started her own investigation. Calling on her great friend and adviser, Tracy Copp, Mary asked if she could identify the source of Busbey's personal criticism. Since Tracy had worked frequently in Illinois, she was able to uncover a friend of Busbey's who had had an "altercation" with Mary during her first two years in VR. Tracy had also activated some of her contacts to reach Busbey. She added that this group had had a major role in Busbey's political destiny.[29] As Mary had predicted, her own study of the audit exceptions showed meagre evidence of fraudulent use of funds. Professional judgment might be questioned, but nothing was apparent that could be classified as maladministration. Within her own shop, Mary chided regional representatives about their slipshod audit reports and pressed them to provide adequate documentation. "We would like to clear up this little chore as soon as possible" was her way of telling the states to clean up their act.[30]

The report from Busbey's sub-committee also suggested a reduction in funding of $2.4 million from the $23 million Mary Switzer had requested and $1.85 million below the current spending level. Mary conferred with E.B. Whitten and strategy was drawn to restore funds.

John Fogarty of Rhode Island remained on the sub-committee as minority leader and had supported rehabilitation in the past. Knowing that the bill would come to the floor of the House for action, Switzer and Whitten approached Fogarty to lead the floor fight. Fogarty accepted, and Whitten mobilized NRA members into a telephone campaign that deluged members of Congress with letters from constituents supporting the increase.

Mary was prepared for the worst. "Somber staff meetings" had been held to decide what could be cut, if John Fogarty was unsuccessful. Thirty positions would be abolished, and the reduction-in-force notices had been prepared.

On the afternoon of May 25, John Fogarty introduced his amendment, restoring the VR appropriation to $23 million. Committee members attacked Busbey for his charges of maladministration, which had not been seen until the sub-committee report was published. Busbey withdrew formal charges of maladministration in the states, but he maintained its presence in OVR and called for a thorough investigation before appropriations were made for 1955.

When the roll was called, the Fogarty amendment passed. It had been presented in two parts, however, and the portion that dealt with increased funds for OVR administrative expenses was approved by a margin of only two votes.[31] Busbey charges had taken their toll. Although the margin was slim, the relief was tremendous in the central office and throughout the states. John Fogarty and Walter Judd were proclaimed heros, and the Congressional Record of May 22 and 25 was made required reading for rehabilitation supporters.

But the matter was still not settled. The Senate sub-committee reduced the House appropriation, and once more a floor fight was organized. An amendment was offered to restore funds to the House level. The sub-committee accepted the amendment without a vote being taken, and the campaign for 1954 appropriations was closed.

Busbey, however, had his revenge. Through a loophole in procedure, he attached a clause to the conference report that was adopted. In the future, for every $100 the Federal government spent on VR, the states had to contribute $75. The ideological problem that had been prevalent during the House sub-committee hearings was resolved in the amendment. In effect, it put a permanent lid on Federal expenditures and lowered the percent share to no more than 57%. For 1955, it meant a cut in the Federal investment from $23 million to $19.5 million.[32]

In retrospect, Congressman Busbey did more than anyone to consolidate the allies of the VR program. NRA members again rose in protest to the amendment, and John Fogarty led a second successful floor fight. Legislators knew rehabilitation had a vocal constituency.

Mary Switzer had her hands full during the summer of 1953, correcting audit problems and dividing up the hard-earned Federal allotment. In August, "everyone who can work mathematics" was assigned the central office task of figuring settlements to states, agency by agency.[33]

The appropriations fracas had drawn Secretary Hobby's attention to VR. By July she had held several staff meetings to identify problems in the programs of the new Department. Nelson Rockefeller had been appointed Under Secretary and had commandeered two staff members of the Rockefeller Foundation as fact-finders. Having repeated and lengthy contact with the top staff of the Department was just what Mary Switzer wanted. And the fact that Rockefeller thought VR's legislative program was the most alive and demanding and had set his assistants to work there first made her hopes leap.[34] Here was the opportunity to inform the Secretary and her staff, as well as to prepare legislation for 1954.

The hearings had made it all too clear that an overhaul of the fiscal provisions of the present law was needed. Mrs. Hobby had instructed Mary Switzer to prepare legislation that would improve rehabilitation services without obligating the Federal government for increased participation. The Secretary had also chastized Mary for quoting dollar amounts to states for the Department's budget requests; Rufus Miles had been offended, as members of his staff concerned with budget matters were "scrupulous."[35] But then, neither Mrs. Hobby nor Rufus Miles was a program advocate, with anxious state directors to appease. Mary was getting pressure from above and below to straighten out the fiscal base of VR.

Mary capitalized on the proximity legislative planning had given her to Secretary Hobby and Nelson Rockefeller. An invitation was issued to Mrs. Hobby from the National Rehabilitation Association to address their membership at a Miami conference.[36] Mrs. Hobby accepted, and NRA's stock soared, along with Mary Switzer's. Mrs. Hobby's mood was ebullient, also, for she had found an answer to President Eisenhower's dilemma.

Eisenhower wanted a new legislative program that would silence his liberal critics and the press that was so critical of Mrs. Hobby's modest approach. Being cartooned as "Secretary of-Not-Too-Much Health, Education, and Welfare" was not the image Republicans wanted of Mrs. Hobby.[37]

A search for a middle of the road domestic program stopped with VR. Here was a program that had existed before the New or Fair Deal, which had as its goal the elimination of dependency, and operated from a tradition of state control. Mrs. Hobby began to talk about rehabilitation in her public appearances; Nelson Rockefeller described the program's goals to Eisenhower. Nixon proclaimed 1953-54 "Rehabilitation Year."

Mary Switzer used her talents to keep rehabilitation in Mrs. Hobby's mind and to translate general ideas into action. By the close of 1953, Mary Switzer, Roswell Perkins, and Nelson Rockefeller had recast the funding and scope of the rehabilitation program for legislative action.[38]

No one anticipated the response of President Eisenhower. He not only expressed his support and related some of his war experiences with disabled officers, he asked Mrs. Hobby how many handicapped citizens she expected to rehabilitate under the expanded program. Mrs. Hobby answered, "100,000 per year," thinking this quite ambitious since the current number of rehabilitants per year was 40,000. The President shot back: "Let's make it 200,000!"[39] That number was to haunt Mary Switzer for many years, but at the moment, she was delighted to see the President's enthusiasm. Rehabilitation was going to have a significant role in the Republican legislative proposals.

Within a difficult year, Switzer had shown that she could sell Democratic or Republican administrations on the "rehabilitation story." By removing disabled welfare recipients from public assistance rolls, the program could be advertised as saving money. It was just the compromise the Republicans wanted to make good on their promises of thrifty Federal spending while heeding the cause of needy citizens.

Mary Switzer had asked for "clear sailing orders" through new legislation for more than two years. Now the wind of an Administration eager to exhibit a its showpiece of a social program might force the legislation Mary wanted.

She had taken the criticism of some of the state directors for suggesting in the appropriations hearings the closing of the appropriations "end." She had asked for legal clarification so that state budget officials could be referred to a law, not an attitude. Now she had the responsibility of striking a compromise within the Department that would not endanger state programs.

In conferences with Secretary Hobby and her staff, Mary was pushed to explain the variation among states in the rate of Federal participation. Staff members surmised that there were no clear-cut reasons; Mary asked for tolerance of the VR program in the states. Since it had been around for so many years and states had built around the expectation of Federal support, programs would suffer greatly if Federal funds were drastically reduced.

The states could not have asked for a more talented advocate, particularly since Mary had publicly stated that she did not care who paid for the work, "so long as the results were secured." Her strategy was to persuade the Department staff that the Federal support should not drop below 60%. What emerged as a Department recommendation was an average Federal share of 55% and a "hold harmless" provision that would maintain state allotments at no less than their 1954 grant level for a period of five years.[40]

The "top staff" of the Department worked determinedly on legislative proposals.[41] Nelson Rockefeller spearheaded the preparation of charts, based on the information received from his investigation, documenting the story of rehabilitation. Mary boasted that VR was the first unit of the Department to conduct a "grand seminar" at which all other Department heads listened.

While the Department staff labored to produce a legislative proposal, Sam McConnell of Pennsylvania, Chair of the House Committee on Education and Labor, told them not to bother. He intended to have his committee write their own bill. The ever diplomatic Mary Switzer, however, testified before the Sub-committee, implanting the same ideas that were being hatched by the Administration.[42]

Some old ghosts came out of the closets during the hearings held by the House Committee in 1953. Paul Strachan was back, wanting to set up a new agency for all Federal programs related to handicapped people and claiming that there were at least 35 agencies doing little useful for handicapped people. He wanted the new agency to be located in the Labor Department, a thrust that Mrs. Hobby had known would come. Speaking to the hearing, Mrs. Hobby recommended that OVR stay in the Department of HEW, and that seemed to settle that.[43]

After extensive hearings and much bickering, the Committee announced that executive sessions would be held in 1954. Meanwhile, during recess, Committee members visited choice rehabilitation facilities: The Institute for the Crippled and Disabled and the Institute of Physical Medicine and Rehabilitation in New York, the Woodrow Wilson Rehabilitation Center in Fishersville, Virginia, and workshops in Birmingham, Alabama, and Washington, D.C.[44] Mary Switzer's wish that Committee members could see "fine operations" had come true, even if Busbey had been unimpressed several months earlier.

When the Administration's proposal went to Congress in 1954, Nelson Rockefeller's charts were again pressed into service.[45] The data presented analyzed the needs of disabled persons, and the recommendation was for a program that could rehabilitate 200,000 persons a year within five years. It was obvious that there was a HEW team: Nelson Rockefeller, Rod Perkins, Mary Switzer, and Donald Dabelstein.

Unfortunately, Mr. McConnell and his Committee felt a great deal of ownership for any bill regarding rehabilitation. After all, they had spent many hours in hearings and had told Mrs. Hobby they would prefer only a letter stating some principles the administration thought important in rehabilitation.[46] A good deal of fence-mending would have to be done in the Executive Sessions.

Mary Switzer was very much present at the Executive Sessions, representing the Government, alongside Nelson Rockefeller and Reginald Conley from the Department of Health, Education, and Welfare. Apparently, the location of OVR was yet unsettled, for there were also representatives from the Department of Labor and the U.S. Employment Service. Mary noticed a representative from the American Federation of the Physically Handicapped, Paul Strachan's group. When she asked Mr. McConnell if NRA should not also be invited, McConnell made no comment. Mary's next stop was E.B. Whitten, who pressed the Chairman for permission to attend. Chairman McConnell no doubt rued the day any nongovernmental representative was allowed to attend, for contention for that recognition added to the tension.[47]

Rather than fence-mending, the Executive Sessions were stormy from beginning to end. Mary made sure her NRA cohort was included, said little as Graham Barden objected to almost everything, and helped feed the committee suggestions through Whitten that would bring the bill out of committee.[48]

On the Senate side the Administration's bill was gladly accepted, and a House-Senate conference was called to reconcile the House and Senate bills. The trade-offs worked to Mary Switzer's and NRA's benefit. Allocations to states with highest per capita income was 60%; training of personnel would extend indefinitely. "Six terrific months of legislative hearings" was Mary's way of describing the Departmental planning and Committee squabbles. "All that goes along with getting complex pieces of business through Congress."[49]

No wonder Switzer wanted a signing ceremony. Within a year what threatened to be an embarrassing defeat had turned into an overwhelming personal victory. There was no question that she would remain Director of

OVR. There was no further question about her "maladministration," in fact, no one heard from Fred Busbey again on the subject. The difficult question of state responsibility for rehabilitation programs had been averted, and Mary had all the pieces of a program she had been building toward for four years.

On August 3, 1954, President Eisenhower signed Public Law 565, with Mary Switzer, Nelson Rockefeller, Howard Rusk, and E.B. Whitten present.[50] Not only had Mary been vindicated, the role of the Federal government in rehabilitation had been expanded greatly. Not only had basic support grants to the 91 states and territorial agencies been authorized, improvement grants to the state agencies had also been authorized. State directors were euphoric. There was no more talk of the decreasing Federal share or of "closing the end" of appropriations. Instead, an entirely new means of financing was created. OVR would estimate the amount of state funds available each year and the Bureau of the Budget would recommend the Federal allotment needed to match state funds. Never again would the central office staff be drafted into the emergency mathematics corps, figuring what the Federal government "owed" various states.

With fiscal policy determined, Mary was able to bring from her background with health agencies the design for research, following the National Institutes of Health model, complete with a national advisory council. Strachan's barbs were extracted with the creation of a training program to produce professionals in several fields that constituted rehabilitation. Now there was a cohesive national program, with service, training, and research as interactive branches.

Nelson Rockefeller stayed little more than a year in the Department of Health, Education, and Welfare. Shortly after his legislative victory, he went to the White House as Eisenhower's Special Assistant. It was Rockefeller's leadership that captured the Administration's attention, for Mary thought Mrs. Hobby too "economy-minded" to have been affirmative early. "He is a wonderful witness and was the indispensable ingredient to what we have now."[51]

Mary knew that the timing had been right also, for 1954 was a Congressional election year, and by November the Democrats had regained control of the Congress. Through a fluke, the Republicans had seized upon rehabilitation as "their social program" and had pushed it through into law.

E.B. Whitten had emerged as a winner, too. NRA was now a political force taken seriously by Congress. The annual October meeting was a celebration. Nelson Rockefeller received an award and delivered a major address. Of course, Mary Switzer was there to introduce him.

John Fogarty, although not present at the signing of the law, had also been instrumental in its passage. Mary Switzer never forgot his support in the darkest hours of 1953, when the narrow vote to continue appropriations for VR administration kept her from losing 30 staff members.[52] John Fogarty was one of the votes. He had not been present at her "thorough going over" at the hands of Fred Busbey, but this would be the only year during his twenty as a Congressman that he did not chair the House Sub-Committee on Labor, Health, Education, and Welfare.

The victory made heroes and heroines out of many of the cast. Howard Rusk, who had thrown himself into preserving Mary Switzer's position, felt gratified. There were not only training dollars earmarked in subsequent budgets for students studying rehabilitation medicine; he had also joined forces with Mary Switzer and the NRA to amend the Hill-Burton Act to allow construction of rehabilitation centers and other rehabilitation facilities with Hill-Burton funds.[53] Howard Rusk was gladdened that rehabilitation centers would be funded alongside general hospital construction.

Two of the Eisenhower Administration's goals in social welfare legislation had been accomplished: the expansion of the vocational rehabilitation program, and Federal assistance to states under the hospital construction act for the building of rehabilitation centers. A third resulted in a compromise, with the passage of an amendment to the Social Security Act to protect disabled workers by "freezing" their benefits at the level they earned when disabled. Without further payments, they would draw retirement benefits when they reached 65. Rehabilitation was drawn into this provision as well, with VR agencies designated as "agency-of-choice" for disability determination.[54] Eisenhower's special messages to Congress had borne fruit. Rehabilitation was the proper approach to solving welfare problems in 1954.

By pleading for time for the states to accept their fuller responsibility for the cost of rehabilitation, Mary Switzer weathered a period of piercing questions. It was startling how quickly those questions ceased, once rehabilitation became a Republican bandwagon. Other bureaucrats, who had come to Washington with the New Deal, left under the Republican administration. Arthur Altmeyer, head of the Social Security Administration, Jane Hoey, head of the public assistance program, and I.S. Falk, Social Security's leading health insurance advocate, left the Federal scene, while Mary Switzer retained her place in Washington. The others, who symbolized the New Deal, returned to their homes. The "grown-up bureaucrat," meanwhile, was practicing her craft of uniting common interests and seeing liberal programs take root. The names of the programs did not matter. Their continuance did.

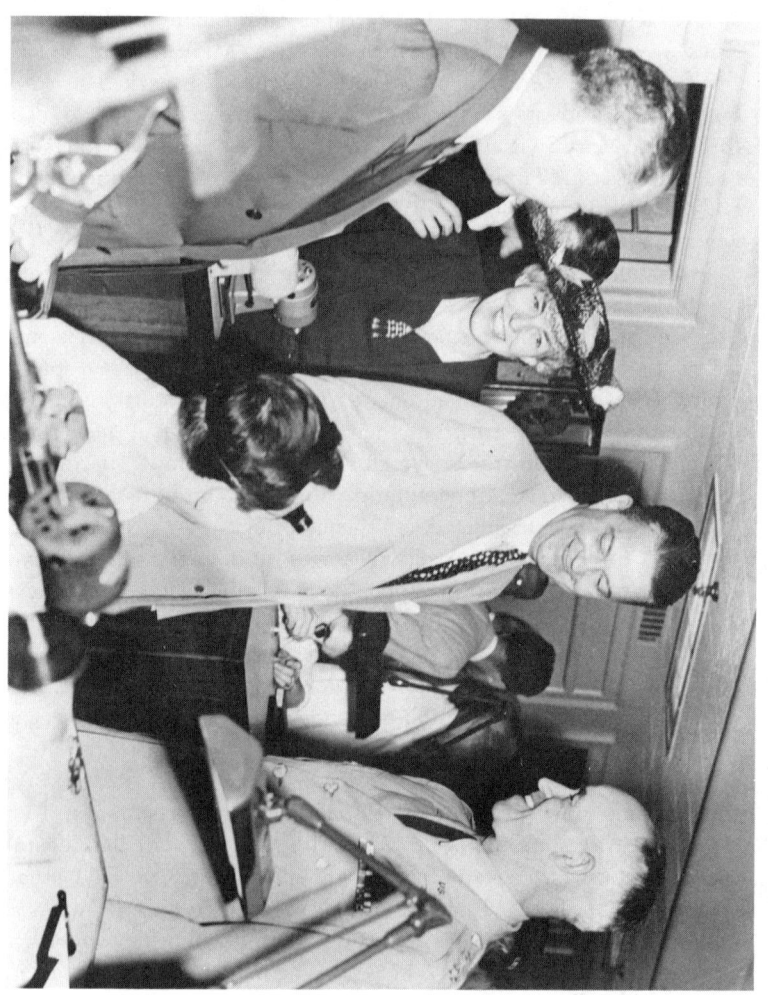

Switzer, Howard Rusk, and General Omar Bradley at Bulova, ca. 1951. (*Courtesy The Schlesinger Library, Radcliffe College.*)

XI
The Joy of Craftsmanship
1954-1959

I believe you will agree to put among the most precious and dependable of our satisfactions the joy of craftsmanship. In that I include all effort to impose upon the outside world an invention of our own: to embody an idea in what I shall ask your leave to call an artifact.

Learned Hand, 1952

Through the long years of seeking a place and enough time to measure up to her Uncle Mike's and Scott Nearing's expectations, Mary had held to her idea of what government could do to give people the chance to be happier. There was a quiet revolution at work, one Mary led and preserved. Something was going to be done about disability in the United States; Mary was determined to impose this justice upon the outside world.

For a brief five years, Mary had the opportunity to practice her craft and develop her "artifact." A new Department, a supportive Administration, a constituency that lavished power on their leader led to the greatest period of growth in rehabilitation's history. Mary knew what was needed to build a program that could expand to reach every disabled person in the United States. She was too busy to keep a diary during these growth years, but her craft can be reconstructed. Her joy shines through the strategy.

Mary Switzer's stock was high with state directors. Almost miraculously, rehabilitation had surfaced from a collection of social programs as the one legislators fought to sponsor. Within a year VR had moved from backstage to center stage, and Mary Switzer was intent on pressing her advantage.

For almost four years Mary Switzer had made plain her discontent with state agencies that turned away difficult cases or failed to garner state funds for rehabilitation. She had testified that VR should "serve the people that no other agency is set up to do anything about."[1] And she had charged state directors with being too restrictive, of being afraid to dare and afraid of failure.[2]

The state directors had gotten even more than they asked for through the 1954 legislation. They wanted adequate funds and a uniform method of distribution to provide a basic support program to states, improvement and expansion, and new service programs. Public Law 565 had provided all that and much more, with a $4 million dollar increase over the prior year. [3]

The tenor of meetings with state directors had changed. Four years earlier, Mary Switzer had been on trial. No one could doubt her effectiveness now; she had gotten the money and the state directors depended on her. An observer thought the state directors seemed half afraid of Mary Switzer and talked to her as if she were the Virgin Mary.[4] In turn, Mary was ruthlessly honest in their exchanges.

All the pieces were assembled. The new Vocational Rehabilitation Act had as its objective the expansion of the program so that 200,000 disabled persons might be restored to productive activity annually. Old services would continue, known as the "basic program," but would operate with increases of Federal monies. Funds for training were authorized to produce specialized personnel to provide rehabilitation services. Financial support was available for research and demonstration in the improvement of rehabilitation practice. Specialized rehabilitation facilities and sheltered workshops could be established or expanded. Voluntary organizations could receive funds, if they joined the "battle against disability."[5]

Mary's inhouse paper, Headquarters News Notes, reminded regional representatives of the goals of the new Act. Throughout 1955, Mary Switzer watched anxiously to see if the states would deliver on promises made to capture more Federal funds. By December of 1955, the number of rehabilitations were only 14.4% of the 1956 goal. Donald Dabelstein wrote:

> We have got to begin to persuade, prod, and push now. . . we have to use our best talent in human relations, education, and persuasion in getting our State administrators to want and actually achieve our 1956 goal."[6]

VR's head count, the number of disabled persons returned to work, was not good news. Like it or not, Mary had to appear before the Appropriations Committees with only seven months of the first year's statistics reported. Perhaps the Committee members had forgotten the claims laid before them one year earlier, or perhaps Mary Switzer was so skillful in reporting the good news that the committee members failed to notice that the number of rehabilitations fell 20,000 below the 1956 goal.

In her testimony, Mary moved on to happier subjects quickly. State support increased by $4 million dollars, joint planning with voluntary groups had increased availability of community resources, 46 research and demonstration grants had been approved, and 124 teaching grants had been awarded. The triad of research, training, and service was indeed "tooling up."[7]

Mary Switzer had recognized the paucity of resources in the system before she became Director. The possibilities she had glimpsed were the addition of trained personnel and additional community resources. At last the capacity of the VR system was being increased. Mary came to VR with strong ties to voluntary agencies. She had the knack of knitting rehabilitation's interests with those of voluntary organizations. Nothing and no one was irrelevant to rehabilitation, in Switzer's view.

The National Association of Manufacturers received one of Mary's "special letters," suggesting they help acquaint management with the value of vending stands operated by the blind.[8]

Mary wrote the National Travelers' Aid Association about the possibility of a cooperative venture in identifying disabled travelers and providing service through VR. Holding out a planning grant of $15,000 as bait, Mary sent along an application.[9] Mark McCloskey would have been pleased that Mary targeted the National Committee on the Employment of Youth in New York City, suggesting that a sheltered workshop might be preferable to the "busy-busy" approach used in many communities to get young boys off the street.[10]

The approach was definitely ecumenical. The Methodist Church women interested Mary, particularly their "educational campaign." Mary envisioned an institute that would "bring ministers into the general orbit and make them more cognizant of the problems and possibilities of handicapped parishioners."[11] Catholic Charities seemed another plausible partner, and she suggested they explore a joint community project.[12] Hers was a fortunate habit, of seeing relationships and believing that rehabilitation was everybody's business. "I have a profound conviction that our work cannot grow in isolation, that what is good for rehabilitation in this country will inevitably be good for vocational rehabilitation."[13]

With such an evangelist, it was no surprise that two-thirds of the expansion grants in 1955 were awarded non-profit organizations. Local voluntary organizations such as Tuberculosis Associations, Goodwill Industries, United Cerebral Palsy, and Associations for Retarded Children received extension and improvement projects.[14]

With Mary Switzer's connections and Federal money authorized by Public Law 565, local communities began to develop rehabilitation facilities and workshops at a rate five times as fast as in the 1920-1954 period. The legacy of the Baruch Committee and "Operation Knoxville" directed the nature of these new rehabilitation centers. Concentrated, comprehensive, specialized services offered under one roof through an individual, integrated plan was the standard. From 1954 to 1960 almost 200 rehabilitation facilities and workshops would be established.[15]

It was an extraordinary display. The discretionary grant funds provided through the 1954 legislation strengthened the basic grant program in just the way Mary Switzer hoped.[16] A sense of unity was created among divergent groups in rehabilitation; communication between disciplines was required,[17] and common problems were solved.

Capacity building sounds dull. Finding the right people and places to widen rehabilitation's reach was anything but dull in the 1950s.

Hank Viscardi was just the person Mary Switzer needed to whip up interest. Viscardi had founded Abilities, Inc. in 1952, putting to the test his belief that physically handicapped persons could work in industry.[18] The five disabled persons he employed grew to more than 200 in the next five years, not only because he believed, but because he could package his ideas.[19]

Coining the phrase, "Just One Break," Viscardi used his own history as evidence that disabled persons did not want special treatment, just an opportunity to show what they could do. Hank Viscardi's experience as a child born without legs and denied "a man's stature" until he was six years old and fitted with artificial legs, made him a potent speaker and writer. Viscardi's ingenuity in reaching the public was obvious: news of him and his center appeared in newspapers, the Reader's Digest, and eight books.[20] Bernard Baruch and Eleanor Roosevelt wrote introductions. Mary Switzer consistently asked Viscardi to send copies of his books to influential persons she thought could be recruited as supporters of rehabilitation. A seventh printing of Viscardi's first book signalled Viscardi's and Switzer's promotional skills.

Viscardi soon expanded the capacity of Abilities, Inc., into a Human Resources Center that retained its focus on competing in the free enterprise system, while adding comprehensive service.[21] Rehabilitation's footing was firmly established on Long Island, and Mary Switzer's combat team was complete. Rusk, Whitten, and Viscardi became familiar to legislators whenever rehabilitation's interests were at stake.

Community resources were being increased through establishment and expansion; they were also being strengthened by the influx of professionals who responded to the challenge of unconventional problems.[22] Rancho Los Amigos was treating severely disabled victims of polio in 1952, and by 1955 it was on its way to becoming an outstanding center for treating other severe disabilities. Orthopedic surgeons stretched beyond their specialty to enter the interdisciplinary world Mary Switzer was bent on constructing.

Standard bearer of converted professionals was Howard Rusk. The contented Missouri internist was no longer recognizable in the flush of authorized expenditures. Rusk had been an apostle for rehabilitation since the end of the Second World War. Private funds had begun his Institute of Physical Medicine and Rehabilitation at Bellevue Hospital. Rusk's column in the *New York Times* had made rehabilitation noteworthy; fate made his Institute newsworthy.

In March of 1958 the great Brooklyn Dodger catcher, Roy Campanella, overturned his car and injured his spinal cord. By May he was transferred to Rusk's Institute, and with him came public attention.[23] The wizard of human interest used Campanella's entry into the world of rehabilitation to advertise the team approach for getting disabled patients from "bed to job."

Howard Rusk, Hank Viscardi, and Mary Switzer all understood the most important element in capacity building. The understanding of rehabilitation by the American people was their goal in all the publicity they engineered. Even in her personal correspondence, Mary Switzer transmitted the message. On the bottom of every letter she wrote appeared the line "transcribed by a blind operator." And the letters were always perfect.

Mary also remembered the great lesson of Eleanor Roosevelt.[24] Personal contact was invaluable. "That you care enough to come, that you remember what you see, that you keep your promises." In this time of expansion and establishment, Mary traveled extensively to new centers that were just beginning to function. Her visits were never forgotten by clients or staff, and her glimpses of what was happening often had immediate repercussions.

Once, while touring a rehabilitation center for the blind, Mary asked the director if the color of the walls must be so drab. The unfortunate director answered: "Well, the clients can't see the walls."[25] The flow of Federal money to that center ended immediately.

Photographs abound of Mary Switzer talking with clients in workshops or watching their operation of equipment. On one such occasion she sat down at a sewing machine and stitched a pair of paper slippers, which promptly fell apart.[26] Mary could laugh at herself and cause clients and nervous staff to feel comfortable within minutes of meeting her by being "homey."

Frank Birdsall remembered one of Mary's trips to the Woodrow Wilson Center, when a surprise snowstorm necessitated a search for a pair of galoshes for Mary. When none could be found, Birdsall wrapped her feet in plastic, and then burlap bags for the trudge to the bus for Washington. Mary made quite an appearance at her Washington office wearing her burlap galoshes.[27]

There was no predicting events on her visits to rehabilitation centers. Mary often had to demonstrate her acceptance of severe disability under the scrutiny of facility staff and clients. Seated next to an armless man for a banquet, Mary appeared completely accustomed to his use of his feet for eating.[28]

At the Carville Leprosarium, while visiting a research and service project she had long supported, Mary insisted on staying in the dormitory overnight. The next morning she appeared in a housedress, saying to Warren Perry, who accompanied her: "We're going to work." She made beds before breakfast, and no one doubted that she did indeed care.[29]

Public Law 565 had called for "temporary assistance in initiating a substantial nationwide expansion of vocational rehabilitation programs in the States."[30] The shape and form of the expansion was infinitely variable, but the impetus was consistent: the Director of OVR who dangled a little money and checked up on its use.

Nothing gave Mary Switzer more satisfaction than the authority to conduct research and demonstrations which "hold promise of making a substantial contribution to the solution of vocational rehabilitation problems common to a number of states."[31] Having worked to develop the National Institutes of Health in the late 1940s, she recognized research as central to the improvement of rehabilitation.

The Rehabilitation Act had established a National Advisory Council on Vocational Rehabilitation, which was appointed by the Secretary for four year terms. The Advisory Council, just as it had been in 1946 in the National Mental Health Act, was the balm the American Medical Association required for passage of the Rehabilitation Act. Doctors would be represented on the Council, which "advised" the Director on which research projects should be funded.[32] The twelve member committee included two of the rehabilitation medicine pioneers: Dr. Frank Krusen and Dr. Henry Kessler. Dr. Klumpp, who had chaired the 1951 Task Force on the Handicapped, Henry Viscardi, and Mrs. Spencer Tracy were also named by Secretary Hobby.[33] The state directors were represented by Voyle Scurlock from Oklahoma, an "elder statesman" Mary Switzer considered the "soul of integrity and honor," who was also determined to make Oklahoma a model for the nation in its commitment to rehabilitation.[34] As she had done for Oscar Ewing years before, Mary Switzer recommended the members of the Advisory Council to Mrs. Hobby and to subsequent Secretaries.

Within the first year 45 projects in 17 states were approved. They ranged from the demonstration of psychiatric techniques with deaf persons to the demonstration of work potential for epileptics. Occupational training centers for mentally retarded adults were begun, and optical aid clinics to provide devices for employable persons with low visual acuity received funds. Priority was given to solving problems of persons with severe disabilities, demonstrating across the country that it could be done.[35]

Five years later Mary Switzer pronounced the research program lacking in the fulfillment of its full potential, but the steady growth of research in cardiovascular, neurological, orthopedic, visual, personality, and speech and hearing disorders prepared the way for more systematic research of the 1960s.[36] In the birth of rehabilitation research, Mary Switzer was often the mid-wife, encouraging mavericks as well as the established to initiate research proposals. The informality suited her; the air crackled with excitement.

It also crackled with controversy as the expansion and experimentation continued. Mary Switzer's largess with voluntary agencies began to concern state directors and regional representatives. "Service-type demonstrations," delivered through private, voluntary agencies, came under attack because they outstripped the public program. Was OVR deliberately creating parallel service arrangements?[37] Mary reassured the state program by suggesting a remedy: determine the most valuable areas to be demonstrated, control the project, and incorporate the results into the public program.

Encouragement of private, voluntary agency involvement in research and demonstration projects continued for almost four years before state directors registered complaints. In the beginning it had been difficult to stimulate their interest in expansion.[38] Many directors were unaccustomed to dealing with community groups, some were afraid of the complexity of new projects, and some were simply opposed to expansion. The voluntary agencies offered proof, not only to the community, but also to the public agency, that new ways of solving difficult problems were possible.

The dispensation of research and demonstration funds remained in the hands of the National Advisory Council, and the balancing of sectors of rehabilitation was insured. Eli Gorodezky, attorney and civic leader in Phoenix, Peter Salmon of the Industrial Home for the Blind in Brooklyn, Chester Hadden, a prosthetic expert from Denver, and Russell Brothers, a Nashville businessman provided ballast.[39] Mary Switzer initiated all new members with personal letters. To the state director on the Advisory Committee, Mary pleaded for the greater good.

> The greatest contribution a State Director makes as a member of the Council is to convey a positive dynamic picture of the State-Federal program, its accomplishments, and potentialities, and, above all, to be objective and open-minded in dealing with the great variety of questions that have to be discussed.[40]

The appointment of the state director to the Advisory Council came to be regarded as a great honor, with the sterling reputation of former state director members always recounted. Pressure to be high-minded, rather than protect the interests of state directors was almost tangible.

But controversy seemed to come with increased dollars to dispense. The expansion grants interested many hospitals in establishing rehabilitation facilities through Hill-Burton funds. Suddenly, proposals flooded the Surgeon General's and Secretary's office. Called "blue-sky" proposals, they were viewed as wishful thinking, impossible to fulfill. "Blue-sky" was a derogatory term attached to any proposal that gave lip-service to comprehensive and integrated services, but really sought only to establish physical medicine within the hospital. Vocational and psychological services cost money, and hospitals claimed to have them "on call," rather than under roof. The Hill-Burton legal requirement was that rehabilitation facilities provide evaluation and services in four basic areas: medical, psychological, social, and vocational.[41] Two old allies were about to part ways over money.

Physical medicine proponents, one of the allies, could be forgiven for leaping at the Hill-Burton money, rather than remaining true to rehabilitation principles. They had had a long and frustrating battle to gain any Federal support for their medical practice. The National Institute of Health had denied them money because physical medicine did not focus on a single disease or part of the body. NIH wanted to aid specialties, not introduce a new philosophy of medical care. When the first hospital construction began in the late 1940s, physical medicine was again excluded. States did not include rehabilitation hospitals as part of their state plans, and so hospital construction money eluded physical medicine.[42]

The provision under the Hill-Burton Act to construct rehabilitation facilities was a last ditch effort. The VR state agencies had even been a disappointment to physical medicine. Before Mary Switzer arrived as Director, their services were used sparingly; severely disabled persons were not typically served. Physical medicine claimed to be the only discipline that could mobilize a wide range of specialists to treat the psychological, emotional, and social problems of a severely disabled person.[43] However, if they could get Hill-Burton funds to establish physical medicine within existing hospitals, perhaps they could get along without these other non-medical specialists.

The toehold must have seemed very attractive to rehabilitation medicine. The small number who had been trained by Rusk, Kessler, or Krusen had found themselves placed in medical school faculties or large hospital programs where they were the sole physiatrist, responsible for organizing and guiding other physicians. They had had no "slow assimilation process" as other specialists who were blessed with proximate role models.[44] Within those settings, physiatrists were constantly having to battle for their legitimacy. Orthopedists, neurologists, pediatricians were operating clinics with a physiatrist technically in charge, but subordinated to other specialties. One researcher had difficulty finding a "real rehabilitation center" to study among those used to rehabilitate miners.[45]

The jealousy with which each specialty guarded its own domain effectively excluded rehabilitation medicine from inclusion or growth in most communities. Rehabilitation medicine simply had no "home base" in medicine to develop comprehensive rehabilitation. Among government agencies, only Vocational Rehabilitation had made a commitment to rehabilitation medicine.

Mary Switzer was a consummate compromiser. Understanding the plight of rehabilitation medicine, she engineered an agreement that allowed physical medicine departments to be established in hospitals if they provided medical services plus one non-medical service.[46] She went further to pursue authority for construction of rehabilitation facilities under the Rehabilitation Act, so that Hill-Burton funds could be used to establish physical medicine departments in hospitals and the OVR program could channel funds to build a wide variety of facilities, such as sheltered workshops, halfway houses, and specialized facilities.[47] And so the Baruch Committee dream began to unravel, with rehabilitation facilities splitting into medical and vocational routes.

Mary Switzer was loyal to Howard Rusk and the philosophy only he and a handful of other gifted doctors seemed able to translate into a rehabilitation center. When the results of a follow-up study to evaluate the effectiveness of the provision of services to disabled miners produced embarrassing results, Mary enjoined the results.[48]

Mary's loyalty had limits, however, and seeing the stalemate and dilution of intent, she struck out in another direction, this time to North Carolina. Duke University was developing a long-range plan to further their influence in medical education. Mary Switzer saw an opening for a research and demonstration program that would support a rehabilitation center with a different look. A project for follow-up and home care attached to the medical center would give each department a separate, but identifiable role. There was no physiatrist among the members of the medical faculty Mary met, rather, all the specialists thought patients were getting better care since their one physiatrist had left. The orthopedic surgeon thought his Department should be the focal point for the rehabilitation program. Mary held out for someone skilled in physical medicine "for the long pull," but left Durham excited about the public program "elevating its contacts" with such a research and demonstration project.[49] Orthopedics was an established medical specialty; Vocational Rehabilitation had an opportunity to do a little social climbing within the medical pecking order through the Duke project. The boundaries within the medical profession were negotiable when Mary Switzer started trading, even if rehabilitation medicine came out the loser.

Mary Switzer discovered new constituencies at every juncture. The small amount of research, demonstration, and training money that was appropriated created new interest groups of educators, researchers, and facilities. Adding research and education to the basic program of VR had multiplied the influence of rehabilitation. The interest groups that grew from the education thrust of P.L. 565 were familiar to Mary Switzer. She had missed the interaction with universities that her involvement with the National Science Foundation and the Patents Board produced. She was experienced in negotiating with universities, but she had never had the companion task of preserving the inter-disciplinary nature of rehabilitation training. It was much easier to route Federal money to universities with established programs, with the hope that new emphasis on rehabilitation would make good team players, automatically.

In the first year under the new Act, 124 teaching grants were made to institutions and 1,177 to individuals. Physicians, social workers, nurses, occupational and physical therapists received instruction in rehabilitation. Thirty-four institutions began graduate training programs in rehabilitation counseling.[50] In no instance were the team members attending the same classes and learning how to work with one another.[51]

Mary Switzer hoped to influence university education through the breaking down of departmental barriers. She believed that knowledge was individual, and that scholars belonged to a universal company. In the training programs she believed the force of the environment could be overcome, that specialties did not have to splinter in order to survive. She thought rehabilitation counseling offered the best chance to cross departmental boundaries.[52]

Rehabilitation counseling was the newest emphasis in rehabilitation education, although it was the oldest of the practices. Thirty years earlier Dr. R. M. Little of New York described the beginnings:

> ...The civilian rehabilitation effort was started without being enveloped in a hectic sentiment and plagued by political influence. The work has been inaugurated in most States without a blast of trumpets and upon a conservative and thoughtful basis... The workers have usually been selected by the civil service process, and for the most part only men and women who are genuinely interested in the effort have been appointed.[53]

Mary's five years of experience with Vocational Rehabilitation had shown that "rehabilitation of the disabled is a highly complex, specialized personal service, which must take form according to the peculiar difficulties and aptitude of each person."[54]

A state supervisor of Vocational Rehabilitation in 1927 declared that rehabilitation called for "the highest type of workers," workers that were "mature enough to work with mature people."[55] The description of the people and the process had a lofty ring through the thirty years in which rehabilitation counselors were born, not made.

Great store was set by the counseling function, particularly at legislative hearings. H.L. Benshoof, Iowa State Director of VR, testified before the Appropriations Committee of the House in 1953 regarding the importance of counseling services:

> Essential counseling services have been curtailed in the face of an ever-increasing demand for rehabilitation services. There are actually fewer professional rehabilitation workers in the State-Federal program now than 3 years ago... Let me say here that counseling is the most important single part of the rehabilitation program and the least understood...
>
> ...The term 'counselor' is really not adequate to explain what a rehabilitation worker does. He is not merely a friend and adviser to his client, but he is actually the human engineer bringing to bear on his client all the community resources which can contribute to his vocational adjustment.[56]

Mr. Benshoof did not fail to point out that the skillful counselor prevented the waste of tax dollars in the purchase of tangible services from physicians, training institutions, or vendors of assistive devices. It had been a near crippling embarrassment when Paul Strachan accused rehabilitation counselors of being "wrapped in a toga of professionalism." Underneath the toga, there really was very little; it took until 1954 for graduate programs in rehabilitation counseling to be instituted.

Donald Dabelstein, Mary's Assistant Director, had been a rehabilitation counselor and State Director in Minnesota before coming to Washington in 1943. His thinking influenced Mary Switzer and the development of a formal, long-term training program.[57] The rehabilitation counselor was a hybrid, Dabelstein thought. Measurement and guidance was drawn from psychology, a case method from social work, and the feature of continuity from referral to placement was unique to rehabilitation counseling.[58]

At last "the key figure in the public program" was to have formal preparation for the job.[59] Mary expected persons recruited into the profession called "counseling" to be able to fit into any setting, getting the job done with the doctor, therapists, social worker, and any team members. She wanted the curriculum to stress philosophy, not techniques, a sense of history and purpose, not profession or agency.

The original thirty programs in rehabilitation counseling depended upon OVR staff and state rehabilitation agencies to help develop a reasonable, but scholarly curriculum. The Federal office funded a workshop in Charlottesville, Virginia, in July of 1955, to produce a document that would serve as a basis for other programs.[60] E.B. Whitten had submitted the grant application for a long-range project of NRA to study problems related to the training of rehabilitation counselors. Twenty-two participants developed a structure for rehabilitation counselor education that has survived three decades. It was a special group, drawn from counselor, supervisor, educator, and administrator ranks.

Mary Switzer was pleased with the results; it seemed the solid foundation needed to refute detractors' charges that rehabilitation counselors were little more than purchasing agents. Two of her most trusted staff members, Cecile Hillyer and James Garrett,[61] took on the major responsibility for nurturing this and other training programs. Mary turned to her promotional and administrative interests, concerning herself with training only when there was trouble.

Trouble did occur as agencies and universities tried to strike a balance of control over the curriculum. A vocal group of educators were also psychologists, and agency administrators thought they were "violently opposed to any suggestions."[62] There were public displays of temper in joint meetings of educators and administrators and repercussions in meetings of the state directors. Mary listened as one state director accused universities of "setting themselves up on a high plane," expecting whomever they selected for university training to be hired. "We will only hire those we figure can produce!" was the threat.[63] Mary Switzer might think training was important, but many of the state directors were accustomed to "fire house boys," genial men who could secure placements for their disabled clients by dropping in at the community gathering place.

When Mary Switzer had described the shortage of trained personnel as "the greatest single obstacle to the more rapid expansion of all types of rehabilitation services" she had no idea how difficult that shortage would be to overcome. Her goal of seeing state agencies staffed by practitioners trained in a mix of social work, psychology and vocational guidance[64] took much longer than the 1955-59 period she initially predicted. She lectured educators and state directors alike, stressing the "essential reciprocation" between public programs and training institutions.

Cecile Hillyer nursed the "infant and emerging discipline" past the shoals of parental rejection and sibling rivalry.[65] Educators and state directors met annually on Joint Committees to keep the university curriculum aligned with state agency needs. Mary Switzer was a true believer in meetings as makers of compromise. OVR paid for many an airing of complaints, and an uneasy truce was the product.

The rivalry within OVR for basic allegiance of this new profession swirled around Donald Dabelstein and Jim Garrett as psychologists, and Cecile Hillyer as social worker.

Both Dabelstein and Garrett had written early articles or textbooks dealing with the psychological aspects of rehabilitation.[66] Their preference was that university programs should be housed in departments of psychology. Cecile Hillyer argued that rehabilitation counselors should understand social forces and develop leadership in public affairs. The stalemate served Mary Switzer's purposes: she did not want "profession-centered" or "agency-centered" persons being trained. Instead, she wanted this new profession to focus on the persons being served and the "fast-changing scene in the community."[67]

The official stand taken by the Office of Vocational Rehabilitation was that the university would decide the location of the rehabilitation counseling courses and that those courses should contain essentials from several fields. The curriculum should be planned as an inter-disciplinary endeavor and should be taught to inter-disciplinary audiences whenever possible.

There were some model programs, where medical and nonmedical personnel who would work in rehabilitation were trained together. "The rehabilitation team" could be brought together for instruction and practical experience.[68] Although 35% of the training money during the first year was allocated to rehabilitation counseling, 21% went to teach physicians "comprehensive medicine" (the importance of social, vocational, and psychological factors in physical restoration) at undergraduate levels or to attract residents to physical medicine as a specialty. Social work received 19% of the training funds, with occupational and physical therapy and nursing disciplines receiving smaller allocations.[69] The thread Mary Switzer and Cecile Hillyer wished to weave through each field was interdependence of the rehabilitation professions. As the training programs became more numerous, Mary relied more heavily upon Cecile Hillyer to construct policy and to keep her informed of developments. Following the example of the National Advisory Committee, Cecile Hillyer recruited a thirteen member advisory committee on training policy. Leaders in education and involved professions met annually at OVR expense to review the problems, challenges and possible new directions for rehabilitation training. In each of the professional fields an additional panel was constructed, so that standards in each field would be preserved through the grant mechanism.[70] Peer review had its beginnings in these councils, as Hillyer and additional staff asked the most respected professionals to judge applications for teaching grants and traineeship support.

Mary Switzer's determination to have a solid rehabilitation training program was mild when compared to Cecile Hillyer's. It was Cecile who prepared long memos for Mary Switzer as she made her rounds of university ceremonies or class presentations. If Miss Switzer were speaking at Brandeis or Harvard, the memo would be particularly detailed; the promoter took the field fully prepared by Cecile Hillyer. Cecile earnestly believed that OVR should "encourage improved practice,"[71] whether that meant financial assistance to professional associations, reorganizing existing curricula, or establishing new training programs.

Mary Switzer had put the training program in the hands of a real perfectionist. Cecile Hillyer made Advisory Council meetings personal, productive, and of sterling quality. Successful people in their own fields, usually six to eight "old-timers" in the field, a state director, and a regional representative would make up a Training Council. Cecile Hillyer set a standard of personally entertaining advisory groups, of expecting members to be prepared and involved, and of producing a planning document with each advisory group during the annual meeting. In the advisory group for rehabilitation counseling, pioneer educators of the ilk of Lloyd Lofquist, Cecil Patterson, John Muthard, John McGowan and Marceline Jaques read applications for days prior to meetings and were rewarded with efficient, stimulating meetings.[72]

It was the sort of quality Mary Switzer desired in her "lieutenants," attention to detail and commitment. Yet the relationship between the promoter and the two women became increasingly strained. Cecile Hillyer was a professional herself, having earned a Master's degree in Social Work. Mary Switzer did not think of herself as a professional and was somewhat suspicious of professionalism. She reminded audiences of the expectations of the 1920s: "if you were going into a job serving people, you got into some agency that would take you and you learned the best way you could what to do."[73] Although Mary Switzer claimed she had given official sanction to the development of the professions making up the rehabilitation team, she viewed some standards as over-professionalism. Like the state directors, Mary Switzer would support training only so long as it increased the number of rehabilitations. Mary's background as a civil servant who rose the hard way influenced her opinion of professionalism, just as did her capacity as a talent scout. She recognized promise and set great store by "capable young people of college calibre."[74] Graduate education was too slow for Mary Switzer; she proposed shortening the time of education through a planned undergraduate emphasis. Her target was liberal arts colleges as producers of a "pool of bright, dedicated young people, who if accepted by public and private agencies could fill the acute need quickly."[75] Mary modeled the "missionary work" she promulgated in trying to interest faculty in offering such a "special exposure."[76] Although a champion of the liberal arts, she did not hesitate to try to bend it to her purposes.

Cecile Hillyer fought for training, earning the respect of university types through her insistence on academic freedom and an intellectual base for practice. The only female coordinator of a rehabilitation counseling program, Marceline Jaques, knew how difficult respect was to earn. Dr. Jaques remembered vividly her introduction to a state agency director, who continued to address his questions to the male faculty member who accompanied her to the state agency offices. Male coordinators may have discounted Cecile Hillyer, but they presented her with an award for her leadership.[77]

For rehabilitation counseling, the profession Cecile created, the start in 1955 had been slow. Five students received their degrees. A dozen years later 800 graduated in one year, and a grand total of 3,300 rehabilitation counselors had been produced.[78]

Cecile Hillyer's problem with established disciplines, such as rehabilitation medicine, physical therapy, occupational therapy, and speech therapy was being sure that teaching grants actually increased the "rehabilitation focus" in the curriculum, rather than sustaining faculty or students in a traditional curriculum. She worked with authorities in each field to identify the "rehabilitation elements" that made a request for funds legitimate.[79]

While Cecile Hillyer labored to develop training policy and processes, Mary Switzer consorted with college presidents increasingly interested in the Federal support for education. Carefully avoiding institutional conflicts, Mary would encourage a university to offer "something rather special" that would not duplicate programs already in operation in the state.[80] In other instances, Mary would turn down a request and redirect the president to greener pastures within OVR grant authority.[81] With unusually prestigious universities, Mary would write the president, dropping names of members of the Board of Regents, and inviting him to continue the university's interest in comprehensive medical rehabilitation.[82] Mary brought the customers in; it was Cecile Hillyer's task to find something that suited them.

Mary practiced her "sky is the limit" philosophy in promoting training for rehabilitation counselors already employed by state agencies. Short courses were taught by leading educators and researchers. When rehabilitation counselors needed to know more about the use of vocational tests in counseling, E.K. Strong, developer of the Strong Vocational Interest Blank, was imported for a short course. When young state administrators were thought to need business approaches, Harbridge House was called into service. Brookings Institute joined the impressive teaching roster at Mary's insistence.[83] The encouragement of professional development required a first class approach.

Cecile Hillyer, the yeoman who made Mary's wishes reality, had a male counterpart. Bill Usdane tried to fit Mary's "finds" into the priorities and policies that had been set by the Advisory Council on Research. Laughingly and lovingly, Bill Usdane would say there was never a dull moment with Mary working the vineyards.[84] New imperatives depended on seating assignments aboard return cross-country flights; no one ever knew whom Mary would meet and lasso into the rehabilitation fold.

Jim Garrett, Assistant Director of Research and Training, knew Mary Switzer's enthusiasms, her pet people, and her pet projects. It was Jim Garrett's responsibility to insure a balanced and reasoned research and training program. Accomodating Mary Switzer's spontaneity sometimes made it difficult. Between Mary's generation of new ideas and applicants and Jim Garrett's systematic approach, both quantity and quality of projects increased. Garrett insisted that research and training projects be of high quality. Mary agreed, "You generate more political support when explaining a justified 'No'."[85] And that was the real pay-off for Mary, the political support, the new constituencies.

Jim Garrett appreciated Mary's breadth of interests and enjoyment of the limelight. She had earned it. The resources were there because of the 1954 legislation. Her classical education, like his, created her diversity and led to casting the world in rehabilitation terms. In the training endeavor, the goals were indeed grand. Rehabilitation medicine was being underwritten, rehabilitation counseling was being legitimized, and other disciplines were being proselytized. Cecile Hillyer and Jim Garrett had an enormous task in carrying out Mary Switzer's dreams.

The dream that demanded resources in communities, personnel, and research was Mary's inheritance from three persons who had taught her about rehabilitation. Tracy Copp, her "gold dust twin" implanted the idea of comprehensive services. Bell Greve, who marshalled public and private support for a rehabilitation center in Cleveland, raised rehabilitation in Mary's mind as the international cornerstone of health and welfare services. Donald Dabelstein, a professional himself, demonstrated what sensitivity meant in the rehabilitation process.[86] These were Mary Switzer's personal rehabilitation resources, and all three died during this assembly and proving period.

Tracy Copp had never found time to write a book about her 34 years in rehabilitation. Instead, she had continued as Mary's unofficial consultant on staff affairs and official consultant for international projects. The Curative Workshop in Milwaukee had also benefited from her retirement in 1947, growing rapidly while she was a Board member. Tracy, the first of Mary's resources, died very suddenly, while playing bridge with friends in Green Bay on March 24, 1955.[87] Mary received notes of condolence from other "old timers" in rehabilitation, those who knew what Tracy meant to Mary.

Bell Greve, whom many knew as "World Citizen of Cleveland," had corresponded with Mary in 1946, when she was searching for a Public Health grant that would help in her Cleveland Rehabilitation Center.[88] Their correspondence and friendship grew, and Mary soon learned that Bell was one of the "saints" of the rehabilitation movement, having been Secretary General of the International Society for the Welfare of Cripples since 1939.[89] Bell instructed Mary on the concept of a modern rehabilitation center and the art of enlisting community support for rehabilitation.

Bell's last "post" was as Director of Public Health and Welfare of the City of Cleveland, and Mary noted that "she ran this vast group of services as she did her center, thinking of each person as an individual and wanting for them the best they could use to be whole again."[90] The week before Bell's death, Mary visited with her in her hospital room. The inspiration was still there, a thousand unfinished tasks in her heart. The unconventional worker who insisted on health and welfare being one, and of understanding "what families were up against" died on January 9, 1957,[91] leaving Mary without either of the women who had been rehabilitation to her for many years.

Donald Dabelstein, or "Dabs" as the central office staff called him, had been Mary's closest associate in Washington since becoming Director of OVR. Mary thought of him as the VR program's most creative thinker.[92] He and Terry Foster had prepared training sessions and casework procedures long before Mary Switzer came to OVR.[93] The rehabilitation counseling process was largely their construction. "Dabs" had helped usher in a new rehabilitation concept, following World War II, in which all handicapped persons were served through a team approach and a comprehensive plan of services.

Mary confessed to "feeding upon the mind" of this man who had weathered conceptual and administrative changes in rehabilitation. When touchy issues arose, it was "Dabs" Mary consulted. He prompted Mary with information about states into which she traveled. When Mary was away, it was "Dabs" who wrote Headquarters News Notes. His capacity to absorb the worries of others and to remain composed and elegant through the pressure of those growth years made him almost indispensable to Mary.[94]

By 1958 "Dabs" was feeling the effects of the workload. A virus refused to depart. After several weeks of rest, he still felt no better, although he kept in touch with the office daily. A heart attack ended his life on October 8, 1958.[95] Mary's personal resources had been heavily reduced during the three years of building the capacity of the rehabilitation program.

But the 1954 legislation was creating a vortex of activity. Mary had gotten what she wanted; she would have to continue without her mainstays. Career civil servants remained in the central office, translating the excitement into requests for proposals, new regulations, and annual reports that cast rehabilitation in the most positive light.

In addition to authority for research, training, and establishment of rehabilitation facilities, the pool of rehabilitation clients had been dramatically increased through changes in the Social Security Act in 1954. A "disability freeze" provision became law, in which benefits for workers were frozen at the age the worker became disabled. The effect of the amendment was to prevent the period of disability from affecting the worker's retirement and survivor benefits.[96] For Mary Switzer, the result was a vast recruiting system for rehabilitation. Disabled workers were referred to the state VR agency, where an initial determination of disability from Social Security guidelines would be made and potential benefits of rehabilitation could be predicted. Mary Switzer believed 125,000 of the 200,000 workers whose benefits were frozen could be rehabilitated.[97] In actuality, from July 1955 to June 1959 over 1,300,000 referrals were made from Social Security to VR, and 140,000 were accepted for rehabilitation consideration.[98] President Eisenhower's goal of 200,000 rehabilitants in a year did not seem too ambitious in 1954, with increased referrals and resources.

Having the authorization and implementing an expanded program proved to be two different matters. For one thing, Mary had hardly completed her conversion of Oveta Culp Hobby when Mrs. Hobby resigned. Contaminated batches of Salk vaccine had panicked millions, and Mrs. Hobby had the responsibility of restoring public confidence.[99] By the summer of 1955, Mrs. Hobby had decided to return to Texas, and Mary wrote her from Cape Cod: "You will always be our first Secretary in point of time, in point of standards of performance, in point of the many qualities which make for uniqueness and excellence in public service."[100]

Since Mary had helped write a memo to Franklin Roosevelt in 1944, describing a department that would offer health, education and welfare as one program, she was grateful to Mrs. Hobby for having been the "indispensable ingredient" in getting the long-imagined department accepted.[101]

Mrs. Hobby's successor was Marion Folsom. Mary's strategy in cultivating new Secretaries was effective. With Folsom, Mary had much in common, for he had come from the Department of the Treasury. Of course, they were both "Treasury alums." On the afternoon of Folsom's swearing in ceremony he met with the top staff of the Department, and Mary Switzer was one of those invited. Three days later, Mary Switzer met with Secretary Folsom privately, later reporting that "he is deeply interested in vocational rehabilitation."[102]

Folsom had taken the job of Secretary of HEW with the understanding that it would be only a two year assignment. His principles of objectivity, flexibility, and economy and efficiency of administration worked so well he was persuaded to stay a third year.[103] Mary Switzer reveled in his tenure. "This has been a wonderful year (l956); I hate to have it end. I had a wonderful talk with the Secretary this week, he really is most remarkable. His willingness to go along and support anything I feel will push the program ahead gives me the most inordinate sense of security."[104] To Folsom, Mary sent a note saying he was "just right for us at this period of history."[105]

Folsom's fortunes in HEW were unwittingly abetted by the launching of Sputnik in September l957. Until that time, his proposals for Federal aid to education had gone unresolved.[106] Suddenly, the impetus was there for expanded and improved educational services and Federal aid of $900 million. The crash educational program made it difficult for rehabilitation "to hold its own" in the budget negotiations, but Folsom "knew when and where to fight," and slight increases were gained. In l957 this was no small accomplishment, for an "economy block" had been formed in the House of Representatives which was determined to put a stop to steady increases in appropriations. President Eisenhower had been embarrassed by his Secretary of the Treasury, George Humphrey, who predicted a depression, resulting from Federal spending, on the same day the President submitted a budget $3 billion higher than the previous year. A shaken President Eisenhower instructed all members of the Cabinet to find places to save a dollar, and Republican Senator Tabor and Representative Williams of Mississippi led the crusade to reduce Federal spending.[107] VR escaped any funding cuts in l957, thanks to the lobbying efforts of E. B. Whitten and the support of Marion Folsom for Mary Switzer's program.[108]

The newly appointed Assistant Secretary for Legislation, Elliot Richardson, found Eisenhower's domestic policy "half-hearted" in l958.[109] Republican insistence on fiscal solvency had been replaced by general acceptance of the government's responsibility to respond to needs of general welfare. Only a change for the better in economic tides prevented the Eisenhower administration from providing benefits to all needy unemployed families.

But the change was only temporary, and by July of l958 the United States was in the third recession since World War II, with l of every l4 Americans unemployed. The fortunes of the Democrats were rising, in tandem with unemployment rates. The expectation that the government should "do something" also continued to rise, and the Department of Health, Education, and Welfare was increasingly pressured with solving the growing number of social ills.[110] It became clear that the job was "truly impossible." Caught between Presidents beset with budget problems and representing the poorest people, the average tenure of Secretaries of HEW during the first twenty years of the Department's existence was 2.2 years.[111]

A ritual of goodbyes and greeting was an outcome of this high level turnover. August 1958 arrived and Secretary Folsom announced his resignation. Mary relayed the leave-taking festivities to the regional representatives, being sure they understood her "incalculable debt to Secretary Folsom," but also the fact that "I know Arthur Flemming well, too, and admire him greatly."[112] She was one of two women invited to a Cosmos Club dinner, where associates from the Cabinet, the Treasury, Congress and HEW gathered to say goodbye. President Eisenhower and Mamie came by briefly, long enough for Mary to tell Ike that he and Mr. Folsom were the "best rehabilitations of the year."[113]

Department parties and in-house humor were also part of the send-off. Mary Switzer presented Secretary Folsom with a Cabinet chair, saying that he was the embodiment of the motto: Hope is the Anchor of Life. Mary pondered the festivities, saying: "Is it not interesting how things like this for some people can be just right and for others, just routine and banal. I believe it all goes to the quality of the individual and what they bring out in all of us."[114]

Arthur Flemming, last of the Republican Secretaries for another decade, had known Mary Switzer since 1932. He had worked with the Civil Service Commission and the War Manpower Commission, and alongside Howard Rusk and Mary in preparing the doctor draft laws. Flemming invited all the top staff to his swearing in, then met with directors individually. Daily reports from each program were to be on his desk by noon each day, for he preferred being able to read about problems before discussing them. In speaking before the OVR staff, he had "glowing" things to say about Mary and the rehabilitation program.[115]

Mary was also jubilant over the appointment of Bertha Adkins as Under Secretary. "I personally take great pride that such a nice accomplished woman could be our Under Secretary," she told the regional representatives.[116] It was lonely for a woman at Mary Switzer's level of government, and Mary welcomed a woman who did not administer a competing program, but acted as stand-in for the Secretary during VR awards parties.

Five years of a frontal attack on disability had passed quickly. Budget battles became ordinary, and Mary talked of "making a pitch" and of getting concessions from the Appropriations Committee. She also referred to walking a tight rope before committees. As the 1950s wore on, the connection between successful rehabilitations and employment became increasingly clear. The "tight rope" was asking for more money to alleviate a problem Federal money had not solved. Successful rehabilitations depended upon the labor market, and the construction of the rehabilitation industry Mary had overseen did not address this key economic determinant.

Mary continued to build the capacity of the rehabilitation industry during some rather lean years. At the close of 1957, Mary attempted to tighten up her ship. Advising regional representatives that gains should be consolidated by reducing committee work and travel and concentrating on "actual grubbing day-by-day activity" to improve the administration of the state programs and service provision, she continued to believe that changing attitudes and abilities of disabled persons would return citizens to work. She was confident that there would be a stream of benefits from the research, training and construction of facilities spurred by her leadership.

At the end of Folsom's term as Secretary of HEW, Mary counted her blessings. "We have had a happy combination of Secretaries since this Department was created, and only someone like myself, who has been through dark and sunny days, can appreciate what it has meant to our program."[117] Eisenhower's administration had been a boon to rehabilitation. The figures showed that the numbers of rehabilitants had increased 45% from 1954 to 1959; states had increased their appropriations by 100%; and federal appropriations had risen from $25 million to $55 million. The goal of 100,000 rehabilitants per year had not been reached, but 80,739 was acceptable.

By the close of the 1950s the diversity and volume of the rehabilitation industry by the close of the 1950s was Mary Switzer's "artifact;" her craft had built a rehabilitation industry. She had also survived a change of administrations, the creation of a new Department, and a change of Secretaries of that Department. The rehabilitation program included research and training ten years before education gained that authority.

The excitement obscured the fact that rehabilitation as a cure for dependency had not been demonstrated. Rehabilitation services were increasingly being concentrated on the removal of an impairment, and rehabilitation counselors were left with the realization that successful remediation did not invariably lead to employment. Aid to families with dependent children was rising steadily; economic security was now thought of as a right by many of the nation's poor. Although a rehabilitation industry had been built, its effectiveness as a philosophy and process remained to be shown.

XII
Categorical Jungle 1960-1965

I came to realize that a democratic society had created a monster--a benevolent one, to be sure, but a monster nevertheless. The unwieldy creature had its own self-serving purposes, its own organic processes, its own insatiable appetites. Surrounded by a dense categorical jungle, protected by layers of bureaucratic barbed wire, and tended devotedly by interest-group representatives, it had become all but inaccessible to broadly based public opinion.

Elliot Richardson, 1976

Departmental programs were just beginning to multiply as the new decade began. One of the results of successful program advocacy was a host of separate funding decisions. Mary Switzer, exhilarated with the program she had strengthened, found new competitors and scarcer funds to be the test of the sixties. In December, 1960, Mary Switzer summoned her staff with orders to prepare a "comprehensive memorandum which sets forth the story of where the vocational rehabilitation program is, how it got there, and the next steps."[1]

Prophetically, Mary greeted the New Year saying, "it is indeed the end, and the beginning, not only of a year, but of a period in history for all of us." She had spent an hour on December 29 with Governor Ribicoff, following the procession of Commissioners of Education and Health. Mary thought Ribicoff found her proposals simple indeed, after grappling with problems of legislation for Federal aid to education and medical care for the aged.[2]

Ribicoff had wanted only the "barest presentation and the price tags" and Mary had been ready.[3] A Task Force, led by Corbett Reedy, had been at work for more than a year, preparing goals for the 1960s. In her hour with Ribicoff, three precise recommendations, one to change the financing of the VR program, one to recognize rehabilitation services under any proposal for hospital and nursing care for the aged, and one to extend VR services to include independent living services and facility development.[4]

Knowing the categorical jungle, Mary had chosen fights she could win. Independent living, as a major legislative proposal during the early months of the new Administration might create jurisdictional controversies that would injure the program. And knowing the nature of her Congressional allies, Mary suggested that the Department advance no legislative proposal in this area, but respond to the proposals that would be introduced by "our friends in Congress," giving them the opportunity to gain credit for sponsoring the proposals. The bare minimum suggested would represent major victories for rehabilitation on policy decisions, if Ribicoff acted on the "affirmative approach" he indicated to Mary in their conference.

The "if" in Mary Switzer's assessment of her success in her first meeting with Ribicoff expanded as the year progressed. At the boundary of the Office of Vocational Rehabilitation, all was not hurrahs. Another experienced jungle strategist, Wilbur Cohen, had been appointed Assistant Secretary for Legislation under Kennedy. Through Cohen's suggestion, Ribicoff's legislative energies were directed to modifying the Social Security Act. Cohen was technically skilled in the workings of social insurance, and built upon the program expansion that had occurred during the Republican administration. As a pragmatist, he sold to the Kennedy administration merchandise he had helped manufacture from 1934 to 1943.[5]

Cohen had repaired to the University of Michigan during the Eisenhower Administration, but had continued to keep in touch with his colleagues in the Social Security Administration. Two important steps had been taken during his "political leave."[6] A disability freeze had been enacted in 1954, and cash benefits to disabled persons over 50 were authorized in 1956. Mary Switzer had had her opportunity to "emphasize the positive" through the referral of disability recipients to the VR system. Based on the logic that disabled persons were now protected by the same system that provided insurance and income distribution to the retired population, legislation had been introduced in 1958 to administer all rehabilitation costs from the Old Age and Survivors' Insurance Trust Fund.[7] A much larger competitor, Social Security, cast its shadow over Mary Switzer's domain.

Now that workers were granted benefits at the onset of disability, the Commissioner of Social Security, Charles Schottland, believed that rehabilitation could be more efficiently administered from his shop,[8] and this was a formidable initiative. The Social Security Administration had a history of program executives with continuity and commitment. They also had a policy planning function in their Bureau of Research and Statistics, which completed internal research based on the assumption that social insurance was the preferred technique for social welfare.⁹ The Bureau of Public Assistance, which had also been created in 1935 by the Social Security Act, was housed in the Social Security Administration, although considered a "despised alternative."¹⁰ Conservatives' fear that the Social Security program would become a general income support program was fed by this administrative location.

For the public, which feared social insurance growing into permanent assistance, rehabilitation was an attractive option. Rehabilitation was a tempting antidote for the public fear of social insurance growing into permanent assistance to those with little expectation of self-support. Reattachment to the labor force was rehabilitation's primary objective, and cash support had never been provided through the VR program. Social Security would much prefer the company of rehabilitation over that of public assistance and its income maintenance program.¹¹

Mary Switzer had been struggling for two years to fight off absorption by the larger agency. Before the re-entry of Wilbur Cohen and the Kennedy Administration, she had used the argument of conservatives, who did not trust the Social Security Administration nor any Federal agency to control medical or rehabilitation services. State and local involvement were crucial, providing "grass roots" support. And, Mary asserted, the Social Security Administration had experience with cash support programs, but not with providing services.

Mary went directly to Secretary Flemming, whom she described as having great personal loyalty to her, stating that she was "unalterably opposed to having rehabilitation in welfare" and predicting that such a move would set rehabilitation back many years. Despite the fact that welfare had bent more "to spread its skirts to include rehabilitation, State welfare workers are not rehabilitation-centered people."¹²

Mary insisted that moving Vocational Rehabilitation to the Social Security Administration would be the first step in abandoning the Federal-State grant system. "Does the administration wish to reverse itself on its often-reiterated principle that the States are a responsible part of this man's government?"¹³

Then she contrasted the welfare state with the "fulfillment society," hailing state and community involvement as a cooperative project aimed at securing greater fulfillment for more human beings. "Rehabilitation does not have all the answers, but we are on the right track, a track this Administration has followed consistently. CAN WE AFFORD TO REVERSE OUR DIRECTION?"¹⁴

Mary warned that the degree to which the Trust Fund was used to underwrite services would have direct bearing on both Federal and State support of the rehabilitation program. "The temptation to dip into the Trust Fund for support of the rehabilitation program rather than support from the general revenue would become irresistible." Mary recalled a discussion with

Secretary Folsom in which she had conceded that rehabilitation would be the "least controversial entering wedge" for comprehensive health insurance coverage. "I opposed it then as I do now. I believe more strongly than ever that this step would lead inevitably to sweeping changes in the method of delivery in paying for health and welfare services in this country."[15] Mary predicted that the Trust Fund would be asked to support difficult-to-finance services, such as care for the aged and chronically ill and rehabilitation. Six years later, her prediction came to be, with the passage of Medicaid and Medicare legislation. For the moment, Mary Switzer's strategy worked, and the Social Security Administration did not have its way in providing a "direct line operation."[16]

Mary Switzer had won the battle to continue state VR agencies as intermediary organizations in Federal involvement in disability insurance and rehabilitation programming. She had also rolled out awesome barbed wire around her category in the jungle. No sooner had the battle been won than a new President and his appointed Secretary of Health, Education, and Welfare required Mary's attention. Battle scars from the last change of administrations remained, and Mary was partially prepared for the threat to her position. Eunice Kennedy's concern for programs in mental retardation was an incalculable influence. Months dragged on before Ribicoff announced his decision. The tension trickled down to each of the states, the thought that VR's expert in categorical jungle warfare might be replaced made the whole system fearful.

Finally, at a meeting of state directors and regional representatives, the waiting came to a head. Ribicoff was invited to be the banquet speaker, and Mary Switzer was seated at the head table on the other side of the chairman for the evening. This was Ribicoff's introduction to a group that owed its recent prosperity to Mary Switzer. He had evidently learned how deep the support ran. Ribicoff began, "Before I get to anything else, there is something I want to clear up. Mary Switzer is being asked to continue as Director." The audience rose with resounding applause. Mary Switzer lowered her head, and this was one of the few occasions when anyone saw her weep.[17] Now she would at least be able to guard her section of the social program preserve.

Wilbur Cohen's return to Washington may have drawn Ribicoff's attention from rehabilitation to Social Security legislative concerns, but it also contributed indirectly to Mary Switzer's career advancement. Cohen was determined to correct some of the more glaring faults in the public assistance program, and with Ribicoff designed the Public Welfare Amendments of 1962. The neglected Bureau of Public Assistance was overtaxed with the administration of enlarged authority and the management of $4 billion dollars in annual welfare grants to states. The Bureau employed only 375 persons in 1962, and when Ribicoff resigned in frustration later that year, new Secretary Celebreeze almost immediately ordered a reorganization that

Mary Switzer stages Rose Garden Celebration with President Kennedy, honoring the 100,000th rehabilitant of 1962, Edward Friskie, "Mr. Rehabilitation.".
(*Courtesy The Schlesinger Library, Radcliffe College.*)

separated social insurance functions of the Social Security Administration from the public assistance and child health and welfare functions.[18]

The Social Security Administration was delighted with the removal of its philosophical opposite, the new Welfare Administration was relieved to have additional resources, and Mary Switzer was elevated to the rank of Commissioner of the Vocational Rehabilitation Administration. Although Mary said she was "amazed that the change in name and title was such a status symbol," and that she "had always acted like a Commissioner anyway," she rejoiced that the Secretary's action indicated the equality of status of Welfare, Social Security, and rehabilitation.[19] Newly appointed Secretary Celebreeze "felt strongly about the independent leadership of vocational rehabilitation." Passage of rehabilitation legislation had to wait while Welfare and Social Security were the center of Department attention, but rehabilitation's status and that of Mary Switzer improved.

Mary Switzer knew how to press her advantage. It was no coincidence that in late August of 1962 the 100,000th rehabilitation was celebrated. The number had been an albatross, ever since Dwight Eisenhower had doubled Oveta Culp Hobby's estimate of how many persons could be rehabilitated in a single year by the Office of Vocational Rehabilitation. Despite the near tripling of Federal funds in 10 years, the numbers of persons rehabilitated had not even doubled.[20] Mary Switzer had suffered from the assembly line mentality of 1952 long enough. Finally, in August of 1962, when the value of this competitor of Social Security and Welfare most needed attention, the 100,000 mark was passed.

"We felt this was worth making a little splash about," said Mary.[21] The rehabilitant was chosen with President Kennedy's experience in mind. The chosen rehabilitant happened to be a young father who had been injured in an automobile accident. He happened to have a three year old son and an attractive wife. Photographs of that Rose Garden day show Mary arranging things even while President Kennedy is addressing the group on the lawn. She leaned over to distract the weary three-year old son of "Mr. Rehabilitation," so that all could hear Kennedy pledge his support for VR to reach the 200,000 mark as soon as possible.

This was one of Celebreeze's first official acts, and President Kennedy paid tribute to him and to Mary Switzer in one breath. Mary Switzer said she would always remember "the pride and excitement and the romance" of the day "Mr. Rehabilitation 1962" was introduced to the press on the White House lawn.[22] Certainly the program that had occasioned such an event should have equal footing with Welfare and Social Security. Celebreeze had been imprinted with rehabilitation on that "perfect Washington day."[23]

Privately, Mary Switzer had bemoaned Kennedy's appointment of Celebreeze. "I'm so dark; the idea of appointing a *mayor* of a city."[24] Following the Rose Garden fanfare, Mary reveled in Celebreeze's presence. Within three months Mary proclaimed him "wonderful." "We go to Congress with the best budget we have ever had; I go into the New Year with the greatest sense of assurance."[25] Unaccustomed to any of the programs and customs of the Department of Health, Education and Welfare, Celebreeze was an active participant in the outpouring of social legislation during 1964 and 1965.[26] As the Eighty-ninth Congress, often called the "Congress of Fulfillment", dished out promises for correction of a host of social evils, Celebreeze waited table. He lasted three years, longer than any other Secretary of HEW, and during that time 60 new programs were established within the Department. [27]

The categorical jungle was getting crowded. So long as Mary Switzer's program was safe from annexation and generously remembered by appropriations committees, she congratulated Kennedy on his naive choice. Celebreeze fit in nicely with the responsive government just getting up momentum. Mary Switzer had taught Ribicoff how difficult management of the Department could be. In appropriations hearings earlier that year, her friend John Fogarty questioned Ribicoff about the Department's recommended cuts for Vocational Rehabilitation. Several days later, when Mary appeared to testify, Fogarty rather proudly said, "The Secretary was here for 2½ days, as you might have known." Mary replied, "We had a rumor to that effect." She went on to contradict Ribicoff's assertion that she was happy with the Department's recommendation, and to win the Committee's support for her request.[28] The budget for the Department was unmanageable with such program advocates at work.

About Celebreeze, Mary conceded that his experience was "fairly extensive from the point of view of a large city's problems" and that his "warm and loving spirit" would prevail. Watching him at a press conference focused on thalidomide incidents, she admired his skill in handling the press in a "quiet, unobtrusive manner," unlike the "former Secretary whose press was universally good, but who gained his attention by flamboyant poses and statements."[29]

Ribicoff had certainly been candid, if not flamboyant, in his explanation of his resignation. It was an impossible job.[30] Mary Switzer did not tolerate anyone speaking ill of the Department, even if the magnitude of its commitments was obviously far outdistancing its capacity to deliver on its promises. Mary Switzer was known for being a person who got things done, even if her work fed the undergrowth in the categorical jungle.

Advocacy run amuck resulted in an array of interest groups aligned with politicians who sponsored legislation addressing a specific problem and setting up a new bureaucracy. Elliot Richardson called it "Capitol Hill's oldest continuous floating shell game."[31] Money had to be moved from title to title, because there simply was not enough for all the jungle inhabitants.

In 1962, the logic of Vocational Rehabilitation had become obvious to competing programs. Vocational Rehabilitation's sales pitch was hard to top:

restoring persons to useful jobs was preferable to sustaining them on the public purse. States were becoming increasingly alarmed at the rising costs of welfare. Realizing that grants-in-aid to states for social services might relieve states of crushing welfare costs, Cohen and Ribicoff designed the 1962 Amendments to the Social Security Act. The blueprint was Vocational Rehabilitation: individual identification of problems, counseling, referral to other community agencies, with the Federal government paying 75% of the costs of services such as public education, medical care, and employment assistance.[32] What was not drawn from the forty year history of VR were the broad social objectives of the Amendments. "Self-support" and "strengthened family life" could not be celebrated on the White House lawn, as could employment.

A category of grants to states for social services, begun in 1962, were touted as having rehabilitation as their focus.[33] For Mary Switzer, they initiated another turf battle. She could define her jurisdiction much more clearly than the law defined services, eligibility, or outcome. Although Mary Switzer made sure no Public Assistance funds were used for Vocational Rehabilitation, she could not protect taxpayers from the exploitation that ensued, using the grant-in-aid system borrowed from VR.

The more sophisticated of states saw the Amendments as a bonanza, transferring workers from one state department to another, so that every state dollar for salaries would be matched by three Federal dollars. They exploited loosely written guidelines and designed programs that fit.[34] State-local effort was replaced through the Federal funds designated to change "relief to rehabilitation." Grantsmanship gone wild added to the ferocity of the categorical jungle.

The impetus for social programs came directly from President Kennedy. "The hand of hope" was extended through crash programs in welfare reform and education and job training programs, designed not to change society, but to alter the victims of poverty.[35] The Community Work and Training Program and the Work Experience and Training Program failed when 90% of monies were used for cash payments to AFDC fathers for work.[36] Little that resembled the rehabilitation components of Vocational Rehabilitation were provided through these early manpower programs for welfare recipients. Instead, the manpower programs drew attention away from the slow-down of industrial productivity in the United States. Aggregate unemployment was becoming the rule. Unemployment was a widespread problem, not confined to the poor or disabled.

Mary Switzer called this period a time of "whirling circles." She had asked for direction in program development from rehabilitation program experts, but had shelved their advice. A Task Force assembled in 1960 plotted the course of rehabilitation for the next decade. In contrast to competing programs, VR had a definable, if ambitious, goal of 200,000 rehabilitants per year and a process that others now wanted to imitate.

In 1959 Corbett Reedy, regional representative and Mary Switzer's great supporter, predicted the growth of social programs. "Our whole national economy and national economic thinking is now attuned to larger amounts," Reedy advised. If rehabilitation were to be sold as the American answer to disability, rather than disability payments, the Director would have to lead the way with a "total mission." He suggested the appointment of a Task Force to blueprint rehabilitation needs, goals, and resources for 1960-70. A "massive push forward" could come with proper leadership from the Federal office.[37]

Within six months, a Task Force on Organization had been formed, with Corbett Reedy as chairman.[38] While Social Security and Welfare jockeyed for jurisdiction, Mary Switzer was building the strongest case possible, that Vocational Rehabilitation not only knew what it was doing, it knew where it was going.

The major assumptions that guided the Task Force on Organization reaffirmed the state-Federal partnership and the emphasis on a tangible goal. The continuance of the Office of Vocational Rehabilitation and the state agencies as the principal public rehabilitation agency was fundamental. A lengthy document was produced by the Task Force, now labeled the Task Force on Program Development. Both the product and the process were symbolic; Mary Switzer had gotten the jump on the planners. A national policy for rehabilitation had been constructed with involvement at state, regional and central office level.

The quality of the Task Force report also gave Mary reason to be proud of her "VR family." She had been in office almost 10 years and had built a staff that was both loyal and talented. When regional representatives and central office staff were asked to critique a draft of the Task Force report, their mettle was tested. Incisive questions were raised: "Is it our objective to strengthen the VR agency unilaterally, or is it our need to develop a rehabilitation force which has as its purpose the strengthening of services to the disabled?" Philip Schafer, a Regional Representative, took issue with the sacrosanct single rehabilitation agency concept. "The historical concept of rehabilitation with authority to buy all services needed by the disabled . . . has been completely upset by the tremendous growth and activity of the voluntary and public health agencies, the welfare agencies, and by the medical profession." Turn away from this "perpendicular machinery," Schafer urged, and move toward inter-relationships with other operating services and organizing the total community resources to meet the problems of the disabled.[39]

Regional representatives, who like Corbett Reedy favored the single state agency concept, found the Task Force report surprising in its visualization of the state agency of the future as "prosperous, progressive, and vital." H.L. Benshoof thought the state agencies would be heartened and challenged by the confidence expressed in them through the report, a "transformation" that would have to be released gently to state agencies.[40]

As the analyses of staff came in, Mary marked each with question marks and marginal comments. She was taking the measure of her staff and of the issues she must resolve for this "massive push forward."

Should she strengthen the hand of the state agencies, as the Task Force report advised? Or should she heed Schafer's concerns and those of Jim Garrett, who doubted that the only way to improve rehabilitation services was through the state VR agency. To do that, Garrett stated, would require the state agency to provide all the services a disabled person and families of disabled persons need. State agencies, Garrett believed, were one facet of the community approach, with other public and voluntary agencies having "clearly demarcated roles."[41]

Related issues of facility operation were also raised by staff. The report had advised state agencies to establish their own facilities. Which pattern of establishment should Mary favor, that of state-operated facilities or consultation with public and private agencies operating facilities? Emily Lamborn favored both approaches, with the state-operated facility being a comprehensive rehabilitation center.[42] Robert Wright, the medical consultant, objected to any comprehensive rehabilitation center being anything other than "the lengthened shadow of a general hospital." It should "be under the nose of the physician, so close he can reach it from the hospital without removing his white coat in the transfer." There should be a counterpart, of course, the "learning workshop" with limited medical service.[43] It was Mary Switzer who would decide the policy directing the flow of establishment grant monies.

The most cautious of Mary's staff members, Sam Martz, who had advised her on budget matters since her arrival at OVR, threw up the most serious caution. The Task Force report had described disability as a national problem and rehabilitation as a national responsibility. To follow that logic to its end, should it not be entirely federally financed and administered? Martz predicted that as the OASI disability program became broader in scope and less restrictive in its definition, it would encompass a larger and larger segment of the disabled population. Martz thought it unlikely that the OASI Trust Fund would turn over large sums of money to VR to administer a service program. The combination of rhetoric about a national problem and proposed payment of rehabilitation costs from the OASI Trust Fund would lead to the abandonment of the Federal-state program.[44]

But broadening the eligibility base within both Social Security and VR had become clear by 1960. Rehabilitation had moved constantly deeper into the problems of the severely disabled, yet under Federal law, VR could not serve anyone who did not have good prospects of becoming employable. Mary Switzer estimated the number of persons needing "independent living services," so that they could take care of themselves, to be two million. She had argued that the cost of caring for these disabled persons through public assistance, municipal and state hospitals and other public resources ran into millions of dollars. Rehabilitation could "get at this dependency" with legislative changes allowing the broadening of the public rehabilitation program to serve this group.[45]

Mary Switzer knew the cost of such a broadening of scope. The old production line mentality, of the number of successful rehabilitations per year, would no longer be VR's outcome measure. Appropriations committees loved that head count, it made at least one human service program understandable. Rehabilitation would go out of the mass production business. As Emily Lamborn put it, "the emphasis should be on services, and any use of numerical goals should be in terms of the number of individuals served, with subordinate emphasis on the results."[46] Mary believed in the need for serving severely disabled persons, but she worried about losing her accountability measure.

Corbett Reedy had proved a productive chairman of an amazingly prompt and prolific Task Force. A 150 page document was duly delivered to Mary Switzer in August of 1960. The goals in the field of disability and rehabilitation were confused and unclear, said the Task Force. Its work was to develop facts and avenues of action. Their message was clear: drive the vertical nail of the state-Federal program straight to the heart of disability. Use the state agencies, not voluntary or private agencies, to expand services so that inefficient multiplication of rehabilitation programs would not occur.[47]

The pressure to direct the VR program through the confusion that lay ahead was acute. Mary had gotten more than she bargained for from the Task Force. Mary's assistant, Russell Dean, suggested an alternative to the bold step recommended by the Task Force. Appoint a group of 10 to 12 individuals, eminent in their own field, and "with the capacity to deal with major national questions" to study the recommendations of the Task Force.[48] The suggestion was itself a departure from the control of line personnel in planning, a move more consistent with involvement of voluntary agencies and other state agencies. Both the vertical and the horizontal approach made Mary Switzer nervous, and when she was unsure, she did nothing. Although Dean thought the Advisory group report could be completed within six months, it was almost six years before it was officially constituted.

Mary Switzer's energy went instead to those things she felt she did well. With Celebreeze, she had a Secretary who thought she could never be given too much money,[49] and she returned year after year to up the ante with Appropriations Committees. This very faculty contributed to the confusion: Mary Switzer was much better at capturing funds than she was in planning for their use.

The "whirling circles" of the early sixties, kept aloft by a responsive Congress and a President whose youthful enthusiasm made all things seem possible, hurried the tempo of the categorical jungle. Each program wanted to expand and to improve its organizational position in these days of plenty. Planning was the catchword for the public bureaucracy, and in mental health a new approach was being tested to include the public in social policy making.

Encouragement from the Kennedy Administration for pre-legislative planning for mental health and mental retardation led to the appropriation of funds for mental health planning in 1963. The belief underlying "State-wide Planning," as this approach was called, was that special "seed money" could encourage states to broaden its planning base.[50] Most programs used in-house evaluations or blue ribbon commissions, like Corbett Reedy's Task Force, for planning. State-wide planning was to be different; it was to use new planning theory and interorganizational patterns for national goal setting.

The assessment that state-wide planning produced was invariably used in enacting new legislation for categorical programs. The bureaucratic surveillance system passed along mental health's success, and by 1965 VR and Health also had received their Federal funds for state-wide planning.[51]

The thrust of Corbett Reedy's Task Force had been magnified by the competitive nature of categorical programs. The Task Force report had advocated strong leadership for the state VR agency, rather than a interagency, cooperative service delivery. This state-wide planning design was even more categorically based. If other agencies were getting money for planning on that basis, VR would follow that lead.

But lined up alongside mental health and mental retardation, VR looked frail in comparison. Both mental health and mental retardation were relative newcomers to the Federal scene. VR had been serving both groups for years, but the newcomers were draining some of Mary Switzer's Congressional bargaining power.

She responded by suggesting that VR, as the agency serving all the handicapped, engage in a leadership role for the statewide planning effort. "Just because a special planning effort is not authorized for this disability, or that disability, should never mean that proper attention is denied to a group."[52] The categorical claim for planning grants produced a maze of Federal-state cooperative programs, each attempting to plan for a health-related purpose. Overview planning became the new goal, and the Comprehensive Health Planning and Public Health Service Amendments of 1966 were the attempt to consolidate planning efforts, rescuing them from categorical competition.

The problem was that planning, optimistically thought capable of directing sudden growth in social programs, was connected to categorical interests, and the Department of HEW had no oversight controls. The mechanism had simply contributed to the outpouring of legislation, for national consensus led to laws and additional Federal grants.

Between the "insatiable appetites" of the categorical programs, and the problems with the planning process itself, broad based public opinion as the root of public policy proved elusive. Instead, state-wide planning became conservatively biased and perpetuated the status quo.

Mary Switzer used her own surveillance system to monitor these ill-fated planning efforts. Internal memos reveal some of the process difficulties and personal deficits that undermined planning efforts. In one state, Mary's informant described state office staff as "suspicious of innovations and unresponsive to working closely with other agencies."[53] Community-wide work was hampered by a consultant who "could see a flaw in any proposed program and the outcome of his 'consultation' was the abandonment of promising projects."[54] The state VR agency's inability to "join established planning groups" and its inclination to "isolate itself thoroughly" were serious barriers to community planning and programming;[55] VR simply did not know how to work effectively on the local level. Plaintively, Mary's contact pinned his hopes for an old agency learning new tricks on her upcoming visit to the state. Perhaps she could inspire cooperation; she seemed to have the knack of preventing fights.

But these were troubling years for Mary Switzer. The lesson learned from Eleanor Roosevelt: "That you care enough to come, that you remember what you see, and that you keep your promises" was becoming more difficult to practice. Mary cared and remembered, but keeping promises was becoming more and more arduous. The promises were of such grand scale!

For the man who had changed the focus of Mary's efforts from a battle against disability to a battle against dependency, Mary had both high regard and sympathy. "Poor President Kennedy! He probably thought he knew a lot of what he was getting into, but I am convinced he did not know the half of it."[56] Shortly after Kennedy's assasination, Mary Switzer spoke of his idealism. "He made a distinction we should remember: a distinction between words and the strength and willingness to follow words with action."[57]

There had been action following his dreams. "Intense activity" in HEW led to the Public Welfare Amendments of 1962 and the Manpower Development and Training Act. The promise had been to "stress services in addition to support, rehabilitation instead of relief, and training for useful work instead of prolonged dependency."[58] Perhaps Kennedy would have kept his promises, had he lived. Mary Switzer received condolences from around the world which reflected the hope Kennedy had inspired.

> He was a liberal without pathos, a man of bright heart and bright mind, one who combined ideals with realism. The youngest President of the United States represented to the world that America that accepted responsibility for the future of this planet and strived accordingly to bring about changes in the structure of its society, in order to be able to carry this responsibility with honor.[59]

The response to Kennedy's death was one of universal concern and deep sorrow, a force that contributed to the mass production of legislation by the

88th and 89th Congress. Kennedy's dreams were suddenly those of hero's, and Federal aid was authorized and appropriated at an astounding rate.

At the program level the task of keeping promises imbedded in the dream became increasing difficult. As new legislation was enacted it affected each of HEW's programs. In 1964 the Civil Rights Act became top priority, and Mary Switzer warned Rufus Miles, now Administrative Assistant Secretary of HEW, that VRA was "spread so thin that the constant shuffle of priorities is creating chaos in the administration of our expanding grants programs."[60] Implementing such an act required review of operations of state agencies and other grantees, a workload the agency could ill-afford to absorb. Just keeping up with the legislative changes supplanted the hope of keeping promises.

Being a program advocate had its occupational hazards: vertigo, from the whirling circles of spreading Federal influence. In its midst, Mary Switzer felt control slipping away. It seemed to her that planning, reorganization, any intervention to tame the monster HEW created more problems than were solved. She clung to two principles, "so long as I am responsible for this program" VRA must "remain intact and it must be a self-contained, independent operation with freedom to move about to accomplish its mission."[61]

Mary Switzer spoke like a true tender of bureaucratic boundaries. However, hers was the wisdom of one schooled in statecraft, who knew the penalty of cooptation disguised as cooperation. She was convinced VR was the instrument to combat disability and dependency.

XIII
There Are Victories
1960-1967

No pollster has dared to ask Americans what they would think of their children growing up to become Washington bureaucrats.

Hugh Heclo

Mary Switzer did not grow up wanting to become a bureaucrat. The process had been slow, and she had survived a world of agency competition and periodic fear of being ousted by a political appointee of a new administration. Her career stretched back to the days when bureaucrats were heroes,[1] struggling for a better social order. By the mid-sixties, public bureaucracies were under fire, and still Mary Switzer was proud of being a bureaucrat. She believed in the leadership of the Federal government. It was the bureaucrat who kept "a place for tomorrow's things."

She began to review her career in 1964, in hopes of writing an autobiography that would amount to a narrative of accomplishment in the field of rehabilitation.[2] Henry Urrows, the writer who encouraged Mary to dictate vignettes from her life, suggested the title, "There are Victories." The fragments Mary dictated were intriguing, but very slow in coming, for her responsibilities as Commissioner claimed most of her time.

The program had been built by identifying problems and daring to innovate in solving them. Research and demonstration projects broke ground, entering areas where there was no service, doing things in a new way, showing the effects, and eventually becoming standard rehabilitation operating procedure.[3]

Mary Switzer had learned from Eleanor Roosevelt the importance of going where service was needed. On her return from many trips, Mary would propose specific demonstration projects, opening up new territory for

Vocational Rehabilitation. The success of Mary Switzer's pioneering varied from project to project. She counted as a victory the demonstration by VR of the capability of mentally retarded persons through evaluation and training projects. Rehabilitation had been ready to capitalize on President Kennedy's concern, establishing comprehensive research and training centers in mental retardation and the inclusion of the mentally retarded program in Social and Rehabilitation Services.

Treading where others feared to tread had made rehabilitation a popular program. New areas of employment were opened for disabled persons, a victory Mary Switzer never failed to mention. Training programs in spoken Russian had been instituted for blind persons who had a special talent for language. Professional opportunities had been created for deaf actors through the Theatre for the Deaf. Mentally ill women were being trained in home economics. Some examples were more dramatic than others, but Vocational Rehabilitation was always shown as being ready to experiment with opportunities in a complex labor market.

All of Mary Switzer's ideas were not instant successes. In 1967, while in Wiesbaden for the World Congress of the International Society for Rehabilitation of the Disabled, Mary had met with parent groups of the Armed Services. They were concerned with the schooling of children who had disabilities. "With a firm commitment in my heart to figure out some way to improve the situation" Mary returned and proposed a meeting with Secretary McNamara through proper administrative channels.[4] Writing Secretary Gardner to explain a series of demonstration projects, Mary enclosed a draft letter for his signature. "It is absolutely imperative that the acceptance of this program come from the Secretary himself; otherwise the delays and resistance will make it difficult to put into effect," she said.[5] The assistant Secretaries of HEW did not think the demonstration projects Mary wanted to institute warranted John Gardner's attention. A note from the Assistant Secretary saying "The proposal letter seems much to do about little"[6] angered Mary Switzer. Wilbur Cohen, then Undersecretary, got a telephone call and a memo with the pencilled message: "I am not replying to Mr. B's memo or Assistant Secretary C's comment at this time. Tell the Secretary I have to cool off!!!"[7] Within a week she had her letter from John Gardner, proposing a series of demonstration projects to be supported by the Vocational Rehabilitation Administration for a period of three years, after which "we are convinced they will have become so essential you will recommend that they be made a permanent part of the educational program of your department."[8]

The research and demonstration projects were often designed to prove something to other agencies or the general population about disabled persons who had been overlooked or discounted as wage earners. Once the point was made and an agency sufficiently alert or embarrassed, VR moved out and on to other neglected areas.

Five years before Congress extended Medicare to persons with end-stage renal disease, Mary Switzer decided that state agencies could use matching funds to pay for kidney dialysis of patients eligible for vocational rehabilitation services. At that time 5,000 Americans were said to have "fatal kidney disease" and the treatment cost $10,000 per year. "This is a good example of the kind of thing we feel we must do. Nobody else was doing it, so we had to," Mary announced.[9] Basic program operation was as innovative as the research and demonstration projects, so long as Mary Switzer was making the decisions.

Through this decision an industry was born. Public financing for medical care to persons under 65 began with a VRA backed project. After 1972 and the extension of Medicare, the cost of dialysis rose steeply. Because Medicare paid 100% of the costs of treatment at a dialysis center and only 80% of the cost for treatment at home, physicians who specialized in this field set up profit-making centers and referred their patients there for treatment. Home dialysis fell from 37% to less than 10% in two years.[10] By demonstrating that persons with renal failure could live and work, so long as they had proper treatment, Mary Switzer introduced public financing to yet another group everyone had given up as hopeless. Inadvertently, she also pointed out a lucrative source of reimbursement for the emerging health care conglomerate.

Human frailty not only followed Mary Switzer's expeditionary trail, it sometimes preceded it. One of the most lasting ideas of Mary Switzer's creations was brought about by a scoundrel. Although Mary Switzer and Jim Garrett had proposed "centers of excellence" in rehabilitation to the Bureau of the Budget in 1960, the idea had been rejected. Mary knew the power that could be gained from developing sites where research, training, and clinical practice were offered. She had assisted in the construction of the National Institutes of Health and longed to bring that same forceful combination to rehabilitation. But leadership did not suffice; a ripe "climate" as Mary Switzer called it, was needed to bring about the establishment of Rehabilitation Research and Training Centers.

A thief created the climate.[11] A former mayor of a Minnesota city had raised funds to begin a rehabilitation center. To the great embarrassment of the university and medical dignitaries who had backed the endeavor, the fund-raiser disappeared with $250,000. A flurry of telephone conversations and a visit by VRA's Deputy Director produced a plan.[12] The Vocational Rehabilitation Act authorized the establishment of regional rehabilitation centers. Congress could allocate $3 million for the initiation of such regional research and graduate training institutes throughout the country for the first year of operation.[13] Two physiatrists, Krusen and Kottke, spoke with John Fogarty, who assured them of his support, and in turn, contacted Lister Hill. The Federal dollars would fill the void left by the absconder, and Mary Switzer would have her wish for a center of excellence.

The climate was ripe, and Congress appropriated $723,000 in 1962 for the Research and Training program. They were to provide a programmatic attack on the complex problems of rehabilitation. In good bureaucratic style, no favoritism was shown, and two centers were ordained: one at the University of Minnesota and the Sister Kenny Institute and one at New York University Medical Center and the Institute of Physical Medicine and Rehabilitation.[14] Rehabilitation had taken a great step. Now there were not only research projects; there were research programs, and they would prove very durable in years to come. Jim Garrett and Mary Switzer, with a little help from a thief, had provided as perfect an environment as possible for the advancement of modern rehabilitation. Universities where medicine and closely allied health professions were trained had been combined with access to selected patients for research and training. Fourteen months later, the University of Washington and Baylor were added as Research and Training Centers, and by 1964 there were 10 universities operating as part of a chain "in the great talent pools of rehabilitation medicine."[15] For Mary, this was the realization of a twenty-year old dream. There was permanence in interactive resources.

Mary Switzer enjoyed being in the forefront of service provision: "Rehabilitation so often leads the way because of all the programs of service we see today, it above all retains its belief in each individual and underlines at all times the moral responsibility to care."[16] For anyone related to rehabilitation who did not share her optimism, Mary Switzer had little regard. During debate on a National Center for the Deaf-Blind, Mary referred to a principal of a school for the blind as a "man of little faith," after he testified that few deaf-blind students could become self-sufficient.[17] The legislation creating a national center was enacted five years later; Mary Switzer had started a trend during the hearings of 1967.

Mary Switzer linked problems with solutions that would dramatize belief in the individual. Riffling her "position cards," she would locate and approach a benefactor to invest in the riskiest of projects. The Repertory Theatre of the Deaf was an example of adventure and victory.

Troubled by the isolation of the deaf, rehabilitation leaders searched for means to involve deaf adults in the mainstream of American culture. During the early 1950s, Anne Bancroft played the lead role in The Miracle Worker, bringing her close to a number of deaf people and introducing her to manual communication. She became one of the promoters of this new "art form." Mary Switzer met with the actress, and the drive was on to find a way to sustain deaf actors as they trained and toured.[18]

A planning grant was soon prepared by Edna Levine of New York University, where a Rehabilitation Research and Training Center on Deafness had been started. Dr. Levine consulted with Helen Mencken, an actress whose parents were deaf and whose first means of communication was sign language. Helen had not spoken until she was five, after making her debut on stage as a fairy in "A Midsummer Night's Dream." Victor Herbert had helped her learn to sing his music, and Helen Mencken became a popular actress of the 1920s and 1930s. Now a member of the Theatre Wing, she became one of those determined to see her first language, signs, appreciated as an art and deaf actors as artists.[19]

Mary Switzer went to work on private sources of funding for this "rather unusual, but very exciting, adventure in rehabilitation of the deaf."[20] The cost of producing a first-class troupe was overwhelming to both the private donors and to government boosters. For several years the idea awaited the right people and enough public support to launch the Theatre of the Deaf.

The Eugene O'Neill Memorial Theatre Foundation, led by David Hays, turned out to be the right troupe to get the idea moving. Boyce Williams, the VRA specialist in deafness, tutored David Hayes in the skill of writing an application for a planning grant, and several pilot productions were reviewed favorably by audiences.[21] Mary Switzer continued to meet with the O'Neill Foundation staff, describing them as "stimulating, eager, and able theatre people." In 1967 a three-year demonstration project was funded to found a professional company of deaf performers, assembled and trained by professional theatrical personnel of recognized stature. The company would tour for twelve weeks at the completion of their training.[22]

The letters David Hays wrote Mary Switzer between tours are informal project reports which revealed how innovative this public investment was. Hays wrote: "Imagine! from a dream that the world thought was crazy, in two short years we are playing the great festivals in Europe!" Hays encountered the stigma attached to deafness on the overseas tour. "My error was in permitting the Royal National Institute for the Deaf to send out press releases and invitations: as a result, no theatre critics considered us professional enough to review."[23]

There were "fences to walk" in choosing performances for deaf audiences. Hayes reported, "We suffer with the deaf whenever we do not do the things they want most, such as 'Arsenic and Old Lace.'"[24] Between conciliatory efforts, Hayes also fielded requests by officials of other governments for assistance in getting their own companies started. The sponsorship of performances soon became international and shared by private donors. Airfare and air freight for the troupe when they extended performances to additional countries were covered by donations from both airlines and foundations.[25]

The three year project ended in 1970, with a cost to SRS of $445,272. The reviews of the Theatre's work were glowing. Amateur troupes were springing up in communities and schools.[26] The producer of the "Today" show had said he was more pleased with the Theatre's program on his show than anything he had ever done. Mary Switzer called it a victory not only as a demonstration of the job possibilities for deaf people in the "vast theatre complex," but as an influence on the attitudes of all employers whose image of the deaf had been changed.[27]

Mary Switzer presided over the spadework of research through most of the 1960s, indirectly lobbying for her favorite projects, which typically seemed a bit eccentric to other reviewers. "Marginal projects are usually ideas which are a little ahead of their time... I'm very susceptible to way-out ideas," she confided. The Theatre of the Deaf was used as an example of projects that were "off the accustomed patterns." When questioned, Mary would point with pride to another dubious project, intervention to stop tremors in Parkinson's disease and cerebral palsy. "People thought it bordered on malpractice, but rehabilitation financed it to its great glory... Members of the Advisory Council had to be cajoled into trying it because 'Mary wants it so much.'"[28]

A project with aesthetic value was almost assured of approval. "The need for beauty in life, especially in the life of a disabled person, is universal,"[29] Mary insisted. Rehabilitation, art, beauty, and music--these were universal languages Mary made sure everyone understood. She doggedly defended the "genius who has people criticizing and holding back." When an old friend chose a peak of a New Hampshire mountain to construct a rehabilitation facility, Mary chided staff who pointed out problems with the remote location. The fact that water had to be piped in was much less important to Mary than the emphasis on the "glory of nature as an inspiration to lift the weary body once more from the floor."[30]

Mary Switzer was even more determined to open museums for blind persons' aesthetic experience. If a museum had only pictures, or if sculpture could not be touched, blind citizens were denied access to works of artists.

> A desire to heighten the awareness of beauty in the blind awakens us to ways and means of conveying aesthetic significance through touch, hearing, smell, emotion, and intellect. This is a cause for the bold and the dedicated.[31]

Mary Switzer spent 16 years developing the cause and recruiting enough people and resources to change the attitudes of the public and governing bodies so that all the public could enjoy museum holdings.

It took the use of every mechanism Mary Switzer knew to reach her goal. The first was locating a man who was not only bold and dedicated, but quite talented as well.[32] Allen H. Eaton was granted a Research Fellowship to collect objects of beauty, develop plans for their display, and to write an essay on beauty experienced through the sense of touch.[33] His book, *Beauty for the Sighted and the Blind*, which was published in 1959, documented the need of blind persons for beauty. That there are other means of perception of beauty as well as eyes, and that the sighted and the blind can derive satisfaction and fulfillment through sharing aesthetic experiences was the thesis Mary wished to prove.

Eaton chose 40 examples of handicrafts, man-made objects serving utilitarian or decorative purposes, which he thought would stimulate emotions and ideas between the sighted and the blind. Now Mary had a spokesman who could enlarge upon her ideas. Her next step was to interest her friend, Mary Semans, who chaired the Duke Foundation.

Mary Semans responded, and the North Carolina Museum of Art in Raleigh opened up glass cases so that blind people could explore works of art donated by the Duke Foundation and Mrs. Semans herself. The example to other curators, of letting things be touched, was thought to be an intermediate goal. VR assisted with staff advice and public information.

In 1966 Mary Switzer took the next step, convincing the Advisory Council that a planning grant to develop and operate a specific gallery for the blind at the North Carolina Museum of Art was a good investment. The year of planning would be followed by three years of demonstration.

Three years later the dream had been fulfilled. The Mary Duke Biddle Gallery for the Blind had profited from the pilot study, learning more about works that evoked particular responses from blind visitors. It pleased Mary Switzer that one of the most popular of the 63 pieces of sculpture was a cat, carved in 2,000 B.C. for an Egyptian tomb. The Gallery was visited by 11,000 blind children and adults and sparked interest in other states and countries. Mary Switzer was one of its best press agents.

> I had the very unusual pleasure just before leaving for work this morning to see you on the 'Today Show,' and to savor a little of your philosophy on what you wish to make out of the great Metropolitan... I have tried to stimulate an interest in developing special programs for the blind and deaf among those responsible for the arts... All of this is to plant in your mind a seed, which might one day grow into a small room at the Metropolitan, in which would be placed some of the treasures that could be enjoyed by the sighted and the blind alike, quietly, but enthusiastically. Could I come and see you about this sometime?[34]

Along with Mary Switzer's letter to the new director of the New York Metropolitan Museum of Art went Allen Eaton's book, her principal recruitment device. Thomas Hoving's reply promised, "We shall start on such a room right away."[35] Mary also inveigled the Smithsonian to try a pilot project using scale models of a NASA exhibit showing the history of flight in the United States.[32] The accomplishments of 15 years began to ripple out into the world, girded by the research and writing of Allen Eaton. The Mary Duke Biddle Gallery for the Blind had an interested and competent curator, with whom Mary Switzer regularly corresponded and suggested purchases of additional pieces.[36]

To critics who asked about the expense and the accessibility of the North Carolina Gallery for persons from other states or international visitors, Mary retorted: "We feel the Twentieth Century, for all its faults, has reached a level of social awareness and competence which permits the world to go quite a little out of its way for blind individuals."[37]

No small part of Mary Switzer's success in setting up a milieu in which research could be done was due to her devotion to her critics. Advisory Committees that reviewed grant applications were typically made up of prominent people with unshakable principles. One such advisor was John Stafford, a psychologist and priest who was the chairman of the Psychology Department at Catholic University. For more than twelve years he countered Mary Switzer's arguments for favored projects, supplying reason and scientific logic. In a mood of grudging admiration, Mary scribbled a note to Jim Garrett: "Jack is going to make me turn Catholic when I'm reincarnated!"[38]

There was no doubt in Mary Switzer's mind that research was the cutting edge of the rehabilitation program. As an "action-oriented administrator" she knew she was not a good researcher, in a pure sense.[39] Her respect for the search for knowledge was limitless, and her awareness of the reputation of researchers was acute. Although there was an elaborate application and review process, she bet on people and on institutions, rather than on the content of the application.[40] By 1968 there were 19 Research and Training Centers with a total budget of $10,225,000. In the same year 175 demonstration projects were funded at $2,716,927.[41] From such research, legislation was shaped to launch Regional Spinal Cord Injury Centers and Rehabilitation Engineering Centers. Mary Switzer was appropriately dubbed "student and mistress of research" by Duke University in 1962, when it awarded her an honorary doctor of humanities degree.[42] The mistress of research had monitored many an Advisory Committee session, appearing to be only half listening as she knitted throughout the discussion, then revealing that she had followed closely the amount of cash approved for each project. If research was the cutting edge of the rehabilitation program, Mary Switzer saw that it remained sharp, and this was a victory.

Mary Switzer was as solicitous of underdog professions as she was of unusual research ideas. Through the investment of public funds, trends were begun in the 1940s that would affect health care for decades. Mary Switzer began her policy of betting on long-shots during those days of developing postwar science and medical policy. Hospital administrators, physiatrists and psychiatrists considered Mary Switzer their benefactress.

When Paul McNutt presented Mary Switzer with the President's Medal of Merit in 1946, the Catholic Hospital Association announced the award, saying

> Any honor which comes to Miss Mary Switzer comes to one who has become for the hospital and medical interests of the country, in her high place, a protector, advocate, and an enthusiastic pleader. Her position enabled her to aid in securing for the hospitals of the country one advantage after the other.[43]

Referring to Mary Switzer as an "informal agent" McNutt applauded her ability to "give herself unreservedly to the service of her Government, especially when she is able at the same time to make that giving of herself in the public interest a personal favor to thousands of admiring and devoted friends."[44]

The informal agent was gate-keeper for the newest specialty, rehabilitation medicine. It was a victory of Mary Switzer's that Federal money and union funds were directed toward the establishment of rehabilitation hospitals and the creation of training programs for physiatrists. Although physical medicine and rehabilitation had received popular attention during the Second World War, rehabilitation doctors had great difficulty getting their slice of the research and construction pie. Respectability, indicated by being recognized as a specialty by the American Medical Association, did not come until 1951. Rehabilitation medicine was too general to fit into the research plans of the National Institutes of Health or the National Institutes of Mental Health. The specialty missed the feast of public investment in medical research and hospital construction.

Mary Switzer saw to it that physical medicine and rehabilitation was not crowded out. Through her friend Warren Draper, who directed the United Mine Workers "250 mile long hospital chain," Howard Rusk's Institute received referrals to fill its bed space. When Mary became Director of the Office of Vocational Rehabilitation in 1950, she increased the utilization of rehabilitation centers by the Office of Vocational Rehabilitation, co-sponsoring projects with the United Mine Workers to send severely disabled mineworkers to New York or to the Kabat-Kaiser Institute in California for treatment. Without the lifeblood of patients, and money invested in research, training, and construction by the Federal rehabilitation program, the specialty that purported to treat the whole man might have foundered in its infancy.

Although psychiatry could not be described as a foundling in 1940, when Mary Switzer first met Karl Menninger, it held an inferior status to those specialties that dealt with acute medical problems. Mary Switzer brought psychiatry under her wing. At the beginning of World War II only 25 medical officers were assigned to psychiatry. By the end of the war more than 2500 psychiatrists were treating mental and neurological problems of the armed forces.[45] The profession of psychiatry was clearly more influential by the end of the war, and Mary Switzer had been the gatekeeper to recognition.

The Procurement and Assignment Board knew very little about psychiatry and "had given no thought whatever to the need of the army for psychiatrists and related personnel" in 1942, when Mary Switzer arranged for Karl Menninger to meet her boss, Paul McNutt. Because McNutt trusted Mary Switzer, he gave his approval to take Karl Menninger and his message to the Procurement and Assignment Board.[46] From that day forward, Karl Menninger and psychiatry had a skillful advocate in Mary Switzer. The growth of psychiatric services within the armed services and the preservation of psychiatric residencies resulted from Mary Switzer's adoption of the little-understood profession.

Karl Menninger recognized Mary Switzer's ability to find investors, whether they were public or private. The Menninger Foundation was just getting started in 1943, and Karl Menninger wanted the bureaucrat's touch on the Board of Directors. Mary Switzer accepted, after pointing out her limited time and even more limited money. She knew the reputation of the Menninger Clinic, even at that early stage. It was a place where innovative things were being practiced, including psychoanalysis. She would be "happy to be associated with the Foundation and to assist in the solution of your many problems." [47]

The assistance Mary provided illustrates what a well-placed bureaucrat can do. Mary became the pathway to Federal funds for the Menninger Foundation, and psychiatry in general. Federal grants began to flow to the Foundation through the National Mental Health Act, which Mary Switzer, Bob Felix, and Lawrence Culp had created. Mary remembered the passage of the act as a victory:

> In the Public Health Service there was very little real interest on the part of the leadership in mental health and psychiatry. . . but by all of us working together and patterning the Mental Health Institute Law on the other institutes that have proved successful, it was finally passed.[48]

When the Menninger Foundation wanted Federal dollars to build training centers, they turned to their "informal agent" for advice. Mary Switzer urged the Foundation to document the need before asking the Federal Security Administration to request $25 million from Congress.[49]

Mary Switzer was in close contact with Mary Lasker during 1947, contributing to the strength of the "noble conspiracy" known as "Mary and her little lambs."[50] Mary Lasker had helped introduce modern advertising techniques to fund raising for medical research, had cultivated key Congressmen, and had perfected the use of the lay lobby to expand the National Institutes of Health. The Lasker lobby had been a powerful influence in the passage of the National Mental Health Act in 1946; Mary Switzer kept in touch with Mary Lasker whenever an interpretation of the act was to be attempted, such as the use of training funds for the construction of training facilities.

Psychiatry needed a defender as well as a fund raiser in the 1940s. An article in The Christian Century accused psychiatrists of inflating their own sense of importance. The length and heat of Karl Menninger's reply revealed how threatened the species was:

> I am shocked at the ignorance and bad taste betrayed by an editorial in which you compare psychiatrists with osteopaths and make the sneering and gratuitous inference that psychiatrists are manufacturing conditions to inflate their own sense of importance. Sixty minutes of your time spent in the psychiatric wards of your nearest military hospital ought to make you feel ashamed of your exhibition of stupidity. There are not thousands but hundreds of thousands and one may almost safely say a million or more men for whom the pressure of military requirements has been in excess of their adaptation capacities and who have reacted with symptoms that not alone psychiatrists but all physicians and I believe I may say all intelligent osteopaths to boot recognize as falling into the category of mental illness.[47]

William Menninger was equally incensed in 1949 when a magazine article appeared in the Catholic journal *Sign* with "nasty, mean" references to both Menningers and their alleged "takeover" of the American Psychiatric Association. He asked Mary Switzer for advice about how to deal with the criticism. Mary Switzer was certainly "one of the family," as she put it, exchanging advice and inside information for friendship and the excitement of helping psychiatry play a role in post-war health care.[52]

Mary Switzer thought the Menningers' influence pivotal in the field of mental health after World War II. And she believed her loyalty to the Menninger Foundation had enabled psychiatry to expand its reputation. Both were victories. Each February Mary received a copy of "Salutation to the Dawn" from the senior Dr. Menninger as a birthday remembrance. The association lasted 25 years, and the memory of her first visits to Topeka remained clear.

> I gained most from my intimacy with Dr. Karl. Whenever I would go to Topeka, I would sit in on the seminars that he would conduct with the advanced psychoanalytic students, and I never came away without having achieved at least one significant insight into problems that had a very direct bearing on my own responsibilities. I remember one evening, . . . listening to a discussion of the relationship of psychoanalysts to their patients and the way in which it was absolutely essential to hold an objective relationship although great human understanding of the problem was also essential. And as he drew the picture of this perfect relationship, it became for me the ideal also of the perfect administrator--the ability to stand outside the situation while at the same time to appreciate it emotionally and, believe me, after ten years of trying, this is not easy even today.[53]

Mary Switzer's respect for psychiatry was grounded in her appreciation of Karl Menninger, with his range of interests which she believed made a "mentally healthy person."[54]

Popularizing psychiatry was an uphill fight. Mary Switzer kept the Menningers abreast of the arguments of psychiatry's detractors. Her friend, Warren Draper, was questioned by Karl Menninger about the United Mine Workers' Welfare and Retirement Fund policy to limit psychiatric care for miners to acute and short term cases. After reading his response to Mary (whom he described as a "charming and gifted member of your Board"), Mary encouraged Dr. Draper to send his less than optimistic letter along.

> Our mining people from the highest echelons down are deep in their conviction that psychiatry does not make much sense, that psychiatrists are for the most part impractical dreamers, that the cost of psychiatric service is out of all proportion to the benefit to be derived, and that money expended for the purpose is largely or wholly wasted. . . I am convinced that on the basis of our present knowledge we can restore a lot more people to health and usefulness through ministering to their physical ills than we could by expending the same amount of money on their mental ills.[55]

Union funds might be withheld on the basis that people did not want psychiatric treatment because they did not believe in it, but Mary Switzer applied her knowledge of how government works to see that public funds were speculatively invested in psychiatry.

A bureaucrat who spent her time "conniving for the good of the world,"[56] Mary Switzer made it her business not only to boost underdog professions, but to use the carrot of Federal money to make factions in rehabilitation work together. Her decisions brought several internecine wars to an end. The use of orientation and mobility training with the blind was an outcome of her intercession.

Blindness had personal significance for Mary Switzer, due to Isabella Diamond's interest in the disability. Two astute VR staff members realized that Miss Diamond, Mary's lifelong friend and "unofficial consultant and sounding board," was a valuable pipeline to Mary Switzer's consciousness. Isabella Diamond was recruited to the cause of blindness by Louis Rives and Warren Bledsoe, being formally "brought into the fold" when she was made editor of *The Blindness Annual*, after retiring from her position as Treasury librarian. Rehabilitation of the blind had a special place on the agency agenda, thanks to the wooing of Miss Diamond.[57]

World War II had brought the conflict in the "armed camps" of workers for the blind to a peak. Suddenly a large group of war blinded men was created, a group amenable to early training, as no large group of blind people had ever been before. Old rivals, some who favored residential schools and others public education, some who thought job placement more important than social and psychological adjustment, vied for possession of this glamorous war blinded group.

The Veterans Administration was authorized to provide rehabilitation for disabled veterans, and the varying philosophies of the warring camps were implanted at the centers for eye care created by the VA. At one Army hospital, Valley Forge, soldiers were flown back to the United States within a few days of being blinded, where they were taught orientation and mobility by sighted instructors. Warren Bledsoe and Richard Hoover, father of orientation and mobility with the cane, had their demonstration center.

Tradition dictated respect for the prerogatives of blind people, including the continued employment of blind instructors. Bledsoe and Hoover ran counter to this thinking, and the impertinence of using sighted helpers and seemingly ignoring the blind leaders who had succeeded without the "long cane," slowed the acceptance of the technique.

Richard Hoover had the experience that made him challenge tradition. When staff at Valley Forge Hospital was asked what the newly blinded soldier needed most, he broke the silence.

> I think the first thing they need to know is how to get around. We've been working on it, but not enough. People say blind people in this country do a good job of getting around. I don't think they do a good job. I think they do a hell of a poor job.[58]

The affront led to the selection of thirty "orientors" who spent hours individually with veterans, teaching "foot travel."[59]

The success of Hoover at Valley Forge proved hard to transplant at nine other eye centers, and when the war ended, Warren Bledsoe persuaded Dr. Donald Covalt, chief of the medical rehabilitation program of the VA Department of Medicine and Surgery, to establish a new program at Hines Hospital where blind veterans could continue to be trained. Opposition almost killed the plan, but General Hawley exercised his authority to launch the center.[60] Mary Switzer represented the Federal Security Agency at meetings designed to promote cooperation between the civilian and veterans' organizations.[61] She was delighted that Hawley pushed the center through, but it was several years before she was able to give orientation and mobility training her own push.

Part of Mary Switzer's job as a bureaucrat was to clear away some of the VR staff that opposed the Hoover approach to rehabilitation of the blind.[62] This she did slowly and mercifully, in turn recruiting Warren Bledsoe himself to the VR central office. Finally, in 1960, she took action to incorporate orientation and mobility training for blind civilians. She wrote the chief of the Veterans Administration that the Office of Vocational Rehabilitation had granted funds to Boston College for training mobility instructors. "Without our mutual action I am afraid a skill which is really useful will not reach the great majority of blind people for many years to come."[63]

Warren Bledsoe likened Mary Switzer to Queen Victoria, who had the habit of writing personal notes. Nothing was ever dull in Queen Victoria's castle, nor in the VR staff. "The Queen is back. Little notes are flying all over the castle, saying, I am here." Mary Switzer's little notes went all around the world. Her note on the letter to the Administration of the VA said, "A fascinating effort but we need to bring the boys together."[64]

The skill that had been bottled up at Hines Hospital for too many years was let loose by Mary Switzer's backing. During the 1960s matching funds were provided by VR for faculty salaries and student fellowships at Boston College, Western Michigan University, and California State to teach orientation and mobility instructors. Thirty demonstration projects introduced state agencies to the new skills.[65] Although respected experts viewed this development as a dubious investment, Mary Switzer continued to put money into the cause and resisted arguments that Federal aid should be phased out, once the projects were successful. A few months before she died she wrote her successor, John Twiname, about the evidence of the effectiveness of training programs in mobility instruction and the inadvisability of cutting training funding.[66] She had helped create a new role in work for the blind. She defended support for the orientation and mobility instructor tirelessly.

It took years, but Mary Switzer made sure that a skill important to the future of blind people escaped the stricture of government agencies and old rivalries. She had worked with blind staff who often guarded the preserve of blind people by saying, "You'll never know what it is to be blind." Orientation and mobility became the apex of cooperation between the sighted and the blind. Training and demonstration dollars changed attitudes that had ruled rehabilitation for the blind for two centuries. The determined bureaucrat made the blind and the sighted work together.

From her position as the head of VR, Mary identified numerous dislocations in rehabilitation services. Federal money proved palliative for rifts in other disability areas, and Mary Switzer was instrumental in drawing opposing groups to the conference table. Here was a bureaucrat who tried to integrate services and service providers.

The quarrels among educators for the deaf and speech and hearing clinicians rested upon one of the issues that also had plagued work for the blind. Just how special and segregated should education for the deaf be? Mary Switzer was concerned because most state schools for the deaf were isolated from the mainstream of public education and from the expertise of audiologists and speech pathologists. Through grant money, Mary brought representatives from the Executives of American Schools for the Deaf and the American Speech and Hearing Association to Miami in 1962. A joint committee was formed that remained active for many years, offering regional meetings for teachers of the deaf and audiologists and publications that promoted exchange and understanding. Today every state and private residential school for the deaf employs at least one audiologist, as opposed to the three schools which did so in 1962.[67]

Some of Mary Switzer's victories were won by dint of steady attention, others with a dramatic nudge toward a decision in the direction she wanted. Gallaudet College, the nation's institution of higher education for the deaf, was one of her long-term interests. Mary had first become acquainted with Gallaudet as the Assistant Administrator of the Federal Security Agency, and as the years went by she continued to exercise her influence as a member of the Board of Trustees. She rarely missed a graduation, bedecked in her Harvard crimson robe and sitting proudly on the speakers' platform. Her behind-the-scene goal was always surveillance of liberal arts standards for this special college. As long as Mary Switzer was on the Board of Trustees, accreditation was a key issue.[68]

Mary would not let the administration of Gallaudet settle for less than first class instruction, and she applied the same principle when a technical institute for the deaf was being considered. When Congress authorized Federal support for a National Technical Institute for the Deaf, Mary Switzer was determined to see it located in the mainstream of technical instruction. Rochester, New York, was the seat of photographic expertise, and deaf students would be able to take coursework with hearing students attending the Rochester Technical Institute.[69] It was the clear choice, in Mary's mind, despite the dissent of those who thought Rochester the "Artic circle." To the

Switzer "barnstorming" in Barrow, Alaska, 1960.
(Courtesy The Schlesinger Library, Radcliffe College.)

skeptical she said, "Go up there and see it!" They did, and the National Technical Institute for the Deaf, federally established and funded, today enrolls 1,000 students from every state in the country, with over 80% receiving financial support from state rehabilitation agencies.[70] When Lyndon Johnson signed the National Technical Institute for the Deaf Act into law, Mary Switzer made sure her valued staff member, Boyce Williams, was present. Williams, himself deaf, had repeatedly instructed Mary in finger spelling, placing her hands in position to spell "VR" when she spoke to deaf audiences.[71] "VR" became the gateway for many deaf adults to exemplary technical training.

Mary Switzer dreamed large dreams, sometimes for disabled persons, always for rehabilitation. She treasured her international experiences, her work on the constitution of the World Health Organization,[72] her attendance at the Fifth World Congress of the Society for the Welfare of Cripples, the first World Congress on Mental Health.[73] Convinced that rehabilitation had the potential for giving people specific reasons to work together in dramatic ways, she built an international program of research and exchange of experts that continues.[74] "Rehabilitation has always been a major instrument for brotherhood," she reminded audiences.[75] How could she forget Bell Greve and her efforts during the first World War? She had seen rehabilitation heal the destructiveness of war and deprivation and worked diligently to see it become "the conscience of the world."

When Mary Switzer attended her first international rehabilitation conference after World War II there were no more than a dozen countries in which rehabilitation was being practiced. In 1964 she wrote:

> Today, there is hardly a country in the world, with the exception of some of those in Africa and Asia that have most recently attained national status, which has not made, or is not making a serious effort to rehabilitate the handicapped and disabled. Even in those less developed countries, where the burden of supporting rehabilitation services weighs heavily on the economy, the sense of national responsibility has taken firm root.
>
> To those of us who have worked for a long period of time in the field of rehabilitation this is a degree of progress that has exceeded our most optimistic hopes.[76]

Mary Switzer's work for international rehabilitation took the form of travel, encouragement of staff members to attend international conferences, and voluminous correspondence. When the State department took the position in 1959 that officials of the United States government could not attend professional meetings where representatives of Communist China were present, Mary protested, calling the policy "extremely short-sighted," and proclaiming that "in the field of health and medical afairs there is no national boundary to the development of new knowledges and the improvement of services, and even Communist China might contribute an idea that would be valuable to us here."[77]

When one of Mary's physician acquaintances left his position at the

University of Texas to direct the Ludhiana Christian Medical College in Punjab, India, Mary wrote her good wishes and added the rehabilitation push:

> I hope that you will be able to incorporate in your teaching the rehabilitation principles we are trying to inculcate all over the world. Everyone does not have to make America's mistakes, and some of the countries, like India, with many and varied disability problems and all sorts of diseases might do well to encourage their young physicians to think about the prevention of disability as a major part of their medical responsibilities."[78]

Such coaching culminated in research projects, once the International Health Research Act of 1960 became law.[79] Mary Switzer had prevailed upon Hubert Humphrey to introduce a bill making the use of funds accumulated in other countries from the sale of U.S. surplus commodities. Such funds would become available for rehabilitation research. With these funds VRA could join the United Nations, the International Society for the Rehabilitation of the Disabled and the World Rehabilitation Fund in international rehabilitation research and expert exchange.[80]

By 1964 the Christian Medical College and Hospital in Vellore, India, was investigating the rehabilitation of persons disabled by leprosy. Surgical reconstruction of hands, and the use of prosthetic appliances was one of 15 projects authorized in India for a three to five year duration.[81] The concern Mary Switzer had shown for lepers during many visits to the Carville Leprosarium in Louisiana produced change in medical and rehabilitation treatment. She had witnessed the results of leprosy, insisting on staying at the Leprosarium. The staff member who accompanied her had been surprised to find her in a housedress the morning after their arrival, saying, "Let's get to work" and proceeding to make the beds of five children.[82] Mary Switzer had kept on working to combat a disability affecting the world.

Mary Switzer sold Congress on the concept of investing in rehabilitation as a type of foreign aid, because it was such simple and clear evidence of American interest in individuals of other countries. While the average citizen might not see the relationship between roads, sanitation, or immunization, and his own well being, it was personally and dramatically effective to see "a person walk when he formerly crawled; to see a man receive his first paycheck; to see a blind man walk alone when he formerly was led by another."[83] Mary Switzer's other justification for international research was the benefit the United States derived. Research and exchange of experts brought benefits to the United States from other countries, Polish techniques for prosthesis fitting, Yugoslavian approaches to teaching deaf children. By 1967 research activities were being carried on in Burma, India, Israel, Pakistan, Poland, Syria, the United Arab Republic, and Yugoslavia.[84] The enterprising bureaucrat had found another source of money for extending rehabilitation, a source that continues.[85]

With a similar, steady, pressure, Mary Switzer furthered other causes. The Washington she came to in 1921 was a segregated city; she had been reminded of that as the young secretary to the Women's International League for Peace and Freedom. As residents of Alexandria, Virginia, Mary Switzer and Isabella Diamond had been "tortured by the problems" of civil rights and frustrated in their inability to change the situation.[86]

The coming of the New Deal changed little for blacks in Washington. Blacks were employed only as messengers and chaffeurs in the Capitol,[87] and Mary's job as Assistant to the Federal Security Administrator, in charge of Freedman's Hospital, made her acutely aware of racial inequities.

Freedman's Hospital had been established in 1865 to provide for the relief of Freedmen and refugees. During the 1940s the entire medical staff of the Hospital was supplied by Howard University Medical School.[88] Mary Switzer struggled to maintain hospital standards and teaching capacity, petitioning the Federal Security Agency to increase the allowances for the Hospital, and the Kellogg Foundation to finance an objective survey of the needs of the Hospital.[89] Once Mary was made Director of the Office of Vocational Rehabilitation she deployed a rehabilitation counselor to survey the need for counseling services at Freedman's.[90] With bureaucratic craft, she pointed out deficiencies and routed resources toward the improvement of patient care at the segregated facility.

Racial barriers to rehabilitation services were part of Mary Switzer's inheritance in 1950. Inquiries as to why blacks were not being treated at the only state-operated rehabilitation center in the country brought about a quiet secession of the Woodrow Wilson Rehabilitation Center from the Virginia county school system.[91] Mary also quietly recruited Jim Burress, a black rehabilitation counselor who had worked in the D.C. area since 1943, to be the rehabilitation counseling specialist for the central office.[92] His "special talents" were put to use in liaison to the National Urban League and the National Medical Association, the minority counterpart of the American Medical Association. "We are particularly anxious not to fall into the habit of thinking of him as an expert in matters concerning either Negro staff or Negro clients," Mary cautioned her Regional Representatives.[93] But soon Jim Burress was making visits to VR offices and making recommendations for improvements. Burress was not a token staff member, and his ability worked as an antidote to prejudice within the VR organization.

While Jim Burress carried on Mary Switzer's interest in Freedman's Hospital, Howard University, and the National Medical Association, Mary worked unobtrusively to extend black representation on influential committees. Among her suggestions for the Board of the National Science Foundation was Dr. Franklin McLean, Professor of Physiology at the University of Chicago, who had promoted graduate training for black physicians and graduate students. "He is a fine liberal as well as a first-class scientist," Mary proclaimed.[94] The barriers for black medical students and physicians included exclusionary internships and hospital privileges, with only Howard and Meharry surviving the "reform" of medical education following the Flexner report.[95] By opening up opportunities for capable black leaders, Mary Switzer hoped to alter attitudes and policies. Federal money should also help, she stated, as more hospital and rehabilitation facilities were built in rural areas through the Hill-Burton Act and the Rehabilitation Act Amendments of 1954. Speaking at Tuskegee Institute, she tried to recruit blacks to rehabilitation fields, where newly available training stipends waited.[96]

Mary Switzer had asked for no assurances that her labor would result in enduring changes or that she would be rewarded for her contributions when she swore allegiance to the bureaucracy. But she was credited with "starting a new science of rehabilitation," and she reveled in accomplishments that lasted.

Typically, the victories were not sudden, but were won over decades. The woman who appeared fresh and unhurried in her office had learned to conserve her energy for important fights. A staff member reported that if she dropped a pencil on her office carpet, she would not pick it up until she needed it the next week, meanwhile, she would have covered a great deal of ground.[97]

Patience and persistence was evident in one of the last battles Mary Switzer fought. As a child, Mary had been taken to see Helen Keller and Annie Sullivan when they came to Boston. As a member of Radcliffe's Board of Trustees, she had been present when a fountain in the Radcliffe College yard was dedicated to Helen Keller. The fountain symbolized the first word Helen Keller learned: "water." Helen Keller symbolized for Mary Switzer the power of the individual to overcome disability. Annie Sullivan symbolized the willingness of a dedicated person to work with a disabled individual to help "share the spirit with the world."[98]

In many trips to Senate and House hearings, Mary Switzer had presented one after another disability as targets for rehabilitation's attack. In August of 1967, she argued movingly for a national center for the deaf-blind, the nation's "most neglected people." She proposed a center to accomodate 300 persons, and brushed aside the argument that 300 deaf-blind adults would be hard to find. "I am a great believer in the divide and conquer rule," she said, and she succeeded in persuading legislators that citizens with Helen Keller's disability required the specialized approach only a national center could provide.[99] The Vocational Rehabilitation Amendments of 1967 established a national center for Deaf-Blind Youth and Adults.[100] Mary Switzer had circled back to an early heroine and called it eloquent evidence of the desire for equality in this country.

When lasting accomplishments and personal recognition were tallied, Mary Switzer differed from other bureau chiefs who were usually frustrated in seeing their deeply held convictions realized.[101] The job of the bureaucrat

Switzer and "Snowshoes," in her Alexandria home, 1967.
(Courtesy The Schlesinger Library, Radcliffe College.)

was the reconciliation of Mary Switzer's dual motives: her need to improve the world and to achieve personal security. As broker for public investments, she had become as influential as any capitalist, had traveled extensively, knew personally leaders of state and stage, owned property and retirement benefits, all without betraying her liberal philosophy. She had harmed no one in her personal advancement, instead, she had unquestionably bettered the lot of disabled persons in the United States.

Switzer meets with President Johnson, Secretary Gardner, and Undersecretary Cohen, 1967. *(Courtesy Warren Perry.)*

XIV
Problems of Plenty
1965-1967

Sometimes I think the problems of plenty are more complex than the problems of poverty. At least, when you do not have enough money or enough resources you always have an alibi.

Mary Elizabeth Switzer, 1965

The decade had passed mid-point before Mary Switzer was able to shepherd the legislation she had proposed to Abraham Ribicoff in 1960 through Congress, calling for the inclusion of independent living services and the extension of facilities. Some of the details had changed in five years, but the thinking of Corbett Reedy's "internal evaluation committee" was the framework.

In July 1965, Mary wrote her friend, Elizabeth Brandeis Rauschenbush, that the bill to amend the Vocational Rehabilitation Act was in a period of uncertainty. The bill itself was a dream come true, a "comprehensive overhaul of the present program and a marvelous foundation for the long pull." In a short time, and with improved Federal funding, Mary believed rehabilitation services could be made available to every disabled person in the United States.[1]

The pressure for change in the law had been building steadily. Competition with Medicare amendments, comprehensive educational aid bills, and dozens of lesser bills had delayed action. Mary wondered if "our Department" would be equal to the challenge of new legislation and new resources. She also worried about her own program and whether the new law would provide so many resources that there would be little excuse for failure.

During the hearings, the amendments had been dramatically advertised as a "bellwether for future efforts."[2] The 1965 VR Amendments were later said to have had the same effect on rehabilitation as Sputnik had on American education.³ It had been 11 years since Public Law 565 became law; it was high time for "sweeping revisions," as Mary Switzer called it.

Two of the major players in 1954 returned for testimony after an eleven year hiatus. E.B. Whitten was back to testify for the National Rehabilitation Association, and Mary Switzer offered testimony for VRA. The Administration was now Democratic, and Mary Switzer thought there was more enthusiasm about the VRA bill than there had been in years.⁴ Edith Green of Oregon was Chair of the Subcommittee on Education, and she had promised E.B. Whitten "good legislation" and appropriation authority earlier that year. Whitten was mindful of that promise, for Green had singlehandedly defeated a NRA amendment to anti-poverty legislation that would earmark funds for services to the disabled poor.⁵

Mrs. Green thought vocational rehabilitation would not suffer from being left out of anti-poverty legislation, and asserted her position on both programs early in the hearings before her Sub-committee. "I think that the vocational rehabilitation program is, without question, the best antipoverty program that we have ever had in this country."⁶ What went unsaid, but was understood, was that President Johnson's war on poverty program fell far short of VR's accomplishments.

Mary Switzer privately called them the "poverty boys" and resented both the creation of the new agency and the billion dollar price tag that went along with its implementation.⁷ It was clear that Mrs. Green and Mary Switzer were on the same team during the hearing. "We have had an anti-poverty program since 1920," Mary said flatly, to which Mrs. Green replied: "I do not know why the poverty program is entitled to 90 percent matching, while there is a limit of funds for rehabilitation programs." Mary concurred, "I must say our constituency feels that quite strongly."⁸ The following day, E.B. Whitten built on Mrs. Green's skepticism of the newer programs by pointing to matching precedents in manpower development training programs, and training services under the Public Welfare Amendments of 1962. "I don't see how anybody can justify a different Federal share for one of these than the other," Whitten contended.⁹

The hearings offered NRA and VRA an opportunity to complain that newcomers to the grant-in-aid programs were getting more state money than VR, simply because they bought a larger Federal share. The argument was convincing, and one of the major changes enacted in the 1965 amendments was a change in financing. Neither E.B. Whitten nor Mary Switzer would ever again have to attempt an explanation of the "formula," a complicated allotment base that defied simplification because, as one amused Congressman noted, "we simply do not know what we are doing."¹⁰

This was the only case of any supporter of the new VR legislation pleading ignorance. Charts and figures were presented to show the growth and impact of the program since 1954. Rehabilitants had increased from 55,000 in 1954 to 135,000 in 1965; Federal investment grew from $35.4 million in 1954 to $157.5 million in 1965. Only 18 research and demonstration projects existed in 1954, in 1965 there were 943. In 1955 there were 77 training programs, in 1965 there were 526.[11] It was an impressive record, a fit prelude for new requests.

There were two new funding authorities being requested in the 1965 legislation which had far-reaching effects: the construction of facilities and a compromise on Independent Living. Vocationally related facilities had not fared well with the provisions of the Hill-Burton Act to build new rehabilitation facilities. Although the funds were jointly approved by the VRA and the Public Health Service, medical rehabilitation facilities received the lion's share of construction funds. As E.B. Whitten testified, "there was a dearth of vocationally oriented rehabilitation facilities" and the proposed legislation would authorize the use of Federal funds for the construction of vocationally oriented facilities.[12] The compromise Mary Switzer made 10 years earlier, allowing hospitals to have "medical plus one" services, had left the vocational counterpart out of the construction scene. The Baruch Committee might not recognize the vestiges of their dream, but Mary Switzer was determined that workshops and vocationally oriented facilities have their bricks and mortar, also.

Mary Switzer had been attempting for five years to change the Rehabilitation Act so that severely disabled persons could be better served. Without evidence that a client had some "vocational potential," VR services could not be rendered. The problem was that both the Public Health Service and the Welfare Administration felt that a program for "self care" should be administered by their agencies. Howard Rusk had suggested in 1962 that a better term would be "Independent Living,"[13] and with this name that seemed quite consistent with rehabilitation philosophy, Mary Switzer and E.B. Whitten set out to finally change the law.

Whitten advocated NRA's position, that all disabled persons needing assistance in achieving rehabilitation goals would be eligible for services from VR. Measures of successful intervention would be broadened from competitive employment alone to include deinstitutionalization to live at home, independent living at home, independent living in home and community, sheltered employment, and home employment.[14]

Anticipating objections that would be raised in the Department of HEW, Mary Switzer hastily conferred with Whitten. What should she do if NRA's proposal was rejected? They agreed that it was important to "get a foot in the door" and that the Vocational Rehabilitation Administration might propose as an alternative an extended evaluation for severely disabled persons. This would allow the agency to serve any disabled individual for six months while determining rehabilitation potential.[15] Services would be limited in time, but not in scope, and a start would be made.

The compromise worked well; the Bureau of the Budget accepted RSA's proposal that same day. Mary was surprised at how easily agreement had been reached. NRA continued its pressure for an "all-out" independent living program, while VRA took a more conservative, but positive stance. At the very least, they expected to get action on the more modest proposal.

During the hearings before the House Subcommittee, William Page, President-Elect of the Association of Rehabilitation Facilities, coupled the two objectives of facility construction and extended evaluation. Calling the evaluation of disabled individuals the "hearthstone of this amendment," Page pointed out need for facilities focused on vocational preparation and emotional adjustment and included sheltered workshops and halfway houses for posthospital mental patients as belonging to this genre of facility. And, for good measure, Page requested funding for initial staffing of such facilities, saying that with "substandard staffing we run the risk of lending the resources of the Federal Government to a facility or workshop which will be unable to render appropriate level of services."[16] Deinstitutionalization was just getting underway as a philosophy and practice. Page saw the opportunity for rehabilitation facilities and VR to provide the critical link from hospital to community.

A coterie of effective witnesses testified at hearings for the amendment of the Vocational Rehabilitation Act, providing support for Mary Switzer's thesis that the rate of increase in services to the disabled was too slow. Centers and workshops were "too few, too far between, and in many cases substandard." The state service program was to be opened up to large numbers of severely disabled people, and program guidelines were to be made more flexible so that state agencies could "move in promptly with community efforts to better serve the poor, the youngsters dropping out of school, and the aging."[17]

The goal was the magic 200,000 rehabilitants in one year. It haunted Mary Switzer that Eisenhower's projection had been so long in coming. The Congress of Fulfillment was certainly the one to provide the authority and the Federal funds to reach that goal.

There was little respite for Mary Switzer during the spring and summer of 1965. After the hearings there was much shoring up of support to be done in the Administration. A new Secretary of HEW had been appointed, and Mary wanted John Gardner to be a buttress, not a barrier. In a long memo to the new Secretary, Mary announced the expectation of the passage of the Amendments and requested Gardner's help.

The doubling of Federal funds wrought by passage of the Amendments and action of the Appropriations Committee would require the doubling of state agency staffs and create "extensive operating problems." While "making every effort to avoid inroads on your time during the next few months," Mary asked Gardner's assistance in the form of a public commitment to the achievement of the legislation's objective and personal letters to the Governors of each State, "to underpin the work which we and the State directors will be doing."[18] "Underpinning" meant making sure the states put up their share of the match, now that it would be more liberal. Mary also laid out the bureaucratic boundaries for Gardner. "For some time we have endeavored to encourage and assist other agencies to extend their objectives and their resources to meet the real problems of several millions of disabled people in this country." Alluding to the statewide planning efforts, Mary stated flatly: "The constituency of the VRA is the disabled population of the United States." She wanted it clearly understood that neither Mental Health, Mental Retardation, nor Public Health would subsume VRA on a constituency basis. "I should like to talk to you before long to secure your ideas about how we might better arrange the Federal government's role in this whole picture of serious disability among the American people."[19]

Knowing that Gardner was an educator, Mary then turned to a subject she thought would strike home, the transition of handicapped young people from school to job training, to employment. The time was right, Mary avowed, to "move this year" to create a more formalized national cooperative program with the Office of Education and the Children's Bureau to reach "these handicapped youngsters promptly."[20]

Mary had tried in 1962 to broaden her administration to include the Children's Bureau and Welfare.[21] The Secretary had not accepted her proposal, and Mary continued to be frustrated by the age boundary for her program. If VR was only allowed to serve adults, then she would embarrass the Children's Bureau and the Office of Education into action.

Reserving the most troublesome issue for the end of her memo, Mary prepared the Secretary for a controversy that was bound to reach his ears. There was internal conflict in the "rehab family" over legislation introduced by Senator Morse to establish new requirements with respect to minimum wages for handicapped workers in workshops.

Mary focused her discussion of the issue on the "long-range picture of workshops in this country" and the danger of the present controversy damaging the image of workshops generally. "I have felt for some time that we will inevitably turn to workshops (conceived and operated quite differently from the present narrow efforts and aims) as a 'base of operations' for attacking many problems arising out of an urbanized and automated society."[22] H.R. 8310, the Amendments to the VR Act represented an effort to overhaul and improve workshops with an eye to the future.

Workshop directors and "nearly all voluntary organizations involved in workshops were violently opposed to the bill," saying it would force some workshops to close and others to reduce the number of severely disabled workers. "Certain organizations for the blind" supported it. There had, in fact, been picketing of some workshops for higher wages. Mary's request of the Secretary was for a proposal to solve the issue within the next four months.[23]

Mary was practicing her skill in "talking to the boss." She picked her time and her method to insure a smooth transition from Celebreeze to Gardner. She was looking ahead, with the problem of plenty weighing heavily before the long-awaited legislation was passed. By 1967, she said, "we go back to Congress for extension of the appropriation authorities, and we must be able to show a clear and positive picture of achievement by then." Could she rely on the new Secretary to help the state agencies "gear up to take advantage of the sharp increase in Federal funds?"[24]

Secretary Gardner was assisted by Wilbur Cohen, having been appointed Under Secretary of HEW in June. Almost immediately, Cohen sent out a memorandum to Lister Hill, Chairman of the Senate Committee on Labor and Public Welfare, supporting H.R. 8310, with permission to quote from his four-page memo, if necessary.[25] Two weeks later, H.R. 8310 passed the Senate.

Mary had rested with Isabella and her sister on Cape Cod before this final push. The respite was sorely needed and strictly observed. No telephone connected their cottage to Washington and work. It was the only time of the year when rehabilitation problems were left behind. Mary swam, made gooseberry preserves, read the novels she had hoarded for months, and visited with friends. Two weeks went by too quickly.

Once back in Washington, the work resumed. Action had still not been taken, not due to opposition, but the flood of legislation pouring from the 89th Congress. The first session of the 89th Congress passed 25 major pieces of legislation affecting the Department of HEW. Mental Retardation and Community Mental Health Centers Construction Act Amendments, Heart Disease, Cancer and Stroke Amendments, the Higher Education Act, and the Social Security Amendments which established Medicare and Medicaid were part of the rush of change.[26] September was frantic for the program advocate responsible for seeing a five-year dream materialize. Mary wrote a friend:

> We got back from the Cape and I immediately plunged into the most trying period of getting legislation through the Congress. We are still negotiating with the Senate and hoping to get some action next week. If citizens only realized the day-to-day irritations and energy consuming tasks that go into getting legislation through, they would be amazed. There are so many wheels within wheels, conflicts between key members of the House and Senate, political moves that must count for more than one thing, and all sorts of constituents to satisfy! It is indeed a great life. Most of the time, it is fun.[27]

It was much more fun on October 1, when the Senate finally passed the bill. Another delay followed, and it was not until November 8 that President Johnson, at his Texas White House, signed Public Law 89-333.[28]

Just as Mary Switzer had predicted, sharp expansion resulted. Within one year, state rehabilitation agencies had twice as much money for services as they had in 1965. State agency staff doubled, and the emergency staffing patterns Mary had outlined to Secretary Gardner had to be adopted.[29] For the first time in the history of rehabilitation's training program, undergraduate education was funded "to bring large amounts of promising young people into the field of rehabilitation counseling."[30]

The VR bonanza reflected the Department of HEW in 1966. Implementing huge new programs enlarged the budget of DHEW from $7.1 billion to 10 billion. Employment within the Department rose from 87,316 to 99,810 within the year. DHEW now administered 200 separate programs, double the number administered in 1960. Of the top 23 posts in the Department, 15 were filled by new personnel in 1966.[31]

Although Mary Switzer participated in the Federal gold rush of 1965-66, she was also aware of the contradictions in American life and mounting international problems.

President Johnson had deployed U.S. Marines to Vietnam in March of 1965. Writing to her confidante, Elizabeth Rauschenbush, Mary described the "wonderful thing" happening with the new legislation. Then she added,

> I wish I could say as much for the foreign field. I confess it is difficult now to decide what to do in the Vietnam situation, but the whole thing 'makes me very nervous,' as Mrs. Roosevelt used to say in days gone by when something troubled her.[32]

Mary Switzer remembered the effect war had on domestic programs, and the knowledge took the edge off her excitement.

This period of plenty was one Mary Switzer had worked desperately to achieve, and having reached such a high water mark made the remaining distance acheiveable.

For years she had worked within the framework she had inherited: a businessman's mentality toward rehabilitation. Her fiscal conservativism was rooted in her family and her own struggle for financial security, and she was a true believer in the work ethic. Still, she had a larger vision of what a society's responsibility was to all its citizens.

At this point of the rehabilitation program's greatest momentum in history, Mary was acutely aware of the problems of greater magnitude than she or rehabilitation had ever faced.

A product of the legislative furor was a "Committee Print," a document published by the Committee on Education and Labor of the House of Representatives to "give an encylopedic account of the public rehabilitation program."[33] RSA staff had prepared the manuscript, and in her letter of transmittal to Adam Clayton Powell, Mary Switzer described the document as "a valuable contribution to the literature in rehabilitation." Retrospectively, its greatest value lies hidden in an Appendix, where Mary Switzer revealed the philosophy that had guided her career in government service.

> Vocational rehabilitation, like many other aspects of human affairs, has evolved through three stages of public attitudes--compassion without action, followed by willingness to act

> for economic reasons, followed by willingness to act for social reasons. It seems to me that we are at a transitional stage between the last two, with almost universal acceptance of the economic soundness of returning disabled people to employment and a slowly growing philosophy that an advanced civilization like ours should so order its system that all disabled people will be restored as fully as possible, regardless of any economic benefits to anyone. [34]

Mary Switzer had defended the "head count" of VR for 15 years; rehabilitated to competitive employment was the only measure that mattered. She had used the cost-benefit ratio and "taxpayers, not taxeaters" line at every turn. But she had done so with the realization of the evolution of public attitudes.

She could remember no time since the 1930s when she was so conscious of the contrast between much and little, and of the crushing problems of poverty, deprivation, and prejudice. The philosophy of the Great Society dealt with the most difficult of problems as part of a national policy. "This is thrilling," she said, "to contemplate as a citizen and a taxpayer."[35]

It was particularly thrilling, when she envisioned the rehabilitation process being extended to all American citizens, as a primary tool of the Great Society, attempting to create an environment where people and institutions could flourish. She had long been the advocate for individualizing rehabilitation services. Now she saw the portent of depersonalization, brought about by "the coming age of technology." She predicted a "great and rising need among humanity for a sense of personal objective, of achievement, of participation, of self as an important entity in a mass of mechanized systems and controls."[36]

The concept of individualized effort was the foundation of rehabilitation programs, programs that had grown remarkably.

> The rehabilitation counselor becomes the instrument for focusing the talents of many different specialties upon the unique problems of one disabled person, to gain a full understanding of the obstacles to be overcome and to make that disabled person an active partner in the process of building his own future.[37]

Mary Switzer had testified before the House Sub-Committee on Education that such an approach, with a client-oriented goal, was the only way of solving the personal problems of poverty.

The temptations of mass production were great, particularly in an age when there were such visible and impressive results of large-scale technical efficiency. If, however, there were truly to be a sharing of the good life, the self would have to be seen as the cornerstone of the future. This can be done, Switzer said, "if we can find a way to attach as much importance to it as we now attach to four-speed transmissions, lunar exploration flights, and irrigation."[38]

Audiences wondered how Mary Switzer always seemed able to speak without notes and to enlist them all in her cause. Perhaps only Josephine Coe, her secretary during the Treasury days and through their task of answering pleas for help from bankrupt farmers, could understand Mary Switzer's source of fervor. Letters came to Mary Switzer now from rehabilitation counselors attempting to cope with the grinding problems of poverty and deprivation, just as they had come from the Dust Bowl during Roosevelt's administration.

David Walls had such an assignment in Harlan, Kentucky. Mary Switzer kept his letter to remind her of a nation's responsibility and the personal toll of ignoring it. Walls described his impotence in "affluent America:"

> On my third day in the area I was Henry and Lois' guest for supper, and they talked with me about the problems of the community, and, incidentally, themselves. Henry had just escaped serious injury in a mine accident which left him bruised and hospitalized a fellow worker. Four of their delightful young children sat with us at the table during supper. The fifth they showed me later, a beautiful thirteen-year-old girl, crippled and mentally retarded from birth, who because of extreme disability was kept in a specially constructed wooden crib in one of the bedrooms. Lois told me of over ten years of efforts to get her daughter the kind of care she required. She had written to three governors of Kentucky and numerous Congressmen, to no avail. I understood well the maze of agencies and offices she must have faced, and I meant to write to you in hopes that one more attempt could be made to unsnarl the red tape. But in my first few days of supervising several VISTA trainees and getting to know the area took a great deal of time, and I put off writing.
>
> On October 22 the Jones' four-room, wooden home burned to the ground in a matter of minutes, killing the thirteen-year-old girl, Marilyn Sue. The two articles in the Harlan Daily Enterprise describe the tragedy and document the long and futile effort of Mrs. Jones to secure care for her child.
>
> Miss Switzer, after two years on various fronts in this war against poverty, I still don't understand why this nation allows such conditions to persist. Marilyn Sue died because her father can find work only in small, dangerous, non-union 'dog-hole' coal mines and can't afford to pay for institutional care for his daughter.
>
> ... I know this case is not in your department, bureaucratically considered, but I hope you will pass this letter on to Mrs. Oettinger of the Childrens Bureau or an appropriate official in the Secretary's mental retardation task force. I think it underscores the need for Federal standards and dollars for comprehensive care, including adequate facilities, in every state. Possibly this letter could move us one iota closer to the day when no other Marilyn Sue will have to die such a terrible and unnecessary death.[39]

Mary Switzer did pass the letter along, and wrote David Walls as well, but the memory of Marilyn Sue remained. David Walls had been asked to sing at Marilyn Sue's funeral, and he had commented on the "fatalistic despair of the families in these coal camps." The chorus of the last song said it all:

> Farther along we'll know all about it,
> Farther along we'll understand why,
> Cheer up my brother, live in the sunshine,
> We'll understand it all by and by.[40]

Twenty-three years earlier, Mary Switzer had seen Agnes Inglis' poem depicting displaced workers. The theme of Agnes Inglis poem and the chorus of the coal camps was identical: the reason for such suffering would be revealed. The reason, for Mary Switzer, was society's abrogation of responsibility for the difficult problems of poverty, isolation, and disability. It was something of an irony that the Appalachian Regional Development Act had been passed among the spate of 1965 legislation. They would build roads within months, ramming into isolated areas and imposing change. Why had it taken decades to build programs to reach the people so in need of rehabilitation and its hope for recovery?

There were no adequate excuses in Mary Switzer's mind for the human toll of program shortcomings. Each letter she received with evidence of program failure was investigated and answered, but this seemed hollow when a disabled person suffered from system malfunction. Whenever Mary Switzer visited field offices she reminded young counselors that each file was a person, not to be forgotten or laid aside.[41]

Mary Switzer had known rehabilitation counselors who understood what she called "the comfort of the shared burden." She had witnessed the reaction of disabled persons who suddenly found themselves no longer mentally or physically on top of life, asking "How can I bear it?" The work of rehabilitation only counted, she believed, if the person served sensed that someone cared enough to share the burden of the struggle to overcome the disability. Disease and disability could be a sharing.[42]

Belle Greve had taught Mary this cardinal principle of rehabilitation and how it could be applied in a rehabilitation facility. In one of the first programs run by volunteers for cerebral palsied children at the Cleveland Rehabilitation Center, caretakers of severely disabled children were given the "comfort of a shared burden" through a few hours freedom from the sole responsibility. Belle Greve founded the Center, and she made sure that those who came no longer felt isolated by disability.

Mary Switzer wanted the Vocational Rehabilitation Administration to be the agency and the people who cared, for she believed that the comfort of the shared burden was much more important than anything else that might be brought to disabled men, women, and children who needed help.

Rehabilitation had come of age by 1965 and was facing the challenge of success. She had dreamed of the day when all disabled people who needed service could get it, now she was about to find out if the dreams had also been plans, plans both realistic and courageous.

With the greatest momentum in its forty years of history, Mary saw her second chance to organize the services of every community to serve all the disabled people who needed them. Her grand plan for post-World War II America had been scrapped along with government involvement in health care. But now it was 1965, and twenty years had changed opinion. Medicare was not what Mary Switzer had hoped for as quality health care for the entire country, but it ended the controversy over health as the business of the Federal government.

The action of the 89th Congress had been described by John Gardner as a "contemporary response to an ever-changing world, demonstrating the concern for the individual and for the maintenance of his freedom and integrity." Mary Switzer saw equality of opportunity as the key characteristic of the new legislation, which she said had always been the keystone of the vocational rehabilitation program.[43]

Mary Switzer was optimistic. Her second chance to mobilize communities in meeting human need arose from a national concern for the "welfare of the stranger and for those who are different." She could not remember there ever being such a commitment to breaking down prejudices and opening doors of opportunity. And there could no longer be the excuse of not having enough money. The albatross "formula" had been jettisoned; now three Federal dollars were available for every state dollar invested in rehabilitation across the country. Mary Switzer had sought social progress for more than forty years; the "speed-up" in the Federal attack on old and new problems was unprecedented.[44]

Social unrest and turbulence were not new to Mary Switzer, but a daily fare of violence was. She was concerned that the personality of the United States had always been marked by its capacity to resolve differences short of violence. There had always been an underlying stability in government and in the people themselves. Now it seemed sustained violence was the pattern: civil rights demonstrations, Vietnam sit-ins, assassinations. Rehabilitation had come of age in a time when, in the tumult, the quiet ones and those smallest in number might be obscured.

Mary Switzer's characteristic optimism was tempered in 1966 by twin concerns: failure to meet the "challenge of success" and fear of disabled persons being lost in the tumult of social protest. In her appearances before Congress and in conversations with John Gardner, she continued to cast Vocational Rehabilitation as the program that "cared."[45] When asked about a new program for correctional rehabilitation, Mary Switzer made sure legislators and administrators of HEW knew that rehabilitation had accepted a challenge other Government agencies had refused. "We often find ourselves in that position,"[46] Mary stated, reinforcing the idea that VR cared enough to attempt the most difficult tasks.

Internally, Mary Switzer was scrutinizing the performance of the VR agency to see if her claim of its being a "caring" agency could be supported. One of the flaws of this image of compassion was the rehabilitation of Social Security referrals. In 1964 rehabilitation counselors were screening out nearly 90% of the applicants, and of the 10% that remained, half were closed before receiving any services.[47] Mary Switzer predicted that the grown up profession of rehabilitation would have an essential role in a complicated society. Selling the VR program to the public could only be done on "sound, solid work with the severely disabled who present multiple problems." Were

Social Security cases too tough for VR? Or had some stone been left unturned?

Mary Switzer's verdict was that everyone "up and down the line" had not given this group of disabled individuals "our best emphasis." Counselors, supervisors, state directors, regional offices, and VRA were all responsible for the "gloomy picture." Still, she maintained that counselors were the key. "Nothing in this field is likely to succeed that does not have the understanding and support of counselors in the field."[48] And counselors had expressed little interest in Social Security referrals.

This was a problem VR could not ignore, Mary thought. Public confidence in the rehabilitation movement would be the price of neglecting the challenge. In a lengthy analysis of the problems of the past nine years, she proposed specific steps to overcome some of the difficulties. But at the end of her lengthy presentation, Mary Switzer gave her "call to service." The VR program could not flag in its energy and patience; there were promises to keep.[49]

And there had been substantial sums invested, based on those promises. By July 1967, Federal and State funds for rehabilitation approached a half billion dollars. State agency staffs had doubled. As Mary Switzer put it: "VRA goes on apace. We seem to gain ground all the while—slowly in some places, less so in others."[50]

Although the Congress of Fulfillment had seemed to provide for any and all social ills, it had held out promises that could not be kept, and this was clear to Mary Switzer by early 1967.

> The legislation passed a year ago is suffering, as all the new programs are, from under-financing and this has a subtle, deflationary effect not only on the projects that have to be postponed, but also on the general morale of the groups.[51]

Mary Switzer's plan for an "all-out" drive to improve workshops and develop modern treatment centers was a casualty of under-financing.

> The token appropriation for this program has been a wet blanket on much of the effort... and it is particularly serious from our point of view since we have to come up before the Congress a year from now for the renewal of our authorization. We cannot have as much to show as we would like if we do not have adequate support.[51]

What had happened to the plenty Mary Switzer feared might end any alibis VR had previously offered? The capacity of the United States government to finance and administer the domestic programs it had created had been outrun by the scale of the country's problems.[53] Government had accepted such a wide variety of new goals in the fields of health, education, manpower training, and reduction of poverty that fiscal resources were rapidly drained.[54] Federal grants-in-aid to state and local governments doubled in the five year period of 1964-69. Plenty evaporated quickly, resembling fool's gold to program advocates who thought everything was possible with expanding authorities.

Public assistance continued to be an embarrassment to administrators. By 1966, the Social Security Administration was congratulating itself for having parted company in 1963 with welfare. The costs of public assistance were sky-rocketing,[55] and the Social Security program was grateful to be spared public criticism leveled at welfare programs.

The public felt misled. Public assistance was billed as a transitional program, which would wither away as contributory insurance components were broadened. But now, in the 1960s it was growing alarmingly. The dichotomy between those who had worked and those with little expectation of self-support was increasingly obvious. The average AFDC payment increased by 67% between 1963 and 1971.[56]

Ellen Winston, North Carolina's Commissioner of Public Welfare, had been persuaded by Wilbur Cohen and Robert Ball, Commissioner of Social Security, to head the new Welfare Administration when it was removed from the Social Security Administration in 1963. Given the choice of transferring to the new Welfare Administration, or staying with the Social Security Administration, a few of the career staff opted to move and help the newcomer to the Federal bureaucracy.[57]

Help was badly needed, for the Public Welfare Amendments of 1962 had initiated a category of grants to the states for social services, attempting to change the approach of welfare from a cash handout to rehabilitation. States were required to provide services to welfare recipients, with the Federal government paying 75% of the costs of services.[58] It was Ellen Winston's task to exhort states to establish service programs and to ensure the quality of the programs.

As two female program executives, Mary Switzer and Ellen Winston were frequently compared, and Mary Switzer was particularly wary of the Welfare Administration's efforts at rehabilitating the nondisabled poor. She had demanded the firmest protection of VR jurisdiction when the Public Welfare Amendments of 1962 were being drafted,[59] and she was determined to see that VR preserved its purchasing power.

Ellen Winston was equally determined to improve the ratios of staff to welfare recipients and to enforce standards for professional personnel. Winston was a professionally trained social worker. She knew that the law did not adequately define services or eligibility. Only a visit to the person's home and the exercise of worker discretion could reduce waste in the welfare program, while individualizing service delivery.[60] Formal educational requirements for welfare workers were dictated by the Welfare Administration, and Ellen Winston became known as "a southern gentlewoman with a fist of steel."[61]

Professionalization, case load and visiting standards seemed sacred to Ellen Winston and to her social work constituency. "Better not to have a service than a poor service," said Ellen Winston.[62] Her belief in good supervision, a clear job description, and good personnel did not get people off the welfare rolls. Instead, the volume of Federal regulations for public assistance grew almost as rapidly as AFDC payments.

As Ellen Winston struggled with the Welfare Administration, she found Mary Switzer's job enviable.[63] VR was focused on a defensible area, whereas she was responsible for a number of related programs, including the Children's Bureau, the Office of Juvenile Delinquency, the Bureau of Aging, the Cuban Refugee program. The Welfare Administration was responsible for a great deal of money, with no statutory limit on expenditures.

Meanwhile, Mary Switzer was frustrated by the restrictions imposed by Federal legislation that gave VR its focus. She was convinced that VR could embark on large-scale programs to serve the socially, educationally, and economically disadvantaged, because VR had demonstrated its effectiveness in serving disabled citizens. The logic of giving the Welfare Administration the authority and money to rehabilitate the largest and most difficult target population contradicted Mary Switzer's belief in the rehabilitation approach. Provision of comprehensive services to meet unique individual needs through a person-to-person relationship was far superior to mass or class approaches. VR had been helping people help themselves for 45 years; what sense did it make to put federal service dollars in the hands of beginners?[64]

It doubled the frustration for Mary Switzer to see new programs cropping up in the mid-1960s that she had envisioned years earlier, only to be claimed by another agency. Some said she never hesitated to go in someone else's backyard to acquire an additional program emphasis,[65] but those observers had seldom been in Washington long enough to know how long Mary Switzer had worked toward an objective suddenly discovered by a rival bureaucracy.

When VR left the Office of Education in 1943, it left behind the educational and vocational concerns of disabled children. Liberation from an agency that seemed unconcerned for disabled youth and adults had worked well for VR, but children with disabilities were left out of the coordinated programs of research, training, and service, characteristic of VR during the 1950s. Mary Switzer was concerned then, expressing a philosophy that became dogma in education for handicapped children.

> The most important thing to stress is the most comprehensive possible services while the children are growing up, the most normal atmosphere, community atmosphere and school atmosphere, and the use of segregated facilities only when that is the sole way to get the kind of education the children ought to have.[66]

As federal aid to education finally made its way to public acceptance, Mary Switzer was surprised and hurt to discover that VR would not be the administrative home for services to disabled children.

It also stung Mary, in 1963, to discover that her near-monopoly of influence on Senator Hill and Congressman Fogarty had been broken by another woman.

Patria Winalski came to Washington from Connecticut as Abraham Ribicoff's aide. The mother of a deaf child, she was determined to discover what the Federal government was doing for handicapped children, and she went about it in a way that made Mary Switzer very uncomfortable. There was a pecking order to be respected; no one went over Mary Switzer's head in matters involving VR, yet Patria Winalski acted as if she was not bound by Switzer protocol.[67]

Captioned Films for the Deaf had been authorized in 1958, aimed at the cultural enrichment and recreation of deaf persons, although its educational impact was clear. It was so successful that later amendments extended its authority to research and development, production, and training teachers to use media.[68] Mary Switzer had helped with the passage of the 1958 legislation and was very interested in the program as it prospered. Patria Winalski had seen Captioned Films at close hand, because it had been started on a volunteer basis at a school for the deaf in Hartford, Connecticut. Patria Winalski wanted teachers trained to work with the deaf, and she cut a wide political swath promoting her ideas.

Mary Switzer heard from her staff member, Boyce Williams, of the Ribicoff aide who was talking to Senator Purtell about legislation to improve education for deaf children. Inviting Patria to lunch in her office, Mary asked why she had not come to her for help. After all, her prowess on the Hill was well known. And she wanted this training program to be part of the Vocational Rehabilitation Administration. "You're not in the education business," was Patria's retort. "They'll never do anything about it over there (in Education)," warned Mary. [69]

But Mary Switzer underestimated Patria Winalski. She gathered her own facts: the number of teachers for the deaf needed, how to encourage students for the field, what universities would be strong training sites. All Mary Switzer's old allies were recruited to Patria's cause. Lister Hill, John Fogarty, and Edith Green played a part in speeding Public Law 87-276 through the legislative process in late 1961, to become one of the first Federal supports to education.[70]

Jack Forsythe, who had been Abraham Ribicoff's Assistant Secretary for Legislation, and who later married Patria Winalski, was a trump card Mary Switzer could not beat. The pattern of legislation that followed placed the Bureau of Education for Handicapped Children in the Office of Education. Mary Switzer's hope of VRA's being the rehabilitation specialist for all disabled persons, regardless of age or disability, was ruined.

As competing bureaucracies took on responsibility for rehabilitation or for disabled citizens, the funding available to VR diminished. The grand plan Mary Switzer described, of an advanced civilization that restored disabled people regardless of economic benefits to society, seemed to be fading in 1965. The Congress of Fulfillment could not guarantee the plenty it authorized. Factors combined to slow progress: the "police action" in Vietnam, rising public assistance demands, and aggressive competitors for Federal funds.

The Task Force on Program Development had warned in 1960 that many government and voluntary organizations were beginning to emphasize rehabilitation in their programs, and that the result would be uneconomical and inefficient. Mary Switzer had given Corbett Reedy an award for chairing the Task Force;[71] by 1967 she considered the report prophetic. The preface had also said that great and enduring things would be accomplished in the decade ahead. Had that also happened?

The push for facility construction and workshop improvement that had been detailed in the 1960 Task Force report became part of the 1965 legislation. Rehabilitation facilities, whether state or privately owned and operated, became the center of service provision for the next two decades.[72] A broadening of the definition of eligibility, suggested in the Task Force report, was also part of the 1965 amendments, with "behavioral disabilities" being added to the population VR could serve, and two Advisory bodies had been established in the 1965 legislation with lasting effects.

The National Commission on Architectural Barriers to Rehabilitation of the Handicapped had been charged with determining the extent of architectural barriers and planning for physical access. On June 3, 1968, the President transmitted the Commission's report to Congress, a report that was to form the basis for legislation to force the use of accessibility standards in the building of any building utilizing Federal funds for construction.[73] Mary Switzer had gotten what she wanted from this Commission. She was known for scolding professional groups of architects: "It's your fault there are barriers in hospitals, schools, libraries, and court houses." Planning for all Americans became a requirement after 1968.

This could surely be called a great accomplishment. A mandated citizens advisory body was another accomplishment of Mary Switzer's. Faced with encroaching programs, Mary sought legislative action to require a VR advisory group.

Mary Switzer was a great believer in Advisory groups when she had a hand in constructing them. When the Committee on Appropriations of the House of Representatives acted on the appropriation request of the VRA in 1965, it provided for the establishment of a citizens' advisory body to study national needs for VR, the current VR program, and to formulate goals and recommendations to meet those goals.[74]

All nominations forwarded to the Secretary by Mary Switzer served on the National Citizens' Advisory Committee on Vocational Rehabilitation. The Chairman was, predictably, Howard Rusk, "long a presidential adviser on health and rehabilitation matters." Other members were suggested for a variety of reasons, all detailed in a lengthy memo to the Secretary. A map of the United States was carefully attached, showing the broad geographic distribution of the persons recommended for the Committee.[75]

When beset with a problem, Mary Switzer would often say, "Let me cast about in my mind" to search for a person who could provide a solution.[76] Her associate, Paul Howard, believed she had a "position card" in her mind for everyone she knew. The composition and rationale of the National Citizens' Advisory Committee illustrated her mental filing system, which showed each nominee's relationship to the program. Phrases like "outstanding radio and TV executive," "one of the South's leading industrialists," "recommended by Congressman Fogarty,"[77] provided a map of personal influence to be harnessed for Vocational Rehabilitation.

For Mary Switzer the process was reminiscent of 1952. Arthur Flemming had been Assistant to the Director of Defense Mobilization, and Howard Rusk had used his position as Chair of the Health Advisory Committee for President Truman to suggest the composition of a Task Force to explore the manpower needs that disabled citizens could fill in a period of defense mobilization.[78] Rusk had suggested Theodore Klumpp, President of Winthrop-Stearns Chemical Company, to chair the Committee. He had also suggested members: Harold Von Achen, Medical Director of the Caterpillar Tractor Company, William Menninger, Henry Viscardi, and Gerard Ungaro, President of the National Society for Crippled Children and Adults.[79]

The criteria for committee appointment were almost identical to those of 1966: personal prominence or representation of a rehabilitation constituency. In 1966 the National Citizens' Advisory Committee included W. Scott Allan, Assistant Vice President of the Liberty Mutual Insurance Company and Past-President of the National Rehabilitation Association, Edgar Forio, retired Senior Vice-President of the Coca Cola Bottling Company, Mary Duke Biddle Semans, Chair of the Duke Foundation, Mrs. Beatrice Burns, wife of the Governor of Hawaii, Burt Risley, Director of the Texas Commission for the Blind, Al Slicer, Director of Illinois Vocational Rehabilitation, Dr. Hester Turner, National Director of the Camp Fire Girls, and William Kuhl, Director of Research and Education for the International Brotherhood of Boilermakers.[80] Following in the tradition of the Task Force on the Handicapped, this national committee was of Mary Switzer's and Howard Rusk's choosing.

Mary Switzer hoped the outcome of the 1966 Committee would be as far-reaching as that of the Task Force. The Task Force Report had been taken as a national policy statement on the utilization of the handicapped; state directors had taken the report as a charge to carry out its recommendations. The policy statement was the first time a national declaration on the handicapped had been made a part of defense plans.

Could the National Citizens' Advisory Committee accomplish a similar feat in carving out rehabilitation's niche among the plethora of social

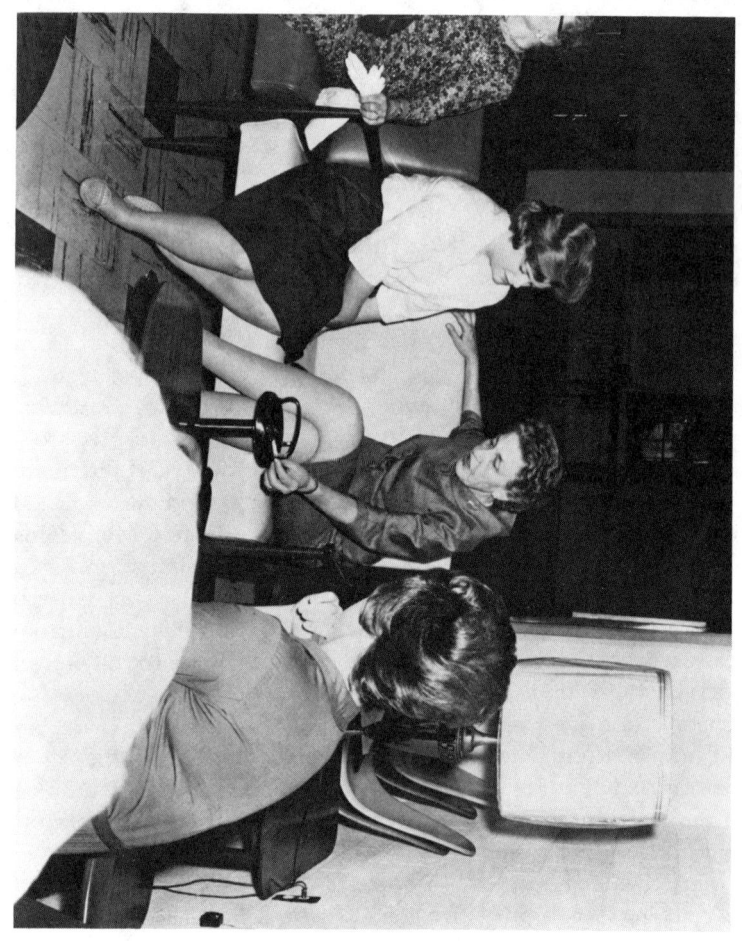

Switzer and students at Christian College, ca. 1966. (Courtesy The Schlesinger Library, Radcliffe College.)

programs? Competing agencies had their blue ribbon committees as well, studying needs and establishing goals, always with their agency as the primary service provider. Mary Switzer called upon the Advisory Committee to "give a fresh approach to rehabilitation," saying, "we need to extend our understanding of dependency."[81]

Howard Rusk and Mary Switzer always put on a good show, and the first meeting of the Advisory Committee was intended to be just that. John Gardner was invited to welcome the Committee. Of course, he stayed to hear Miss Switzer's remarks and to see Howard Rusk's slides on the "many aspects of rehabilitation." The film on a hemicorporectomized patient, a laundry worker whose hip joints and legs had been amputated, yet had returned to walking and to work, was the most persuasive evidence of rehabilitation know-how that could be found.[82]

John Gardner agreed that rehabilitation was "a work of great validity," but he went on to say that this was a great period of transition in all "social-help fields."[83] Efforts needed to be coordinated and related to the grass roots level. Rehabilitation could retain its vitality and conviction, and still fit itself in with other programs.

Mary Switzer would prefer other programs fit in with rehabilitation. By practicing the "divide and conquer rule" Mary Switzer had mobilized an agency to address a long list of disabling conditions. "Anytime you can highlight anything and tackle it, break it off from the broad base, you can achieve your goals," she said. This wisdom she attributed to her experience with the development of the National Institutes of Health. Now she would like to attack the problem of public assistance, or dependency, with the rehabilitation approach.[84]

The 1967 Rehabilitation Amendments were a first step in the breaking off of another disability to conquer. Migratory workers were to be served with rehabilitation dollars. The Advisory Committee Report, when it emerged in 1968, argued for a law to enable VR to serve "all those who are vocationally disabled, regardless of the cause.[85]

Problems of poverty and of plenty, although what emerged as most plentiful were competing bureaucracies, were propelling VR and Mary Switzer toward a testing of the "rehabilitation approach." The veteran bureaucrat knew that John Gardner was sizing up each of the Administrations and their Administrators. He did it through memos that posed difficult questions and set one-week deadlines.[86] Only the most facile and informed could pass that test. Six months later, John Gardner called VR "his Marine Corps;"[87] he had located a small, tough group with a mission and a master sargeant.

Mary Switzer admired John Gardner, saying, "He has some imaginative ideas about the need to get faster into the core areas of the cities and unify the Department's approach to them, but it is slow work when you have an empire like HEW."[88]

Mary Switzer's sector of the empire was in order, and she was credited with VR's accomplishments. Lister Hill paid Mary Switzer a great compliment during the 1967 August Senate hearings. Quoting Emerson, he said: "An institution is the lengthened shadow of one man," and added, "you are that individual in rehabilitation."

XV

A Rescue Mission
1967-1970

Secretary Cohen has said that if our nation has big headaches, it is because our people have big dreams.

Mary E. Switzer, 1968

Mary Switzer had lived through so many reorganizations that she could feel them in her bones. A Washington Post article proclaimed in November of 1966 that VR would be moved to the Health camp.[1] Reverberations of the reorganization proposal spread throughout the states, and staff rushed to influence Mary Switzer in her recommendation to Secretary Gardner.

It was an "age-old chestnut," as one state director put it.[2] Even the initial suggestion of Secretary Gardner was not new, that HEW be patterned after the Department of Defense, with an overall Secretary who would be a Cabinet member and separate secretaries for each of the three divisions. That solution had been proposed by Senator Taft when HEW was created. Both medical and education interest groups had insisted upon having an assistant secretary for health and education. Secretary Hobby had listened to the Bureau of the Budget, however, and held out for top-level assistants to aid her, not special interest groups. The most powerful of the pressure groups, the American Medical Association, succeeded in wresting a compromise from Mrs. Hobby. One of the assistant secretaries was designated Assistant Secretary for Health and Medical Affairs, although it was distinctly a staff position. The other two assistant secretaries were assigned to Legislation and Federal State relations, and Secretary Hobby had a tiny staff, but one of her own choosing.[3]

The idea had been to keep assistant secretaries from empire-building, loyal to the Secretary, and attentive to issues that cut laterally across HEW.

Because health and education were easily definable and had vocal constituencies, Secretary Hobby did well to emerge from the controversy with two objective staff advisors, and the third only partially tainted by loyalty to health pressure groups.

Mary Switzer remembered the problems of subordinate agencies when HEW had been created. Arthur Altmeyer, she recalled, had tried to persuade Oscar Ewing to place VRA under the Social Security Administration, rather than enlarge the independence of the Office of Vocational Rehabilitation. The Welfare establishment would have had a much clearer voice in affairs of the agency if all its parts had been grouped under one. Of course, Social Security was Altmeyer's choice.[4] The cost of unity was independence, and Mary Switzer was sure that VRA's subsequent success stemmed from Mr. Ewing's rejection of Altmeyer's suggestion. "Ability to function within the Department and capacity to follow through its mission in the long future" was at stake now, even as it had been in 1953.

Secretary Gardner needed some principles and some person to shape up the welfare sector of the Department. It seemed ironic that in 1953 one of the suggested titles for the Department had been "The Department of Welfare." By 1966 the word "welfare" was so stigmatizing that Health and Education wished they had been placed in another Department. HEW resembled a holding company, with largely autonomous units placed there for convenience, rather than any functional relationship.[5] Public assistance had contaminated the entire Department with its reputation of accelerating costs. The unpopularity of the Welfare division of the Department accentuated the problems of coordination between the three divisions of HEW. As in the past, VRA floated among all three fields in its function and philosophy. Which of the three areas was most appropriate for VRA? This was the "age-old chestnut." While John Gardner called VR his "Marine Corps," others dubbed it the "orphan brother" of Vocational Education.[6] Reorganization was certain to affect Vocational Rehabilitation.

The dialogue that Mary Switzer evoked with her assignment to staff of "an exercise in thought"[7] to decide which of the areas was most advantageous to VRA was rich with pride and paranoia. Public health was said to have "glamour at the federal level," but at the local level the public health officer was on the bottom rung of the medical totem pole. What was more crucial, if VRA was to be associated with county health units, they might be just across the hall from "that other agency" that administered relief to the poor. The plea was that VRA should find more "venerable or acceptable godfathers."[8]

And education got no higher marks from Mary's advisors. After all, VRA had a history of "being in the educational basements throughout the land." In particular, Vocational Education was castigated. "Never was so straight an arrow guided so amiss from its proper target!" Its "extraordinary non-leadership" had been ridiculous in contrast to the growth of the private trade school movement, which vocational education was supposed to preclude.[9]

For almost two decades VRA had been recognized by Democrats and Republicans as a dynamic program with considerable glamour of its own. It was quite painful for staff to "accept a destiny within one of the three major service areas of HEW," but better that than "awaken an old but now 'sleeping dog' over in the Department of Labor and really invite a jurisdictional donneybrook."[10]

Jim Garrett was not about to accept less status than he had helped VRA earn. With cold reason he built a strategy on VRA's strengths and the contribution it could make to the "thinking of other agencies." Garrett urged Mary to seize upon this as an opportunity to reorient Social Security payments, welfare, and aging programs to a rehabilitation philosophy. Focusing the positive aspects of individual and family services, and changing those who were or were potentially dependent individuals into contributors to society was a task VRA alone could accomplish.[11]

> It is all well and good to think of the VRA--David using his meager sling-shot of pressures to slay the Health or Education--Goliath . . . but our total program could compete more equitably in an Individual and Family Services army than it could in Health or Education.

Garrett warned against the behemoths and stressed the importance of keeping the VRA mission and program of services intact. "To have a meaningful vocational rehabilitation program, it is necessary to have an integrated program of services, facilities, research and training." In its totality of services, VRA would come to the other agencies with real strength. None of the other agencies had construction programs, and VRA's research and training budgets were more than double those in the Public Assistance, maternal and child welfare, Children's Bureau, juvenile delinquency, and Administration on Aging programs. This was a "not inconsiderable factor" in maintaining both VRA identity and integrity.[12]

Mary Switzer liked Garrett's combination of offense and defense. Perhaps VRA could take charge; John Gardner had himself proposed a division of the Department of HEW into Health, Education, and Individual and Family Services when he had been appointed Secretary.[13] The plan had dropped from sight, but the philosophy of dealing with the whole person probably had not. Defending the "identity and integrity" of VRA would be a natural consequence of ascension to a leadership position in a regrouping.

Mary asked her chief supporter in time of trouble, Howard Rusk, to add weight to the argument. As Chairman of the National Citizens' Advisory Committee on Vocational Rehabilitation, it was almost a routine matter for Rusk to submit a recommendation to Secretary Gardner. "In the reorganization, the VR program must maintain its organizational integrity" was the directive of the group Secretary Gardner had met only a few months earlier. They "respectfully" suggested a grouping of programs that were directly

Another swearing-in -
Switzer becomes Administrator of the Social and Rehabilitation Services, 1967.
(The Schlesinger Library, Radcliffe College.)

concerned with service to disabled people,[14] words taken almost verbatim from Jim Garrett's memo. A month later, John Gardner called out the Marine Corps of HEW. Vocational Rehabilitation was to provide leadership during and after reorganization. The age-old chestnut was being cracked differently this time.

Between February and August of 1967 the plans were finalized, a name for the new division chosen, and Mary Switzer was given the job of an assistant secretary, without the title. Instead, she was named as Administrator of the new Social and Rehabilitation Services on August 15, 1967.

Once more, Howard Rusk played a key role in Mary's promotion. As Rusk remembered it, they had had lunch with Gardner three months before he made the decision to ask for new legislation to construct the Social and Rehabilitation Services. At that meeting he said he would not attempt the organizational change unless Mary stayed to "see it off the ground." What impressed Rusk was Gardner's determination to give the problems of aging and welfare the same strength, vibrance and leadership that rehabilitation had. [15]

Publicly, John Gardner "owned up to the fact" that his department should be doing a better job of making those on relief independent, and that he was combining four of HEW's "do-good" activities under Mary Switzer's leadership.[16]

Announcements of the appointment described Mary Switzer as moving deliberately, out of the success of motivating severely disabled persons. "If anyone is qualified to find solutions to the complex problems, Miss Switzer is," proclaimed reporters.[17]

"I went to bed one night with what I thought was a tremendous budget of more than 300 million dollars and when I awoke the next morning I found it was six billion dollars," was Mary's recollection of the change from Commissioner to Administrator.[18] It was the budget of an empire, and she called it that. The newspapers used the same term, and underscored the responsibility she also inherited:

> "Whether her new empire really embodies a revised approach, or whether Miss Switzer merely presides over a broadened bailiwick doing more of the same, is the acid test she faces."[19]

Nothing diminished Mary's enjoyment of her appointment. The trip to the White House with John Gardner and Wilbur Cohen was one of the happiest occasions of her life. She relished the hour spent with Lyndon Johnson as evidence of his confidence that she could solve some of the problems which had beset his administration. It took little persuasion for her to recount part of the Presidential hour:

> We were sitting down having the photographers putting the cameras to and fro, and as some of you may know, the President has a habit, as do I, of leaning over and putting his hand on your arm. I found myself sitting next to him and putting my hand on his, talking

earnestly about something, and then I was conscious of the fact that the photographers were focused fast on us. So I said, 'Mr. President, I am afraid that they are taking our picture holding hands, do you mind?' He answered, 'I love it!' The picture has had wide circulation, perhaps because of that happy incident.[20]

Mary's excitement was matched with her conviction that she and "the small battalion of forces" constituting Social and Rehabilitation Services could contribute to the solution of problems facing American society.[21]

The rescue mission had been launched. John Gardner's dream of reducing dependency had been sharpened by Jim Garrett and Mary Switzer into an extension of rehabilitation. It seemed that David had slain some smaller scale Goliaths in the reorganization. As she began her job, Mary embraced the vanquished, including them in the "new family" and calling upon their best in "salvaging more lives."[22]

Gardner described it as the merger of three existing agencies: welfare, vocational rehabilitation and aging. The aim of the reorganization was to provide better services to the public. "It is our duty to make government manageable," Gardner said. "Poor organization, duplication, cross-purposes and confusion are a source of frustration to good workers and an obstacle to the accomplishment of good purposes." He had shaped the reorganization so that determination of income eligibility and provision of services would be separated. Perhaps now the process would be simpler, more dignified, and would free scarce manpower to provide services to those who needed them. He had placed rehabilitation at the heart of the new agency, because it had taught that rebuilding broken lives required the knowledge of many disciplines and the work of many hands. With rehabilitation principles and techniques "we can restore a sense of belonging to those outside the mainstream of society--the people in the urban ghettoes and rural slums, the needy and disadvantaged."[23]

John Gardner knew that fragmentation of services could not be cured by changing an organization chart. The cures were the ability to see the whole program, the willingness to work together and to subordinate one's personal interest in favor of the larger goal. "I have no illusions about the difficulty of this task," he said.

> *It amounts to asking the rehabilitation workers of this country to expand the concept of rehabilitation, so that it embraces millions instead of thousands, to relate itself to some of our massive social problems, and to maintain the kind of excellence which has marked the emergence of modern rehabilitation programs for the handicapped.*[24]

John Gardner went further. "In all the so-called helping professions, none rivals your own in ardent commitment to the possibility of human betterment. You have a never-say-die spirit in these matters that should stand as an example to everyone."[25]

The laurels were gladly received by rehabilitation workers, but did little to further the willingness of the four other agencies taken in by the merger. In the margin of one of her speeches, in which Mary emphasized the importance of inter-agency cooperation, she wrote: "We stand or fall together."[26] John Gardner acknowledged the fact that Mary Switzer had taken on an "immensely difficult assignment... the largest operational responsibility of any woman in government." He asked that she be given support and predicted that "she will make history for all of us."[27]

August and September were months of celebration. A banquet was held in honor of Mary's appointment. The guest list was so distinguished that a secretary suggested there be revolving seats at the head table.[28] There were a few guests who had been in Washington long enough to remember Mary Switzer as Paul McNutt's and Watson Miller's staff assistant. No guest realized that Mary had been passed over in 1946 for a role similar to the one she now assumed.[29] It was ironic that 20 years of building the strength of one statutory bureau earned Mary leadership of the most inclusive branch of HEW. Now she must change her parochial view to one more comprehensive, the perspective she had had in 1946, long before the bureaucratic borders of Health and Education made Department-wide planning moot.

The hiatus had increased Mary Switzer's experience as a program advocate and her Civil Service rating to an 18,[30] but it had been a costly interlude for knitting the related functions of HEW. Wilbur Cohen stated: "I can think of no other person who could so well lead us on the vigorous new course that has been set."[31] That course was a rescue mission, and Mary Switzer knew it to be perilous. "This is a daring program and thus has its dangers. I share with you a sense of urgency. I share with you an awesome responsibility. I share with you a hope and a dream."[32]

The priorities set for the new Social and Rehabilitation Service were certainly awesome. Improvement of conditions in cities, expanding services to older persons to prevent or alleviate financial and social dependency, increasing early identification, diagnosis and treatment of handicapped children, developing joint programs by VR and Public Assistance agencies for rehabilitation of the "socially disadvantaged," all called for program coordination and cooperation.

Mary Switzer set out to gain cooperation in much the same way she had won VR state directors in 1950, by contact and persuasion. The barn-storming began once more, but now there were two targets. VR personnel were not entirely pleased with the reorganization, although many of the newly appointed regional SRS commissioners came from their ranks. Accustomed to having Mary Switzer's entire attention, they were jealous of the many new programs and people who claimed her time.[33] Welfare workers were also taking a "wait-and-see" approach. Their loyalty had been to Ellen Winston, who had fought for their professional qualifications, and now she had returned to North Carolina. Mary Switzer had to enlist the help of both groups to complete her rescue mission.

In the VR circle, Mary appealed to pride. "Vocational rehabilitation has developed the techniques and the programs, and 200,000 disabled persons closed as rehabilitated during the fiscal year just ended are now sharing in the American dream."[34] Speaking to groups across the country, Mary stressed rehabilitation as a broad concept, broader than vocational rehabilitation. The name of the new agency reflected the new emphasis, that rehabilitation applied to young children and old people and to bringing people to the level of self-care, not always to the vocational success level. This reorganization had "placed a rehabilitation philosophy in all the programs that serve those who cannot achieve their rightful place in our society without some assistance."[35] The rhetoric was inspiring and logical; yet disciplinary action would soon have to be taken when the number of rehabilitants on Public Assistance actually fell.[36] "The position of rehabilitation in the new SRS program makes it even more important that the state rehabilitation agencies take the leadership in this area," Mary insisted.[37] To the Welfare audiences, Mary began in a soothing tone: "Work with us." Invariably, the new Administrator would refer to John Gardner's having "set a high star to steer by" and added Gardner's statement of the mission of SRS:

> That mission is to strive toward the elimination of all the conditions that stunt individual growth or impair human dignity. It is to foster the strengths and capabilities that enable individuals to function as free and responsibile citizens. It is to create the institutional arrangements that enable individuals to have greater freedom of choice.
>
> Too many children and too many adults in this free society still live under the subtle but powerful tyrannies of ignorance, disease, want, discrimination, physical handicap or mental illness. Those tyrannies keep them dependent. We want them to be free and strong.[38]

Mary Switzer's style was to appeal to the best in her listeners, and she would typically end her speech with a poem exhorting all to "reach out beyond your reach," to "give, beyond stint or measure."[39]

For almost twenty years, Mary Switzer had considered VR her "family," and SRS should not be different. The new organization was really only a means to an end, she reminded SRS personnel. This was a new family, hoping to meet major problems confronting the country. Services to the people where they live was the end, and new thinking was absolutely essential. "The exciting thing about it is that with a new look at each other, and with the hope and faith that we can change our emphasis, change our focus, and make our talents go further."[40]

The collaborative spirit Mary Switzer spoke about in her barn-storming of welfare bastions was contradicted by press releases and several of her ill-considered statements. "Welfare Head Calls Program a Disgrace" blared one headline.[41] A Time article quoted her as saying the answer to welfare programs was more work, by both welfare workers and recipients. Neither characterization won friends for Mary Switzer among the group she so desperately needed to support her.

Other comments distanced Mary from welfare workers. "I am not an expert in public welfare or social work, but I am an expert in finding ways to make programs more responsive."[43] Time referred to her as a 67-year-old spinster who gloried in the "often maligned name of bureaucrat." Mary Switzer's loyalty was and always had been to government, not to a professional group. That allegiance made her quite different from Ellen Winston and the majority of welfare workers.

Advisors who knew the welfare system and wanted Mary to succeed warned her of particularly sensitive subjects. For one thing, no social worker needed to be reminded of Mary's rehabilitation background. "You are 'Miss Rehabilitation' and need not stress that issue," came the advice.[44] Desist in blaming public assistance, it was only part of the problem and will not be the solution, she was told. It had been only a recent development that people receiving public assistance had any incentive, and still there were problems of day care, subsistence while being trained, and finding the right training. The problem is poverty, Mary's loyal critic pronounced.[45]

There simply seemed to be too many groups to appease and an intractable problem. A glance at the progression of organization charts leading to the formation of SRS foretold difficulty in uniting this new agency. Three Administrations had been abolished, and two new ones were created in the reorganization. The Children's Bureau was known for the personal relationships which had kept it intact since 1912.[46] Mary Switzer remembered the pain of its transfer to the Federal Security Agency in 1946 and realized how thick the links of loyalty to Martha Eliot and Kay Oettinger were.[47] The antipathy for a prior rival program advocate was as strong from this quarter as it was from anyone formerly associated with the Welfare Administration. Abolition did not lead to an easy coalition within SRS.

Mary Switzer expected reluctance, although she preached dedication. She also prided herself on having predicted the collision of affluence and poverty long before becoming Administrator of SRS.[48]

Like her ideal, Eleanor Roosevelt, Mary Switzer made sure she visited poor people to hear their problems firsthand. The "practical solace" of an Eleanor Roosevelt seemed directly applicable to the present. Being a "beacon of hope" was what Mary Switzer aspired to be in 1967, as Mrs. Roosevelt had been to NYA workers in 1939.[49] In the "little informal meetings" Mary scheduled around the country with ghetto women, she found a serious condition: welfare workers were communicating rejection, not caring. While VR personnel were accustomed to Mary's memos, reminding them of program or personnel failures, workers in the new Assistance Payments Administration and Medical Services Administration were not. Without this control mechanism, Mary was limited in her influence.

It was ironic that Mary's longing for an opportunity to improve the delivery of medical care in the United States was realized in 1967. She had seen the possibilities twenty years before, only to see plans for national health insurance rejected. At long last she now would administer Medicaid, a program of medical assistance to needy persons.

Although it had been twenty years since she worked with the procurement and assignment of physicians, Mary had tended her ties to the medical establishment. She knew them well, and she also knew that poverty was one patient disability most physicians tried to avoid.

> ... the most disadvantaged are not attractive patients. They do not think as a physician thinks. They don't take responsibilities that he thinks they should. They stink. They are not a good advertisement in the waiting room. They don't follow up. They don't have the money to buy their medicine... How do we get physicians to give comprehensive and goal oriented care to these bottom of the barrel persons widely regarded as relatively undesirables?[50]

Mary had distinguished herself from experts in public welfare by saying she was an expert in making programs more responsive. A reporter had called SRS an "acid test." Problems of poverty and problems with personnel combined to make a severe test. The size of Mary's task also constituted a problem. With 1900 employees she was responsible for aiding 7,600,000 (4% of the population in 1967) who received welfare payments; 6,000,000 needy who received medical services through Medicaid; 600,000 children needing adoption or foster care, 450,000 handicapped children receiving special medical services; more than 250,000 birth control recipients, and millions of elderly citizens.[51] To this, Mary Switzer was to bring administrative efficiency and to deliver speedily an increasing range of essential services to people in need.[52]

Civil rights and welfare rights movements were affecting the numbers of persons receiving assistance. As poor people were advised of their rights, more applied for aid, and the numbers increased. Illegitimacy rates continued to rise, and with them the number of illegitimate children receiving AFDC aid. The trajectory of poverty, social injustice, poor housing, and inadequate health care called for more than reorganization, but Mary Switzer had taken the job.[53]

She prescribed the only valid and reliable remedy she knew: rehabilitation. Improvements in assistance would be accompanied by a major effort to rehabilitate public assistance recipients through work experience and training projects that also provided adult basic education, medical assistance, and day care for children. A second major effort would be concentrated on reducing illegitimacy and improving family planning. Finally, Mary Switzer wanted to change the public image of people living in poverty. The reasons people needed assistance were important: four out of seven needed help because they were aged, blind, disabled, or because the father had died or was disabled. Seven out of ten children were not illegitimate. Mary Switzer thought citizens could only feel comfortable about the expenditures for SRS services when

Switzer and Wilbur Cohen meet with Hosea Williams and the Southern Christian Leadership Conference, 1968. (Courtesy Wilbur Cohen.)

job training and opportunities for becoming self-supporting were a vital component of all public welfare programs.[54]

No one underestimated the enormity of the problem SRS had been created to solve, least of all Mary Switzer, but no one could have predicted John Gardner's sudden resignation at the end of December 1967. His tenure had been longer than the average Secretary of Health, Education, and Welfare (2.2 years),[55] but the loss to Mary Switzer and her dreams was substantial. Wilbur Cohen supported her in every way for the year he served as Secretary, but the philosopher-spokesman was missed.

Historians write of 1968 as a year of "unprecedented violence and turmoil," and this was Mary Switzer's first year as Administrator of SRS. On the afternoon of the day Martin Luther King was killed, Mary stayed in her office to sign papers, although the guards asked her to leave.[56] Mary had seen Resurrection City, she had spoken with representatives from the Poor People's Campaign, and she seemed unafraid of any physical danger.

> How pleased we all are to be so comfortable within our own private shells of material comforts! I wish you could see in reality how things are at Resurrection City. No TV camera can portray what the eye sees when one passes by--a mass of humanity, mud make-shift homes, and terribly inadequate facilities for cooking and bathing.
>
> However remote the Poor People's Campaign may seem, it is as close to your doorstep as it is to mine. They are our neighbors. And I hope you can sense their plight as I feel their presence--in our camp, in my office, in our Department's cafeteria or auditorium.[57]

It was Mary Switzer who accompanied Wilbur Cohen to the HEW Auditorium for a meeting with the Southern Christian Leadership Conference.[58] From Resurrection City, the poor marched into the Department hallways, chanting, "We want Cohen, we want Cohen." Declaring they would stay all day and all night until they saw "the head," Hosea Williams suggested the crowd "take a tour of the building, to run their bare feet through some of those thick carpets."[59]

Suddenly Cohen appeared with Mary Switzer, saying welcome, but could they please give a little notice before their next visit. The appeasement process began, supported by a 34 page response to the group's demands. The crowd left, some feeling satisfied with their confrontation of Brother Cohen. In photographs of that exchange, Mary Switzer appears earnest, but relaxed. Taking on the burdens of the poor meant making the government less foreign. It was a day when soul met soul in an auditorium where, moments earlier, even cameramen had been afraid to stay.[60]

Mary believed that government was still the most powerful instrument to harness the country's resources, so that Martin Luther King's dream could come true. "I am concerned with our responsibility and our commitment for helping the poor, the deprived, the disabled, the hopeless, to move from the road down, onto the road back."[61] SRS was "Mr. Gardner's dream" in Mary Switzer's mind, the injection of rehabilitation philosophy to break the cycle of dependency. She had been in Washington and seen social changes occur without provision to head off problems.

> We have not been wise enough to establish the right training programs at the right times... to open up avenues of work... to see the effects of rejection and failure... to enforce Civil Rights... to have equal justice before the law... to recognize what has been happening in our cities.[62]

The violence of 1968 seemed the inheritance of the years of denial, and Mary Switzer and her fledgling agency were caught in the vortex.

Less than a year after being called in to correct the problems of dependency, Mary Switzer knew how difficult that would be. "It is very obvious that responsibility is so divided that no agency can tackle a problem with any hope of really achieving a meaningful solution," she confided to the Assistant Secretary. She pled for a small, capable organization, something like the Council of Economic Advisors, to focus on "our social ills."[63]

On the anniversary of the creation of the Social and Rehabilitation Services, Mary asked if SRS had spoken to or with the people. Had they dominated or shared the decision making process? And she made a birthday promise. There would be greater emphasis on the airing of opinions and the participation of staff.[64]

Criticism for not soliciting advice hurt. On the morning of the anniversary party, which was held in the North Building Auditorium,[65] Mary rose early and wrote personal notes to persons who had supported her during the past year.[66] Their loyalty touched her, in the midst of overwhelming problems.[67]

Time was running out for Mary Switzer to make real John Gardner's dream. College-aged youth were mesmerized by Eugene McCarthy's call for a shift in foreign policy. On March 31, Lyndon Johnson announced that he would not seek a second term as President. The battle for the Democratic nomination that ensued between McCarthy and Robert Kennedy was ended on June 5th by an assassin. The violence seemed to have no end, and the Democratic convention in Chicago became an anti-war demonstration as well as a shattering of party unity. Hubert Humphrey emerged as the Democratic nominee, struggling to free himself from Johnson policies on Vietnam. Richard Nixon stressed his "new policies" to end the war and cast Humphrey as an "uncompromising defender of the Johnson Administration." When the votes were counted in November, Nixon had won a clear majority, and some saw his election as the "death knell of New Deal-Fair Deal-New Frontier-Great Society liberalism."[68]

Wryly, Wilbur Cohen described the effect of the election upon his professional career: "I was involuntarily retired from my position. And it's no secret that I wasn't particularly happy about it at the time... I look back on the position as the high point of my professional experience." Cohen had loved the job. "A splendidly rich and gratifying stewardship," he called it. He had been the seventh Secretary of Health, Education, and Welfare, and he served the shortest period, less than a year. "The clock ticks fast in the United States--and at the Department of Health, Education, and Welfare," he said.[69] Too fast for Wilbur Cohen. On January 22, 1969, Robert Finch was sworn in as the eighth Secretary of Health, Education, and Welfare.

"There is much we have done in the last eight years; there is much yet to be done" wrote Wilbur Cohen in his transmittal letter of the Department's Annual Report to Lyndon Johnson. Lyndon Johnson told his Cabinet members that they could be proud of the record of new programs and policy. "We have had five wonderful and productive years," Johnson said.[70] But what was to come? Accustomed to the uncertainty of new administrations, Mary Switzer listened intently to Nixon's Inaugural address for some hint of his direction. The keynote seemed to be the recruitment of volunteers, with HEW being "the place where the action is." Nixon had stated that "we are approaching the limits of what Government alone can do. Our greatest need now is to reach beyond Government to enlist the legions of the concerned and the committed." There was nothing new about that in Mary Switzer's mind; Vocational Rehabilitation had been enlisting the concerned and committed for 50 years. She was relieved that there was no dismantling of the SRS program suggested, or another reorganization.[71]

As with every change of administration, Mary Switzer knew her position was in jeopardy. The difference was that this time she was 69 years old, due to retire in February of 1970, unless the Secretary asked her to stay.

She had hardly had a fair chance to rescue public assistance from the derision of the public through the application of rehabilitation philosophy. It had been difficult to explain to the new administration what the Social and Rehabilitation Service was "all about." Being the devoted bureaucrat, Mary expected slowed progress during this "time of change."

> When any new Administration comes into Washington, and especially into a large Department like ours, it's an opportunity for good things and bad things to happen. And people who are there and remain have a tremendous responsibility for trying to sort out . . . the things that they feel are most important so that their emphasis and their energy and talent can be devoted to pushing that because you can't push everything at once in a changing time.[72]

She was "bearing the bureaucratic burden" now, after having been "preoccupied" with the administrative problems of the Public Welfare Amendments of 1967 for more than a year. Devising new ways of delivering services had suffered from the necessity to clean house, but Mary was proud of the fact that resources were growing in centers where the poorest people lived.

There had been a rush of activity to make the most of the legislation while Democrats were still in office. Between the election and the Inauguration, the speeding up of effort to respond to the Welfare Rights organization had run afoul of some of the state administrators of Public Welfare programs. They had been caught between taxpayer revolt and Welfare rights' demands, leading state legislatures to "hold Federal money like a gun to our chest."[73]

Mary Switzer had looked down both barrels of state welfare systems' demands. The Social Security Amendments of 1967 contained a provision which was called the AFDC freeze. On July 1, 1968, Federal financial participation was limited in each state to a certain number of children under the age of 18 who were eligible for AFDC. The number was determined by the average of children receiving AFDC during a three month period early in 1968. The state agency in Georgia promptly retaliated by amending its AFDC plan and forming waiting lists for children affected by the freeze. Mary Switzer informed the agency that they had violated the principle of equitable treatment required for public assistance programs, and that she would not approve Georgia's AFDC plan, curtailing any Federal participation. Hearings were held, at which Mary Switzer presided. Welfare Rights organizations and Legal Aid Society representatives were allowed to testify.[74] For the organization woman who had cherished the maxim: "First, let's kill all the lawyers,"[75] this was a duel she did not care to repeat.

The attention of the new administration was directed toward the solution of the Public Welfare problem, the most dramatic within SRS. Mary thought this typical of new administrations. There had been a change, however, in the past two years. Until then welfare was thought of as a small charity. Now it was a tremendous social problem, involving millions of people needing to develop their own centers of power. Mary Switzer had been in the middle of the fray and had little respect for "planners" who had not heard the individual complaints of welfare recipients. And, although she was critical of the "administrative peculiarities and anachronisms of the Welfare System," she was also sympathetic to the stress state or city welfare administrators experienced. "They really are on the firing line in a degree that no other administrator in the country is." "This is the real hot spot of government today, because there is no answer to it."[76]

Mary had been with Secretary Finch when he spoke with a welfare mother, just after he took office. "If you could only make us feel that you think we can be decent and are decent," the woman had said. As Mary Switzer listened to complaints, the gap between administrators of Public Welfare and recipients was apparent. "People in this business have to remember they are holding the destiny of human beings in their hands," thought Mary.[77]

It was not only Public Welfare Administrators whose sensitivity she questioned. On June 24, 1969, the National Citizens' Conference on Rehabilitation of the Disabled and Disadvantaged was held at the Mayflower Hotel in Washington. The Conference had been discussed since 1966 and was seen as a positive way to emphasize the Committee's findings.[78] But 1967 brought change for the Vocational Rehabilitation Administration. Mary Switzer became Director of the Social and Rehabilitation Services, and suddenly the focus of the long awaited conference changed to include social and economic disabilities and a vital role for consumers.

The National Citizens' Advisory Committee served as "secretariat" for the Conference; sixty planning groups from public, private, and consumer sectors labored and brought forth a conference of "different character."[79] The only similarity between this and former conferences was the dignitary configuration. Howard Rusk was general chairman, Mary Switzer and Scott Allan co-chairmen. No speeches were scheduled, instead dramatic presentations and films were used to portray the needs of disabled and disadvantaged groups. Small discussion groups followed.[80]

Seven hundred persons attended this conference that almost did not happen. It had been written out of the Department's budget for 1969. Mary Switzer looked around and found the legal authority to fund the proposed conference through a Vocational Rehabilitation expansion grant, and the show began.[81]

Mary Switzer expected a great deal of her rehabilitation constituency; she had advertised them as "caring" and the rehabilitation process as applicable to problems of poverty. What became obvious during the Conference was that minority participants knew little about rehabilitation and that many rehabilitation professionals were being exposed for the first time to the language and bitterness of minority groups. Some of the SRS Regional Commissioners valued the initiation, others were offended. "I was greatly disappointed that the concept of rehabilitation was not set forth during the Conference, nor was it defended when participants spoke in opposition to the rehabilitation concept," said one participant.[82] "I believe we can find people who will tell it like it is, people who will call us to task and make us reconsider our objectives, without the obscenity and vulgarity and without the belligerency that alienates rather than illuminates," said another.[83] "I would not recommend a Conference of this type in my Region. Too much militancy," was yet another evaluation.[84]

For some, the opportunity to see and hear firsthand what was happening in the country was valued. Breaking from the old mold and feeling unsettled in the process was a small price to pay for the experience.

> I believe the group that needs this kind of horizon lifting most strongly is our own people in rehabilitation. There is still the strong desire to cling to traditional ways and to continue to select clients with whom our predominantly white middle class counselors feel most comfortable.[85]

Much as Mary would have liked VR to lead the way to consumer participation and counselor compassion, the outcome of the Conference made that possibility less likely. To discover that "needless and thoughtless disregard to the sensibilities of the assistance applicant or client" was not confined to welfare workers and existed among her top level staff was a cruel awakening.[86]

Mary's observations of some SRS Regional Commissioners' reactions to the Conference caused her additional concern during that same week at a

Camp David meeting with Secretary Finch and other top-level HEW staff. The recommendation to decentralize authority had come from Finch, on the heels of Mary's having seen evidence of negative attitudes from Regional Commissioners toward disadvantaged persons. And these were the persons whose authority Finch planned to expand. "Along with decentralization of authority must go the selection of regional staff capable of exercising these authorities," Mary reminded the Secretary.[87]

Mary had ridden to Camp David with Finch and the Undersecretary. The wooing process that had preserved her job many times before had run aground. She had had little opportunity to talk with Secretary Finch since he took office, and on the way to the meeting "pending matters were settled."[88] Although Mary Switzer was known for her never-say-die attitude, this time she was beaten. None of the support she had been able to garner netted her retention as Administrator of Social and Rehabilitation Services. When February 1970 arrived, she would be retired and replaced by a Republican appointee, John Twiname. There seemed to be nothing even Howard Rusk could do. Old friends like Claude Pepper had also tried to help, but unsuccessfully.[89]

She just was not ready to retire yet. There was much left to be done. So little progress had been made in providing social services, to organize communities to spend money while appropriations were open-ended and their investment could be recovered from Federal funds. There was the push to meet manpower problems through undergraduate training. The improvement of university-affiliated centers in the mental retardation program was something she longed to undertake.[90]

Some objectives had been almost untouched in Mary's brief administration of SRS. Other unfinished business caused her equal regret. The Children's Bureau had been a sore point from the moment it was transferred into Social and Rehabilitation Services. Martha May Eliot resented the splitting of Crippled Children's Service from maternal and child health and accused Mary Switzer of the dirty deed, when she "brought about her organization of the program."[91]

Bad blood between SRS and the Children's Bureau resulted in "ambiguous or nonexistent communication," and "low morale and interagency confusion" within the Children's Bureau. In January of 1969, Mary Switzer reported:

> *For 1 and ½ years I have been trying to introduce a priority into the Children's Bureau concern for children: to help the poor... We have been less successful than we would have been if the Children's Bureau had fully cooperated... The problem is philosophy, structure and people, particularly those in the top spots of the Children's Bureau.*[92]

Mary thought her problems with the Children's Bureau revolved around the fact that she was not a professional. "The Children's Bureau is one of those organizations that has a great sense of its own destiny... they get very upstage when you tell them they have neglected poor children."[93]

Everything seemed to be falling apart that August. On August 1, 1969, the Children's Bureau was transferred to the Office of the Secretary, where it became part of the newly created office of Child Development. The categorical nail was quickly used to split the Social and Rehabilitation Services Mary Switzer, John Gardner, and Wilbur Cohen had tried to reinforce.

As if the keystone had been removed, more props fell. Joe Hunt resigned as Commissioner of Rehabilitation Services Administration in October of 1969.[94] For the first time, VR was headed by an appointee who had not come from the career government service ranks. On December 7, 1969, the last of Howard Rusk's columns appeared in The New York Times.[95] It was no accident that Pearl Harbor day was his finale; the first column had appeared on December 7, 1945. Although Dr. Rusk wrote in an optimistic tone, saying the benefits of rehabilitation had been achieved, for Mary Switzer it was a sad passing of an era. The atmosphere in her office had been tense for months. Hearings on the Family Assistance Act had been difficult; "simply being able to sell your program does not go as far as it used to," she told Central Office staff. Everything seemed "up in the air."[96]

By December 17, 1969, when Robert Finch announced he was accepting Mary Switzer's resignation "with regret," her family and close friends had known for months that Mary had lost her final, and most personal lobbying effort. Mary Switzer held her own press conference on that same afternoon. The reporter described Mary as "gray-haired and sparkling eyed" as she talked about her 48 years of government service.[97]

About the present, Mary had no public sour grapes, only reminders of what she would like to see happen in SRS. The merging of services for the individual at the local level required interaction of bureaus. "Health and welfare deal mainly with institutions. And sometimes the institutionalized structure stops before they ever see a person. SRS reaches down to the individual."[98] There had been no change in Mary Switzer's belief that the government provides the glue to put services together.

The Poor Peoples' March had been the "greatest eye opener" of the difficulty involved in getting something done at the local level. Mentioning that she was active in Alexandria community affairs, Mary warned: "It's essential when you have a job like mine, where you are telling people what to do in the communities, to do it yourself and find out how difficult it really is." There was just one derisive note in the virtuoso performance. "In the Rehabilitation Administration, I had every letter of complaint followed up immediately. Now I've adopted that program in welfare, but I've found the welfare people are not as responsive. I suppose after years in the field they become kind of tough."[99]

Some of Mary's supporters thought her dream had been sabotaged by the "welfare people."[100] Others thought her VR staff had let her down.[101] SRS Regional Commissioners who had come from the VR ranks pointed out the inconsistency of the Republicans' "flattening out finances for the program while pushing for more services."[102] Measuring the effect of rehabilitation leadership was premature for this reason, and because it often took more than a year to complete a rehabilitation plan.[103]

Mary Switzer had had less than two years to rehabilitate welfare. Short as the time was, and tardy as it might have been, it was the best opportunity that would come to glue together services to poor and disabled individuals. The post she held would never again be occupied by a career civil servant. Instead, political appointees rotated through the Administrator's office. Two layers of administrative continuity were abolished that fall of 1969: the Rehabilitation Services Administration, also, was never again directed by a bureaucrat with program loyalty. Politics subjugated the frail ideal of the Social and Rehabilitation Services and VR.

Mary Switzer thought the frustrations of 1969-70 to be the worst she had ever known. Budget problems, congressional intransigence, "all this flim-flam about money," the inability or unwillingness to make decisions, and the perpetual solving of problems by committees were coming together to make it difficult for an administrator, "even one who has had a great deal of success." [104]

Rufus Miles believed SRS had no chance from the start. The public expectation that those responsible for administering the AFDC program could stanch the growing tide of beneficiaries by getting people employed and self-reliant was unrealistic. There was an attitudinal difference between rehabilitation clients and the AFDC caseload: rehabilitation clients had learned the discipline of work and had confidence in themselves to do more than society expected of them; AFDC clients had the reverse situation, with society expecting more of them than they could produce. The result was psychological defeat. Miles reckoned that Mary Switzer's rescue operation would have had to have been launched at least a decade earlier to have any chance at success.[105]

Another scholar in governmental affairs, Martha Derthick, believed that the troubles SRS encountered were due to Mary Switzer's administrative style. VR was accustomed to a much more casual approach to regulation, giving brief and general guidelines to the states and trusting state directors' discretion. Public assistance, on the other hand, had a greater volume of expenditures with no statutory limit, and the administrative style for decades had been highly regulatory. Mary Switzer's loose and free-wheeling approach did not suit public assistance, in its potential for fraud, waste, and abuse. It was a natural consequence, in Martha Derthick's analysis, that expenditures continued to climb for social services.[106]

Jim Garrett, defender of Mary Switzer's administrative style, insisted on defining regulation. "What welfare calls administrative oversight and control is just a lot of paper-checking." Although the state-Federal VR program might appear laissez-faire, Garrett pointed to program audits as well as fiscal audits as evidence of administrative control. If weaknesses were discovered in the program, a program analysis followed to determine what could be done to solve the problem. VR was checked programmatically; welfare was checked on expenditures, not whether people were getting the services.[107]

Other faithful hands in the VR program had their own opinions about the end of the Mary Switzer era. "One reason the VR program was so acceptable was that its cost was under a billion dollars. It had the charm of a little program," said Joe LaRocca,[108] who had known and worked with Mary Switzer since 1938. LaRocca thought Mary had been asked to do the impossible. Promising jobs to those who wanted to work depended upon the private sector to provide the jobs. The poverty in the United States during the 1960s was proof that a public works program was needed, but none had been constructed to anchor the rehabilitation philosophy being preached.

Sam Martz, Mary Switzer's budget expert, was a man of few words. His judgment was a one-liner. "No one can avoid hard questions with emotional answers anymore."[109] Mary's ability to extract money for VR had won the loyalty of that constituency in 1950. She, herself, had said a sales job was no longer sufficient, and her new constituencies in SRS were getting cut back, not prospering.

Perhaps each of the analysts spoke plainly and perceptively because they spoke from a distance of years. In the moment, Mary Switzer either had no such insights or chose to place no blame. She relished having the largest administrative responsibility of any woman in government. Relinquishing it was painful: she ignored her sister's urging to "beat the gun" and retire without being told to retire.[110] Her "great family" had made progress, she believed, and she had faith in them and the patience to see it unfold.

The February 28, 1970 issue of the SRS Newsletter was a memo from the staff to Mary Switzer. Their goodbye was pages filled with "personal glimpses of the Chief at work" and those who had worked with her. The photographs are largely unposed: Mary Switzer at her desk, eyeglasses in place, reaching for a pen to sign yet another document; Mary with her "reticule" and fur jacket, visiting a rehabilitation facility; Mary greeting a black dignitary with arms flung wide; Mary cuddling her cat "Snowshoes" in her den at home.[111]

A last message from Mary was the feature of the Newsletter. It began with Latin: Salve atque vale! Hail and farewell!

> The Social and Rehabilitation Service was created to revolutionize static, traditional and complacent programs which were not otherwise about to change their course. It is necessary to understand the drives of every decade to make them serve the ends for which one has a special mission.
>
> I feel strongly--very strongly--that during the past two and one half years, the SRS

family has, despite an overabundance of turmoil, come to understand itself and its members much better. But we must continue to break the barriers of fear of differences. . . The most tragic development of the 70s for the disabled, the aged, the poor, and our children would be if their government failed them.

The name 'Social and Rehabilitation Service' was not chosen whimsically. It was chosen to provide a goal toward which we could struggle. . . We must resolve to shoulder the onerous tasks ahead. . .to make real for all our programs the rehabilitation philosophy.[112]

Switzer with six Secretaries of the Department of Health, Education and Welfare, February 24, 1970. *from the left*: Wilbur Cohen, Marion Folsom, John Gardner, Mary Switzer, Robert Finch, Abraham Ribicoff, Anthony Celebrezze. (*Courtesy Richard Switzer.*)

XVI
The Wind at Her Back
1970-1971

It is not what you have lost that matters, but what you have left that counts.

Mary Elizabeth Switzer

It began with a serenade from an audience of over a thousand. At the Sheraton Park Hotel six Secretaries of Health, Education and Welfare gathered at the head table. Mary Switzer's successor was to be sorely tested as Master of Ceremonies for her Retirement Dinner, for this was designed to be a world class celebration.

On February 16, 1970, Mary reached compulsory retirement age. Hoping President Nixon would make an exception and ask her to stay on as Administrator of the Social and Rehabilitation Services, Mary had made every effort to avert this evening commemorating her retirement.[1] This time no amount of persuasion rescued her. Mary was determined to bow out with as much grace and style as possible, and the Nixon administration was obliged to supply the fanfare.

Invitations embossed with the seal of the Department of Health, Education, and Welfare were issued by Secretary and Mrs. Finch. The banquet was carefully planned. For two women who served meals of typically small portions in their home,[2] the menu Isabelle Diamond and Mary Switzer chose was sumptuous. A healthy slab of roast beef and an ice cream bombe awaited guests who had paid $15 to be at the event. If she was leaving, Mary Switzer wanted to be sure the send-off was fitting. Seating charts had been carefully prepared, dignitaries had been invited. While Nixon himself was not present due to a state visit of French President Pompidou, the response to invitations had been overwhelming.

Despite the bitter cause for the retirement dinner, the tone of the evening was very like a family reunion to honor its most illustrious member. Mother Bernadette DeLourdes repealed some rancor with the Irish blessing she used in the invocation:

> May the road rise up to meet you,
> May the wind be always at your back,
> May the sun shine warm upon your face,
>   the rains fall soft upon your fields and,
>   until we meet again,
>   May God hold you in the palm of his Hand.

John Twiname,[3] the Nixon appointee who had been Mary Switzer's understudy for the past six months, began by mentioning his early skepticism at being asked to come to Washington to "report to a woman." Leaving a lucrative business for such an assignment had seemed onerous indeed, but Twiname stated that Mary Switzer soon made him "captive to her cause."

Twiname, as the new Administrator, dutifully pointed out the section for deaf guests who would need to be able to see the interpreters, and called attention to the Brailled programs. Then he turned to introductions of those seated at the Head Table. Six former Secretaries of HEW were introduced, as well as Reverend Jack Greenawalt of Union Theological Seminary, an old friend whose program, "Religion and Psychiatry," Mary had helped found. Helen Dunn, the rehabilitant of the year, retired from life because of blindness and restored to work as a masseuse through rehabilitation services, was seated among the Secretaries. And Howard Rusk, whom Isabelle Diamond called "Mr. Rehabilitation," was there between the Twinames, ready to speak later in the program. Only one person in the audience was recognized in Twiname's introduction: Isabella Diamond. John Twiname pointed out Mary's companion and friend of almost a lifetime, seated just in front of the Head Table. Acknowledging the intimacy and humor of Isabella's and Mary's relationship before a gathering of this size was an unusual action. John Twiname shifted quickly into the introduction of Mary's favorite forms of entertainment: the Federal budget, and barbershop quartets. The "Federal City Four" kept the mood light with "Ain't She Sweet" and "She's Got the Whole World in Her Hands."

Then the roll call of Secretaries began, and their personalities and experience of Mary Switzer were clear to all. Mary herself, and a very few others, knew of incidents that were not recounted that evening, but came rushing back with the voice and presence of each former Secretary.

Oveta Culp Hobby was unable to attend, but sent a telegram saying no one had done as much as Mary in rebuilding human bodies and human hopes, nor was so genuinely admired. As Mary and Howard Rusk listened, they must have remembered 1953 when Mrs. Hobby had been told Mary must go as Director of the Office of Vocational Rehabilitation. Nixon had someone from California in mind for the job. Only Howard Rusk's intervention with Eisenhower's personal physician and key legislators had saved Mary's job.[4] Mary credited Mrs. Hobby with the creation of the Department of Health, Education, and Welfare and viewed her as the hardest worker of all her "bosses."[5] Their correspondence had continued over the years, with Mary thanking Mrs. Hobby for teaching her the will to delegate.

Secretary Folsom, distinguished by his white hair and smile, was introduced by John Twiname as having helped draft the original Social Security Act. Marion Folsom described the special bond that existed between "Treasury Alumni" and pointed to Mary's skill with budgets as an outcome of her years at the Treasury. The same benevolence conveyed by his voice and demeanor was present in 1958, when Mary expressed her sadness at his leaving. He had communicated security to his staff, and although he seemed uncomfortable with women executives, he was always supportive of her.[6] Mary was clearly delighted by his presence at her retirement dinner.

Although Arthur Flemming was not present at the dinner, his telegram contained a plaudit that was later frequently quoted: "Mary Switzer places in any list of the ten public servants who have done most for our country."

Abraham Ribicoff spoke warmly of Mary, referring to "his day" when Mary's "empire" was not so extensive as today. Ribicoff told, in masterful style, the story of Kennedy's order to hold the budget line and the assurance he received from his staff that a modest increase for Vocational Rehabilitation would satisfy Mary. "Some advice!" Ribicoff snorted, "It's like playing golf with Spiro Agnew: Look the other way and she'll take your head off! By the time she got finished with me, she got what she wanted, and HEW got a $4.65 increase." Ribicoff stated the First Rule of the Budget: Whatever Mary wants, Mary gets.

The voice and debonair manner of Secretary Ribicoff was little changed from the impression Mary had of him after several months of working under his direction. Mary wrote her staff:

> He is very different from any Secretary we have had--handsome, composed, and direct. He talked only about legislation and wanted only the simplest and bearest (sic) presentation with our recommendations and the price tags.[7]

As Mary listened to Abraham Ribicoff recall a quotation she had used, the memories of difficult days amplified Victor Hugo's words: "Greater than the tread of mighty armies is an idea whose time has come."[8] Ribicoff ended by praising the idea of rehabilitation and the woman who knew how to get things done.

Anthony Celebreeze stood next at the podium, his voice as solid as his grip on the edge of the wooden stand. Mary sat to his left, leaning on her elbows, with her hands folded against her chin. She seemed to listen intently as Celebreeze added his account of being "Mary's boss."

> I had a habit when I went on a new job to get someone to tell me about key people. They said about Mary: 'Let her think she's out-smarting you.' So I went on for two years and

finally came to the realization that she was out-smarting me. She came in and wanted more funds. I said, 'Mary, I can't do that; the President's putting the lights out at the White House to save money.' Mary paused just a moment and said, 'Mr. Secretary, did anyone ever tell you you look like Pope John?'

The dinner guests laughed loudly, showing their familiarity with Mary's wooing procedures. When the group quieted, Celebreeze confessed his reply: "Mary, the lights just went on again." Then the former Secretary turned to Mary and said: "So long as Mary lives, she'll be turning on lights for people." The affection was real and shared.

Then a tanned, handsome John Gardner stood, and Mary's hands moved to the same constrained position. The clear, strong voice began:

When I came to HEW I received advice about the cast of characters. The advice on Mary Switzer was misleading. I was told that Mary would be a source of considerable difficulty. She was strong-minded, knowing in the ways of bureaucracy, and I would have difficulty. It is true that she is rugged and knows the 'Cambodian trails' of bureaucracy. But they forgot to tell me that she has the breath of life in her, that her warmth and spirit light the landscape around her. They forgot to tell me of her vibrant love of her work.

This nation needs Mary, needs her now more than at any other time. In the long perspective of history, nations rise and fall. Historians write their epitaphs. The epitaph I don't want a historian to have the right to say about this country is that we were a potentially great people who forgot we were interdependent, forgot what we owed each other.

That's what Mary does, reminds us of the simple human truth that we need each other.

The audience was still, still as it had been throughout, except for an "Amen" flung from a corner of the room. Mary was also still and close to tears. The Secretary who called Vocational Rehabilitation his "Marine Corps" and had subsequently elevated its Director to the leadership of the Social and Rehabilitation Services had left office so quickly, before any of their mutual dreams had been realized. She also felt she was needed yet; how different things might have been if John Gardner had stayed.

The shift to the jaunty, feisty Wilbur Cohen seemed abrupt. A peak had been reached prematurely. Mary and her admirers were touched by Gardner's remarks. Suddenly they were jerked to the present by Cohen's insistent jabs at the Republican administration. It was an interlude lacking synchrony with the mood of the audience. Finally, the Secretary who appreciated Mary's career because of his own history, which began in Washington in 1934 with the preparation of the Social Security Act, moved to the temper of the moment: "You honor Mary Switzer tonight because she typifies many dedicated public servants in this Department; Mary, you are a great spirit and a great lady."

There was a break in the march of former Secretaries. Helen Dunn spoke of being one handicapped person who was just beginning to live because of Mary Switzer. David Hayes, Director of the Theatre of the Deaf, described the three companies of deaf players who were fully employed because the country wanted to see their talent--and because of Mary's ideas. President Kennedy's Inaugural Address, "I Have A Dream" was spoken and signed by two members of the Theatre of the Deaf. Fellow dreamer, Howard Rusk, announced scholarships for international rehabilitation that had been established in Mary's name. Unable to resist a quip, he complimented the audience for standing for each speaker, a boon to circulation and a demonstration of rehabilitation technique. Abruptly serious, Rusk predicted Mary's sentiments as being those of William Allen White's: "I am not afraid of tomorrow, I have known yesterday, and I have loved today." The wind seemed truly at Mary's back as she rose to introduce Nanette Fabray who would sing Mary's favorite song: "To Dream the Impossible Dream."

The small woman in the above-the-knee skirt filled the entire room with her voice. Once more, a crescendo was reached and followed by a Secretary dwarfed by the emotion created. Robert Finch resorted to humor and reference to the testimony of the evening about how Mary had "manipulated all the Secretaries." Then he bestowed upon Mary Switzer the flag of the Department of Health, Education, and Welfare, with the motto: "Hope, the Anchor of Life." Usually an honor reserved for Secretaries alone, this was a tangible tribute that touched Mary deeply. And finally, the floor was hers.

The Boston accent wrapped the audience in the particular charm that was Mary Switzer's. Holding her half glasses in her right hand, standing perfectly erect behind the well-used podium, Mary began: "Mr. Secretary... All Mr. Secretaries, I never wanted any flag but the Assistant Secretary's, and now I have the Department flag." The crowd laughed, understanding that Mary had never had the official title of Assistant Secretary, although her responsibilities and rank should have accorded her that honor. Chuckling, Mary turned toward Secretary Ribicoff: "I've done it again, haven't I?" Again, laughter. Then a long pause before her last address as Administrator of the Social and Rehabilitation Services.

"I feel very solemn and very touched... we would never have thought we'd see this, that day in the elevator coming down, did we Howard?" Her mind had traveled back to the day in 1950 when Oscar Ewing first suggested she direct the Office of Vocational Rehabilitation. Howard Rusk had been with her in the elevator where the idea was broached. Twenty years, yet many of the people in the room had traveled alongside Mary to reach this night. Some had watched many times as she pointed her toes carefully outward, having been taught as a child by Dominican nuns that this was essential in public address.[9] Untold orchid corsages and banquet fare lay behind this moment; she had earned "her night."

The evening had been like Mary herself—informality mixed with dignity, and now it moved on to Mary's description of herself and of her career. "In my position as propagandist, prodder, and designer of programs, I have been

Secretary Finch awards Mary Switzer
the Flag of the Department of Health, Education, and Welfare, 1970.
(Courtesy Richard Switzer.)

sustained by the hidden talents of special people for half a century." The woman who compartmentalized her life began to reveal the divisions of her heart and mind.

"A half a century seems a long time when you say it, and yet it doesn't seem long to me as I have lived it at all. And yet, day by day, added together, it is a long time." Turning to one of the tables before the rostrum, Mary spoke to the Switzer family, one of the "pillars of hidden talent" that had always supported her. For Anastasia, Mary's younger sister, it was precious notice to be singled out as a family member who had followed in her footsteps by her work with the mentally retarded in Connecticut. Although Mary did not name her, she had arranged the seating plan that accorded her a place of honor, equal to that of Isabella Diamond. A difficult balancing act, this bringing together of all the components of a lifetime, some competing, some complementary. But Mary was addressing each of the sectors with the diplomacy learned over that half-century. It was indeed a great performance.

Arthur, Mary's younger brother and twin of Anastasia, was seated at another table with his wife, May. May had been instrumental in re-establishing the family bonds. When Julius Switzer left Boston with eight year old Arthur, Mary and Anastasia did not see their brother again until he married May. And May had seen to it that Thanksgivings were spent in New York, reuniting the three Switzers at least once a year.[10] Arthur beamed with pride in his "big sister," while May sported an orchid as large as Mary's.

With May and Arthur sat Dick and Patty Switzer. Dick had been a favorite of Mary's, the youngest son of Arthur and May who was born with cerebral palsy. Mary had operated quietly in Dick's life, never providing any rehabilitation services, except referrals to surgeons for corrective procedures and offering counsel to Dick when he visited her in Washington. It was Dick that Mary also described as a member of her family who had followed in her footsteps. Now headmaster of a school for handicapped children, the large, lovable Dick glowed with the momentary spotlight. "And that's the Switzer family," signalled the audience that one category was complete; another was about to be introduced.

"Then I have my Alexandria family. You heard mentioned tonight Miss Isabella Diamond, my friend through all of these years, also a distinguished Treasury alumni, who has made her home with me almost ever since I came to Washington." At another table the now 79 year old Isabella sat proudly erect, dressed in red brocade and pearls, enjoying the tribute and remembering the trials. Mary remembered also, saying, "Without her staunch support, her perspective, and understanding of the frailties of Irishers who sometimes see themselves as bigger than they are, I probably would not be where I am today at all." Only a few in the audience knew how seriously Isabella believed what Mary said. Among close friends, Isabella would chide Mary for her lack of administrative skills. "She can't organize a thing at home; I have to do it all" had been Isabella's complaint.[11] But she had enjoyed participating in decisions Mary had made since 1950, when she had stood behind the new Director's chair for photographs on the day Mary took over the Office of Vocational Rehabilitation. Reflected power had been glorious for Isabella. Tonight was no exception.

The "Alexandria family" included Anna Parker, Mary and Isabella's housekeeper for 38 years. Anna sat at the table with Isabella, seeing those select friends of Mary's and Isabella's whom she had served at small dinners in a very different light.[12] Tonight she was being served and recognized by Mary as the person who sustained both Isabella and Mary.

Mary paused for a moment, then moved on to her "Office family," making plain that she meant the intimate family, not dignitaries or Bureau chiefs. Part of that family stretched back to Treasury days. Josephine Coe, retired since 1965, had begun work with Mary in 1933. Through thirty years, Jo Coe had seen little change in Mary. Quite simply, she saw Mary as having the brains and charm to keep people from fighting. Jo Coe listened to Mary's voice and observed that she could still talk someone into anything she wanted. The great persuader had needed someone as a confidante, and Jo Coe had kept her secrets well.[13] Mary included Jo Coe in her list of tributes as "a strong, staunch servant and inner talent in my life, ever since I first knew her."

Her current Office family was Frances Curtis, her secretary since 1951, who handled her files and travel plans. Frances knew how distressed Mary was that she was the last of the career civil servants to hold the position of Administrator of the Social and Rehabilitation Services, and that her request to have her retirement delayed had been refused by Nixon. Mary had fought battles for Fran in the past, battles that allowed Fran to demonstrate her competence despite her wheelchair.[14] Fran was particularly sad this night, for her loyalty and understanding of Mary caused her to sense the pain of the evening, through the panoply.

Missing from Mary's "Office Family" was Ann Verano, home sick with "the bug." Ann was the newest of Mary's secretaries and not the least submissive. Ann had walked off the job many times in frustration, only to be called several hours later by Mary, apologizing for whatever had transpired.[15] As the executive in charge of the management of the office, Ann had had little time to herself and her own career due to Mary's demands. Perhaps it was "the bug" that kept her away this night, or perhaps it was ambivalence toward the woman she respected, yet resented for claiming so much of her life.

Mary traveled quickly from the missing member of her "Office Family" to the final hidden talent, a pillar of support through her career.

> And then, as I look around and see how the past generation repeats itself in the present generation, and look back and think where I got my first start in really transferring from the Treasury to the human services, by way of the Public Health Service, I think of one who has been my counselor, advisor, teacher--Dr. Warren Draper.

Eighty-seven year old Dr. Draper sat with his daughter, Ann, watching the performance of this woman who seemed as vibrant at 70 as she had been at 32, with her hair braided around her head, enamored of the doctors in the Public Health Service. She had opened a door for him in 1948, starting a second career as John L. Lewis' right hand man in the UMW Hospital system. He had been her abiding link with medicine, an alliance that saved her job several times.[16] Warren Draper, with Isabella Diamond, was the only person in the ballroom that shared professional and personal depths with Mary Switzer.

Rounding out the accolades, and returning to the political, Mary swung to Henry and Ruth Morgenthau. "How strange life is, who would have dreamed, we would be celebrating together, the son of the man who gave me my first real chance in the Treasury." Full circle, and now onto what Mary made of her life.

> It's been a great career. I wish I could get across to people who wonder about the government, the great excitement I have had in every phase of my government life. I wish I could dramatize for people the thing that Eunice Shriver said in her telegram, that government can make a difference, and does make a difference, and will make a difference, if we give ourselves to its service. I am deeply grateful and happy to be able to think of the new Administrator in the person of John Twiname, because I think he has the touch.

The politician Mary gave way to the prodder Mary, as she added: "If I can only get him to go out and visit the projects, he will get the feeling of what it takes to make this program." The audience laughed. Mary was at it again, leaning on her successor to preserve her program. And then she gave a warning, drawn from her most recent and painful experience:

> Bureaucracy is a terrible thing unless you can tranlate it into service to people. All of the letters that I have received have emphasized this contribution that people think I have made, and I think I have made it, too. And that is: Never forget the individual at the end of the statistics. If you do, you are lost. And I hope and pray that our Department of Health, Education, and Welfare will never forget that they are in business to serve people. To serve them well and efficiently, but to remember the people, even if they have to be a little inefficient in doing it.

The gavel had been passed with sledgehammer force. Control of her program was no longer Mary's. John Twiname had been warned of the consequences of management by less than human objectives.

With the gavel went the gloves. The fighter relaxed, the tone of voice changed, Mary looked out over the audience to thank them for what was real, yet magic about this night.

> And, finally, I would like to repeat again the deep gratitude I have for this evening. From the very moment of Mother Bernadette's inspiring prayer to now, it has all been a life-giving and life-building experience for me, and I will carry it forward as a pillar in my own deep heart. And I do express to all of you the deepest gratitude I can possibly say.

Howard Rusk called the evening a "capstone of a lifetime of dedicated service to mankind" in his New York Times column.[17] Guests treasured the small paperweights inscribed with the seal of the Department of Health, Education, and Welfare which was given them. Each had left a message for Mary, written on stationery headed, "Mary Elizabeth Switzer, February 24, 1970," and bordered with her favorite saying: "Life is faith, and love, but most of all, hope."

It was a crowning moment in Mary Switzer's career. Isabella Diamond carefully collected each of the messages guests wrote and assembled a scrapbook for Mary. All the photographs of the evening were lovingly labeled, and a recording of the evening was preserved for all the "old troopers" who wanted a reminder of the celebration.

Meanwhile, Mary stepped off into her new ventures, as a private citizen. In her letter of resignation, addressed to Robert Finch, Mary had informed him that the Board of the World Rehabilitation Fund had elected her Vice-President.[18] Howard Rusk had once more come to Mary's rescue. She would not be retired to inactivity, instead, she had the new responsibility to open an office of the World Rehabilitation Fund in Washington.[19]

Now Mary Switzer could provide consultation to organizations who wanted to build stronger relationships with the Federal government, and she was in great demand. The American Society for Allied Health Professions provided her with an office at 1 Dupont Circle;[20] the National Association of Hearing and Speech Agencies asked her to be National Chairman of Better Hearing and Speech Month;[21] Gallaudet College named her to their Board of Directors.[22] Secretary Finch requested Mary's assistance on the Secretary's Committee to Study the Public Health Service Commission Corps.[23] She was as forceful and articulate as a private citizen as she had been a public administrator.

Her reputation in statecraft led to invitations to speak to young aspirants. On one occasion, a morning seminar for three young men sporting no little arrogance in their new knowledge, Mary's first words were: "Well, boys, when the revolution comes, we've got to be ready for it."[24] She had spent her life in readiness, always wishing to be part of the "passion of our time." She retold Martin Luther King's story of Rip Van Winkle, the man who slept through a revolution,[25] to urge young people to stay awake to fashion the revolution to their liking.

The three young men who had come to "disparage and ignore" knew nothing of the Radcliffe radical or the Irish revolutionary in Mary's past. In the course of the morning, however, she convinced the three that if all bureaucrats were like her, the world might yet be saved. And she made them feel that she liked them and understood how they felt. She had lost none of the "short-wave sixth sense" with which she communicated.[26]

But she was losing strength. Her knees had troubled her for years, sometimes causing her to use a wheelchair at work.²⁷ She had never felt so tired before. She missed her friend, Warren Draper. His death in March, following her retirement, had been sudden, and Sunday mornings seemed empty with out the telephone call she had come to expect from him.²⁸ Mary knew hundreds of physicians, but she rarely asked their help for her personal health problems.²⁹ One evening, Anna Parker heard the garage door opener whir and expected Miss Switzer to walk through the kitchen. When she did not appear, she went to the garage and found her slumped over the wheel of her car. "I'm just tired," she said.³⁰

Isabella thought a trip to Cape Cod to visit Anastasia would help. Together they flew to the Cape, where she needed a wheelchair and a makeshift lift to deplane. Anastasia and Helene Goepner, a friend who also lived on the Cape, were shocked at Mary's appearance.³¹ Still, Isabella was determined that this be a vacation like others they had spent. Mary made attempts to do the things she most loved on the Cape, cooking, reading, talking. But it was far from the visit Isabella envisioned. Instead, Isabella became ill, and Anastasia and Helene urged Mary to call Howard Rusk.

Her fellow conspirator in good deeds urged Mary to come to the New York University Medical Center, where he could involve himself in her treatment. Alone, Mary flew to New York, where a series of tests explained her weakness, vomiting, and weight loss. "Sweet hour, I have had tests I did not know existed!"

She had suspected that something was very wrong for months. Earlier, when someone who had not seen her for several months said, "I wish I knew your secret to losing weight," Mary had replied, "No, you don't."³² Howard Rusk explained to Isabella and Anastasia that Mary had "massive cancer" and that nothing could be done, except to make her comfortable.³³ He knew that Mary wanted to go home, so he dispatched a nurse to accompany her on flight back to Alexandria.

It was impossible for Isabella to accept what Mary had guessed. A neighbor, who was also a nurse, came into their home for almost two weeks, trying to care for Mary, while supporting Isabella in her determination that nothing had really changed. Anna cooked lamb again, and Mary carved. There was a brief reprieve from reality, but Mary was getting increasingly weak. Anastasia arrived and approached Isabella and Mary about rehospitalization. Mary agreed this was best, and the ambulance was called to take her to George Washington University Hospital.³⁴

The silent cancer had so weakened Mary that her final hospital stay was short. Anna came with her favorite foods. May and Arthur Switzer were called, and May bathed Mary every evening.³⁵ Isabella avoided the hospital, but finally focused on what was now impossible to avoid. When Mary died at 4 A.M. on October 16, 1971, Isabella had her obituary ready. There was little she could do for Mary at the hospital; Isabella made sure the public would remember properly.³⁶

"Mary wanted no funeral, she's going to be cremated," Isabella announced to Dick Switzer.[37] Mary, like her Uncle Mike, had thought of herself as a "renegade Catholic." Although there was no controversy over cremation at Mary's death, part of the family was offended that no wake was held. Isabella took charge, asking Dick Switzer to help her.[38]

Washington newspapers for Sunday, October 17th, carried long articles about Mary Switzer, "Ex-U.S. Welfare Official," and announced a memorial service to be held at Grace Episcopal Church in Alexandria. Rather than flowers, donations to the World Rehabilitation Fund and the National Rehabilitation Association were suggested.[39]

More than 700 people attended the Tuesday memorial service, where Isabella's touch showed. "Nothing lugubrious about it," said a friend.[40] The Episcopal Order for the Burial of the Dead was followed closely, with hymns chosen by Isabella. The only personal reference in the program followed her name and the dates, February 16, 1900 - October 16, 1971: "A distinguished civil servant who truly loved her neighbor."[41] The casket was closed; only Anastasia, Isabella, Anna Parker, Arthur, May and Dick Switzer, and Joe Hunt were present for the interment in Ivey Hill Cemetery, in a plot that reserved space for Isabella and Anastasia.[42]

The news of Mary Switzer's death was a shock to many. Only six days before her death she had sent a telegram to the National Rehabilitation Association Conference, saying, "Although I cannot be there with you this year, I am with you in heart and spirit. Keep up the good work."[43] She had been scheduled months before to be in Rome on October 16th for a meeting of the Executive Council of the International Society for Rehabilitation of the Disabled.[44]

Jim Burress was one of her friends surprised by her death. He was just introducing John Twiname at a national meeting of Parents of Retarded Children when a message was handed him, saying Mary was dead. The meeting was abruptly adjourned, and Jim hurried to inform others and get on to Washington.[45]

Mary's rehabilitation "family" wanted a memorial service of their own. Jim Burress arranged a service held in the HEW auditorium on October 21st, befitting "the prime architect of a workable rehabilitation service."[46] The Overbrook School for the Blind Chorus sang Mozart's "The Gloria" and Schubert's "Omnipotence." Secretary of HEW, Elliot Richardson spoke of the woman who made a difference. Robert Smithdas from the National Center for the Deaf-Blind was introduced by Ed Newman, Commissioner of the Rehabilitation Services Administration. Mary Switzer herself was present as speaker in a film where she described rehabilitation. All the "little people" were represented by James Downer, an aide who said he and other lower grade workers would miss the mutual respect she evidenced. A message from Howard Rusk was read by John Twiname. Gallaudet College's Dance Group performed "The Lord's Prayer."⁴⁷

The memorial services expanded to memorials almost immediately. Jack Taylor, Mary's friend and advisor for years, directed the acknowledgement of contributions that flowed to the World Rehabilitation Fund. He had visited her every afternoon when she was at the New York University Medical Center; now he continued to correspond with Isabella, forwarding "eloquent quotations and expressions of devotion to Mary."⁴⁸ On November 15th, he had directed a memorial tribute for the New York City Chapter of the National Rehabilitation Association at the New York University Medical Center. Governor Nelson Rockefeller had asked to speak, remembering days of being Undersecretary of HEW when Oveta Culp Hobby was the first Secretary. It seemed Howard Rusk was right; hundreds of persons considered Mary one of their closest friends.⁴⁹

Mary had been born and had died on the 16th of the month. That coincidence was repeated on January 16, 1973. On that chilly day, the first Federal building to be named for a woman civil servant was dedicated. Once more, Mother Bernadette D'Lourdes offered an opening prayer, repeating the Irish blessing from the retirement dinner of 1970. Elliot Richardson expressed his hope that the Mary E. Switzer Memorial Building would "forever continue to focus the conscience and understanding of all Americans on the illumination of the dark silhouette of disabled persons."⁵⁰

Congress had voted to name this building for Mary Switzer. Hubert Humphrey had introduced a bill on December 3, 1971 "to pay lasting and appropriate tribute to one of the great women of our Nation."⁵¹. On December 15, 1971, John Brademas had introduced Humphrey's bill to the house, saying "the name of Mary Switzer stands for dedicated service to human beings;" the "extraordinary service" merited approval of the bill.⁵²

It was not a particularly impressive building Congress voted to dedicate to Mary Switzer's memory. As John Twiname said, it was only five stories high, "too small to stand beside the towering achievements of her career in public service."⁵³ Still, it was a model of how existing buildings could be modified, and it was adorned for this dedication day with a speaker's platform shielded with an awning, and flanked by the Joint Armed Forces Color Team and the United States Marine Band. John Twiname recalled the informal name first given the HEW South Building, "Switzerland." The formality of the dedication only made public what its occupants knew. This was the house that Mary built.

The platform was shared by dignitaries, old friends and family. Anastasia represented the family, leaning over the podium as Mary might have, and urging the audience to "keep the show on the road."

A plaque was unveiled by Elliot Richardson, which would be placed on the side of the building. Isabella sat at the rear of the platform, near Howard Rusk. Shortly after Mary's death, she had written Howard Rusk, saying she would think of Mary as by her side always; she had not been cancelled out by death.[54] She had asked an old friend, Lee Johnson, to share this day with her. Mary's room had been kept as she had left it, and Lee had stayed overnight there.[55] What Isabella missed most was the talk from "sun-up to sun-down," the mutual enjoyment she and Mary had found in their shared lives. Her position on a public platform was of much less consequence.

Isabella was often described as a woman of iron, and her life after Mary's death seemed to reflect her determination. She continued her usual routine, lunching at the National Democratic Club, occasional trips to Cape Cod to visit Anastasia. She shook her head over changes in the rehabilitation program and vowed Mary Switzer would not be forgotten.

Isabella had not only been named executor of Mary's will, she also assumed the informal role of executor of her memorials. Although Mary had agreed to have her official papers included in the Schlesinger Library at Radcliffe, she realized it was no place to house the plaques, figurines, paperweights, gavels, and framed letters that had once decorated her office. Before she died, Mary made a decision to keep such evidence of her accomplishments intact. Isabella Diamond was instrumental in seeing that her intent was followed.

Corbett Reedy, now Deputy Commissioner of Vocational Rehabilitation, had talked with Mary frequently after her retirement as Administrator of the Social and Rehabilitation Services. He proposed a solution. Why not create archives at the Woodrow Wilson Center? Rehabilitation workers who came to see the Center could also visit Switzer's Archives. It took a comparable action by the State of Virginia to found the Mary E. Switzer Building for Clinical and Professional Services at Fishersville.[56] Mary Switzer never saw the paneled room where the flag of HEW that she was given hangs, her seventeen honorary doctorates are displayed, nor her 116 awards exhibited. Isabella Diamond supervised the packing and unpacking of all, including the original Grandma Moses painting that Allen Eaton had given them.[57]

For Isabella, a Bryn Mawr graduate who never believed Radcliffe paid sufficient homage to Mary Switzer, the dedication of the Mary Switzer Building on May 30, 1973 was particularly satisfying. Let Radcliffe and the Schlesinger Library have Mary's official papers; Woodrow Wilson would house her distinctions. Although she engineered the near-shrine, Isabella was not scheduled to speak at the Dedication ceremony. Again, Anastasia made a few remarks, and Henry Viscardi filled in for Elliot Richarson.[58] Only the faithful rehabilitation worker would travel to the southwest corner of Virginia to see the Center Mary Switzer had helped establish, but each would be rewarded with an understanding of why Mary Switzer was called "the most honored woman in America."

Isabella had her favorite memorials, contributing directly to those she preferred. Warren Perry was a special friend to both Isabella and Mary. His association with the American Society of Allied Health Professionals had led to Mary's post-retirement job at 1 Dupont Circle. The membership of the Society had approved the establishment of the Mary E. Switzer Memorial Lectures on November 3, 1971.[59] Isabella was particularly touched with the alacrity of the Society's action and the intent of the lectures. The speaker would be expected to focus on the future. Both Woodrow Wilson and the Society for Allied Health Professions were written into Isabella's will in 1975; Woodrow Wilson because "all of Mary E. Switzer's memorabilia are so admirably housed," and the Schools for the Allied Health Professions because "of their many courtesies to Mary E. Switzer when she left the Department of Health, Education, and Welfare."[60]

Isabella was not so fond of the National Rehabilitation Association and its memorial for Mary, perhaps because she was not continually consulted regarding its use.[61] The NRA campaign for funds was launched immediately following the dedication of the Mary E. Switzer Building in Washington. Each chapter was asked to appoint a committee, and a veteran fund raiser, Olive Banister, of Cleveland, was asked to head the committee. Mrs. Banister had succeeded Bell Greve as Director of the Cleveland Rehabilitation Center and was a great admirer of Mary Switzer. With the funds collected from NRA members, the Mary E. Switzer Seminar was instituted. "How Mary would have enjoyed the discussions that produced this first report!" Olive wrote. "Memories of her charm and vitality and her demand for relevance in conference were humbling forces to all who participated."[62]

Another building was soon named for Mary Switzer: the Mary E. Switzer Rehabilitation Building at the Helen Keller National Center, Sands Points, Long Island.[63] Peter Salmon asked Isabella to write an account of Mary's professional life for the occasion; Frances Curtis typed "Mary E. Switzer: The Dedicated Bureaucrat." The last line in Isabella's fifteen page description of Mary Switzer's life follows a list of Administrators of the Federal Security Agency and Secretaries of the Department of Health, Education, and Welfare:

> And to help--even guide--each of them--from July 1, 1939, until February 16, 1970:
> Mary Elizabeth Switzer.

The companion of forty years knew just how much guidance Mary Switzer had offered each of the administrators. From the day Paul McNutt and Mary unlocked the door of a small marble building on the Naval Hospital grounds to make room for the new Federal Security Agency,[64] Isabella had been privy to Mary Switzer's bureaucratic sophistication. Anyone searching through her papers at the Schlesinger Library would say Mary Switzer was an opaque character. Isabella Diamond understood that this was only the armor of the bureaucrat. Great deeds had been accomplished, some in the name of Mary's superiors, some bore her name. She had delayed personal recognition for more than a quarter of her professional life, readying for the golden opportunity to use what she had learned to become "defender and advocate of the lame, the halt, the blind, the deaf, and the poor."[65]

Mary Switzer had led a quiet revolution. Disabled persons would never again be viewed as they had in 1950, when she had committed her future to theirs. She had said "my intellectual activity was influenced by a basic commitment to a revolutionary point of view for accomplishing justice in the world."[66] Uncle Mike had bequeathed her the commitment; observation of his frustration had enabled Mary to find a way to make revolutionary ideas reality. Others might say that bureaucratic labor seldom leads to enduring changes in policy or behavior;[67] Mary Switzer found government service a channel for a woman to influence social policy. The products were attributable to her, and they were lasting. At her memorial service, Howard Rusk said: "We have lost a cherished friend. The disabled of the world have lost their great champion."[68]

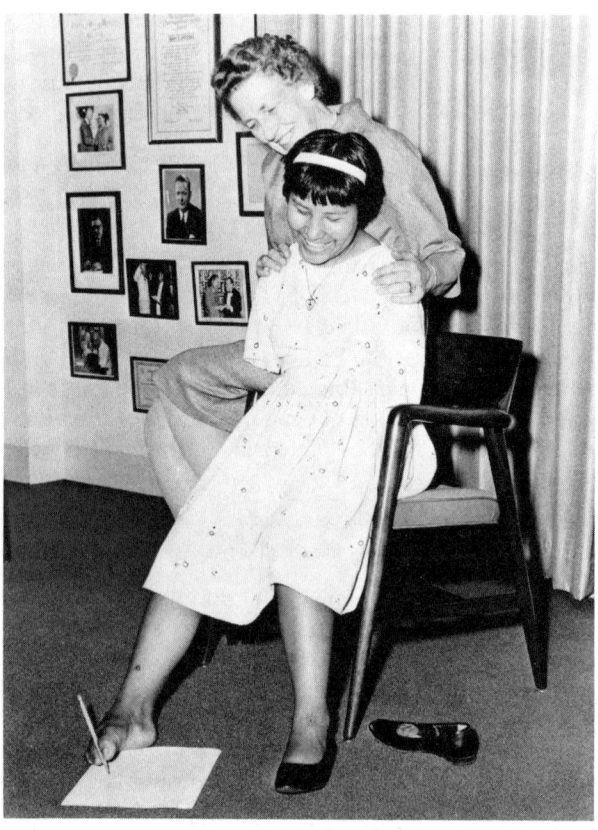

Switzer and Teodoria Martinez Silva of Boliva, 1964 *(Courtesy The Schlesinger Library, Radcliffe College)*.

General Sources

Interviews

Katharine Arneson, August 11, 1981, Washington, D.C.
Frank Birdsall, August 14, 1981, Afton, Virginia
Warren Bledsoe, August 11, 1981 and March 14, 1984, Bethesda, Maryland
Sterling Brinkley, August 11, 1981, Washington, D.C.
James Burress, November 7, 1981, Washington, D.C., and November 1, 1982, Kent, Ohio
Josephine Coe, August 13, 1981, Greenbelt, Maryland
Wilbur Cohen, July 5, 1982, Ann Arbor, Michigan
Frances Curtis, August 11, 1981, Washington, D.C.
Palmer Dearing, March 9, 1982, Washington, D.C.
Ann Draper, November 15, 1982, Washington, D.C.
Douglas Fenderson, May 13, 1983, Washington, D.C.
Patria Forsythe, November 16 and 17, 1982, Washington, D.C.
James Garrett, March 8, 1982 and March 15, 1984, New York City
Sheila Hackett, November 7, 1981, Washington, D.C.
Paul Howard, August 12, 1981, Alexandria, Virginia
Marceline Jaques, March 11, 1983, Buffalo, New York
Dorothy Kirkbride, March 15, 1984, Washington, D.C.
Joseph LaRocca, November 16, 1982, Washington, D.C.
Kathleen Lloyd, November 11, 1981, Washington, D.C.
Edward Martin, October 19, 1982, Albertson, New York
Samuel Martz, August 12, 1981 and March 10, 1982, Washington, D.C.
Martin McCavitt, September 18, 1984, Washington, D.C.
Rufus Miles, March 8, 1982, Princeton, New Jersey
John Newdorp, March 9, 1982, Washington, D.C.
Anna Parker, August 12, 1982, Washington, D.C.
Warren Perry, March 11, 1983, Buffalo, New York
Ethel and Felix Putterman, October 10, 1981, Orleans, Massachusetts
Jennings Randolph, March 15, 1984, Washington, D.C.
Elizabeth Brandeis Rauschenbush, October 20, 1983, Madison, Wisconsin
Corbett Reedy, August 17, 1981, Abingdon, Virginia
Elliot Richardson, February 5, 1982, Washington, D.C.
Al Rotundo, September 22, 1983, Washington, D.C.
Howard Rusk, October 9, 1981, New York City
Fred Sachs, March 10, 1982, Washington, D.C.
Richard Seggel, March 10, 1982, Washington, D.C.

Mary Duke Biddle Semans, November 11, 1982, Durham, North Carolina
Harold Shay, March 10, 1982, Washington, D.C.
Miriam Stubbs, March 9, 1982, Washington, D.C.
Anastasia Switzer, October 9, 1981 and May 16, 1982, Orleans, Massachusetts
May Switzer, October 19, 1982, Sayville, New York
Richard Switzer, November 24, 1981, Albany, New York
Frieda Ullian, May 14, 1982, Cambridge, Massachusetts
Ann Verona Lyden, August 12, 1981, Washington, D.C.
Henry Viscardi, October 19, 1982, Albertson, New York
Margaret Washington, July 11, 1982, Nashville, Tennessee
E.B. Whitten, August 13, 1981, Washington, D.C.
Boyce Williams, August 11, 1981, Washington, D.C.
Ellen Winston, November 10, 1982, Raleigh, North Carolina

Manuscript Collections

The Arthur and Elizabeth Schlesinger Library on the History of Women in America, at Radcliffe College houses Mary E. Switzer's official papers. Extensive use of the Switzer Collection was made in completing her biography; permission was granted by the Schlesinger Library for the use of quotations from the Switzer Collection. Permission was also granted by several individuals to use papers from their private collections. Richard Switzer allowed the publication of autobiographical materials in his possession.

Mary Anderson papers, Schlesinger Library, Radcliffe College.
Martha May Eliot papers, Schlesinger Library, Radcliffe College.
Mary Elizabeth Switzer papers, Schlesinger Library, Radcliffe College.
William Faulkes papers, Wisconsin Historical Society; Madison.
Paul Rauschenbush papers, Wisconsin Historical Society.
Jules Sugarman papers, National Archives, Washington.
Women in the Federal Government Oral History Project, Schlesinger Library, Radcliffe College
Records of the Social Security Administration, National Archives, Washington.
Records of the Department of HEW, National Archives, Washington.
Records of the Department of HEW, Department of Health and Human Services Library, Washington.
Records of the Department of HEW, Social and Rehabilitation Services, Immediate Office of the Administrator, Federal Records Center, Suitland, Maryland.

Records of the Department of HEW, Office of the Secretary and Assistant Secretary, Federal Records Center, Suitland, Maryland.
Records of the Department of HEW, States VR Council, Federal Records Center, Suitland, Maryland.
Records of the Department of HEW, VRA, Federal Records Center, Suitland, Maryland.
Mary Elizabeth Switzer Archives, Woodrow Wilson Rehabilitation Center, Fishersville, Virginia.
Howard Rusk papers, courtesy of Howard Rusk, New York.
Warren Bledsoe papers, courtesy of Warren Bledsoe, Washington.
J. Warren Perry papers, courtesy of J. Warren Perry, Buffalo.
Richard Switzer papers, courtesy of Richard Switzer, Albany.
Radcliffe College Archives

Books

Acheson, Dean. *Morning and Noon*. Boston: Houghton Mifflin, 1965.
Addams, Jane, Balch, Emily, and Alice Hamilton. *Women at the Hague*. New York: MacMillan, 1915.
Altmeyer, Arthur. *The Formative Years of Social Security*. Madison: University University of Wisconsin Press, 1966.
Berkowitz, Edward. *Disability Policies and Government Programs*. New York: Praeger, 1979.
Berkowitz, Edward. *Rehabilitation: the Federal Government's Response to Disability, 1935-1954*. New York: Arno, 1980.
Berkowitz, Edward, and Kim McQuaid. *Creating the Welfare State*. New York: Praeger, 1980.
Berkowitz, Munroe, Johnson, W., and E. Murphy. *Public Policy toward Disability*. New York: Praeger, 1976.
Beschloss, Michael R. *Kennedy and Roosevelt, the Uneasy Alliance*. New York: Norton, 1980.
Bickel, Alexander. *The Unpublished Opinions of Mr. Justice Brandeis*. Cambridge: Howard University Press, 1957.
Blum, John Morton. *From the Morgenthau Diaries: Years of Crisis, 1928-1938*. Boston: Houghton Mifflin, 1959.
Blumberg, Dorothy. *Florence Kelley*. New York: Kelley, 1966.
Blumberg, Dorothy. *Florence Kelley: the Making of a Social Pioneer*. New York: Kelley, 1968.
Burkhauser, R., and R. Haveman. *Disability and Work: the Economics of American Policy*. Baltimore: Johns Hopkins Press, 1979.
Burns, James MacGregor. *The Lion and the Fox*. New York: Harcourt, Brace, and World, 1956.

Council of State Governments. *Federal Grants in Aid*. Chicago: Council of State Governments, 1949.

Dawson, Nelson. *Louis D. Brandeis, Felix Frankfurter, and the New Deal*. Hamden, Connecticut: Archon, 1980.

Dean, Russell. *New Life for Millions*. New York: Hastings House, 1972.

Derthick, Martha. *The Influence of Federal Grants*. Cambridge: Harvard University Press, 1970.

Derthick, Martha. *Uncontrollable Spending for Social Services Grants*. Washington, D.C.: Brookings, 1975.

Farnsworth, Beatrice. *William C. Bullitt and the Soviet Union*. Bloomington: Indiana University Press, 1967.

Furman, Bess. *A Profile of the United States Public Health Service*. Washington, D. C.: Department of Health, Education, and Welfare, 1960.

Godfrey, Drexel. *The Transfer of the Children's Bureau*. New York: Bobbs-Merrill, 1952.

Goldmark, Josephine. *Impatient Crusader*. Urbana: University of Illinois Press, 1953.

Gwynn, Denis. *Traitor or Patriot:the Life and Death of Roger Casement*. New York: Jonathan Cape and Harrison Smith, 1931.

Harris, Richard. *A Sacred Trust*. New York: New American Library, 1966.

Heclo, Hugh. *A Government of Strangers: Executive Politics in Washington*. Washington, D.C.: Brookings, 1977.

Hobbs, Edward. *Behind the President: A Study of Executive Office Agencies*. Washington, D.C.: Public Affairs Press, 1954.

Ickes, Harold L. *The Secret Diary of Harold L. Ickes*. New York: Simon and Schuster, 1953.

Jaffe, Philip. *The Rise and Fall of American Communism*. New York: Horizon, 1975.

Jones, Richard. *A History of the American Legion*. New York: Bobbs-Merrill, 1946.

Kaufman, Herbert. *The Administrative Behavior of Federal Bureau Chiefs*. Washington, D.C.: Brookings, 1981.

Leiby, James. *A History of Social Welfare and Social Work in the United States*. New York: Columbia University Press, 1978.

Krislov, Samuel. *Representative Bureaucracy*. Englewood Cliffs, N.J.: Prentice-Hall, 1981.

Love, Philip. *Andrew Mellon and his Work*. Baltimore: F. Heath Coggins, 1929.

Lubove, Roy. *The Struggle for Social Security, 1900-1935*. Cambridge: Harvard University Press, 1968.

Maddux, Thomas. *Years of Estrangement*. Tallahassee: University Presses of Florida, 1980.

Maney, Patrick. *"Young Bob" LaFollette*. Columbia: University of Missouri Press, 1978.

Marwick, David. *Work and Welfare Go Together*. Baltimore: Johns Hopkins Press, 1972.

Martin, George. *Madam Secretary*. Boston: Houghton Mifflin, 1976.

Miles, Rufus. *The Department of Health, Education, and Welfare*. New York: Praeger, 1974.

Morrison, Theodore. *Chautauqua*. Chicago: University of Chicago Press, 1974.

Muthard, John.*The Vocational Rehabilitation of Public Welfare Assistance Recipients*. Tallahassee: University of Florida Rehabilitation Research Institute, 1976.

Nathan, Maud. *The Story of an Epoch-making Movement*. New York: Doubleday, 1926.

Nearing, Scott. *The Making of a Radical: A Political Autobiography*. New York: Harper and Row, 1972.

Obermann, C. Esco. *A History of Vocational Rehabilitation in America*. Minneapolis: Denison and Company, 1965.

Pearson, Drew, and Robert Allen.*The Nine Old Men*. New York: Doubleday, Doren, and Company, 1936.

Perkins, Frances. *The Roosevelt I Knew*. New York: Viking, 1946.

Richardson, Elliot. *The Creative Balance*. New York: Holt, Rinehart, and Winston, 1976.

Pickett, Clarence. *For More Than Bread*. Boston: Little Brown, 1953.

Redkey, Henry. *Rehabilitation Centers in the United States*. Washington, D.C.: National Society of Crippled Children and Adults, 1953.

Roosevelt, Eleanor. *This I Remember*. New York: Harper and Brothers, 1949.

Rourke, Francis. *Bureaucratic Power in National Politics*. Boston: Little, Brown, 1972.

Rowe, H.*Tercentenary History of Newton, 1690-1930*. Newton: City of Newton, Massachusetts, 1930.

Rusk, Howard. *A World to Care For*. New York: Random House, 1977.

Schaffter, Dorothy. *The National Science Foundation*. New York: Praeger, 1969.

Schlesinger, Arthur.*The New Deal in Action, 1933-1939*. New York: MacMillan Company, 1940.

Schlesinger, Arthur. *History of American Presidential Elections, III*. New York: McGraw-Hill, 1965.

Schultze, Charles. *The Politics and Economics of Public Spending*. Washington, D.C.: Brookings, 1968.

Searles, Charles. *Harry Hopkins and the Depression*. Syracuse: Syracuse University Press, 1963.

Seidman, Harold. *Politics, Position, and Power*. New York: Oxford University Press, 1970.

Stack, John. *International Conflict in an American City: Boston's Irish, Italians, and Jews, 1935-1944*. London: Greenwood Press, 1979.

Starr, Paul. *The Social Transformation of American Medicine.* New York: Basic Books, 1982.
Sundquist, James. *Politics, Position, and Policy.* Washington, D.C.: Brookings, 1968.
Taylor, Lloyd. *The Medical Profession and Social Reform.* New York: St. Martin's Press, 1974.
Tugwell, R. G. *The Brains Trust.* New York: Viking, 1968.
Viscardi, Henry. *A Man's Stature.* Middlesbury, Vermont: Eriksson, 1952.
United Mine Workers. *Rehabilitation of the Disabled.* New York: Cornelius, 1952.
Ware, Susan. *Women and the New Deal.* Cambridge: Harvard University Press, 1981.
Wittke, Carl. *The Irish in America.* Baton Rouge: Louisiana State University Press, 1961.
Wright, George. *Total Rehabilitation.* Boston: Little, Brown, 1982.

Government Publications

Annual Reports:

    Federal Security Agency, 1939/40, Washington, D.C.
    Federal Security Agency, 1941/42, Washington, D.C.
    Office of Vocational Rehabilitation, 1944, Washington, D.C.
    Federal Security Agency, 1948/49, Washington, D.C.
    Department of Health, Education, and Welfare, 1952/54, 1954/56, 1956/58, 1958/60, 1961/62, 1962/63, 1964/65, 1966, 1967, 1968, 1969, Washington, D.C.

Hearings:

    Department of Labor-Federal Security Agency, Appropriations Sub-Committee for the House of Representatives, 1952 and 1953.
    Department of Labor-HEW, Appropriations Sub-Committee for the House of Representatives, 1961, 1964, 1967.
    Senate Sub-Committee, Labor and Public Welfare, 1967.

Rehabilitation Services Administration, Social and Rehabilitation Services, *Rehabilitation Record,* Washington, D.C., 1970.
United States Department of Health, Education, and Welfare, Office of the Secretary. "A Common Thread of Service," Washington, D.C. 1971.
United States Department of Health, Education, and Welfare. "Grants in Aid and Other Financial Assistance Programs," Washington, D.C., 1967.

United States Department of Health, Education, and Welfare. "The DHEW Under the Administration of President Lyndon B. Johnson," Washington, 1967.

Office of Vocational Rehabilitation, DHEW. "Rehabilitation in the Decade of the 60's, A Report of the Task Force on Program Development," Washington, 1960.

Office of Defense Mobilization, Manpower Policy Committee. "Task Force on the Handicapped, Report to the Chairman," Washington, D.C., 1952.

Unpublished Material

Berkowitz, Edward. "Mary Switzer: the Entrepreneur within the Welfare State."

Diamond, Isabella. "The Dedicated Bureaucrat."

Greenberg, George Douglas. "Governing HEW: Problems of Management and Control at the DHEW," (unpublished doctoral dissertation, Harvard, 1972.)

Melia, Richard P. "Statewide Planning in Four Health-Related Programs: a Conceptual Analysis" (unpublished doctoral dissertation, University of Massachusetts, 1973.

Switzer, Mary E. Unpublished autobiographical material, 1964-67.

Whitten, E.B. "A Poor Man's Lobby."

Acknowledgments

I am indebted to many persons and several institutions who have believed in the purpose of this volume and in my ability to do justice to Mary Elizabeth Switzer. Cornelia Throssel deserves credit for getting me started. Brockman Schumacher, Joe Fenton, Lewis Davis, and Hal Shay were also early enthusiasts, who pointed out resources and affirmed the importance of what I wanted to do.

The National Rehabilitation Association, through the Switzer Memorial Committee, Kent State University, and Radcliffe College contributed to my progress through small grants supporting travel for interviews and archival research. The National Institute on Handicapped Research awarded me a Senior Research Fellowship for a year of research and writing. I want to express my thanks to Dr. Douglas Fenderson, then Director of the Institute, for his constant interest, and to Dr. James Garrett, who was instrumental in my receiving the Fellowship.

During my research I was expertly assisted by archivists and librarians. I wish to thank Walter Weaver, Librarian for the Department of Health and Human Services, for his good humor and consultation. Betsy Shenton and Jane Knowles, of the Schlesinger Library, were also very helpful.

I was aided by many of Mary Switzer's friends, who gave me photographs or their personal papers. Ann Draper, Margaret Washington, Corbett Reedy, Sam and Helen Martz, Warren Perry, Martin McCavitt, and Jim Burress were generous with their private "Switzer collections." Warren Bledsoe added his perceptiveness and artistry to the information he relayed about Mary Switzer and Isabella Diamond.

The Switzer family welcomed me many times, entrusting me with family photographs and keepsakes. Richard Switzer, Miss Switzer's nephew, had preserved the only autobiographical notes Mary Switzer wrote. I am very grateful to him for allowing me this glimpse of Mary Switzer's personal life. Ann Switzer, Mary's sister, showed me the Cape Cod Mary Switzer loved, and through her voice and gestures, so like her sister's, made Mary Switzer come alive for me.

Friends and colleagues of mine who read the manuscript include Steve Simon, Ann Meyer, and Ed Berkowitz. Each strengthened the narrative through their criticism. Members of my family also read my work and commented, adding their considerable writing prowess to their emotional support. I am grateful to Betty Lentz, Perry Lentz, and Burke Walker. Martha Baden saw at least three versions of the biography, combining her editorial skills with an understanding of her mother.

Robert Walker deserves a special note of thanks. He was devoted to the completion of Mary Switzer's biography, committing not only a substantial portion of the family commons and his time to the cause, but also his unshakable encouragement.

Footnotes

CHAPTER I
That Foreign Element

1. John Stack's *International Conflict in an American City: Boston's Irish, Italians, and Jews, 1935-1944* (Greenwood Press, 1979).
2. Michael R. Beschloss' *Kennedy and Roosevelt: the Uneasy Alliance* (W.W. Norton and Company, 1980, p. 25-30.
3. H. Rowe's *Tercentenary History of Newton 1690-1930* (City of Newton, 1930).
4. *Newton Assessed Polls of 1891.*
5. Ibid.
6. *The Newton Centennial 1873-1973.*
7. Switzer's unpublished autobiographical material
8. Correspondence with Priscilla Ritter, Newton City Archivist, 6/7/82.
9. *The Newton Graphic*, February 1915.
10. Ibid.
11. Michael Moore's letter to Switzer, 5/1/34.
12. Switzer's "Reminisces about Uncle Mike", 9/13/65, p. 3.
13. John Stack's *International Conflict in an American City: Boston's Irish, Italians, and Jews, 1935-1944* (Greenwood Press, 1979).
14. Switzer's "Reminisces about Uncle Mike," 9/13/65, p. 2.
15. Ibid., p. 2.
16. Ibid, p. 1.
17. Switzer's unpublished autobiographical material, August 1966, p. 9.
18. Michael Moore's letter to Switzer, 10/11/35.
19. Switzer's letter to Michael Moore, 9/19/35.
20. Switzer's unpublished autobiographical material, 8/66, p. 15.
21. Ibid.
22. Switzer's unpublished autobiographical material, 11/28/66, p. 2.
23. Ibid, p. 14.
24. Ibid, p. 17.
25. Ibid, p. 16, 17.
26. Switzer's unpublished autobiographical material, 8/66, p. 16.
27. Interview with Anastasia Switzer, l0/9/81.
28. Switzer's unpublished autobiographical material, 11/28/66, p. 1.
29. Interview with Joe Hunt, 8/10/81.
30. Interview with Anastasia Switzer, 10/9/81.
31. Switzer's "Reminisces About Uncle Mike", p. 4.
32. Interview with Anastasia Switzer, 10/9/81.
33. Switzer's "Reminisces about Uncle Mike," p. 5 and 6.
34. Interview with Anastasia Switzer, 10/9/81.

35. Switzer's unpublished autobiographical material, 11/28/66, p.2.
36. Switzer's "Reminisces about Uncle Mike," 9/13/65, p.5.
37. Ibid, p. 6, 7.
38. Carl Wittke's *The Irish in America* (Louisiana State University Press, 1961, p. 26).
39. Switzer's unpublished autobiographical material, 8/66, p. 5.
40. Denis Gwynn's *Traitor or Patriot: The Life and Death of Roger Casement* (Jonathan Cape and Harrison Smith, 1931).
41. Carl Wittke's *The Irish in America* (Louisiana State University Press, 1961, p. 250.)
42. Switzer's unpublished autobiographical material, 8/66, p. 20.
43. Ibid, p. 8.
44. Ibid, p. 9.

CHAPTER II
Across the River to Respectability

1. Alton Gal's *Brandeis of Boston* (Harvard University Press, 1980).
2. Switzer's unpublished autobiographical material, 8/66, p. 18
3. Correspondence with Jane Knowles, Radcliffe College Archivist, 9/16/82.
4. Interview with Frieda Silbert Ullian, 5/17/82.
5. *Radcliffe Yearbook*, 1921.
6. Interview with Frieda Silbert Ullian, 5/17/82.
7. Oscar Handlin's *Louis Brandeis and the Progressive Tradition* (Little, Brown, 1981).
8. Ibid.
9. Switzer's unpublished autobiographical material, 8/66, p. 1.
10. Ibid, p. 20.
11. Switzer's commencement address, Milwaukee-Downer Seminary, 6/14/57, Switzer Collection, Schlesinger Library, Radcliffe College, MC 293 210.
12. Switzer's article for the *Radcliffe Quarterly*, vol. 43, no. 1, February 1959, Switzer Collection, MC 293 717, p.2.
13. Women in the Federal Government Oral History Project, interview with Esther Lawton, Schlesinger Library.
14. Correspondence with Jane Knowles, Radcliffe College Archivist.
15. *The Radcliffe News*, April 15, 1921, and March 4, 1921.
16. Interview with Frieda Silbert Ullian, 5/17/82.
17. Switzer's unpublished autobiographical material, undated, p.1.
18. *The Radcliffe News*, 2/21/21, p.2.
19. *The Radcliffe News*, 5/20/21, p. 2.
20. Switzer's unpublished autobiographical material, undated, p. 1 and 2.
21. *The Radcliffe News*, 5/27/21, pp. 2 and 5.
22. 1964 Reunion Report, Radcliffe Class of 1914, p. 25.
23. 1921 *Radcliffe Yearbook*, p. 73.
24. Interview with Frieda Silbert Ullian, 5/17/82.
25. Remarks of Frieda Silbert Ullian at 50th reunion of Radcliffe Class of '21, *Radcliffe News*, vol. 43, no. 1, February.
26. Switzer's article for *Radcliffe Quarterly*, 1959.
27. Switzer's letter to E. Rauschenbush, 12/18/59, Switzer Collection, MC 293 633.
28. Gilbert's letter to Switzer, 6/21/63, Switzer Collection, MC 293 993.
29. Switzer's letter to Polly Bunting, 5/18/64, Switzer Collection, MC 293 993.

30. Switzer's commencement address to Milwaukee-Downer Seminary, 6/14/57, Switzer Collection, MC 293 993, p. 3.
31. Ibid, p. 3.
32. Ibid, p. 5.
33. Blackwell Family Papers, Schlesinger Library.
34. Switzer's unpublished autobiographical material, 8/66, p. 22.
35. Ibid, pp. 22-23.
36. Ibid, pp. 23-24.
37. Ibid, p. 18.
38. LeBaron Briggs' letter to Carnegie Endowment Committee, 3/10/21, Radcliffe College Presidents' papers.
39. Unsigned faculty recommendation, 10/11/21, College Archives, vol. 5.
40. Switzer's unpublished autobiographical material, 8/66, p. 20.
41. Switzer's unpublished autobiographical material, undated, p. 1.
42. Radcliffe College Alumnae Association papers, 1928 survey.
43. Switzer's note to alumnae, Class of 1921, 2/9/61, Switzer Collection, MC 293 997.

CHAPTER III
One Step At A Time

1. Scott Nearing's *The Making of a Radical: A Political Autobiography* (Harper and Row, 1972).
2. Theodore Morrison's *Chautauqua* (University of Chicago Press, 1974).
3. Switzer's "Hope, the Anchor of Life," *Radcliffe Quarterly*, XLIII, Feb. 1959.
4. David Bruner in Arthur Schlesinger's *History of American Presidential Elections, III* (McGraw-Hill, 1971).
5. Dean Acheson's *Morning and Noon* (Houghton-Mifflin, 1965).
6. Switzer's unpublished autobiographical material.
7. Nelson Dawson's *Louis D. Brandeis, Felix Frankfurter, and the New Deal*, (Archon, 1980).
8. Dean Acheson's *Morning and Noon* (Houghton-Mifflin, 1965).
9. Russell Dean's *New Life for Millions, Rehabilitation for America's Disabled*, (Hastings House, 1972).
10. Esco Obermann's *A History of Vocational Rehabilitation in America* (Denison and Company, 1965).
11. Switzer's unpublished autobiographical material.
12. Switzer's letter to Miss Mooar, 7/21/21, Radcliffe College Archives.
13. Switzer's letter to Miss Mooar, 8/26/21, Radcliffe College Archives.
14. Switzer's letter to Miss Mooar, 9/13/21, Radcliffe College Archives.
15. Josephine Goldmark's *Impatient Crusader* (University of Illinois Press, 1953).
16. Alexander Bickel's *The Unpublished Opinions of Mr. Justice Brandeis* (Harvard University Press, 1957).
17. Switzer's unpublished autobiographical material.
18. Maud Nathan's *The Story of an Epoch-Making Movement* (Doubleday, 1926).
19. Dorothy Blumberg's *Florence Kelley* (Kelley, 1966).
20. Conversation with Oberlin College Archivist 10/82.
21. Switzer's unpublished autobiographical material.
22. Switzer's letter to Mr. Biddle, 8/10/22, Switzer Collection, MC 293 2.
23. Switzer's unpublished autobiographical material.
24. Ibid.

25. Switzer's "Hope, the Anchor of Life," *Radcliffe Quarterly*, vol. XLIII, no. 11, Feb. 1959.
26. Mary Wiegers' "Mary Switzer: Welfare, Work, and Wisdom," *The Washington Post*, December 18, 1969.
27. Philip Love's *Andrew Mellon and His Work* (F. Heath Coggins, 1929).
28. Switzer's "Reveries of an Old Bureaucrat," *Bulletin of Personnel Administration*, 12/10/46, Switzer Collection, MC 243 719.
29. Switzer's unpublished autobiographical material.
30. Cotterill letter to M. Carey Thomas, 3/13/18, Bryn Mawr Archives.
31. Correspondence with Lucy Fisher West, Archivist at Bryn Mawr College, 11/81.
32. Tracy Copp's obituary, in Faulkes papers, Wisconsin Historical Society.
33. Esco Obermann's *A History of Vocational Rehabilitation in America* (Denison, 1965).
34. Interview with Margaret Washington, Nashville, Tennessee, July 1982.
35. E. B. Whitten's unpublished history of the National Rehabilitation Association.
36. Patrick Maney's *"Young Bob" LaFollette* (University of Missouri Press, 1978).
37. Switzer's unpublished autobiographical material.
38. Esco Obermann's *A History of Vocational Rehabilitation in America* (Denison, 1965), p. 240-242.
39. George Wright's *Total Rehabilitation* (Little-Brown, 1980), p. 158.
40. Dorothy Rigdon's *Rehabilitation Record* (U.S. Dept. of Health, Education and Welfare, 1970).
41. James J. Davis, in Esco Obermann's *A History of Vocational Rehabilitation in America* (Denison, 1965), p. 260.
42. Esco Obermann's *A History of Vocational Rehabilitation in America* (Denison, 1965), p. 251.
43. Mary Anderson's letter to John King, 7/27/51, Switzer Collection, MC 293 598.
44. Switzer's unpublished autobiographical material.
45. John Kratz in Obermann's *A History of Vocational Rehabilitation in America* (Denison, 1965), p. 258.)
46. Switzer's unpublished autobiographical material.
47. Ibid.
48. Correspondence with Morton Pepper, 6/7/82.
49. Switzer's employment record, Switzer Collection, MC 293 793.
50. Switzer's memo to Mr. Birgfeld, Switzer Collection, MC 293 793.
51. Switzer's employment record, Switzer Collection, MC 293 793.
52. Switzer's unpublished autobiographical material.
53. Ibid.
54. Rufus Miles' *The Department of Health, Education, and Welfare* (Praeger, 1974).
55. Lawrence Fuchs in Arthur Schlesinger's *History of American Presidential Elections* (McGraw-Hill, 1971).
56. Switzer's unpublished autobiographical material.
57. Lawrence Fuchs in Arthur Schlesinger's *History of American Presidential Elections* (McGraw-Hill, 1971).
58. Esco Obermann's *History of Vocational Rehabilitation in America* (Denison, 1965).
59. Rufus Miles' *The Department of Health, Education, and Welfare* (Praeger, 1974).
60. Esco Obermann's *A History of Vocational Rehabilitation in America* (Denison, 1965).
61. Switzer's memo to Mr. Finley, 12/30, Switzer Collection, MC 293 2.
62. Switzer's unpublished autobiographical material.
63. James MacGregor Burns' *Roosevelt: The Lion and the Fox* (Harcourt, Brace, and World, 1956.)
64. R. G. Tugwell's *The Brains Trust* (Viking, 1968), p. 12, 31.

CHAPTER IV
A Shipboard Look

1. Interview with Josephine Coe, Greenbelt, Maryland, 8/13/81.
2. John Morton Blum's *From the Morgenthau Diaries: Years of Crisis, 1928-1938* (Houghton-Mifflin, 1959).
3. James MacGregor Burns' *The Lion and the Fox* (Harcourt, Brace, and World, 1956).
4. Switzer's unpublished autobiographical material.
5. John Morton Blum's *From the Morgenthau Diaries* (Houghton-Mifflin, 1959).
6. Eleanor Roosevelt's *This I Remember* (Harper and Brothers, 1949).
7. Harold Ickes' *The Secret Diary of Harold L. Ickes* (Simon and Schuster, 1953).
8. Switzer's unpublished autobiographical material.
9. Ibid.
10. Ibid.
11. Ibid.
12. John Morton Blum's *From the Morgenthau Diaries* (Houghton-Mifflin, 1959).
13. Switzer's letter to Victor Weybright, 6/7/34, Switzer Collection, MC 293 652.
14. Isabella Diamond's "The Dedicated Bureaucrat," 1973.
15. Interview with Josephine Coe, 8/13/81.
16. Switzer's biographical sketch of Josephine Roche, 3/7/40, Switzer Collection, MC 293 634.
17. Rachel Greenfield Minkoff's "The Tale of a Coal Miner's Daughter," *Vassar Quarterly*, Winter 1983, pp. 25-28.
18. Ibid.
19. Switzer's letter to *Radcliffe Class News*, 6/13/36, Switzer Collection, MC 293 993.
20. Interview with Palmer Dearing, 3/19/82.
21. Switzer's letter to Michael Moore, 2/4/36, Switzer Collection, MC 293 437.
22. Nelson Dawson's *Louis Brandeis, Felix Frankfurter, and the New Deal* (Archon Books, 1980)
23. Michael Moore's letter to Switzer, 6/3/35, Switzer Collection, MC 293 437.
24. Drew Pearson and Robert Allen's *The Nine Old Men* (Doubleday, Doran and Company, 1936).
25. Switzer's letter to Michael Moore, 1/21/36, Switzer Collection, MC 293 437.
26. Arthur Schlesinger's *The New Deal in Action 1933-1939* (MacMillan Company, 1940).
27. Switzer's unpublished autobiographical material.
28. Michael Moore's letter to Switzer, 5/1/34, Switzer Collection, MC 293 437.
29. Switzer's letter to Michael Moore, 6/30/36, Switzer Collection, MC 293 437.
30. Philip Jaffe's *The Rise and Fall of American Communism* (Horizon, 1975).
31. Bess Furman's *A Profile of the United States Public Health Service* (U.S. Department of HEW, 1960).
32. Lloyd Taylor's *The Medical Profession and Social Reform, 1885-1945* (St. Martin's Press, 1974).
33. Ibid.
34. Switzer's unpublished autobiographical material.
35. Lloyd Taylor's *The Medical Profession and Social Reform, 1884-1945* (St. Martin's Press, 1974).
36. Roy Lubove's *The Struggle for Social Security 1900-1935* (Harvard University Press, 1968).
37. Edward Berkowitz and Kim McQuaid's *Creating the Welfare State* (Praeger, 1980).
38. Ibid.
39. Nelson Dawson's *Louis Brandeis, Felix Franfurter, and the New Deal* (Archon, 1980.)
40. Interview with Wilbur Cohen, Ann Arbor, Michigan, 7/5/82.
41. George Martin's *Madame Secretary* (Houton-Mifflin, 1976).

42. Ibid.
43. Switzer's unpublished autobiographical material.
44. Lloyd Taylor's *The Medical Profession and Social Reform, 1885-1945* (St. Martin's Press, 1974). 45. Ibid.
46. Edward Berkowitz' *Disability Policies and Government Programs* (Praeger, 1979).
47. Switzer's unpublished autobiographical material.
48. Switzer's letter to Malcolm Bryan, 7/7/35, Switzer Collection, MC 293 437.
49. Ibid.
50. Edward Berkowitz' *Disability Policies and Government Programs* (Praeger, 1979).
51. Ibid.
52. Lloyd Taylor's *The Medical Profession and Social Reform, 1885-1945* (St. Martin's Press, 1974).
53. Roosevelt's letter to Roche, 7/15/38, Switzer Collection, MC 293 98.
54. Switzer's letter to Elizabeth Rauschenbush, Switzer Collection, MC 293 98.
55. Lloyd Taylor's *The Medical Profession and Social Reform, 1885-1945* (St. Martin's Press, 1974).
56. Ibid.
57. Switzer's letter to Elizabeth Rauschenbush, 11/22/35, Switzer Collection, MC 293 633.
58. Ibid.
59. Ibid.
60. Ibid.
61. Emily Blair Newell's "He Ran From Success," *Washington Star*, 12/5/37.
62. Rufus Miles' *The Department of Health, Education, and Welfare* (Praeger, 1974).
63. Switzer's unpublished autobiographical material.
64. Parran correspondence, Switzer Collection, MC 293 32.
65. Rufus Miles' *The Department of Health, Education, and Welfare* (Praeger, 1974).
66. Bess Furman's *A Profile of the United States' Public Health Service* (Department of Health, Education and Welfare, 1960).
67. Rufus Miles' *The Department of Health, Education, and Welfare* (Praeger, 1974).
68. James MacGregor Burns' *The Lion and the Fox* (Harcourt, Brace and World, 1956).
69. Ibid.
70. Switzer Collection, MC 293 605.
71. Paul Starr's *The Social Transformation of American Medicine* (Basic Books, 1982,), p. 277.
72. Switzer's unpublished autobiographical material.
73. Ibid.
74. Ibid.
75. Bess Furman's *A Profile of the United States' Public Health Service* (U.S. Department of Health, Education, and Welfare, 1960).
76. Switzer Collection, MC 293 605.
77. Rauschenbush's letter to Switzer, 11/11/37, Switzer Collection, MC 293 633.
78. Switzer's letter to Rauschenbush, 11/22/37, Switzer Collection, MC 293 633.
79. Ibid.
80. Ibid.
81. James MacGregor Burns' *The Lion and the Fox* (Harcourt, Brace, and World, 1956).
82. Switzer's letter to Weybright, Switzer Collection, MC 293 652.
83. Draft of Weybright article, Switzer Collection, MC 293 652.

CHAPTER V
The Luckiest Thing That Ever Happened

1. Rauschenbush's letter to Switzer, 11/11/37, Switzer Collection, MC 293 633.

2. Switzer's letter to Rauschenbush, 1/22/37, Switzer Collection, MC 293 633.
3. Martha Derthick's *Policy Making for Social Security* (Brookings, 1979), p. 31.
4. Switzer correspondence with Josephine Roche, 11/28/38, Switzer Collection, MC 293 634.
5. Switzer's unpublished autobiographical material.
6. Ibid.
7. Rufus Miles' *The Department of Health, Education, and Welfare* (Praeger, 1974), p. 17.
8. Ibid, pp. 18-20.
9. Switzer's unpublished autobiographical material.
10. Michael R. Beschloss' *Kennedy and Roosevelt, the Uneasy Alliance* (Norton, 1980), p. 201.
11. Rufus Miles' *The Department of Health, Education, and Welfare* (Praeger, 1974), p. 20.
12. Isabella Diamond's "The Dedicated Bureaucrat," 1973, p. 4.
13. *Radcliffe Quarterly*, 1939, XXXIII, p. 75.
14. Ibid.
15. Isabella Diamond's "The Dedicated Bureaucrat," 1973, p. 5.
16. R. Ayres letter to Switzer, 1/15/40, Switzer Collection, MC 293 431.
17. Michael R. Beschloss' *Kennedy and Roosevelt, the Uneasy Alliance* (Norton, 1980), p. 200.
18. Switzer's unpublished autobiographical material.
19. Switzer's letter to Carl Booth, 5/28/37, Switzer Collection, MC 293 437.
20. Interview with Georgina Flannery, Newton Free Library Librarian, May 1982.
21. *Newton Graphic*, 10/23/36.
22. Switzer's letter to V. Weybright, 3/25/40, Switzer Collection, MC 293 653.
23. Proceedings of the Bar of the Supreme Court of the United States and Meeting of the Court in Memory of Associate Justice Louis D. Brandeis, 12/21/42.
24. Nelson Dawson's *Louis D. Brandeis, Felix Frankfurter, and the New Deal* (Archon, 1980).
25. Switzer's letter to Rauschenbush, 10/27/39, Switzer Collection, MC 293 633.
26. Switzer Collection, MC 293 633.
27. Dorothy Blumberg's *Florence Kelley: the Making of a Social Pioneer* (Kelley, 1966).
28. Switzer's letter to V. Weybright, 5/35, Switzer Collection, MC 293 652.
29. Interview with Palmer Dearing, 3/9/82.
30. Draper letter to Barrett, 10/11/43, Switzer Collection, MC 293 605.
31. Draper letter to Switzer, 6/30/37, Switzer Collection, MC 293 671.
32. Switzer's letter to Parran, Switzer Collection, MC 293 32.
33. Correspondence between Parran and Switzer, Switzer Collection, MC 293 33.
34. Switzer's memo to Burdine, 3/25/40, Switzer Collection, MC 293 371.
35. George Martin's *Madam Secretary* (Houghton-Mifflin, 1976).
36. Anderson Degree Committee, Switzer Collection, MC 293 591.
37. Switzer's letter to Comstock, 6/20/40, Switzer Collection, MC 293 591.
38. Comstock's letter to Switzer, 6/26/40, Switzer Collection, MC 293 591.
39. Switzer Collection, MC 293 591.
40. Ibid.
41. Kelchner's letter to M. Weisman, 5/16/46, MC 293 655.
42. Switzer's letter to Mary Lasker, 4/11/42, Switzer Collection, MC 293 622.
43. Switzer's letter to C. Pickett, Switzer Collection, MC 293 128 1/12/42.

CHAPTER VI
The New Reformers

1. Switzer's memo to Burdine, 3/25/40, Switzer Collection, MC 293 371.
2. Ibid.
3. Weisman's letter to Switzer, 9/21/39, Switzer Collection, MC 293 655.

4. Weisman's letter to Switzer, 8/22/41, Switzer Collection, MC 293 655.
5. Charles Searle's *Minister of Relief: Harry Hopkins and the Depression* (Syracuse University Press, 1963).
6. Switzer's memo to W. Miller, 11/14/46, Switzer Collection, MC 293 2.
7. Switzer's memo to Burdine, 3/25/40, Switzer Collection, MC 293 371.
8. Edith Stern's "The Recreation of Independence," Switzer Collection, MC 293 615.
9. Ibid.
10. McCloskey's letter to Ewing, 1/12/51, Switzer Collection, MC 293 615.
11. McCloskey's letter to Switzer, 9/17/46, Switzer Collection, MC 293 615.
12. Ibid.
13. Switzer Collection, MC 293 615.
14. E. Roosevelt's letter to McNutt, 3/25/40, Switzer Collection, MC 293 127.
15. Ibid.
16. Clarence Pickett's letter to Advisory Committee, 5/20/41, Switzer Collection, MC 293 127.
17. Senator Byrd's *Congressional Record*, 6/10/43, p. 5734.
18. Ibid.
19. Glenn Work's letter to Switzer, 6/6/40, Switzer Collection, MC 293 127.
20. "First Lady Speaks at Homesteads," Elkins Intermount, 5/22/40, Switzer Collection, MC 293 127.
21. Switzer's draft of letter to Helen, unpublished autobiographical material.
22. Switzer's unpublished autobiographical materials.
23. Ibid.
24. Ibid.
25. Ibid.
26. Ibid.
27. Ibid.
28. Ibid.
29. Ibid.
30. Clarence Pickett's *For More Than Bread* (Little, Brown, 1953).
31. Pickett's letter to Switzer, 7/10/42, Switzer Collection, MC 298 128.
32. Switzer's letter to McCloskey, 8/6/45, Switzer Collection, MC 293 625.
33. Pickett's letter to Switzer, 11/13/42, Switzer Collection, MC 293 128.
34. Ibid.
35. Switzer's letter to Pickett, 4/20/43, Switzer Collection, MC 293 128.
36. Clarence Pickett's *For More Than Bread* (Little, Brown, 1953).
37. Pickett's letter to Switzer, 11/29/48, Switzer Collection, MC 293 128.
38. Agnes Inglis' report, Switzer Collection, MC 293 98.
39. Switzer's letter to Pickett, 4/20/43, Switzer Collection, MC 293 128.
40. Ibid.
41. Elizabeth Brandeis' "Centralization and Democracy," Reprint from the *Survey Graphic*, 12/46, Switzer Collection, MC 293 633.
42. Ibid.
43. Switzer's speech to National Committee on Voluntary Organizations, Switzer Collection, MC 293 185.
44. List of Switzer's speaking engagements, Switzer Collection, MC 293 709.
45. Susan Ware's *Women and the New Deal* (Harvard University Press, 1981).
46. Switzer's "Reveries of an Old Bureaucrat," 12/10/46, Switzer Collection, MC 293 719.
47. Switzer's memo to Miller, 11/15/46, Switzer Collection, MC 293 2.
48. Cosmos Club dinner announcement, Switzer Collection, MC 293 374.
49. Interview with Palmer Dearing, 3/9/82.

50. Interview with Paul Howard, 8/12/81.
51. Anderson's memo to Switzer, 3/3/44, Switzer Collection, MC 293 432.
52. Ibid.
53. Switzer's memo to Taft, 6/23/41, Switzer Collection, MC 293 646.
54. Parran's memo to Chief of Emergency Medical Section, 6/16/43, Switzer Collection, MC 293 33.
55. Miller's memo to Jackson, 1/27/47, Switzer Collection, MC 293 8.
56. Parran's memo to Switzer, 9/23/43, Switzer Collection, MC 293 33.
57. Switzer's memo to Parran, 10/9/43, Switzer Collection, MC 293 33.
58. Switzer's memo to Parran, 6/10/37, Switzer Collection, MC 293 32.
59. Switzer's telegram to Parran, 6/10/44, Switzer Collection, MC 293 34.
60. Switzer's letter to Davis, 5/6/47, Switzer Collection, MC 293 373.
61. Purpose of Saint Elizabeth's Hospital, Switzer Collection, MC 293 371.
62. Overholser's letter to McNutt, 10/11/43, Switzer Collection, MC 293 371.
63. Overholser's letter to McNutt, 12/9/43, Switzer Collection, MC 293 1000.
64. McNutt's letter to Smith, 10/30/44, Switzer Collection, MC 293 999.
65. "Some Questions," Switzer Collection, MC 293 1001.
66. Lorenz' letter to Miller, 5/14/45, Switzer Collection, MC 293 1001.
67. Switzer's memo to Miller, 5/20/45, Switzer Collection, MC 293 1001.
68. Overholser's letter to McNutt, 6/24/45, Switzer Collection, MC 298 1002.
69. Transcript of telephone conversations, Switzer Collection, MC 293 1002.
70. *Annual Report of the Federal Security Agency*, 1945.
71. Correspondence dated 7/22/40, Switzer Collection, MC 293 372.
72. Description of Duties, 4/1/51, Switzer Collection, MC 293 2.
73. *Annual Report of the Federal Security Agency*, 1945.
74. Correspondence dated 7/22/40, MC 293 372.
75. Transcript of telephone conversation, 1/29/46, Switzer Collection, MC 293 37.
76. Ibid.
77. Frank Lahey's speech to the Medical Association of the District of Columbia, 12/9/42, Switzer Collection, MC 293 665, p. 5.
78. Ibid.
79. Sheldon's letter to Pratt, 7/28/44, Switzer Collection, MC 293 98.
80. Switzer's speech, "New Directions in Rehabilitation," 12/12/69, given at the Institute for the Crippled and Disabled, New York.
81. Switzer's remarks before the School of Nursing, South Baltimore General Hospital, 4/25/45, Switzer Collection, MC 293 2.
82. Switzer's memo to Chairman, War Manpower Commission, 1/15/45, Switzer Collection, MC 293 106.
83. Interview with Palmer Dearing, 3/9/82.
84. Lloyd Taylor's *The Medical Profession and Social Reform, 1885-1945* (St. Martin's Press, 1974).
85. Fishbein article, Switzer Collection, MC 293 606.
86. Draper's letter to Wyman Barrett, ll/10/43, Switzer Collection, MC 293 605.
87. Switzer's letter to Paullin, 5/7/43, Switzer Collection, MC 293 98.
88. Fishbein article, Switzer Collection, MC 293 606.
89. Gregg's letter to Merck, 5/20/43, Switzer Collection, MC 293 630.
90. Description of duties, 4/1/51, Switzer Collection, MC 293 2.
91. Mary Wieger's "Mary Switzer, Welfare, Work, and Wisdom," *Washington Post*, 12/18/69.
92. Interview with Joseph Hunt, 8/10/81.
93. Switzer Collection, MC 293 1.
94. Switzer's letter to Paullin, 5/7/43, Switzer Collection, MC 293 98.

95. Exhibit 2, Assistant to Administrator, 9/1/39-10/20/50, Switzer Collection, MC 293 2.
96. Lahey's letter to McNutt, 2/21/46, Switzer Collection, MC 293 2.
97. McNutt's letter to "Gentlemen," Switzer Collection, MC 293 2.
98. Isabella Diamond's "The Dedicated Bureaucrat," 1973, p. 5.
99. Switzer's letter to Miller, 11/15/46, Switzer Collection, MC 293 2.

CHAPTER VII.
Bureaucratic LeapFrog

1. Edward Hobbs' *Behind the President: A Study of Executive Office Agencies* (Public Affairs Press, 1954).
2. Esco Obermann's *A History of Vocational Rehabilitation in America* (Denison, 1965).
3. Ibid, p. 268.
4. Ibid, p. 273.
5. Switzer's letter to Copp, 4/27/38, Switzer Collection, MC 293 596.
6. Switzer's memo to Coy, 7/25/40, Switzer Collection, MC 293 370.
7. Switzer's letter to Weisman, 9/25/43, Switzer Collection, MC 293 655.
8. Ibid.
9. Esco Obermann's *A History of Vocational Rehabilitation in America* (Denison, 1965).
10. Switzer's letter to Copp, 3/12/41, Switzer Collection, MC 293 596.
11. Tate's memo to Miller, 6/7/45, Switzer Collection, MC 293 8.
12. Switzer's memo to Administrator and staff, 6/28/46, Switzer Collection, MC 293 8.
13. Edward Berkowitz' unpublished paper, "Mary Switzer, the Entrepreneur within the Welfare State."
14. Organizational plan, 7/16/46, Switzer Collection, MC 293 8.
15. Switzer's letter to Weisman, 5/27/46, Switzer Collection, MC 293 990.
16. Truman's memo, 9/13/46, Switzer Collection, MC 293 8.
17. Miller's memo to Switzer, 10/1/46, Switzer Collection, MC 293 8.
18. Miller's memo to Switzer, 12/20/46, Switzer Collection, MC 293 2.
19. Rosenfeld's memo to Ewing, Switzer Collection, MC 293 8.
20. Jackson's letter to Miller, 1/7/47, Switzer Collection, MC 293 8.
21. Switzer's draft memo, 2/4/47, Switzer Collection, MC 293 8.
22. Ibid.
23. Richard Jones' *A History of the American Legion* (Bobbs-Merrill, 1946).
24. Switzer's letter to Copp, 6/20/42, Switzer Collection, MC 293 598.
25. House Congressional Record, 3/5/43, pp. 5686-5697.
26. Esco Obermann's *A History of Vocational Rehabilitation in America* (Denison, 1965).
27. Senate Congressional Record, 6/22/43, p. 6345.
28. Rosenfield's memo to Ewing, 9/9/47, Switzer Collection, MC 293 8.
29. Rufus Miles' *The Department of Health, Education, and Welfare* (Praeger, 1974).
30. Esco Obermann's *A History of Vocational Rehabilitation in America* (Denison, 1965), p. 298.
31. Rufus Miles' *The Department of Health, Education, and Welfare* (Praeger, 1974), p. 23.
32. Arthur Altmeyer's *The Formative Years of Social Security* (University of Wisconsin Press, 1966); Paul Starr's *The Social Transformation of American Medicine* (Basic Books, 1982), p. 284.
33. Switzer's letter to Rauschenbush, 1/3/49, Switzer Collection, MC 293 633.
34. Rufus Miles' *The Department of Health, Education, and Welfare* (Praeger, 1974), p. 23.
35. Willcox's memo to Collins, 1/27/47, Switzer Collection, MC 293 8.
36. Switzer's memo to Miller, 3/18/49, Switzer Collection, MC 293 145.
37. Rufus Miles' *The Department of Health, Education, and Welfare* (Praeger, 1974), p. 200.
38. Arthur Altmeyer's *The Formative Years of Social Security* (University of Wisconsin Press, 1966).

CHAPTER VIII
Offspring of the Brains Trust

1. Switzer's address to the National Conference of Women's Auxiliaries, 9/21/48, and the National Committee on Mental Health, Switzer Collection, MC 293 185; Switzer's address to State Advisors on Women's Activities, The National Foundation for Infantile Paralysis, 11/7/49, Switzer Collection, MC 293 422.
2. Switzer's unpublished autobiographical material, 11/6/66, "Recollections of Karl Menninger."
3. Ibid.
4. Edward Berkowitz and Kim McQuaid's *Creating the Welfare State: The Political Economy of Twentieth Century Reform* (Praeger, 1980).
5. Felix's memo to Switzer, 8/3/45, Switzer Collection, MC 293 882.
6. Switzer's letter to Menninger, 3/14/45; Menninger's letter to Switzer, 4/7/45, Switzer Collection, MC 293 882.
7. Menninger's letter to Switzer, 4/7/45, Switzer Collection, MC 293 882.
8. James Leiby's *A History of Social Welfare and Social Work in the United States* (Columbia University Press, 1978), pp. 305-307.
9. National Neuropsychiatric Institute Act Hearings, 2/6-2/8/46, Switzer Collection, MC 293 391.
10. Switzer's unpublished autobiographical material, 10/6/66.
11. Switzer's description of duties, Switzer Collection, MC 293 2.
12. James Leiby's *A History of Social Welfare and Social Work in the United States* (Columbia University Press, 1978), p. 287.
13. Russell Dean's *New Life for Millions* (Hastings House, 1972), p. 141.
14. Switzer's letter to Lasker, 3/13/45, Switzer Collection, MC 293 391.
15. Rufus Miles' *The Department of Health, Education, and Welfare* (Praeger, 1974), pp. 174-177.
16. Switzer's description of duties, Switzer Collection, MC 293 2.
17. Switzer's memo to Administrator, 9/29/49, Switzer Collection, MC 293 146.
18. Switzer's memo to Thurston, 3/22/50, Switzer Collection, MC 293 42.
19. Thurston's memo to Dawson, 4/28/50, Switzer Collection, MC 293 42.
20. Switzer's memo to Thurston, 3/22/50, Switzer Collection, MC 293 342.
21. Dorothy Schaffter's *The National Science Foundation* (Praeger, 1969), p. 108.
22. Harold Seidman's *Politics, Position, and Power* (Oxford University Press, 1970).
23. Rufus Miles' *The Department of Health, Education, and Welfare* (Praeger, 1974), p. 23.
24. Switzer's address to State advisors on Women's Activities, 11/7/49, Switzer Collection, MC 293 422; Switzer's address to National Conference of Women's Auxiliaries, 9/21/48, Switzer Collection, MC 293 422.
25. The Council of State Governments' *Federal Grants-in-Aid* (1949); Martha Derthick's *The Influence of Federal Grants* (Harvard University Press, 1970).
26. Paul Starr's *The Social Transformation of American Medicine* (Basic Books, 1982) p. 348.
27. Miller's memo to Truman; Miller's memo to Bailey, 8/7/46, Switzer Collection, MC 293 394.
28. Richard Harris' *A Sacred Trust* (New American Library, 1966).
29. Draper's letter to Barrett, 11/10/43, Switzer Collection, MC 293 605.
30. Biographical sketch of Warren Draper, 5/1/56, Switzer Collection, MC 293 605.
31. Rachel Minkoff's "Josephine Roche: The Tale of a Coal Miner's Daughter," *Vassar Quarterly*, Winter 1983.
32. Edward Berkowitz' *Rehabilitation: The Federal Government's Response to Disability, 1935-1954* (Arno, 1980).
33. United Mine Workers' Welfare and Retirement Fund "Rehabilitation of the Disabled," p. 2, RG 363 Accession # 71A 1382, Carton 64.

34. Ibid.
35. "A Hospital Chain 250 Miles Long," *Architectural Forum*, Aug-Nov 1953, RG H363 Accession # 71A 1382, Box 64.
36. Ibid.
37. United Mine Workers' *Rehabilitation of the Disabled* (Cornelius, 1952).
38. Switzer's unpublished autobiographical material.
39. Howard Rusk's *A World to Care For* (Random House, 1977), p. 101.
40. Russell Dean's *New Life for Millions* (Hastings House, 1972).
41. United Mine Workers' *Rehabilitation of the Disabled* (Cornelius, 1952).
42. Rusk's letter to Draper, 3/13/56, Switzer Collection, MC 293 671.
43. Ibid.
44. United Mine Workers' *Rehabilitation of the Disabled* (Cornelius, 1952).
45. Personal correspondence of Warren Draper, letter to Peterson, 2/12/51.
46. Warren Draper's "The Quest of the United Mine Workers of America Welfare and Retirement Fund for the Best Medical Care Obtainable for its Beneficiaries," presentation to the American Association for the Surgery of Trauma, 11/1/57, in Draper papers.
47. Warren Draper's "Facts Pertaining to the Medical and Hospital Care Program of the UMWA Welfare and Retirement Fund, *The Pennsylvania Medical Journal*, vol. 61, 9/58, pp. 1185-1189.
48. Warren Draper's "Steps Taken by the UMWA Welfare and Retirement Fund to Assure the Quality of Medical Care," presentation to the National Conference on Labor Health Services, 6/16/68, in Draper papers.
49. Draper's letter to McIntire, 7/19/57, in Draper papers.
50. Dan Wakefield's "Dr. Jekyll and the AMA," *The Nation*, 6/22/57.
51. Norman Walker's "Labor Girding to Fight AMA on Medical Care," *Washington Star*, 5/4/58.
52. Howard Rusk's "One of Baruch's Deeds," *The New York Times*, 8/23/64; Russell Dean's *New Life for Millions* (Hastings House, 1972), p.89; Margaret Coit's *Mr. Baruch* (Houghton Mifflin Company, 1957); Bernard Baruch's *The Public Years* (Holt, Rinehart, and Winston, 1960).
53. Ray Wilbur and Frank Krusen's "The Baruch Committee on Physical Medicine Report on a Community Rehabilitation Service and Center (Functional Plan), 1946.
54. Russell Dean's *New Life for Millions* (Hastings House, 1972), p. 104.
55. Interview with Frank Birdsall, 8/14/81 and Corbett Reedy, 8/17/81.
56. Interview with Frank Birdsall, 8/14/81.
57. Switzer's speech to the National Committee on Mental Hygiene and Switzer's address to the National Conference on Women's Auxiliaries, 9/21/48, Switzer Collection, MC 293 185.

CHAPTER IX
Taken by the Nape of the Neck

1. Copp's letter to Switzer, 1949, Switzer Collection, MC 293 596.
2. Isabella Diamond's "The Dedicated Bureaucrat," 1973.
3. Interview with Mary Switzer by R. Novogrod, 2/12/70, in Rusk papers.
4. Personal correspondence with John Thurston, 12/11/82.
5. Edward Berkowitz' *Rehabilitation: The Federal Government's Response to Disability* (Arno, 1980), p. 139-142.
6. Switzer's unpublished autobiographical materials.
7. Ed Berkowitz' "The Federal Government and the Emergence of Rehabilitation Medicine," *The Historian*, p.542.

8. Interview with Joseph Hunt, 8/10/81; Tracy Copp's letter to Switzer, 1/10/50, Switzer Collection, MC 193 596.
9. E. B. Whitten's "A Poor Man's Lobby" (unpublished, 1980, pp. 118-119).
10. Tracy Copp's letter to Switzer, 1/10/50, Switzer Collection, MC 293 596.
11. Personal correspondence with John Thurston, 12/11/83.
12. Faulkes' papers in the archives of the Historical Society of Wisconsin; Faulkes' testimony before the House of Representatives, 6/10/43 (*Congressional Record*, p. 5695-6).
13. Esco Obermann's *A History of Vocational Rehabilitation in America* (Denison, 1965, p. 304).
14. E.B. Whitten's "A Poor Man's Lobby" (unpublished, 1980, pp. 133-143).
15. Ibid.
16. Interview with Joseph Hunt, 8/10/81; "Fifty Years of VR in the USA," Switzer Collection, MC 293 715.
17. *Annual Report of the Federal Security Agency*, Office of Vocational Rehabilitation, 1949.
18. Esco Obermann's *A History of Vocational Rehabilitation in America* (Denison, 1965, p. 305).
19. Martha Derthick's *Uncontrollable Spending for Social Services* (Brookings, 1975).
20. Switzer's speech to NRA, 1951, Switzer Collection, MC 293 246; Tracy Copp's "New Concept of Disablement and Rehabilitation," *Social Service Review*, XVIII, no. 4, Dec. 1937, pp. 163-166.
21. Tracy Copp's "Federal-State Cooperation Tested in Vocational Rehabilitation," *American Labor Legislation Review*, 22, no. 4, Dec. 1937, pp. 163-166.
22. Mike Shortley's memo to staff, 11/10/50, Switzer Collection, MC 293 15.
23. News release, Switzer Collection, MC 293 15.
24. Tracy Copp's letter to Switzer, 1/10/50, Switzer Collection, MC 293 596.
25. Ibid.
26. Tracy Copp's letter to Switzer, undated, Switzer Collection, MC 293 596.
27. Ibid.
28. Ibid.
29. Switzer's memo to Regional Representatives, 1/19/51, Switzer Collection, MC 293 407.
30. Interview with Corbett Reedy, 8/17/81.
31. Headquarters News Notes, 2/1/51, Switzer Collection, MC 293 407.
32. Headquarters News Notes, 5/10/51, Switzer Collection, MC 293 407.
33. Headquarters News Notes, 11/2/51, Switzer Collection, MC 293 407.
34. Ibid.
35. Tracy Copp's letter to Switzer, 1/10/50, Switzer Collection, MC 293 576.
36. *Annual Report of the Federal Security Agency*, 1951.
37. Switzer Collection, MC 293 189.
38. Headquarters News Notes, 9/16/51, Switzer Collection, MC 293 407.
39. Switzer Collection, MC 293 266.
40. Switzer's speech, "What Price Rehabilitation?" 10/26/51, Switzer Collection, MC 293 243.
41. Switzer's speech,"The Public Agency Looks at its Rehabilitation Program," 5/15/51, Switzer Collection, Switzer Collection, MC 293 243.
42. Switzer Collection, MC 293 678.
43. Hearings on Appropriations, Committee on Labor-FSA, April 16, 1951, p. 385-405.
44. Ibid.
45. Ibid.
46. Ibid.
47. Headquarters News Notes, 7/18/52, Switzer Collection, MC 293 407.
48. Ibid.
49. Clunk's letter to Switzer, 6/8/51, Switzer Collection, MC 293 595.
50. Switzer's letter to Clunk, 1/1/53, Switzer Collection, MC 293 595.

51. Switzer's memo to staff, 7/27/52, Switzer Collection, MC 293 409.
52. Switzer's memo to John Thurston, 7/28/52, Switzer Collection, MC 293 39.
53. Headquarters News Notes, May 1952, Switzer Collection, MC 293 407.
54. Switzer's "The Politics of Administrative Leadership," Switzer Collection, MC 293 336.
55. Switzer's memo to the Secretary, 10/29/59, Switzer Collection, MC 293 230.
56. Headquarters News Notes, 1/18/52, Switzer Collection, MC 293 407.
57. Fred Hyde's *The Giamo Amendment: A Case Study of Congressional Health Appropriations* (Yale School of Medicine, 1972).
58. E.B. Whitten's "A Poor Man's Lobby" (unpublished, 1980).
59. Fred Hyde's *The Giamo Amendment: A Case Study of Congressional Health Appropriations* (Yale School of Medicine, 1972).
60. Switzer's draft of speech to NRA Conference, 1951, Switzer Collection, MC 293 246.
61. Ibid.
62. Edward Berkowitz' *Rehabilitation: The Federal Government's Response to Disability* (Arno, 1980).
63. Dabelstein's memo to Regional Representatives, 9/26/52, Switzer Collection, MC 293 407.
64. Ibid.
65. "Fifty Years of VR in the United States," Switzer Collection, MC 293 715.
66. Flemming's memo to the Manpower Policy Committee, 4/10/51, Switzer Collection, MC 293 161.
67. Rusk's memo to Fleming, 1/13/51, Switzer Collection, MC 293 161.
68. Report of the Task Force on the Handicapped, 1/25/52, Rusk papers.
69. Ibid.
70. Ibid, pp. 39-41.
71. Ibid.
72. Switzer's memo to Thurston, 7/28/52, Switzer Collection, MC 293 39.
73. Headquarters News Notes, 11/24/52, Switzer Collection, MC 293 407.

CHAPTER X.
The Embattled Advocate

1. Interview with Howard Rusk, 10/9/81.
2. Howard Rusk's article in the *New York Times*, 9/14/52, Switzer Collection, MC 293 407.
3. Rufus Miles' *The Department of Health, Education, and Welfare* (Praeger, 1974, p. 25).
4. Ibid, pp. 25-28.
5. US Department of Health, Education and Welfare's "A Common Thread of Service" (1970).
6. Harold Seidman's *Politics, Position, and Power* (Oxford University Press, 1980).
7. Switzer's letter to Gibbons, 4/19/53, Switzer Collection, MC 293 913.
8. Isabella Diamond's "The Dedicated Bureaucrat," unpublished 1973; and interview with Joe Hunt, 8/10/81.
9. Rufus Miles' *The Department of Health, Education, and Welfare* (Praeger, 1974, p. 29).
10. Switzer's memo to Hobby, Switzer Collection, MC 293 993.
11. Interview with Howard Rusk, 10/9/81.
12. Ibid.
13. Ibid.
14. Switzer's letter to George Merck, 8/14/53, Switzer Collection, MC 293 630.
15. Ibid.
16. Ibid.

17. Switzer's letter to Lois Wheelwright, 8/20/53, Switzer Collection, MC 293 993.
18. Headquarters News Notes, 3/13/53, Switzer Collection, MC 293 407.
19. Hearings before the House Subcommittee on Labor-Federal Security Agency Appropriations, 1954, p. 297.
20. Ibid.
21. Switzer's memo to Miles, 1/18/53, Switzer Collection, MC 293 46.
22. Harold Seidman's *Politics, Position, and Power* (Oxford University Press, 1980).
23. Hearings before the House Subcommittee on Labor-Federal Security Agency Appropriations, 1954, p. 319.
24. Ibid, p. 312.
25. Ibid, p. 322.
26. Ibid, p. 345.
27. Switzer's memo to regional representatives, 3/13/53, Switzer Collection, MC 293 407.
28. E.B. Whitten's "A Poor Man's Lobby," unpublished, 1980, p. 176.
29. Copp's letter to Switzer, 7/53, Switzer Collection, MC 293 598.
30. Switzer's memo to regional representatives, 5/2/53, Switzer Collection, MC 293 407.
31. E.B. Whitten's "A Poor Man's Lobby," unpublished, 1980, pp. 177-178.
32. Ibid, pp. 179-186.
33. Switzer's memo to regional representatives, 8/21/53, Switzer Collection, MC 293 407.
34. Switzer's letter to George Merck, 8/14/53, Switzer Collection, MC 293 630.
35. Miles' memo to Hobby, 3/27/53, Record Group 235, General Files of FSA and Office of Secretary of HEW, GDS 450 215, National Archives.
36. E.B. Whitten's "A Poor Man's Lobby," unpublished, 1980, p. 190.
37. Edward Berkowitz' "Mary Switzer: The Entrepreneur within the Welfare State," unpublished paper, Switzer Collection.
38. Rufus Miles' *The Department of Health, Education, and Welfare* (Praeger, 1974, p. 32).
39. Switzer's memo to Thurston, 7/28/52, Switzer Collection, MC 293 39; Switzer's memo to Miles, 1/8/53, Switzer Collection, MC 293 46.
40. Switzer's letter to regional representatives, 9/16/53, 10/23/53, 12/10/53, Switzer Collection, MC 293 407.
41. Switzer's letter to regional representatives, 10/23/53, Switzer Collection, MC 293 407.
42. Conley's memo to Russell Larmon, 9/16/53, Record Group, 234, General Files of the FSA and the Secretary of HEW, General Decimal Series 450 215.
43. E.B. Whitten's "A Poor Man's Lobby," unpublished, 1980, p. 191.
44. Hearings before the House Subcommittee on Appropriations for Labor and Federal Security Agency, 3/11/53, p. 319.
45. E.B. Whitten's "A Poor Man's Lobby," unpublished, 1980, p. 193.
46. Russell Dean's *New Life for Millions* (Hastings House, 1972, p. 119).
47. Esco Obermann's *A History of Vocational Rehabilitation in America* (Denison, 1965, p. 313).
48. E.B. Whitten's "A Poor Man's Lobby," unpublished, 1980, p. 200.
49. Ibid, p. 212.
50. Switzer's letter to E. Rauschenbush, 12/25/54, Switzer Collection, MC 293 633.
51. Russell Dean's *New Life for Millions* (Hastings House, 1972, p. 120).
52. Switzer's letter to E. Rauschenbush, 12/25/54, Switzer Collection, MC 293 2.
53. "Tribute to John Fogarty," 10/2/67, Switzer Collection, MC 293 335.
54. Edward Berkowitz' and Kim McQuaid's "Welfare Reform in the 1950's," *Social Science Review*, March 1980.

CHAPTER XI.
The Joy of Craftmanship

1. Hearings of the Senate Sub-Committee for Appropriations, Labor-Federal Security for 1952, 81st Congress, 4/16/51, p. 403.
2. Hearings of the Senate Sub-Committee for Appropriations, Labor-HEW for 1952, 82nd Congress, 2/11/52, p. 244.
3. Report of the Finance Committee to the Executive Committee of the States Council, 10/25/53, MC 293 407.
4. Interview with Maceline Jaques, 3/11/83.
5. Statement of Mary Switzer before the Senate Finance Committee, 2/16/56, Switzer Collection, MC 293 117.
6. Dabelstein's memo to regional representatives, 12/8/55, Switzer Collection, MC 293 407.
7. *Annual Report of the Department of HEW*, 1954-56, pp. 271-287.
8. Switzer's letter to John Convery of the National Association of Manufacturers, 7/6/56, Switzer Collection, MC 293 420.
9. Switzer's letter to Savilla Simons of the National Travelers' Aid Association, 3/26/64, Switzer Collection, MC 293 420.
10. Switzer's letter to Salvatore G. DiMichael, 1/5/61, Switzer Collection, MC 293 420.
11. Switzer's letter to Margaret Washington, 6/20/55, Switzer Collection, MC 293 420.
12. Switzer's letter to Father Suedkamp, 11/8/56, Switzer Collection, MC 293 420.
13. Switzer's letter to Corbett Reedy, 8/27/53, Switzer Collection, MC 293 620.
14. Statement of Mary Switzer to Senate Finance Committee, 2/16/56, Switzer Collection, MC 293 117.
15. Henry Redkey's *Rehabilitation Centers in the United States* (The National Society of Crippled Children and Adults, 1953.)
16. Interview with Fred Sachs, 3/10/82.
17. Personal correspondence with Freeman McConnell, 2/18/82.
18. Henry Viscardi's *A Man's Stature* (Eriksson, 1952).
19. Russell Dean's *New Life for Millions* (Hastings House, 1972, p. 123).
20. John Reddy's "The School that Love Built," *Reader's Digest*, September 1971.
21. Switzer's letter to Viscardi, 11/5/52, Switzer Collection, MC 293 649.
22. Russell Dean's *New Life for Millions* (Hastings House, 1972, p. 125).
23. "Back to Life," *Time*, 5/12/58.
24. Switzer's unpublished autobiographical material.
25. Interview with Warren Perry, 3/11/83.
26. "Stories told by Bill Usdane," Switzer Collection, MC 293 367.
27. Interview with Frank Birdsall, 8/14/81.
28. Interview with Warren Perry, 3/11/83.
29. Ibid.
30. Rehabilitation Act, Public Law 565, August 3, 1954.
31. Statement of Mary Switzer before Senate Finance Committee, 2/16/56, Switzer Collection, MC 293 117.
32. Edward Berkowitz' *Rehabilitation: The Federal Government's Response to Disability, 1935-54* (Arno, 1980).
33. Russell Dean's *New Life for Millions* (Hastings House, 1972, p. 121.)
34. The Rehabilitation Service Administration's *Rehabilitation Record*, May-June 1970, p. 17.
35. Ibid.
36. Switzer's memo to Governor Ribicoff, 12/28/60, Switzer Collection, MC 293 52.
37. Reedy's memo to Switzer, 10/9/59, Switzer Collection, MC 293 10.
38. Regional Representatives Conference, Summary of Major Problems, 10/4/55, Switzer Collection, MC 293 200.

39. List of Members of the Advisory Council, Switzer Collection, MC 293 230.
40. Switzer's letter to Don Russell, 7/30/64, Switzer Collection, MC 293 620.
41. Regional Representatives Conference Summary, 10/3/55, Switzer Collection, MC 293 200.
42. Ed Berkowitz' *Rehabilitation: The Federal Government's Response to Disability* (Arno, 1980, p. 131).
43. Ibid, p. 12.
44. Worthingham's letter to Switzer, 1/56, Switzer Collection, MC 293 203.
45. Ort's letter to Switzer, 6/23/54, National Records Center Records Group 363, Accession number 71A1382, Box 64.
46. Redkey's memo to Garrett, 11/12/59, Switzer Collection, MC 293 231.
47. "Tip Sheet for talk to Hill-Burton Committee," 3/27/61, Switzer Collection, MC 293 251.
48. Switzer's letter to Ort, 3/28/55, National Records Center, Record Group 363, Accession Cumber 71A1382, Box 64.
49. Switzer's memo to staff, 3/12/60, Switzer Collection, MC 293 239.
50. Switzer's statement to Senate Finance Committee, 2/16/56, Switzer Collection, MC 293 117.
51. Switzer's letter to Tait, 7/21/59, Switzer Collection, MC 293 231.
52. Switzer's address to Third Rehabilitation Counselor Training Workshop, 2/19/59, Switzer Collection, MC 293 224.
53. R.M. Little's "Economic and Social Significance of the Vocational Rehabilitation Program," at the National Conference on Vocational Rehabilitation of the Civilian Disabled, 2/4/24, p. 8, in Faulkes papers, State Historical Society of Wisconsin.
54. Ibid, p. 9.
55. Percy Angove's "Administration of VR by a State" in *Bulletin #121, Civilian Vocational Rehabilitation Series #14*, June 1927, in the Faulkes papers, State Historical Society of Wisconsin, p. 5.
56. Statement of H.L. Benshoof before the Labor-Federal Security Agency Appropriations Committee, 1953, p. 761-762.
57. Russell Dean's *New Life for Millions* (Hastings House, 1972, p. 128).
58. Donald Dabelstein's "Counseling in the Rehabilitation Service," *Journal of Clinical Psychology*, 1946, 2, pp. 116-122.
59. *Annual Report of the Department of HEW*, 1952-54, p. 235.
60. National Rehabilitation Association's *Rehabilitation Counselor Preparation*, 1956.
61. Correspondence with Cecile Hillyer, 8/27/56.
62. Andrew Marrin's letter to Switzer, 3/31/58, Switzer Collection, MC 293 214.
63. Charles Feike's statement at meeting of States VR Council with OVR, May 1958, in minutes of meetings, Library of Department of Health and Human Services.
64. Switzer's address to Rehabilitation Counselor Training Workshop, 12/18/59, Switzer Collection, MC 293 224.
65. Correspondence with Cecile Hillyer, 8/27/82.
66. James Garrett's *Psychological Aspects of Physical Disability* (OVR, 1942), and Donald Dabelstein's "Counseling in the Rehabilitation Service," *Journal of Clinical Psychology*, 1946, 2, pp. 116-122.
67. Mary Switzer's "The Role of the Federal Government in VR," Switzer Collection, MC 293 200.
68. Switzer's letter to Dr. J. Wayne Reitz, 11/4/57, Switzer Collection, MC 293 620.
69. Hillyer's memo to Switzer, 11/28/60, Switzer Collection, MC 293 236.
70. List of Advisory Council members, Switzer Collection, MC 293 230.
71. Hillyer's memo to Switzer, 1/28/60, Switzer Collection, MC 293 236.
72. Interview with Warren Perry and Marceline Jaques, 3/11/83.
73. Switzer's speech at the University of Arizona (1967), Switzer Collection, MC 293 328.

74. Switzer's "Let's End this Personnel Shortage," 1961, Switzer Collection, MC 293 767.
75. Switzer's memo to Garrett, 5/9/67, Switzer Collection, MC 293 330.
76. Switzer's letter to Harold Rodes, 10/24/56, Switzer Collection, MC 293 240.
77. Interview with Marceline Jaques, 3/11/83.
78. Switzer's speech "Serving is a Privilege, not a Problem," 1967, Switzer Collection, MC 293 329.
79. Hillyer's memo to Switzer, 10/31/60, Switzer Collection, MC 293 236.
80. Switzer's letter to Donald Stone, 12/5/55, Switzer Collection, MC 293 240.
81. Switzer's letter to Willa Player, 1/19/61, Switzer Collection, MC 293 240.
82. Switzer's letter to Robert Sproul, 5/18/56, Switzer Collection, MC 293 240.
83. Interview with Douglas Fenderson, 5/1⅓3.
84. Interview with Bill Usdane, 1/77.
85. Interview with James Garrett, 3/8/82.
86. Levine's letter to Switzer, 6/28/65, MC 293 309; Switzer's tribute to Bell Greve, 1/18/57, MC 293 611; Switzer's letter to Ben Brainerd, 7/29/52, Switzer Collection, MC 293 596.
87. Faulkes' letter to Switzer, 3/28/55, Switzer Collection, MC 293 596.
88. Switzer's tribute to Bell Greve, 1/18/57, Switzer Collection, MC 293 620; personal correspondence with Don Fillmer, 10/14/83; John Bruere's "Bell Greve-World Citizen of Cleveland," 1/20/57 transcript of radio address.
89. Switzer's unpublished autobiographical material.
90. Ibid.
91. Ibid.
92. "Dabs' Questions," 7/6/56, Switzer Collection, MC 293 411.
93. Robert Thomas' "The First Twenty-Five Years" in *The Rehabilitation Record*, June 1970.
94. Edna Levine's letter to Switzer, 6/28/65, Switzer Collection, MC 293 309.
95. "Tip Sheet for Regional Representatives Meeting," 10/10-12/58, Switzer Collection, MC 293 221.
96. Ed Berkowitz' *Disability Policies and Government Programs* (Praeger, 1979); Monroe Berkowitz, William Johnson, and Edward Murphy's *Public Policy Toward Disability* (Praeger, 1976, p. 48).
97. Switzer's speech, "The Legislative Story of VR," 11/15/65, Switzer Collection, MC 293 329.
98. George Wyman and Switzer's memo to HEW Secretary Flemming, Switzer Collection, MC 239 231.
99. Rufus Miles' *The Department of Health, Education, and Welfare* (Praeger, 1974, p. 22).
100. Switzer's letter to Hobby, 7/24/55, Switzer Collection, MC 293 46.
101. Switzer's letter to Rusk, 1/11/55, Switzer Collection, MC 293 636.
102. Switzer's Headquarters News Notes, 8/4/55, Switzer Collection, MC 293 407.
103. Ibid.
104. Switzer's Headquarters News Notes, 12/14/56, Switzer Collection, MC 293 407.
105. Switzer's memo to Folsom, 12/2/56, Switzer Collection, MC 293 46.
106. Rufus Miles' *The Department of Health, Education, and Welfare*, (Praeger, 1972, p. 34.)
107. Elliot Richardson's *The Creative Balance* (Holt, Rinehart, and Winston, 1976, pp. 123-124.)
108. E.B. Whitten's "A Poor Man's Lobby," unpublished, p. 229.
109. Elliot Richardson's *The Creative Balance* (Holt, Rinehart, and Winston, 1976, p. 124.)
110. James Sundquist's *Politics and Policy* (Brookings, 1968, p. 115).
111. Rufus Miles' *The Department of Health, Education, and Welfare* (Praeger, 1972, p. 121.)
112. Switzer's Headquarters News Notes, 8/21/58, Switzer Collection, MC 293 407.
113. Ibid.
114. Ibid.
115. Ibid.
116. Ibid.
117. Ibid.

CHAPTER XII.
Categorical Jungle

1. Switzer's memo to Assistant Director, 12/29/60, Switzer Collection, MC 293 52.
2. Headquarters News Notes, 12/30/60, Switzer Collection, MC 293 407.
3. Ibid.
4. Dean's memo to Directors, 12/13/60, Switzer Collection, MC 293 52.
5. Rufus Miles' *The Department of Health, Education, and Welfare* (Praeger, 1972, pp. 41-42).
6. Switzer's memo to Richardson, 3/11/58, Switzer Collection, MC 293 48.
7. Richard Burkhauser and Robert Haveman's *Disability and Work: the Economics of American Policy* (Johns Hopkins Press, 1982, p. 41).
8. Martha Derthick's *Policymaking for Social Security* (Brookings, 1979, pp. 18-20).
9. Ibid.
10. Ibid, p. 160.
11. David Marwick's *Work and Welfare Go Together* (Johns Hopkins Press, 1972, pp. 70-71).
12. Switzer's memo to Secretary Flemming, 10/5/58, Switzer Collection, MC 293 50.
13. Switzer's memo to Richardson, 10/1/59, Switzer Collection, MC 293 48.
14. Ibid.
15. Ibid.
16. Wyman and Switzer's memo to Secretary Flemming, 10/28/59, Switzer Collection, MC 293 231.
17. Interview with Corbett Reedy, 8/17/81.
18. Rufus Miles' *The Department of Health, Education, and Welfare* (Praeger, 1972, p. 42).
19. Headquarters News Notes, 12/19/62, Switzer Collection, MC 293 407.
20. Division of Statistics and Studies' *Statistical History, Federal-State Program of VR 1920-1969* (DHEW, 1970).
21. Switzer's address to National Labor Conference on Rehabilitation, 12/5/63, Switzer Collection, MC 293 359.
22. Headquarters News Notes, 8/14/62, Switzer Collection, MC 293 421.
23. Ibid.
24. Interview with Joe Hunt, 8/10/81.
25. Switzer's letter to Rauschenbush, 12/25/62, Switzer Collection, MC 293 633.
26. Rufus Miles' *The Department of Health, Education, and Welfare* (Praeger, 1972, p. 44).
27. Ibid, p. 46.
28. Hearings before the House Appropriations Subcommittee on Labor, Health, Education, and Welfare, 1/30/62.
29. Headquarters News Notes, 8/14/62, Switzer Collection, MC 293 407.
30. Rufus Miles' *The Department of Health, Education, and Welfare* (Praeger, 1972, p. 43).
31. Elliot Richardson's *The Creative Balance* (Holt, Rinehart, and Winston, 1976).
32. David Marwick's *Work and Welfare Go Together* (Johns Hopkins Press, 1972, p. 71).
33. Martha Derthicks's *Uncontrollable Spending for Social Service Grants* (Brookings, 1975, p. 7).
34. Ibid, p. 30.
35. David Marwick's *Work and Welfare Go Together* (Johns Hopkins Press, 1972, p. 70.)
36. John Muthard's *The Vocational Rehabilitation of Public Welfare Assistance Recipients* (University of Florida Rehabilitation Research Institute, 1976, pp. 4-5).
37. Reedy's memo to Switzer, 10/9/59, Switzer Collection, MC 293 10.
38. Reedy's memo to Switzer, 6/29/60, Switzer Collection, MC 293 8.
39. Schafer's memo to Switzer, 8/8/60, Switzer Collection, MC 293 10.
40. Benshoof's memo to Switzer, 9/16/60, Switzer Collection, MC 293 10.
41. Garrett's memo to Switzer, 9/19/60, Switzer Collection, MC 293 10.
42. Lamborn's memo to Switzer, 9/16/60, Switzer Collection, MC 293 10.

43. Wright's memo to Switzer, 9/28/60, Switzer Collection, MC 293 10.
44. Martz's memo to Switzer, 9/22/60, Switzer Collection, MC 293 10.
45. Switzer's memo to Ribicoff, 12/28/60, Switzer Collection, MC 293 52.
46. Lamborn's memo to Switzer, 9/16/60, Switzer Collection, MC 293 10.
47. OVR's Report of the Task Force on Goals for the 1960's (VRA, 1960).
48. Dean's memo to Switzer, 6/29/60, Switzer Collection, MC 293 10.
49. 1964 Hearings before the Appropriations Committee for the Departments of Labor, and Health, Education, and Welfare, 2/18/63.
50. Minutes of National Citizens Advisory Committee on VR meeting, 5/6/66, Switzer Collection, MC 293 166.
51. Switzer's testimony before the Senate Committee on Labor and Public Welfare, Subcommittee on Health, 3/29 and 30/65, p. 41.
52. Frost's memo to Switzer, 3/9/64, Switzer Collection, MC 293 283.
53. Ibid.
54. Ibid.
55. Ibid.
56. Switzer's letter to Rauschenbush, 7/27/61, Switzer Collection, MC 293 633.
57. "Tip Sheet for Miss Switzer" for Florence Heller Graduate School for Advanced Studies in Social Welfare, Brandeis University, 12/63, Switzer Collection, MC 293 281.
58. Switzer's letter to Agnes Callahan, 12/18/63, Switzer Collection, MC 293 422.
59. Ariel Fink's letter to Switzer, 12/27/63, Switzer Collection, MC 293 422.
60. Switzer's memo to Miles, 7/7/64, Switzer Collection, MC 293 419.
61. Ibid.

CHAPTER XIII.
There are Victories

1. Francis Rourke's *Bureaucratic Power in National Politics* (Little, Brown, 1972, p. 380.)
2. Switzer's letter to H. Urrow, 9/29/64.
3. Switzer's "Rehabilitation: An Act of Faith," in Senate Congressional Record, 12/19/69, p. S17274.
4. Switzer's memo to the Secretary, 3/24/67, Switzer Collection, MC 293 52.
5. Ibid.
6. Babington's memo to Carter, 3/21/67, Switzer Collection, MC 293 52.
7. Switzer's memo to Cohen, 3/24/67, Switzer Collection, MC 293 52.
8. Gardner's memo to McNamara, 4/18/67, Switzer Collection, MC 293 52.
9. "Getting the Disabled on their Feet," Medical World News, March 3, 1967.
10. Paul Starr's *The Transformation of American Medicine* (Basic Books, 1982, p. 442.)
11. Interview with Jim Garrett, 9/22/83.
12. Ferebee's memo to Switzer, 4/18/61, Switzer Collection, MC 293 256.
13. U.S. Department of Health, Education, and Welfare *Grants-in-Aid and Other Financial Assistance Programs* (GPO, 1967, p. 325).
14. Tip Sheet for Miss Switzer at First Conference of Research and Training Centers, 3/18-19/63, Switzer Collection, MC 293 274.
15. Switzer's dedication at Temple Research and Training Center, 1964, Switzer Collection, MC 293 322.
16. Ibid.
17. Switzer's testimony before House Subcommittee on Education and Labor, July 18, 1967, p. 137.
18. Ann Bancroft's letter to Switzer, 4/11/61, Switzer Collection, MC 293 414.

19. Biographical sketch of Helen Mencken, Switzer Collection, MC 293 210.
20. Switzer's memo to Salvatore DiMichael, 3/13/62, Switzer Collection, MC 293 420.
21. Switzer's memo to Jim Garrett, 3/18/66, Switzer Collection, MC 293 417.
22. National Theatre of the Deaf Tip Sheet, Switzer Collection, MC 293 417.
23. David Hays' letter to Switzer, 6/23/69, Switzer Collection, MC 293 417.
24. Ibid.
25. Ibid.
26. Tipsheet for Mary Switzer, 7/11/69, Switzer Collection, MC 293 417.
27. "Project Summary" 12/13/67, Switzer Collection, MC 293 317.
28. Interview with Switzer in 1970 AAWB Annual, p. 2.
29. Ibid.
30. Correspondence in Switzer Collection, Switzer Collection, MC 293 610.
31. Switzer's Christmas message, 12/10/58, Switzer Collection, MC 293 47.
32. Switzer's letter to Allen Eaton, 10/16/55, Switzer Collection, MC 293 201.
33. Switzer's "The Enjoyment of the Arts: Another Aspect of Rehabilitation," in 1967 AAWB Annual, Switzer Collection, MC 293 424.
34. Switzer's letter to Thomas Hoving, 5/16/67, Switzer Collection, MC 293 420.
35. Thomas Hoving's letter to Switzer, 5/24/67, in Warren Bledsoe's personal files.
36. Switzer's letter to Blanchett Arnaud, 1966, Switzer Collection, MC 293 424.
37. Switzer's "The Enjoyment of the Arts: Another Aspect of Rehabilitation," in 1967 AAWB Annual, Switzer Collection, MC 293 424.
38. Interview with Jim Garrett, 5/1/84.
39. Interview with Switzer in 1970 AAWB Annual, p. 2.
40. Interview with Jim Garrett, 9/22/83.
41. Wilbur Cohen's Introduction to the Annual Report of The Department of HEW, 1968, pp. 188-193.
42. Switzer Collection, MC 291 360.
43. Ibid.
44. Ibid.
45. Paul Starr's The Social Transformation of American Medicine (Basic Boods, 1982, pp. 344-345.)
46. Switzer's unpublished autobiographical material, 10/9/66.
47. Switzer's letter to Karl Menninger, 4/5/43, Switzer Collection, MC 293 911.
48. Switzer's unpublished autobiographical material, 10/9/66, p. 5.
49. Switzer's letter to Charles Ernst, 7/31/47, Switzer Collection, MC 293 917.
50. Paul Starr's The Social Transformation of American Medicine (Basic Books, 1982, pp. 346-347.)
51. Karl Menninger's letter to Charles Ernst, 7/31/47, Switzer Collection, MC 293 917.
52. Bill Menninger's letter to Switzer, 11/2/49, Switzer Collection, MC 293 910.
53. Switzer's unpublished autobiographical material, 10/9/66, p. 6.
54. Ibid, p. 3.
55. Draper's letter to Karl Menninger, 11/17/52, Switzer Collection, MC 293 605.
56. C. Warren Bledsoe's "Originators of Orientation and Mobility Training" in Foundations of Orientation and Mobility, p. 615.
57. Ibid, p. 617.
58. Ibid, p. 587.
59. Ibid, pp. 587-588.
60. Ibid, pp. 603-606.
61. Interview with C. Warren Bledsoe, 3/15/84.
62. Switzer's letter to Joe Clunk, 1/1/53, Switzer Collection, MC 293 595.
63. C. Warren Bledsoe's "Originators of Orientation and Mobility Training," in Foundations of Orientation and Mobility, pp. 617-618.

64. Personal correspondence from C. Warren Bledsoe.
65. C. Warren Bledsoe's "Low Vision and the Office for the Blind and Visually Handicapped," in *Optical Journal and Review of Optometry*, 113, #12, pp. 56-59.
66. C. Warren Bledsoe's "Originators of Orientation and Mobility Training," in *Foundations of Orientation and Mobility*, p. 621.
67. Personal correspondence from Freeman McConnell, 3/30/84.
68. Interview with Boyce Williams, 8/11/81.
69. The Department of Health, Education, and Welfare's "A Common Thread of Service," (GPO, 1970, p. 18.)
70. George Wright's *Total Rehabilitation* (Little, Brown, 1982, p. 266.)
71. Interview with Boyce Williams, 8/11/81.
72. Switzer's "Expanding Concepts in Rehabilitation," 9/17/67, delivered at the Eleventh World Congress of the Disabled in Dublin, p. 7, in Health and Human Services Library.
73. Switzer's "The Impact of the Rehabilitation Amendments Act of 1965 on Psychiatric Rehabilitation," 5/11/67, Switzer Collection, MC 293 330.
74. Switzer's letter to Clarence Pickett, 1/1/54, Switzer Collection, MC 293 128.
75. Switzer's "Expanding Concepts in Rehabilitation," 9/17/67.
76. VRA's *Rehabilitation of the Disabled in 51 Countries* (GPO, 1964, p. iii.)
77. Switzer's memo to Robert Kevan, 8/18/59, Switzer Collection, MC 293 620.
78. Switzer's letter to Dr. Melvin Casberg, 3/25/60, Switzer Collection, MC 293 420.
79. Switzer's memo to Abraham Ribicoff, 12/28/60, Switzer Collection, MC 293 200.
80. Switzer's "Hope, the Anchor of Life," 5/1/68, in Health and Human Services Library.
81. The Department of Health, Education, and Welfare's *Rehabilitation of the Disabled in 51 Countries*, (GPO, 1964).
82. Interview with Warren Perry, 3/22/83.
83. Switzer's memo to Abraham Ricicoff, 12/28/60, Switzer Collection, MC 293 200, p. 3.
84. "Getting the Disabled on their Feet," *Medical World News*, 3/3/67.
85. The Department of Health, Education, and Welfare's *Grants-in-Aid and Other Financial Assistance Programs*, 1967 Edition, p. 327.
86. Switzer's letter to Reverend Edward A. Cahill, 2/26/59, Switzer Collection, MC 293 224.
87. Interview with Ethel and Felix Putterman, 10/10/81.
88. "Freedman's Hospital," Switzer Collection, MC 293 371.
89. Ibid.
90. Switzer's letter to Dr. Graham Davis, 5/6/47, Switzer Collection, MC 293 373.
91. James Burress' letter to David Amato, 4/20/51, Switzer Collection, MC 293 373.
92. Switzer's memo to Secretary Folsom, 9/16/58, Switzer Collection, MC 293 50.
93. Headquarters News Notes, 8/8/52, Switzer Collection, MC 293 407.
94. Switzer's memo 6/24/47, Switzer Collection, MC 293 624.
95. Paul Starr's *The Social Transformation of American Medicine* (Basic Books, 1982, p. 124 and 167.)
96. Switzer's "Neglected Disability: A National Problem," *Journal of the National Medical Association*, July 1955, pp. 262-247.
97. Charles A. Cerami's "Women in Government," *Women's Day*, 9/65, p. 44, Switzer Collection, MC 293 778.
98. Switzer's article for *Radcliffe Quarterly*, Feb. 1959, Switzer Collection, MC 293 717.
99. Switzer's testimony before Senate Subcommittee on Labor and Public Welfare, 8/14/67, p. 19.
100. The Department of Health, Education, and Welfare's "A Common Thread of Service," (GPO, 1970, p. 25.)
101. Herbert Kaufman's *The Administrative Behavior of Federal Bureau Chiefs* (Brookings, 1981, p. 161.)

CHAPTER XIV
Problems of Plenty

1. Switzer's letter to Rauschenbush, 7/18/65, Switzer Collection, MC 293 633.
2. Statement of William Page before the House Special Subcommittee on Education of the Commitee on Education and Labor, 4/14/65.
3. Switzer's letter to Margolin, 6/2/67, Switzer Collection, MC 293 620.
4. Headquarters News Notes, 12/29/64, Switzer Collection, MC 293 407.
5. E.B. Whitten's "A Poor Man's Lobby," unpublished, p. 257.
6. Edith Green's statement before the House Subcommittee on Education, 4/14/65, p. 88.
7. Switzer's letter to Rauschenbush, 7/18/65, Switzer Collection, MC 293 633.
8. Green-Switzer exchange before Special Subcommittee on Education, 89th Congress, 1st Session, 3/13/65, p. 40.
9. E.B. Whitten's testimony before the Special Subcommittee on Education, 4/14/65, p. 75.
10. Remarks by Mr. Sickles, in hearings before the Special Subcommittee on Education, 4/14/65, p. 73.
11. Committee Print, "Restoring Disabled People to Jobs and Useful Living," Committee on Education and Labor, House of Representatives, 1965.
12. E.B. Whitten's testimony before House Special Subcomittee on Education, 4/14/65, p. 67.
13. E.B. Whitten's "A Poor Man's Lobby," unpublished, p. 258.
14. Ibid, p. 253-254.
15. Ibid.
16. William Page's testimony before House Special Subcommittee on Education, 4/14/65, pp. 83-90.
17. Ibid.
18. Switzer's memo to the Secretary, 8/11/65, Switzer Collection, MC 293 54.
19. Ibid.
20. Ibid.
21. Ibid.
22. Ibid.
23. Ibid.
24. Ibid.
25. Wilbur Cohen's memo to Lister Hill, 9/14/65, Switzer Collection, MC 293 614.
26. The Department of Health, Education, and Welfare's "A Common Thread: An Historical Guide to HEW," (GPO, 1970.)
27. Switzer's letter to Grace Lynch, 9/20/65, Switzer Collection, MC 293 623.
28. Russell Dean's *New Life for Millions* (Hastings House, 1972, p. 148).
29. Switzer's speech to American Psychiatric Association, 5/12/67, Switzer Collection, MC 293 276.
30. Switzer's memo to the Secretary, 8/11/65, Switzer Collection, MC 293 354.
31. The Department of Health, Education, and Welfare's "A Common Thread: An Historical Guide to HEW," (GPO, 1970.)
32. Switzer's letter to Rauschenbush, 7/18/65, Switzer Collection, MC 293 633.
33. House Committee on Education and Labor Committee Print, 1965, p. 81.
34. Ibid.
35. Switzer's speech to 52nd Annual National Hadassah Convention, 8/14/66, in Department of Health and Human Services Library.
36. Switzer's speech to Devereaux Foundation, "The Compleat Society," 5/32/65, in Department of Health and Human Services Library.
37. House Committee on Education and Labor Committee Print, p. 81.
38. Switzer's speech to Devereaux Foundation, "The Compleat Society," 5/3/65, in the Department of Health and Human Services Library.

39. David Walls' letter to Switzer, 11/1/66, Switzer Collection, MC 293 420.
40. Ibid.
41. Interview with Sheila Hackett, 11/16/81.
42. Switzer's "The Comfort of the Shared Burden," 1965 Donald Dabelstein lecture, National Rehabilitation Association, Washington, D.C.
43. Switzer's "Rehabilitation -- Hope for Recovery," 8/15/66, in the Department of Health and Human Services Library.
44. Switzer's "The Impact of Rehabilitation Amendments Act of 1965 on Psychiatric Rehabilitation, 5/12/67, Detroit, Michigan, in the Department of Health and Human Services Library.
45. Switzer's testimony before House Special Subcommittee on Education of the Committee on Education and Labor, 89th Congress, 4/14/65, p. 50.
46. Switzer's "Rehabilitation and Social Security on Trial," Switzer Collection, MC 293 983.
47. Ibid.
48. Ibid.
49. Switzer's "Impact of the Rehabilitation Amendments of 1960 on Psychiatric Rehabilitation," 5/12/67, in the Department of Health and Human Resources Library.
50. Switzer's letter to Rauschenbush, 2/6/67, Switzer Collection, MC 293 633.
51. Ibid.
52. Ibid.
53. James Sundquist's *Politics and Policy* (Brookings, 1968, p. 536).
54. Charles Schultze's *The Politics and Economics of Public Spending* (Brookings, 1968, p. 14).
55. S. Levitan, M. Rein, and D. Marwick's *Work and Welfare Go Together* (Johns Hopkins Press, 1972, p. 7).
56. Ibid, p. 14.
57. Interview with Ellen Winston, 11/10/82.
58. Martha Derthick's *Uncontrollable Spending for Social Service Grants* (Brookings, 1975, p. 23).
59. Ibid.
60. Interview with Ellen Winston, 11/10/82.
61. Martha Derthick's *The Influence of Federal Grants* (Harvard University Press, 1970, p. 172).
62. Interview with Ellen Winston, 11/10/82.
63. Ibid.
64. Report of the National Citizens' Advisory Committee on Vocational Rehabilitation (GPO, 1968.)
65. Interview with Boyce Williams, 8/11/81.
66. Switzer's letter to Helen Ross, 9/17/52, Switzer Collection, MC 293 420.
67. Interview with Patria Forsythe, 11/16/82.
68. Edward Martin's "Legislative History," in *Exceptional Children*, March 1968.
69. Interview with Patria Forsythe, 11/16/82.
70. DHEW's "A Common Thread of Service: An Historical Guide to HEW," p. 12, in Department of Health and Human Resources Library.
71. Office of Vocational Rehabilitation's "Rehabilitation: The Decade of the Sixties," August 1960.
72. Correspondence with Corbett Reedy, 4/14/84.
73. House Committee on Education and Labor's Committee Print (GPO, 1965), and VRA's "Vocational Rehabilitation," in the Department of HEW During the Administration of President Lyndon B. Johnson, in the Department of Health and Human Services Library, H 91 A32.
74. "Report of the National Citizens' Advisory Committee on Vocational Rehabilitation," (GPO, 6/26/68, 0-306-412).
75. Switzer's memo to F. Robert Meier, 1/19/68, Switzer Collection, MC 293 166.

76. Interview with Paul Howard, 8/12/81.
77. Switzer's memo to F. Robert Meier, 1/19/68, Switzer Collection, MC 293 166.
78. Rusk's memo to Flemming, 3/13/51 and Rusk's memo to Symington, 1/12/51, Switzer Collection, MC 293 161.
79. Flemming's memo to member of the Manpower Policy Committee, 4/10/51, Switzer Collection, MC 293 161.
80. Switzer's memo to F. Robert Meier, 1/16/66, Switzer Collection, MC 293 166.
81. Switzer's memo to John Thurston, 7/28/52, Switzer Collection, MC 293 39.
82. Minutes of May 6, 1966 meeting of the National Citizens' Advisory Committee on Vocational Rehabilitation, Switzer Collection, MC 293 166.
83. Ibid.
84. Switzer's testimony before Senate Sub-Committee on Labor and Public Welfare, 8/14/67, p. 19.
85. "Report of the National Citizens' Advisory Committee on Vocational Rehabilitation," (GPO, 6/16/68, 0-306-412, p. 29).
86. Phillip Lee's memo to Commissioners of Welfare, Education and VR and the Surgeon General, 9/12/66, Switzer Collection, MC 293 54.
87. Switzer's letter to Rauschenbush, 2/6/67, Switzer Collection, MC 293 633.
88. Ibid.

CHAPTER XV.
A Rescue Mission

1. W. Grant's article in the *Washington Post*, 11/15/66.
2. Ralph Peckham's memo to Switzer, 11/15/66, Switzer Collection, MC 293 13.
3. Rufus Miles' *The Department of Health, Education, and Welfare* (Praeger, 1972, p. 28).
4. Switzer's memo to Executive Staff, 9/8/66, Switzer Collection, MC 293 13.
5. George Greenberg's *Governing HEW: Problems of Management and Control at the DHEW* (Harvard University, 1972, p. 9).
6. Ralph Peckham's memo to Switzer, Switzer Collection, MC 11/15/66.
7. Switzer's memo to Executive Staff, 9/8/66, Switzer Collection, MC 293 13.
8. Ralph Peckham's memo to Switzer, 11/15/66, Switzer Collection, MC 293 13.
9. Ibid.
10. Ibid.
11. Jim Garrett's memo to Switzer, 11/16/66, Switzer Collection, MC 293 13.
12. Ibid.
13. Rufus Miles' *The Department of Health, Education, and Welfare* (Praeger, 1972, p. 9).
14. Rusk's letter to Gardner, 1/25/67, Switzer Collection, MC 293 13.
15. Rusk's "Mary Elizabeth Switzer: A Tribute," in *The Journal of Allied Health*, Spring 1974, p. 89-92.
16. Vera Glaser's "Welfare Head Calls Program a Disgrace," *Pensacola News*, June 4, 1968.
17. "Organization Woman," *Time*, 9/1/66, p. 14.
18. Switzer's "Remarks," delivered at meeting of SRS Personnel, 8/22/67, in Health and Human Services Library.
19. Vera Glaser's "Welfare Head Calls Program a Disgrace," *Pensacola News*, 1/4/68.
20. Switzer's "Remarks," delivered at meeting of SRS personnel, 8/22/67, in Health and Human Services Library.
21. Switzer's "The Image of Welfare--1968," delivered to the American Public Welfare Association, 12/8/67, Switzer Collection, MC 297 338.
22. Ibid.

23. Gardner's "Remarks," delivered to the National Rehabilitation Association, 10/2/67, Switzer Collection, MC 293 335.
24. Ibid.
25. Ibid.
26. Switzer's "Priorities and New Directions," presented to SRS Conference, 2/19/68, Switzer Collection, MC 293 340.
27. Gardner's "Remarks," delivered to the National Rehabilitation Association, 10/2/67, Switzer Collection, MC 293 335.
28. Guest list, Switzer Collection, MC 293 334.
29. Switzer Collection, MC 293 8.
30. Switzer's civil service ratings, Switzer Collection, MC 293 793.
31. Wilbur Cohen's "A Tribute to Mary E. Switzer," presented at the Columbia Rehabilitation Association meetings, 9/19/67, Switzer Collection, MC 293 334.
32. Switzer's address to the Hawaii State Vocational Rehabilitation General Assembly, 5/21/68, Switzer Collection, MC 293 366.
33. Interview with Jim Garrett, 3/14/84.
34. Switzer's "The Many Faces of Rehabilitation as a Function and as Social Policy," presented to Hawaii State VR General Assembly, 5/21/68, Switzer Collection, MC 293 366.
35. "Tip Sheet" for meeting of Associate Regional Commissioners for Rehabilitation Services, 9/19/68, Switzer Collection, MC 293 350.
36. Switzer's memo to Joe Hunt, 2/10/68, Switzer Collection, MC 293 340.
37. Ibid.
38. Switzer's "Year of Urgency--Our Joint Commitment," 4/3/68, Switzer Collection, MC 293 343.
39. Switzer's "New Opportunities and Responsibilities in our Changing Society," 1/25/68, Switzer Collection, MC 297 339.
40. Ibid.
41. Vera Glaser's "Welfare Head Calls Program a Disgrace," *Pensacola News*, 1/8/68.
42. "Organization Woman," in *Time*, 9/1/67, p. 14.
43. Ibid.
44. Lisle Carter's memo to Switzer, 1/22/68, Switzer Collection, MC 297 339.
45. Ibid.
46. Elliot Richardson's *The Creative Balance* (Holt, Rinehart, and Winston, 1976, p. 196).
47. Oral history of Martha May Eliot, Schlesinger Library, p. 369; Martha May Eliot papers, Switzer Collection, MC 229 280 411.
48. Switzer's "New Opportunities and Responsibilities in our Changing Society," 1/25/68, Eliot Collection, MC 297 339, pg. 3.
49. Switzer's "Rehabilitation--Hope for Recovery," 8/15/66, Switzer Collection, MC 293 200.
50. Switzer's presentation to the SRS National Advisory Committee, 11/4/68, Switzer Collection, MC 293 352.
51. "Organization Woman," *Time*, 9/1/67, p. 14.
52. Switzer's "Our Nation's Commitment to Children," 3/20/68, Switzer Collection, MC 293 432.
53. "Tipsheet for Miss Switzer," Medical Assistance Advisory Council, 7/26/68, Switzer Collection, MC 293 348.
54. Switzer's "Public Assistance," 11/2/68, Switzer Collection, MC 293 336.
55. Rufus Miles' *The Department of Health, Education, and Welfare* (Praeger, 1972, p. 51).
56. Interview with Joe Hunt, 8/10/81.
57. Switzer's "Our Moral Obligation to Care," 6/15/68, Health and Human Services Library.
58. Interview with Wilbur Cohen, 7/5/82.
59. Maude Dorr's "No Miracle in Mud Flats," in the *Village Voice*, 6/20/68.

60. Ibid.
61. Switzer's "To Make the World a Brotherhood," address at Hofstra University, 6/15/69, Switzer Collection, MC 293 360.
62. Switzer's "Changing Mission for the Helping Professions," First Switzer Memorial Lecture at the State University of New York at Buffalo, 1970.
63. Switzer's memo to Simpson, 2/28/68, Federal Records Center, Record Group 71A2593, Box 21.
64. Switzer's "SRS Anniversary," 8/15/68, Federal Records Center, Record Group 71A2593, Box 19.
65. Ibid.
66. Switzer's notes to friends, 8/15/68, Federal Records Center, Record Group 71A2593, Box 19.
67. Ibid.
68. Wilbur Cohen's "Looking Toward the Future," delivered to the American Medical Association, 2/22/80, published in *Inquiry* 17:115-119.
69. Cohen's "Secretary Introduction," of the 1968 *Annual Report of the US Department of Health, Education, and Welfare* (GPO, 1969, p. 1-3).
70. "Opening statement of the President at Cabinet meeting" 12/4/68, Federal Records Center, Record Group 71A2593, Box 19.
71. "Tip Sheet for Miss Switzer: New Directions in Rehabilitation," presented to George Washington University, 2/28/69, Switzer Collection, MC 293 355.
72. Switzer's presentation to Graduate School of Social Welfare, Brandeis, 4/1/69, Switzer Collection, MC 293 357.
73. Ibid.
74. "Instructions for Hearing," Switzer Collection, MC 293 342; and William Burson's memo to John Gardner, 2/21/68, Switzer Collection, MC 293 342.
75. Martha Derthick's *Uncontrollable Spending for Social Service Grants* (Brookings, 1975, p. 21.)
76. Switzer's presentation to Graduate School of Social Welfare, Brandeis, 4/1/69, Switzer Collection, MC 293 357.
77. Ibid.
78. *The DHEW during the Administration of Lyndon B. Johnson* (12), in Health and Human Services Library, H 91 A32, p 155-157.
79. Russell Dean's *New Life for Millions* (Hastings House, 1972, p. 164).
80. News release from Conference office, 6/23/69, Switzer Collection, MC 293 361.
81. Joel Cohen's memo to Switzer, 10/30/68, Switzer Collection, MC 293 361.
82. Richard Grant's memo to Switzer, 7/30/69, Switzer Collection, MC 293 361.
83. Ibid.
84. Ibid.
85. Ibid.
86. Switzer's "Administration and the Concept of Social Service," presented to the 1968 National Conference on Public Administration, 3/29/68, Switzer Collection, MC 293 342.
87. Switzer's memo to Finch, 8/1/69, Switzer Collection, MC 293 362.
88. Ibid.
89. Interview with Patria Forsythe, 11/16/82.
90. Switzer address to Gradute School of Social Welfare, Brandeis University, 4/1/69, Switzer Collection, MC 293 357.
91. Oral history of Martha May Eliot, Schlesinger Library.
92. Jules Sugarman papers, in National Archives, Record Group 235, Stack 2E2.
93. Switzer's address to Graduate School of Social Welfare, Brandeis University, 4/1/69, Switzer Collection, MC 293 357.
94. Russell Dean's *New Life for Millions* (Hastings House, 1972, pp. 165-6).
95. Ibid.

96. Minutes of the Administrator's meeting with SRS Regional Commissioners, 10/22/69, Switzer Collection, MC 293 365.
97. Congressional Record, 12/19/69, p. S17172.
98. Ibid.
99. Ibid.
100. Interview with Kay Arneson, 8/11/81, and Corbett Reedy, 8/17/81.
101. Interview with Jim Burress, 11/2/82.
102. Interview with Sam Martz, 1/1/82.
103. Minutes of Administrator's meeting with SRS Regional Commissioners, 10/20-22/69, Switzer Collection, MC 293 365, p. 9.
104. Interview with Switzer, conducted by R. Novogrod of Long Island University, 2/12/70, from personal files of Howard Rusk, p. 9.
105. Rufus Miles' *The Department of Health, Education, and Welfare* (Prager, 1972, p. 137-8).
106. Martha Derthicks' *The Influence of Federal Grants* (Harvard University Press, 1970, p. 21.)
107. Interview with Jim Garrett, 3/14/84.
108. Interview with Joe LaRocca, 11/16/82.
109. Interview with Sam Martz, 8/12/81.
110. Interview with Anastasia Switzer, 10/9/81.
111. Special issue of SRS Newsletter, vol. 2, #10.
112. Ibid.

CHAPTER XVI.
The Wind at Her Back

1. Interview with James Garrett, 3/18/82.
2. Interview with Warren Perry, 3/13/83.
3. Recording of Retirement Dinner Program, 2/24/70, courtesy of O.E. Reese.
4. Interview with Howard Rusk, 10/9/81.
5. Switzer's letter to Howard Rusk, 1/11/55, Switzer Collection, MC 293 636; Switzer's letter to Oveta Culp Hobby, 3/3/63, Switzer Collection, MC 293 11.
6. Switzer's letter to Rauschenbush, 10/11/58, Switzer Collection, MC 293 633.
7. Switzer's Headquarters News Notes, 12/20/60, Switzer Collection, MC 293 407.
8. Ibid.
9. Interview with Joe Hunt, 8/10/81.
10. Interviews with Richard Switzer, 11/24/81; May Switzer, 10/19/82; Anastasia Switzer, 10/9/81, 5/16/82.
11. Interview with Warren Perry, 3/12/83.
12. Interview with Anna Parker, 8/12/81; Interview with Paul Howard, 8/12/81.
13. Interview with Josephine Coe, 8/13/81.
14. Interview with Frances Curtis, 8/11/81.
15. Interview with Ann Verano Lyden, 8/12/81.
16. Interview with Ann Draper, 11/15/82.
17. *The New York Times*, 3/1/70.
18. Switzer's letter to Robert Finch, 12/5/69.
19. HEW Press Release, 12/17/69.
20. Ibid.
21. *Hearing and Speech News*, March/April, 1971, p. 3.
22. *News from Gallaudet*, 5/21/70.
23. Interview with Richard Seggel, 3/9/82.
24. Warren Bledsoe's "Dedication to Mary Elizabeth Switzer" in *1972 AAWB Annual*, p. xi.

25. Switzer's "The Moral Obligation to Communicate," Commencement Address at Gallaudet College, 6/3/68, Gallaudet College Archives.
26. Rufus Miles' "Tribute to Mary Elizabeth Switzer," 10/26/71, in Richard Switzer personal papers.
27. Interview with Frances Curtis, 8/11/81.
28. Interview with Ann Draper, 11/15/82.
29. Interview with Anastasia Switzer, 5/16/82.
30. Interview with Anna Parker, 8/12/81.
31. Interview with Helene Goepner, 10/10/81; interview with Anastasia Switzer, 10/9/81.
32. Interview with Paul Howard, 8/12/81.
33. Interview with Patria Forsythe, 11/16/82.
34. Interview with Howard Rusk, 10/9/81.
35. Interview with Anastasia Switzer, 5/16/82.
36. Interview with May Switzer, 10/19/82.
37. Interview with Warren Bledsoe, 3/14/81.
38. Interview with Anastasia Switzer, 10//9/81; interview with Richard Switzer, 11/24/81.
39. *The Washington Post*, 10/17/71, p. 38; *Sunday Star*, 10/17/71.
40. Interview with Ann Draper, 11/15/82.
41. Program for Mary E. Switzer Memorial Service, 10/19/71, Grace Episcopal Church, Alexandria, Virginia, in Warren Bledsoe's personal papers.
42. Interview with Paul Howard, 8/12/81.
43. Switzer's telegram to the National Rehabilitation Association Conference, 10/10/71, Switzer Collection, MC 293 5.
44. Isabella Diamond's "The Dedicated Bureaucrat," 1972, p. 9.
45. Interview with James Burress, 11/2/82.
46. Quote from Albert Lasker Award, 1960, Woodrow Wilson Rehabilitation Center Switzer Archives.
47. SRS Newsletter, Switzer Collection, MC 293 5.
48. Jack Taylor's letter to Isabella Diamond, 11/8/71, in personal papers of Warren Perry.
49. SRS Newsletter, Switzer Collection, MC 293 5.
50. House Congressional Record, 1/26/73, p. H468.
51. Senate Congressional Record, 12/3/71, p. S20513.
52. House Congressional Record, 12/15/71, p. H12635.
53. Transcript of Dedication Ceremony, 1/16/73, in Richard Switzer personal papers.
54. Isabella Diamond's letter to Howard Rusk, 11/1/71, in Howard Rusk personal papers.
55. Lee Johnson's letter to Isabella Diamond, 1/19/73, in Warren Perry personal papers.
56. Interview with Corbett Reedy, 8/17/81.
57. Inventory of Mary E. Switzer Archives, from Woodrow Wilson Rehabilitation Center, Fishersville, Virginia.
58. Interview with Henry Viscardi, 10/19/82.
59. Resolution of the American Society of Allied Professions, 11/3/71.
60. Last Will and Testament of Isabella Stevenson Diamond, p. 3, City of Alexandria Clerk's Office, Book 123, p. 397.
61. Isabella Diamond's letter to Warren Perry, 4/16/73, in Warren Perry personal papers.
62. NRA's "Report of the First Mary E. Switzer Memorial Seminar," Cleveland, Ohio, May 20-25, 1975, p. iv.
63. Isabella Diamond's "Mary Elizabeth Switzer: The Dedicated Bureaucrat," 1973.
64. Ibid, p. 5.
65. Rufus Miles' "Tribute to Mary Elizabeth Switzer," 10/26/71, p. 2, in Richard Switzer's personal papers.
66. Switzer's "Reminisces about My Uncle Mike," unpublished autobiographical material, 9/13/65, p. 7.
67. Herbert Kaufman's *The Administrative Behavior of Federal Bureau Chiefs*, (Brookings, 1981, p. 173.)
68. Howard Rusk in the *Journal of Allied Health*, Spring 1974, p. 91.

INDEX

Abbott, Grace, 73, 76
Acheson, Dean, 29-30, 44, 72
Adams, Sherman, 143
Addams, Jane, 28, 73, 77, 82
Adkins, Bertha, 173
Administration on Aging, 233
Allan, Scott, 227
Altmeyer, Arthur, 55-56, 67, 74, 103, 153, 238
American Association of University Women, 26, 27
American Federation of the Handicapped, 128, 151
American Federation of Labor, 48
American Friends Service Committee, 38, 84-85
American Medical Association, 53-54, 56, 60-64, 71, 74, 95, 108, 117, 121-123, 170, 206, 231
American National Red Cross, ll7
American Society of Allied Health Professions, 262, 267
Anderson, Mary, 36, 76-78
Anderson, Richard, 123-124
Arthudale Project, 83-84
Association of Rehabilitation Facilities, 214
Association for Retarded Children, 167
Atomic Energy Commission, 82
Avery, Martha Moore, 4

Ball, Robert, 223
Banister, Olive, 267
Barden, Graham, 151
Barkley, Alben, 69
Baruch, Bernard, 123, 168
Baruch Committee, 123, 162
Baruch Plan, 126, 172
Baylor University, 192

Benshoof, H.L. 164
Berger, Victor, 7
Birdsall, Frank, 123, 169
Blain, Daniel, 113
Bledsoe, C. Warren, 200-201
Blindness, 200-201
"Blue-sky" Proposals, 171
"Bluestocking," 14
Boston, 1-2, 4, 8, 10, 18, 22, 81
Boston College, 201
Braceland, Frank, 113
Brademas, John, 265
Brahmin, 15
Brandeis, Elizabeth (Rauschenbush), 15, 21-22, 24, 27-28, 61, 64, 67, 72-73, 87, 211, 217
Brandeis, Louis, 15, 24, 27, 29, 30, 34, 40, 49, 50, 54, 72-73, 79
Brookings Institute, 179
Brooks, Eleanor Stabler, 18, 71
Brothers, Russell, 171
Brownlow, Louis, 69
Bryn Mawr College, 32, 77, 266
Burress, James, 206, 264
Bunting, Polly, 20
Bulova Watch Company, 146
Bureau of the Budget, 68-69, 101, 142, 152, 191, 214, 231
Bureau of Education for Handicapped Children, 225
Bureau of Narcotics, 68
Bureau of Public Assistance, 177-178
Bureau of the Mint, 68
Bureau of Research and Statistics, 176
Burns, Beatrice, 227
Busbey, Fred, 143-148, 152-153

Cabot, Hugh, 60
California State University, 201

306

Campanella, Roy, 159
Cambridge, 14, 17, 22
Carnegie Endowment for International Peace, 28
Carville Leprosarium, 169, 205
Casement, Sir Roger, 10
Catholic Charities, 167
Celebreeze, Anthony, 178, 180-181, 185, 216, 255
Charlottesville Workshop on Training for Rehabilitation Counselors, 175
Children's Bureau, 38, 59, 62, 76, 104, 215, 233, 239, 247, 248
Christman, Elizabeth, 36, 77, 79
Civil Rights, 240
Civil Rights Act, 188
Civil Service Commission, 173
Civilian Conservation Corps, 69
Clark, Hans, 115
Coast Guard, 68
Coe, Josephine, 43, 67, 131, 218, 260
Coffin, Jo, 77
Cohen, Wilbur, 55, 109, 176-178, 182, 190, 216, 223, 235, 237, 242-244, 247, 256
Committee on Administrative Management (1937), 68, 69
Committee on the Costs of Medical Care, 53
Committee on Economic Security, 54-55
Committee on Education and Labor, 217-218
Common Council for American Unity, 88
Community Work and Training Programs, 182
Conley, Reginald, 151
Consumer's League, 28, 55, 81, 104
Coolidge, Calvin, 16, 18, 32, 34
Copp, Tracy, 26-27, 33-36, 40, 58, 77, 94, 102, 116, 125, 127, 129, 131-132, 147, 169-170
Cosmos Club, 88, 173
Coy, Wayne, 69-70
Cumming, Hugh, 53, 61
Curative Workshop of Milwaukee, 170
Curtis, Frances, 258, 267

Dabelstein, Donald, 128, 133, 144, 151, 156, 164-170, 175-176, 179-180
Davis, Hallowell, 22
Deaf, 202-204

Debs, Eugene, 4, 8, 52
Dean, Russell, 138, 144, 185
DeLourdes, Bernadette, 252, 261, 265
Department of Labor, 36, 55, 77-78, 105, 128, 142, 150-151, 233
Department of Health, Education, and Welfare, 110, 142, 144, 149, 150-152, 172, 181, 188, 213, 216-217, 232, 233, 235, 237, 244, 251, 262, 267
Derthick, Martha, 249
Diamond, Isabella, 32-33, 37, 64, 77, 84, 99, 131, 206, 216, 252, 259-261, 263-267
Diehl, Harold, 112
Disability benefits "freeze," 153, 171
Discretionary grant funds, 158, 168, 170, 173
"Disease of the month club," 114, 126
Doak, William, 55
Downer, James, 264
Draper, Ann, 259
Draper, Warren, 61, 64, 74-75, 91, 95, 99, 117-119, 121-123, 131, 199, 261, 263
Duke Foundation, 195
Duke University, 173, 196
Dunn, Helen, 256

Eaton, Allen H., 194-195, 266
Eisenhower, Dwight, 141-142, 149, 152-153, 171-172, 174, 176, 180, 214
Eliot, Martha May, 59, 239, 247
Ewing, Oscar, 70, 106, 108, 115-116, 125-126, 134, 141, 232

Fabian society, 9
Fabray, Nanette, 257
Falk, I.S., 56-57, 153
Farm Security Administration, 62
Faulkes, William, 33-34, 58, 127-128
Federal aid to education, 172
Federal Board of Vocational Education, 25, 33, 35, 40, 102
Federal Security Agency, 69-70, 74-76, 81-82, 86-90, 92, 98, 101-102, 104-105, 107, 110-111, 114, 126-128, 134-135, 140-142, 144, 202, 206, 239, 267
Felix, Robert, 113, 115, 198

Financing of Vocational Rehabilitation program, 144-148, 150, 152, 166, 182
Finch, Robert, 245, 247-248, 251, 257, 262
"Fire house boys," 165
Fishbein, Morris, 56, 60, 95-96
Fitzgerald, John F., 2
Flemming, Arthur, 137, 173, 177, 227, 255
Fogarty, John, 114, 147-148, 152, 181, 224-225, 227
Folsom, Marion, 171-174, 178, 255
Food and Drug Adminstration, 93, 104
Forbush, Gabrielle, 45-46
Forio, Edgar, 227
Forsythe, Jack, 225
Frankfurter, Felix, 49
Freedman's Hospital, 91, 206
Freeman's Journal, 11
Freeman Magazine, 17
Friends' Ambulance Service, 85

Gaelic American, 11
Gaelic Society, 10
Gardner, John, 190, 214-217, 221, 228, 231-233, 235-238, 242-243, 247, 256
Garrett, James, 166, 169, 184, 191, 233, 235-236, 249-250
Gallaudet College, 202, 262, 264
Gilbert, Helen, 19
George Washington University Hospital, 263
Goepner, Helene, 263
Gold standard, 44
Goldstein, David, 4
Goodwill Industries, 167
Gorodezky, Eli, 171
Grants-in-aid, 116, 145, 111
Green, Edity, 212, 225
Green, William, 48-49
Greenawalt, Jack, 254
Gregg, Alan, 96, 112
Greve, Bell, 169-170, 204, 220, 265
Griffith, Louise, 77
Gulick, Luther, 69

Hadden, Chester, 171
Hale, Swinburn, 19
Hamilton, Alice, 59, 61, 73, 78
Harbridge House, 179
Harding, Warren, 31-32
Harrison, Gladys, 77

Harvard University, 13-14, 17, 64, 167, 202
Hawthorne, Nathaniel, 2
Hayes, David, 193, 256
Headquarters News Notes, 132, 170, 176, 180
Health Crusades, 98
Health Resources Advisory Committee, 137
Helen Keller National Center, 267
Hill, Lister, 114, 116, 191, 224-225
Hillyer, Cecile, 166-169
Hobby, Oveta Culp, 141-145, 148-152, 170-171, 180, 231-232, 254-255, 265
Hoey, Jane, 83, 153
Hoover, Herbert, 39-41, 44, 135
Hoover, J. Edgar, 88
Hoover, Richard, 200-201
Hopkins, Harry, 54, 56-58, 69, 81
Hospital Survey and Construction Act (Hill-Burton), 116-117, 153, 161-162, 207, 213
House Appropriations Committee, 144-147, 166, 183, 214, 226
House Committee on Education and Labor, 150-151
House Sub-Committee on Labor, Health, Education, and Welfare, 153
Hough, Eugene, 9
Howard, Paul, 227
Howard University Medical School, 206-207
Human Resources Center, 168
Humphrey, Hubert, 243, 265
Hunt, Joe, 128, 133, 144

Ickes, Harold, 45, 69, 73
Independent living, 176, 184, 213
Inglis, Agnes, 219
Interdisciplinary focus, 158, 163, 165-166
International Health Research Act of 1960, 205
International rehabilitation research, 205
International Society for Rehabilitation of the Disabled, 190, 264
Institute for the Crippled and Disabled, 150-151
Institute of Physical Medicine and Rehabilitation, 151, 168, 192
International Health Conference, 78

International Society for the Welfare of Cripples, 170
Irish, 1-2

Jaques, Marceline, 167-168
Johnson, Lee, 266
Johnson, Lyndon, 217, 235, 243, 244
Joint Liaison Committees, 176
Judd, Walter, 148
"Just One Break," 168

Keller, Helen, 9, 207
Kelley, Florence, 28, 55, 73
Kennedy Administration, 177, 186
Kennedy, John F., 176, 180, 182, 187-188, 190, 257
Kessler, Henry, 121, 124, 160-172
Kidney dialysis, 191
King, Martin Luther, 242, 262
Klotz, Henrietta, 46, 87, 94
Klumpp, Theodore, 112, 15, 138, 143, 170, 227
Kottke, Frederick, 160
Krusen, Frank, 160, 162, 191
Kratz, John, 34, 58, 131-132
Kuhl, William, 227

LaDame, Mary, 77
LaFollette, Robert, 33-34, 63
Lahey, Frank, 94-95, 98, 112
Lamborn, Emily, 144, 184-185
Lasker, Albert, 79, 114
Lasker, Mary, 79, 114, 124, 198
Laski, Harold, 18
League of the Cross, 5
Lenroot, Katherine, 107
Levine, Edna, 192
Lewis, John L., 47-50, 118, 123
Liberal Club, 16-18, 22, 25
Lippmann, Walter, 17
Litvinov, Ambassador, 51
Lofquist, Lloyd, 167

Macy, Anne Sullivan, 9
Mann, Horace, 2
Manpower Development and Training Act, 187
Martz, 184
Mary E. Switzer Memorial Building, 265
McCarthy, Eugene, 243
McCloskey, Mark, 82-83, 86, 167
McConnell, Sam, 150-151

McCormick, Wright, 30
McGowan, John, 167
McLean, Franklin, 115, 206
McNamara, Robert, 190
McNutt, Paul, 69-70, 74, 76, 92, 98-99, 101, 106, 112, 196-197, 231
Medicaid, 178, 211, 220, 240
Medical Advisory Committee, 56
Medicare, 178, 216
Mellon, Andrew, 31-32, 40, 43
Mencken, Helen, 192-193
Menninger Clinic, 113
Menninger, Karl, 112, 137, 197-199
Menninger, William, 227
Mental Health, 215-216
Mental retardation, 190, 215, 216
Merck, George, 112, 115, 143
Merriam, Charles, 69
Methodist Church, 167
Miles, Rufus, 149, 188, 249
Miller, Leo, 103
Miller, Watson, 70, 92-93, 98, 104-106, 116, 237
Minimum Wage Board, 24, 27
Mooar, Eva, 20-21, 26
Moore, Mary, 7-8
Moore, Michael Jeremiah, 2-5, 7-11, 15-16, 18-20, 43, 49, 50-52, 71-72, 155, 264, 268
Morgenthau, Elinor, 46, 83-84
Morgenthau, Henry, 44-47, 54, 68, 87
Morgenthau, Henry and Ruth, 261
Mount Holyoke, 13, 78
Muthard, John, 167
Myles, Gertrude, 9, 13

National Association of Manufacturers, 167
National Center for the Deaf-Blind, 192, 207, 264
National Citizens' Advisory Council on Vocational Rehabilitation, 170-171, 176, 194, 196, 246, 226-228, 233
National Citizens' Conference (1969), 245-246
National Commission on Architectural Barrier to Rehabilitation, 226
National Democratic Club, 266
National Health Assembly (1948), 108
National Health Conference (1938), 59-61
National Institutes of Health, 114-114, 152, 162, 191, 198, 229

National League of Decency, 89
National Mental Health Act, 112-113, 115, 137, 198
National Recovery Administration, 48-50
National Rehabilitation Association, 35, 127, 135-136, 149, 151, 153, 212-214, 264-266, 267
National Science Foundation, 114-115, 163
National Science Foundation Act, 115
National Security League, 18
National Task Force on the Handicapped (1951), 138-141, 170, 227
National Technical Institute for the Deaf, 202-203
National Travelers' Aid Association, 167
National Youth Administration, 69, 81-82
Nearing, Scott, 23, 155
New Deal, 41, 43-44, 63-65, 68, 76, 87-88, 153, 206
Newman, Edward, 264
Newton, Massachusetts, 64
Newton Classical High School, 9
Newton Free Library, 4, 71
New York Times, 168, 262
New York University, 172, 263, 265
Nixon, Richard, 244, 253-254, 260
North Carolina Museum of Art, Mary Duke Biddle Gallery for the Blind, 195

Obenauer, Marie, 78
O'Day, Caroline, 78
Oettinger, Katherine, 239
Office of Community War Services, 82
Office of Education, 69, 102, 104, 215, 224
Office of Special Services, 104
Office of Vocational Rehabilitation, 125-126, 134-135, 137, 140, 147-148, 150, 152, 165, 176, 180, 183, 232, 252, 257
Old Age Survivors' Insurance Trust Fund, 176-178
"Operation Knoxville," 138-139, 167
O'Sullivan, John, 15
Overbrook School for the Blind, 262
Overholser, Winfred, 91-93, 112

Page, William, 214

Parker, Anna, 260, 263
Parran, Thomas, 61-63, 75, 90-91, 97, 104, 113
Patents Board, 163
Patterson, Cecil, 167
Peer review, 177
Pepper, Claude, 247
Perkins, Frances, 47, 54-58, 73, 78
Perkins, Rod, 151
Perry, J. Warren, 169, 266
Phi Beta Kappa, 19
Physical Medicine and Rehabilitation, 123, 161-162, 171-172, 197-199
Pickett, Clarence, 38, 83, 85-86
Poor Peoples' March, 248
Powell, Adam Clayton
Priest, Percy, 113
Procurement and Assignment Service, 94-98, 112, 197
Professionalism, 177-178
Progressives, 24
Psychiatry, 113, 197
Public assistance, 223, 239
Public Health Service, 45, 47, 52, 57, 61-64, 67, 69-70, 75-76, 88-91, 93, 95-96, 102, 109, 113-114, 117, 213, 215, 232
Public Law 113 (VR Act of 1943), 103, 106-107, 116
Public Law 565, 152, 166-173, 181
Public Welfare Amendments of 1962, 178, 187, 212, 223, 244

Quakers, 38, 84

Radcliffe College, 10-11, 13-14, 16-23, 47, 64, 77, 144, 262
Racliffe News, 17
Radcliffe Quarterly, 69-70
Rancho Los Amigos, 168
Rapaport, David, 115
Rauschenbush, Paul, 73
Reader's Digest, 168
Reedy, Corbett, 123-124, 132, 175, 183, 185-186, 211, 226, 266
Regional Spinal Cord Injury Centers, 196
Rehabilitation Act Amendments, 207, 211, 214, 216, 229
Rehabilitation counseling, 164-166, 168, 170, 180
Rehabilitation counselor, 129, 139, 165-168, 174, 218

Rehabilitation educators, 165-166
Rehabilitation Engineering Centers, 196
Rehabilitation facilities, 153, 156-157, 162, 171, 226
Rehabilitation Services Administration, 248-249
Rehabilitation training, 163-168, 174
Research and demonstration grants, 156-157, 160, 167, 171-173, 184, 189-190
Research and Training Centers, 191-192, 196
Research in rehabilitation, 156, 160, 174
Ribicoff, Abraham, 175-176, 178, 181-182, 211, 15, 153
Richardson, Elliot, 172, 181, 264-266
Rives, Louis, 200
Rockefeller, Nelson, 148-152
Roche, Josephine, 46-53, 55-56, 58-60, 63-64, 70, 72, 78, 94, 96-97, 103, 112, 117
Rocky Mountain Fuel Company, 47, 118
Roosevelt, Eleanor, 38, 51, 73, 83-84, 86, 94, 168-169, 187, 239
Roosevelt, Franklin D., 41, 43-45, 50, 55-56, 58-59, 63, 67-69, 79, 81, 101, 111, 201, 219
Ross, Nellie Taylor, 68
Rubinow, Isaac, 53-54
Rusk, Howard, 119-121, 124, 126, 132, 134, 137-138, 141, 143, 152-153, 158-168, 197, 213, 226-228, 233, 235, 246-248, 254-255, 257, 262-265

Saint Elizabeth's Hospital, 91-92, 104
Salmon, Peter, 171, 267
Schlesinger Library, 266
Schneiderman, Rose, 36, 55
Schottland, Charles, 176
Scientific Research Board, 115
Scurlock, Voyle, 170
Semans, Mary, 195, 226
Senate Appropriations Committee, 134
Senate Committee on Labor and Public Welfare. 216
Shafer, Philip, 183-184
Shaw, George Bernard, 9
Sheltered workshops, 214-215, 222
Shortley, Michael, 127-128, 131-132
Sister Kenny Institute, 192
Slicer, Al, 227

Smith, Alfred, 39
Smith, Hank, 138
Smithdas, Robert, 262
Social and Rehabilitation Services, 190, 236, 237-240, 242-245, 247-249
Social Security, 221
Social Security Act, 56-57, 62-63, 153, 182, 216, 256
Social Security Administration, 176-177, 180, 232
Social Security Amendments, 245
Social Security Board, 67, 69, 74, 104, 109
Socialist party, 8
Soldier's Rehabilitation Act, 25
Southern Christian Leadership Conference, 242
Soviet Union, 51-52
Speech and hearing, 202-204
Spellman, Cardinal, 2
Stafford, John, 196
Stanley Motorcar Company, 2
State agency directors, 145, 149-150, 165, 167-168
State agency problems, 146, 166, 174, 187, 214
Stephens, M.A., 144, 146
Strachan, Paul, 128-129, 150-152, 164
Strecker, Edward, 113
Strong, E.K., 179
Supreme Court, 49-51, 72
Survey Graphic, 64, 87
Switzer, Anastasia, 7, 259, 263, 266
Switzer, Arthur, 7, 259, 263
Switzer, Julius, 2, 5-6, 259
Switzer, May, 259, 263
Switzer, Margaret Moore, 2, 7, 9
Switzer, Richard, 259, 263
Swofford, Jewell, 77, 104
Symington, Stuart, 137

Taber, John, 144, 147, 202
Taft, Charles P., 82, 142, 231
Task Force on Program Development, 183-185, 226
Task Force on the Handicapped (see National Task Force on the Handicapped)
Taylor, Jack, 265
Technical Committee on Medical Care, 60-62
Terrell, Mary Church, 28-29

Theatre for the Deaf, 190, 192-194, 154-257
Thurston, John, 126
Tracy, Mrs. Spencer, 170
Training Council, 167
Treasury Department, 30-32, 43-46, 49, 63-64, 67-70, 75, 81, 101, 219, 253, 260
Troyenevsky, Ambassador, 51
Truman, Harry, 101-102, 104-105, 108, 111, 115-117, 135, 141, 227
Tuberculosis Association, 167
Twiname, John, 201, 247, 254, 261, 264-265

United Cerebral Palsy, 167
United Mine Workers, 47-48, 118
United Mine Workers' Welfare and Retirement Fund, 118-119, 121-122, 126, 132, 136, 197, 199
United Nations, 205
United States Employment Service, 69, 151
University of Minnesota, 192
University of Texas, 205
University of Washington, 192
Upper Newton Falls, 2, 4, 13, 22
Urrows, Henry, 189
Usdane, William, 169

Verano, Ann, 260
Veterans Administration, 200-201
Viscardi, Henry, 158-160, 227, 266
Vocational Rehabilitation, 58, 102-104, 106-107, 111-112, 17, 123, 127, 129, 135, 141, 143, 174
Vocational Rehabilitation Administration, 188, 190-191, 212, 215, 220-222, 232-233, 238, 244-245
Voluntary agency involvement in Vocational Rehabilitation, 156-157, 160-161, 167, 171
Von Achen, Harold, 227

Wagner-Murray-Dingell legislation, 95, 108
Wallace, Henry, 50, 54, 56, 69
Walls, David, 219
War Manpower Commission, 94, 98, 173
War Relocation Centers, 90
War Research Service, 98
Warner, Estella Ford, 78
Watertown, 14
Weisman, Margaret, 81
Welfare Administration, 215, 223-224, 232, 238-239
West, Olin, 60
Western Michigan University, 201
Weybright, Victor, 64-65
Whitten, E.B., 135-136, 147, 151-152, 168, 182, 212-213
Williams, Boyce, 193, 204, 225
Williams, Hosea, 242
Williams, Ralph, 62
Wilson, George Grafton, 15-16, 28-29, 37
Wilson, Woodrow, 24, 26, 102
Winalski, Patria, 225
Winslow, C.E.A., 60
Winston, Ellen, 223-224, 237
Witte, Edwin, 55-56
Women's Bureau, 27, 36, 38, 76, 77
Women's International League for Peace and Freedom, 28-29, 34, 38, 73, 206
Women's Trade Union League, 77-79, 86
Woodin, William, 44
Woodrow Wilson Rehabilitation Center, 124, 169, 206, 266-267
Workmen's Compensation, 121
World Congress on the Society for the Welfare of Cripples, 204
World Congress on Mental Health, 204
World Congress on the Society for the Welfare of Cripples, 204
World Health Organization, 204
World Rehabilitation Fund, 262, 264-265
Wright, Robert, 184

About the Author
Martha Lentz Walker

Educated at Vanderbilt University and the University of Tennessee, Martha Lentz Walker teaches graduate students of Rehabilitation Counseling at Kent State University. The daughter of a Public Health Officer, she became aware of community health problems as a child and developed her interests in rehabilitation through volunteer activities. Her professional rehabilitation career began as a speech and hearing clinician in Nashville, Tennessee. Now a Certified Rehabilitation Counselor and Rehabilitation Counselor Educator, she is a Past President of the National Council on Rehabilitation Education and has received state and national awards for her leadership in the rehabilitation field.